~

PRESIDENTAL PRAISE

~

MERCER
UNIVERSITY PRESS

Endowed by
TOM WATSON BROWN
and
THE WATSON-BROWN FOUNDATION, INC.

PRESIDENTIAL PRAISE

OUR PRESIDENTS AND THEIR HYMNS

C. Edward Spann and Michael E. Williams, Sr.

Mercer University Press, Macon, Georgia

MERCER

MUP/H763

© 2008 Mercer University Press
1400 Coleman Avenue
Macon, Georgia 31207

First Edition.

Books published by Mercer University Press are printed on acid free paper that
meets the requirements of American National Standard for Information
Sciences—Permanence of Paper for Printed Library Materials.

Mercer University Press is a member of Green Press initiative (greenpressinitia-
tive.org), a nonprofit organization working to help publishers and printers
increase their use of recycled paper and decrease their use of fiber derived from
endangered forests. This book is printed on recycled paper.

Library of Congress Cataloging-in-Publication Data

Spann, C. Edward.
Presidential praise: our presidents and their hymns
C. Edward Spann and Michael E. Williams, Sr.
1st ed.
p. cm.
Includes bibliographical references (p.   ) and index.
ISBN-13: 978-0-88146-117-6 (hardback: alk. paper)
ISBN-10: 0-88146-117-2 (hardback: alk. paper)
1. Hymns, English—United States—History and criticism
2. Presidents—United States—Religion
I. Williams, Michael E. (Michael Edward), 1960-
II. Title
ML2911.S63 2008
782.270973—dc22
2008030513

This book is dedicated to

Dr. Gary R. Cook,

President of Dallas Baptist University,

a Christian educator who

appreciates the influence of hymns.

Acknowledgments

It was a privilege to work on this book with my colleague Dr. Mike Williams. His writing of the biographies of the presidents provided an excellent foundation for each chapter. I am indebted to the library staff of Dallas Baptist University (DBU) for their assistance.

The archivists of several presidential libraries were exceptionally helpful in providing needed information. The editorial staff of Mercer University Press was especially encouraging during the process. Jerre Simmons, an English teacher and friend, was invaluable as a proofreader, who suggested numerous corrections that made the text clearer, more readable, and stronger.

The president of DBU, Dr. Gary Cook, has been most encouraging. The CD that is included in the book was made possible by an institutional grant from DBU. Special thanks goes to Dr. Stephen Holcomb and the DBU Presidential Hymns Ensemble for their recording. Assisted by Dr. Terry Fansler and recording engineer

Randy Adams, this CD makes the hymns "come alive" for the reader. I also want to express gratitude to Sharon Spann, who served as a historical consultant and, with her husband Dee, suggested the book title. Joe Theige and Ronnie Turney were extremely important in preparing the presidential portraits. Beverly Theige was invaluable as the music engraver for all the hymns included in the book.

There are many others who aided in research, offered encouragement, and sacrificed time and effort in order to make this book become a reality. I want to especially thank my wife Jan, who served as typist, coordinator, and final proofreader for the entire project. Most of all, I am grateful to the Lord. May this book bring honor and glory to Him.

C. Edward Spann

I am most grateful to my friend and colleague Dr. Ed Spann for giving me the opportunity to work on this book. This project has been his from its inception, and he has been patient in working with me as I have been simultaneously working on another project for Mercer University Press. I am especially grateful for the opportunity to work on the brief biographies of each of the presidents. Having studied American history, the presidents, and their administrations, it was especially rewarding for me to examine their lives, administrations, and faith. Their faith backgrounds and viewpoints have been as multifaceted as the people of the United States whom they have served.

In addition to Ed, I am especially grateful to my wife, Robbie, our three sons, Michael, Josh, and Carey, and to my administrative assistants, Wanda Allen and Jillian Pryor, for their patience with me as I have worked on this project.

Michael E. (Mike) Williams, Sr.

Introduction

A minister at the funeral of Franklin D. Roosevelt stated, "You can tell the kind of man he was by the hymns he loved." This comment began my thinking on this subject. Knowing how much hymns mean to me, I began to research those hymns loved by President Roosevelt. I was further encouraged when I learned that President George W. Bush chose as a title for his autobiography *A Charge to Keep I Have*, the name of a Charles Wesley hymn. These references to hymns stirred my curiosity about the influence of hymns on the lives of all our presidents, from George Washington to the present day. Since hymns have been so significant in the lives of people throughout the history of Christianity, there is reason to believe that hymns have affected the leaders of our nation.

My search was further sparked by the discovery of a small, long out-of-print book called *Our Presidents and Their Hymns*. Written and published in 1933 by John Benjamin Merrill, the thirty-nine-page booklet amounts to only a listing of presidential hymn favorites to that time. This information was valuable, however, because Merrill had contacted many family members of presidents and extensively studied earlier presidents' choices of favorite hymns. Obviously, other research had to be done, from President Truman through President George W. Bush, to make the book complete. This was accomplished through the help of presidential libraries, biographies, autobiographies, colleagues, family members, and other sources.

In my research of three years, consulting over 100 sources, I discovered that many of our presidents loved hymns, and some even had "hymn sings" regularly in the White House. At least one president not only wrote hymns, but also versified all of the 150 psalms and put them in meter so they could be sung. Some presidents went to certain church services especially to enjoy singing the hymns of that denomination. One president was so fond of a hymn that an opera company included his favorite hymn in an opera, much to the surprise of the critics. My study revealed many interesting stories about the presidents and their hymns.

To begin each president's chapter, noted historian Dr. Michael E. Williams, Sr., renders a concise biography of each president's path to the White House and his accomplishments and failures as president. Following this, I introduce how that president regarded music, whether or not he was musical, and music in the White House during each president's administration. The book focuses on hymns that may have been used in the presidential mansion as well as in other venues. Each president's favorite hymn was determined according to research done by myself or other scholars. Amazingly, the hymns reflected aspects of each president's life and administration. The hymn may have influenced the president in his spiritual journey, his personal struggles, and even crucial decisions. After this, the story of how the hymn was written, both the words and the music, is presented. Even the stories of the people who wrote the hymns seem to relate to the president in a unique way. This study revealed how some presidents left a legacy reflected by the selection of their favorite hymn. Sometimes being influenced by their choice of inaugural scripture, often by the circumstances of their era, even in collaboration with the First Lady, the hymn seems to fit very well in the life of each president. Some presidents' general theological position can be noted in their hymn choice.

This study became a unique panorama of English hymnody. It has been noted that the songs of the English-speaking world primarily have been hymns. This was especially true of the earliest New England colonists, who enjoyed simple functional music, mainly of a religious nature. Music was an activity to praise God through one of the noblest forms of human nature—singing psalms and, much later, hymns. The rise of congregational singing in America paralleled the development of singing in England for many years.

Because of this, the vast majority of presidential hymns were penned and composed by Englishmen. Even though a hymn may not be classified as an excellent poem, if it provides comfort to the president or to the private citizen during a time of spiritual need, it will serve each as a meaningful sacred song. Hymns often provide an oasis of rest, giving help in the middle of extreme anxiety of difficult decisions. Many American presidents lived through unimaginable dark hours of indecision when they communicated with God through prayers, often expressed in a hymn.

My goal has been to document how hymns affected the nation's presidents. The premise is that hymns serve the same purpose in the life of the commander in chief as they do in the life of a private citizen. The hymns a person sings, whether in public or private, inform us of that person's faith. This study reinforced my belief that strong, biblically based hymns, sung from the view of one's faith, are more memorable than mere words. It is my prayer that this book will inspire the reader to appreciate the legacy of hymns as you read about their importance to our nation's leaders from the beginning of our country to the present day.

C. Edward Spann

~

PRESIDENTAL PRAISE

~

GEORGE WASHINGTON

1732–1799

First President (1789–1797)

No American, save perhaps Abraham Lincoln, is more idolized than George Washington. Perhaps no one, even Lincoln, has had a greater influence upon the development of the United States. Regarded even in his lifetime as "first in war, first in peace, and first in the hearts of his countrymen," Washington's legacy has become, in fact, larger than life.

Born in colonial Virginia on 22 February 1732 (New Style Calendar), Washington's father died when Washington was only eleven years old. Mentored by his older half-brother, Lawrence, and a Virginia aristocrat named William Fairfax, Washington's education was limited, but his training was immense. He worked initially as a surveyor and grew to manhood in this capacity on the Virginia frontier. He first attracted colonial-wide attention as a surveyor and a militiaman, being in part responsible for the French and Indian War. Washington experienced his first real combat and achieved his first real notoriety in that conflict, becoming a genuine hero at the disastrous British defeat on the Monongahela River in 1755.

After the end of the French and Indian War, Washington established himself in Virginia society, married a wealthy widow, Martha Custis, and developed his Mount Vernon plantation, which included many slaves. He participated somewhat in Virginia and colonial politics and found himself increasingly involved as the crisis with Great Britain deepened. Virginia selected him as one of its representatives to the First Continental Congress and, after the first shots were fired at Lexington and Concord, the Second Continental Congress. Congress selected Washington as the commander of the colonial forces in 1775, a position he held throughout the American Revolution. No great tactician or strategist, Washington held Continental armies together through the darkest days of the Revolution by his strength of character and personal will. He staved off defeat in 1776 and early 1777 with surprise victories at Trenton and Princeton. He managed to hold together his army when nothing but defeat seemed to beckon through the bleak winters at Valley Forge and in New Jersey, and parried attempts to replace him as commander in chief.

With the fledgling country being run by state governments and a loosely constructed Continental Congress, Washington emerged as the symbol to which most patriots looked to hold the nation together. Washington ultimately developed the strategy that resulted in British defeat at Yorktown in 1781, and he consistently recognized leadership gifts in untried subordinates such as Henry Knox and Nathaniel Greene, who contributed mightily to the colonial victory.

Washington also worked to rally political and public support to the colonial cause. In the interim as the two nations' diplomats negotiated peace, Washington again kept the army intact as a reminder to the British of American resolve. After final victory was achieved in 1783, Washington renounced any attempts to make him a dictator or king and returned to Mount Vernon. There he worked diligently to make Mount Vernon more efficient and sought to make the Potomac River a major commercial artery to the all-important West.

In 1787 Virginia summoned Washington to public life again to represent the state in the Constitutional Convention. Selected as the presiding officer, he supervised the development of the Constitution and served as a calming influence during some of the convention's tumultuous meetings. After its ratification, the Electoral College unanimously elected him as the nation's first president. Even though he had few real guidelines for serving as the Republic's president, Washington placed the nation on sound footing in the eight years, 1789–1797, that he served. He wisely selected brilliant men such as Alexander Hamilton and Thomas Jefferson to serve as his first cabinet officials. He calmed civil unrest, suspicious of a stronger central government and taxation. As expected, he arbitrated disputes fairly and steered the ship of state through stormy international waters as war erupted in Europe. He also clearly rejected the establishment of any form of hereditary monarchy and established a number of precedents that were followed by presidents in succeeding years. Despite the emerging conflict, which ultimately led to the creation of a two-party system, Washington largely managed to stay above partisan squabbles. Through it all, he maintained the type of quiet dignity and measured response to issues that arose for which he had become famous.

After his retirement in March 1797, Washington returned to his beloved Mount Vernon, where he settled back into the life of a Virginia planter, although he once more found the nation clamoring for his military leadership as possible war loomed with France. Once the crisis was defused, however, Washington quickly reverted to a more simple life. He also struggled with the question of slavery. Eventually, he rewrote his will in response to his changing convictions about the evils of slavery, stating that certain slaves be freed upon his and Martha's deaths. Unfortunately, his idyllic retirement was short-lived as he contracted a bacterial infection that resulted in his death on 14 December 1799.

Washington's religious beliefs have been debated vigorously. American church historian Mark Noll writes that Washington "served faithfully on the vestry of his Anglican parish, but his faith was mostly a social convention." Noll also quotes one recent biographer, who stated, "[Washington] was a Christian as a Virginia planter understood the term. He seems never to have taken communion; he stood to pray, instead of kneeling; and he did not invariably go to church on Sundays." Washington's most recent biographer, Joseph Ellis, records that at Washington's death, "there were no ministers in the room, no prayers uttered, no Christian rituals offering the solace of everlasting life."[1]

Nevertheless, in another of Noll's works, *America's God,* Noll lists Washington among those founding fathers who were "profoundly religious" despite the fact that they "did not [always] uphold traditional Christian convictions." Some aspects of Washington's background and religious interests may be ascertained through the choice of his favorite hymn.[2]

Even as the first president set the tone politically by his honest and unique governing character, helping guarantee a sound democracy, he also established some musical precedents that were followed by his successors to the present day. The Washingtons lived in three executive mansions: two in New York City and one in Philadelphia. At least twice weekly, the first family held receptions that became high social events. These receptions, which were held for ambassadors, foreign dignitaries, and members of Congress and their families, featured musical performances, as Washington was a devotee of music. In 1777, Washington stated, "Nothing is more agreeable and ornamental than good music."[3]

Music at the president's home was similar to a chamber recital, perhaps better termed an intimate amusement. The piano was at the center of the event since it reigned as an elegant image of court life in democracy during this era of American history. Washington had purchased one of the first American-made *pianofortes* for his adopted granddaughter Nelly Custis when she was ten years old. Even though Washington could neither sing well nor play any musical instrument,[4] he made sure that his stepchildren and stepgrandchildren had music lessons of some type. Often, Alexander Reinagle, Nelly's piano teacher, would perform on the piano for these social events, sometimes playing his own compositions. Later, Nelly herself performed for these occasions. She became an accomplished musician. A foreign visitor said that Nelly played and sang better than the usual woman of America or even of Europe.

Washington was also familiar with Moravian music. Both he and Benjamin Franklin were impressed by the excellent music they heard at the Moravian settlement in Bethlehem, Pennsylvania. Franklin wrote his wife about his musical impressions in 1756. Washington spent a night at Bethlehem during the Revolution and found great pleasure in a concert of chamber music he heard there.[5]

Washington also enjoyed other musical concerts and theater productions, including opera. The first president's favorite opera was *Poor Soldier*, composed by William Shield. Irving Lowens, historian of early American music, states that Washington particularly enjoyed "Rose Tree," a popular song from Shield's now forgotten opera.[6] Reinagle, Nelly's piano teacher, included this song in his 1789 *Collection of Favorite Songs*. Washington also was quite fond of dancing, even though at that time some church leaders called dancing "a pollution of the body." This social activity was very popular at Mount Vernon, which became the presidential residence about two or three months yearly. Hymns were sung often at Mount Vernon. Jane Cook states that each evening Martha and George prayed, read the Bible, and sang hymns with Nelly in preparation for bedtime.[7] It is known that Washington copied a hymn into one of his personal letters. The year of Washington's inauguration, 1789, also marked the publication of the *American Prayer Book*. The book contained twenty-seven hymns, including "While Shepherds Watched," which quickly became a national favorite.

Washington had a relative in England who was especially interested in hymns. Selina, Countess of Huntingdon, was co-heiress of Washington, Earl of Ferras. Linked to the English royal family, George Washington was kin to Lady Huntingdon and corresponded with her. She even sent a Thomas Gainsborough portrait of herself to Washington.[8] As a young girl, Selina prayed to marry into a "serious family." This was granted when she married Theophilus Hastings, the ninth Earl of Huntingdon, in 1729. After Lady Huntingdon found personal assurance of her salvation, she became interested in the work of John and Charles Wesley, who had gone to America in 1735 as missionaries to the new colony of Georgia. Boyd Smith, hymnologist, states that Selina had a lifelong relationship with the work of the Wesleys. Also, she evidently was interested in missions because she wrote George Washington, expressing a desire to start mission work among the American Indians. This desire was not realized because of the Revolutionary War.

Lady Huntingdon had the support of her husband in her Christian endeavors following her conversion. Unfortunately, she became a widow at age thirty-nine. Having borne and educated seven children, she evidenced a strong Christian faith and calling. She started a college for the training of ministers in Wales near the home of the fervent Welch preacher Howell Harris. Through her wealth, she supported evangelical pastors, building over forty "chapels" for their ministry. She even sold her jewels to build a chapel in Brighton. The association of "chapels" eventually became known as "Lady Huntingdon's Connexion." [sic]

Because hymnals were needed in these congregations, Lady Huntingdon began editing and publishing hymn collections in 1780. These books included hymns by John Newton, William Cowper, Isaac Watts, Philip Doddridge, Charles Wesley, John Wesley, John Cennick, Anne Steele, and others. One can assume that Washington knew of the work of Selina, Countess of Huntingdon, and her love for evangelical hymns. Six of the American presidents' favorite hymns are included in the 1780 collection of Countess Huntingdon. She commissioned Felice de Giardini, the Italian violist, to write tunes for four hymns.

The choice of Washington's favorite hymn reinforces his love for good music as well as very significant lyrics. It has been noted by John Merrill that the first president's most loved hymn was "How Happy Is He Born and Taught," written by Englishman Henry Wotton in 1614. This hymn truly exemplifies Washington's philosophy and desire to serve as the initial president of the new nation. However, even in the president's few public expressions, one can detect that personal wishes were far down his list of priorities as compared to his obligation as president. That the office was greater than the man filling it was Washington's personal philosophy of his presidency.

Henry Wotton, born in 1568, was educated at Oxford, after which he spent nine years on the European continent. He lived for some time in Florence, Italy, where he became known as "Octavio Baldi." Interestingly, the Grand Duke of Tuscany sent Wotton to Britain to inform James VI of Scotland of an attempt on his life. When James became the English king, Wotton was knighted and rewarded by being made ambassador to the Republic of Venice. In 1623 he was made provost of Eaton College, where he died in 1639.[9] Isaac Walton published Wotton's poems in 1651, after which they were reprinted several times. Evidently George Washington sang the hymn "How Happy Is He Born and Taught" in regular Episcopal services at Christ Church in Alexandria and Pohick Church near Mount Vernon.

The words of each stanza of Wotton's hymn reflect something of meaning about Washington's life and his service to the country. Stanza one emphasizes the blessedness of man who serves others through honesty and simple truth. Stanza two points out the controlling of passions in preparing one's soul for death while de-emphasizing the world's concern about fame. Stanza three speaks of following one's conscience and not worrying about rumors. It also instructs one not to seek flattery because it never develops great men. Stanza four talks about God's grace, which is given to man in abundance. It also mentions God as a close brother and friend. Stanza five speaks of the freedom to hope, which helps man neither to fall nor fail. In addition, it says that man is master of his soul by the decisions he makes, ending with eternal life.

The music for "How Happy Is He Born and Taught" was written by noted English composer Thomas Tallis.[10] It was the eighth of nine psalm tunes composed by Tallis for Matthew Parker's *Whole Psalter Translated into English Metre*, published between 1561 and 1567. In its original version, it was set to a paraphrase of Psalm 67. While this tune has had at least twelve different names, it was eventually called TALLIS' CANON because of its melodic construction. "How Happy Is He Born and Taught" could be sung to any tune with four lines of eight syllables each for every stanza. The music to the universal "Doxology," by Thomas Ken, could have been sung to this text.

It is not known exactly when TALLIS' CANON arrived in America, but we do suspect that it was sung to Ken's popular evening hymn "All Praise to Thee, My God This Night" in England as early as 1732. Many hymnologists

How Happy Is He Born and Taught

Words: Henry Wotton, 1614
Music: Thomas Tallis, 1560

L.M.
TALLIS' CANON

1. How hap - py is he born and taught, That serv - eth not an - oth - er's will, Whose ar - mor is his hon - est thot, And sim - ple truth his ut - most skill.
2. Whose pas - sions not his mas - ters are, Whose soul is still pre - pared for death, Not tied un - to the world by care, Or pub - lic fame or pri - vate breath.
3. Who hath his life from ru - mors freed, Whose con - science is his strong re - treat, Whose state can nei - ther flat - terers feed, Nor ru - in, make op - pres - sors great.
4. Who God doth late and ear - ly pray More of his grace than good to lend, And walks with man, from day to day, As with a bro - ther and a friend!
5. This man is freed from ser - vile bands Of hope to rise, or fear to fall, Lord of him - self, though not of land, And hav - ing noth - ing, yet have all. A - men.

believe that it was sung to Isaac Watts's hymn "Praise to the Lord; 'Tis Good to Raise" which appeared in John Wesley's *Charles-Town Collection* of 1737. Wesley also used this tune in his first tune book called the *Foundrey Collection* in 1742. In addition, a version of this tune appeared in George Whitefield's *Divine Musical Miscellany* in 1754. So we know that TALLIS' CANON appeared in America some time during Washington's lifetime. Nineteenth-century hymn editors arranged it in four-part harmony with the melody in the soprano. Today's hymnals have used it in this form since its first setting in *Hymns Ancient and Modern* in 1861.

"How Happy Is He Born and Taught" is a humble stating of the happiness of an honest man in his Christian faith. It is a personal expression of the importance of living without guile, being truthful and depending on God's grace in daily life even through trials. The humanity of man is stressed; hence, the material nature of mankind is recognized, but what is ultimately important is man's soul. This is an appropriate hymn for a president of a new country, particularly a man who had such a sterling character as Washington. Remember that he refused to consider any hint of a royal title as the first president; more importantly, he stepped down from the presidency after two terms.

TALLIS' CANON is easily recognized as a classic tune and has been arranged in various ways. The harmony in the four-part arrangement is emotionally moving and very well suited to the text. Whether used as a choral or instrumental arrangement, it is always beautiful. Perhaps it is significant that "How Happy Is He Born and Taught" is printed in the latest edition of *The Harvard University Hymn Book*. George Washington's choice of this hymn as a favorite indicates that he was a good judge of excellent music and lyric poetry. As is true of so many of his actions, President Washington set a noble standard in his choice of this exceptional hymn.

JOHN ADAMS

1735–1826

Second President (1793–1797)

Serving as president of the United States has always been a daunting task. Serving in that office in the formative years of the Republic carried with it special challenges. Following a great president can be an equally daunting task. Following a legend might be more than should be asked of anyone. The second president of the United States, John Adams, faced all this adversity and more with the same intrepid spirit that he faced the multifaceted challenges of his public and private life.

John Adams was born into a typical New England family as a direct descendent of Puritan pioneers who settled in Massachusetts in the first decade of that colony's settlement. He spent his early childhood on the family farm near the small village of Braintree, set between Boston and Plymouth. He inherited the stern and devout values of his Puritan family, who educated him in a small private school not far from the family farm. Moving on to Harvard, he received the finest college education offered in the colonies in those days and gave some consideration to a career in the Congregational ministry before deciding to study law. He succeeded as a small-town attorney and married Abigail Smith, the woman who became his lifelong soul mate. She would bear five children, four of whom would survive to adulthood.

As conflict developed between the British colonies in North America and the British Crown, John Adams took a leading role in the unfolding drama. Recognized early on because of his skills as an attorney and an administrator, he served as a leading spokesman for independence in the Second Continental Congress. Together with Benjamin Franklin, Roger Sherman, Robert Livingston, and mainly Thomas Jefferson, he drafted a declaration of independence for the colonies. After adoption of the declaration, he continued in various leadership roles in the Congress, probably being the most important congressman in terms of keeping the war effort going. His extensive committee work and administrative skills became legendary. He sacrificed his health and his family life in those crucial years. He also returned home to Massachusetts, where he drafted a new state constitution. This state constitution has often been regarded as a significant model for the US Constitution, which came less than a decade later. Finally, Congress sent him as an emissary to Europe to gain support for the colonial cause. He served in France with Benjamin Franklin and also in Holland, where he secured important financial support for the young nation. When the war turned in American favor, he helped negotiate the Treaty of Paris (1783), which secured American independence. Adams missed the Constitutional Convention because Congress had sent him back to Europe as the American ambassador to Great Britain. Despite obvious tension with the former mother country, Adams worked diligently to earn respect for the fledgling nation.

After serving as ambassador, Adams returned home in 1788 to a hero's welcome. He soon accepted the nation's call to become its first vice president. As so often has been the case, he was frustrated by the insignificance of the vice president's office. However, after eight years, when George Washington decided not to run for a third term, Adams became his logical successor and candidate of the Federalist Party. His long-time friend, colleague, and sometime adversary Thomas Jefferson opposed him as candidate of the Democratic-Republican Party. When the election ended and Adams was elected president, the unusual conditions of the original version of the Constitution stated that Jefferson, having received the second most electoral votes, would be his vice president. Divided by disagreements on the new nation's nature, the two notable leaders and friends became bitter enemies and political rivals.

Tremendous adversity faced Adams's presidency. Not only did he deal with replacing a legend, but he faced the awkward balancing act of preserving the American neutrality that Washington promoted while war raged in Europe between revolutionary France and Great Britain and her allies. The United States found itself divided between those who wished to maintain neutrality and those who urged alliance with either France or Great Britain. Conflict and intrigue tore apart his own party as Alexander Hamilton undermined Adams's authority. Jefferson and his allies criticized Adams's every decision. Ultimately, Adams chose to maintain American neutrality even though he knew it would probably cost him reelection. In fact, defeat occurred for Adams in the election of 1800 when Thomas Jefferson won the presidency in a close election decided by the House of Representatives.

Somewhat embittered, Adams retired to his farm at Braintree with Abigail. Despite tragedy striking three of their four surviving children, Adams gradually healed from his bitterness, reestablished his friendship with Jefferson after Jefferson completed eight years as president, and rejoiced when his son John Quincy Adams was elected to the White House in 1824. Living to be more than ninety years old, John Adams died on the fiftieth anniversary of Independence Day, within a few hours of his old adversary and friend, Thomas Jefferson.

John Adams came to be noted for his strong Puritan work ethic and values and his tremendous devotion to his family, community, and nation. Reared in a strict Congregationalist home, his father served as a deacon in that denomination. Gradually, Adams drifted from his Congregationalist roots and in the last decades of his life embraced the rationalistic Unitarian denomination, which many former Congregationalists adopted. Ironically, one discussion that helped bring Adams and Jefferson together was their discussion of their unorthodox ideas on religion. Still, Adams cannot be separated from his Congregationalist roots.[11]

The Adamses had only modest musical interests and tastes. There are no records of John or Abigail Adams owning or purchasing musical instruments for the White House.[12] Of course, they only resided in the Washington residence for about four months. However, the Adamses were responsible for bringing the young US Marine Band to the White House. This alone indicates the importance placed on music as a vital part of the spirit and social flair of the presidency, following George Washington's lead. The Marine Band played for the Adamses' first reception on 1 January 1801. This set the precedent of "the president's own" band until the present day.

The Adamses' lack of musical interest may reflect their austere Puritan background. However, their sons were musically inclined: Charles sang with a light but pleasant voice while John Quincy played the flute. Evidently John's extensive service abroad had a lasting effect on the family's memories and musical tastes. In a letter written by Abigail, we learn that the *Messiah* performance she heard at the Handel commemoration in 1778 at Westminster Abbey was "the most powerful effect of music I ever experienced."[13]

President Adams also enjoyed religious music in the services of various denominations. His description of an elaborate Catholic service at Christ Church in Philadelphia contains these words: "the assembly chanted most sweetly. Here is everything which can lay hold of the eye, ear, and imagination. Everything which can charm and bewitch the simple and ignorant. I wonder how Luther ever broke the spell."[14] Adams also admired the Methodists' singing. He wrote in his diary when the Continental Congress was meeting in Philadelphia in 1774, "In the evening, I went to the Methodist meeting [which must have been at the old St. George's Church].... The singing here is very sweet and soft indeed; the [finest] music I have heard in any society, except the Moravian, and once at church with organ."[15]

According to hymnologist Harvey Marks, both John Adams and Thomas Jefferson were very interested in hymns. During their retirement, these two statesmen, who lived long lives, discussed hymns through personal correspondence. In answer to Jefferson's 12 October 1813 letter, Adams wrote to him on 14 November 1813, "The Psalms of David, in sublimity beauty, pathos and originality, or in one Word, in poetry, are superior to all the Odes, Hymns and Songs in any language. But I had rather read them in our prose translation, than in any version I have seen. Why have those verses been annihilated? I suspect platonick [*sic*] Christianity, pharisaical Judaism, or machiavilian [*sic*] Politicks, in this case."[16] Actually, in 1741, Benjamin Franklin had printed on his new press a collection to be used for congregational singing called *Psalms and Hymns* by Isaac Watts.

John Merrill's research revealed that the hymn recognized as the most favored by John Adams is "How Lovely Are Thy Dwellings Fair," written by John Milton in 1648. Milton, the author of great Christian literary works, was born in London in 1608 and died there in 1674. After traveling extensively in Europe, where he wrote some of his most beautiful poems, he returned to England and quickly rose in influence. Under Cromwell, Milton became the Latin secretary of state. While performing these duties, he went blind, forcing him into retirement. It was during that time that Milton com-

How Lovely Are Thy Dwellings Fair

Words: John Milton, 1648
Music: William Croft, 1708

C.M.
ST. ANNE

1. How love - ly are thy dwell - ings fair! O
2. Hap - py who in thy house re - side, Where
3. They jour - ney on from strength to strength, With
4. For God the Lord, both sun and shield, Gives

Lord of hosts, how dear The pleas - ant tab - er -
thee they e - ver praise; Hap - py whose strength in
joy and glad - some cheer, Till all be - fore our
grace and glo - ry bright: No good from them should

na - cles are Where thou dost dwell so near!
thee doth bide, And in their hearts thy ways.
God at length In Zi - on do ap - pear.
be with - held Whose ways are just and right. A - men.

posed his most significant works, including *Paradise Lost* and *Paradise Regained*. Milton made metrical versions of nineteen psalms, but one of his best was written when he was only fifteen years old. This is a setting of Psalm 136, titled "Let Us with a Gladsome Mind." This hymn is one of two psalm settings of Milton in common use today. The other is based on Psalm 84 and is titled "How Lovely Are Thy Dwellings Fair."[17] Although seven of these psalm settings appeared in Unitarian collections, the metrical setting of Psalm 84 has been published rather extensively. The setting has been used as a beautiful hymn.

As with other versifiers, Milton had to deal with three conflicting demands: the common meter, his own imaginative poetic art, and a biblical text. A man with skills in many languages, his original manuscript notes for Psalm 84 were in Hebrew.[18] Because of his brilliant academic resources, he was able to smooth out the difficulties evident in the 1562 *Sternhold and Hopkins* version of this psalm. The text thus became significant for the second president of the United States.

The music for this hymn was composed by William Croft, the first organist of St. Anne's Church in Soho, London. As an important hymn tune composer, Croft followed Jeremiah Clarke at the Chapel Royal. In 1708 he succeeded John Blow as organist at Westminster Abbey. Croft's most significant sacred work was *Musica Sacra* of 1724, the first church music to be engraved in score on plates. The ST. ANNE tune today is very well known as the music for Isaac Watts's "O God, Our Help in Ages Past." However, the music is well suited to Milton's text when sung smoothly and with sincerity. The melody, although having many skips, always rests easily as the cadences at the end of each phrase are approached by half-steps. This results in a powerful yet joyful melodic treatment. Erik Routley, an outstanding twentieth-century hymnologist, calls it "the most celebrated of all English tunes."[19] The melody is even more recognizable than HANOVER, Croft's other outstanding hymn tune. The harmony of ST. ANNE, although containing different chords in each progression, is very smooth and logical.

In analyzing each stanza individually, the reader realizes that the music is very expressive of the text. Stanza one takes the singer immediately to the glories of heaven, away from the trials below. Psychologically speaking, this thought must have been like a balm to Adams's soul. The happiness is further reinforced in stanza two as it tells of the strength in the Lord's ways. Stanza three builds on this strength, which appears to gain momentum as believers approach God's throne. It also indicates glad and joyous cheer, which must have been consoling to Adams in his presidency. Stanza four offers final reassurance of a just reward as the text encourages man to always act with justice and do what he believes is right in God's sight.

The text of each stanza must have provided a solace for President Adams during the many difficult decisions he faced during his tenure. Not only was he required by the Constitution to have his rival serve as vice president, but his decision to remain neutral in the European war between Great Britain and France undoubtedly was a difficult choice. The words of this hymn and their theme certainly reflect an influence on some of the major decisions of our second president, John Adams.

THOMAS JEFFERSON

1743–1826

Third President (1801–1809)

When he served as president of the United States, John F. Kennedy hosted a state dinner for all the nation's living Nobel Prize winners. When he stood up to welcome the group and address them, Kennedy commented, "This is the greatest collection of minds ever assembled in the White House except for when Thomas Jefferson dined alone." While Kennedy delivered his statement in jest, there was a certain amount of truth in it. Thomas Jefferson was probably the most intelligent individual ever to serve as this nation's president. Not only was he one of the nation's greatest political minds, but his inquisitive mind led him to become a leading scientist and architect as well as an inventor, author, philosopher, and agriculturist. Additionally, he apparently was a fine musician. For all of his brilliance, however, Jefferson might have remained a mediocre leader were it not for one crowning achievement in his first term.

Thomas Jefferson was born in 1743 on the edge of the Blue Ridge Mountains. The son of a planter, he received the finest tutorial education possible in that part of Virginia before matriculating to the College of William and Mary. A diligent student, young Jefferson mastered not only his studies in the classical tradition of higher education in those days, but he also became an accomplished violinist. He graduated from William and Mary when he was nineteen and went to Williamsburg to study law. In keeping with tradition, Jefferson studied law by apprenticing himself to another attorney.

After five years of studying law, Jefferson returned to build his home on land inherited from his father, was elected to the Virginia House of Burgesses, and married Martha Wayles Skelton, a wealthy young widow. In addition to his obvious intelligence, observers noted that, like George Washington, he was tall with unusually straight posture and reddish hair, and with a distinguished bearing.

Jefferson's emergence upon the political scene occurred at precisely the right moment. Tensions had been building between the colonies and Great Britain, and his fellow Virginia legislators quickly recognized Jefferson's excellent literary gifts, though they did not always agree with his seemingly radical ideas. When the tension resulted in conflict, Jefferson, representing Virginia in the Second Continental Congress, took a prominent role in the colonies' response. Ultimately, the Congress selected Jefferson to serve as the primary author of the Declaration of Independence, his chief claim to American fame. Afterward, Jefferson served as the governor of Virginia during the American Revolution, fleeing reluctantly when British invaders approached and burned the state capitol, Richmond, and narrowly avoiding later capture at his home at Monticello, near Charlottesville.

After the Revolution, the Continental Congress selected Jefferson to serve as its ambassador to France. It was a difficult time for Jefferson. His wife had died from complications of childbirth after allegedly making him promise that he would never remarry. During those tumultuous days, Jefferson served as a single parent to his daughters and observed France as the French Revolution began. He also was absent when the Constitutional Convention, presided over by George Washington and under the influence of his friend and fellow Virginian James Madison, adopted the Constitution. After its ratification, Jefferson returned home when President Washington drafted him to serve as the nation's first secretary of state.

Jefferson served an important but tumultuous time as Washington's secretary of state. He frequently found himself in conflict with Alexander Hamilton, Washington's equally strong-willed secretary of treasury. Ultimately, the disagreements between the two led to the formation of the nation's first two political parties. One party, led by Hamilton and Vice President John Adams, known as the Federalists, favored a strong central government and tended to take a pro-British attitude in foreign affairs as war erupted in Europe. The other, led by Jefferson and James Madison, was known as the Democratic-Republicans and favored a weaker central government and tended to be pro-French. Ultimately, Jefferson's disagreements with Hamilton led Jefferson to run against Adams for the presidency in 1796. Narrowly defeated, he served in the unusual position of being Adams's vice president due to the way the Constitution was structured at the time. He and Adams served together for an uncomfortable four years that often found Jefferson away from Washington, DC, leading the opposition to Adams.

The election of 1800 proved to be a repeat of the election of 1796 and also one of the most bitterly contested presidential elections in US history. It was so fiercely contested that the results of the Electoral College threw the election to the House of Representatives, where Jefferson was chosen. Despite his obvious dislike of a strong central government, Jefferson found himself forced to deal with some of the most vexing problems in early American history, most notably the ongoing war in Europe. In many ways, his presidency was an ineffective one—save for one outstanding achievement. In 1803 Jefferson seized the opportunity to purchase the Louisiana Territory from France, thus securing the western destiny of the young country, peacefully doubling its size for the cost of fifteen million dollars, and serving as the crowning achievement of his presidency. In addition to these successes, he also initiated and authorized the Lewis and Clark expedition that explored the newly acquired land and also went all the way to the Pacific coast, staking claim to those western lands. The popularity of the Louisiana Purchase ensured his reelection in 1804.

Upon completion of his second term, Jefferson retired to Monticello, where he pursued his many scholarly and business interests. Unfortunately, he failed to manage his finances effectively and died deeply in debt. His death occurred within a few hours of his old friend and adversary John Adams, on the fiftieth anniversary of the Declaration of Independence. Ironically, Jefferson never considered his presidency one of his most outstanding achievements. His tombstone, which he designed, reads, "Author of the American Declaration of Independence, Author of the Statute of Virginia for Religious Freedom, and Father of the University of Virginia."

Jefferson's religious interests might rightly be interpreted as those of a Deist. He deeply distrusted organized religion and throughout his political career sought to achieve a separation of church and state so that neither body would be unduly influenced by the other. He also fiercely protected religious liberty so that all Americans might worship freely and thus avoid the sectarian strife that he believed destroyed freedom. While rejecting evangelical and orthodox Christian beliefs, he did regard the teachings of Jesus Christ as good moral guidelines and as important components of the development of a civil religion in the fledging nation.[20]

Thomas Jefferson was one of the most musically sensitive presidents. Having learned to play the violin quite well by the age of fourteen, he valued music highly throughout his life. At the age of seventy-four, he considered music as "the favorite passion of my soul." The art of music for him was a delightful recreation. Jefferson was an accomplished musician and played a number of instruments. He enjoyed performing chamber music and was adept at improvisation. Jefferson often played with a group of noted amateur musicians in Virginia as well as violin duets with his friend Patrick Henry.

Upon receipt of Francis Hopkinson's collection of *Seven Songs for the Harpsichord or Piano-forte* (1788), which was dedicated to George Washington, Jefferson acknowledged his appreciation with this note: "I will not tell you how much they have pleased us, nor how well the last of them merits praise for its pathos, but relate a fact only, which is that while my elder daughter was playing it on a harpsichord, I happened to look toward the fire and saw the younger one all in tears. I asked her if she was sick? She said, 'No, but the tune was so mournful.'"[21]

Of Jefferson's six children, only two survived to adulthood, Mary and Martha. Both were musically talented, as was their mother, Martha Wayles Skelton, who died at age thirty-four, leaving Jefferson a widower until his death. However, he saw to it that his daughters were musically trained, especially on the keyboard. He bought each of them their own fine Kirkman harpsichord. Even though Jefferson was not a keyboard player, he always had a keyboard close by even when he was president. He was fascinated with the *pianoforte*, being among the few Americans to own a piano. However, he never purchased one for the White House because of lack of funds.

Jefferson's feeling toward music in America during his generation is best described in a letter he wrote to a correspondent in France: "If there is a gratification which I envy any people in this world, it is your country its music. This is the favorite passion of my soul, and fortune has cast my lot in a country where it is in a state of deplorable barbarism."[22] While Jefferson was president, he had several sheaves of music bound into volumes, indicating that he valued their preservation.

At one point Jefferson had expressed his desire to import Italian musicians who could provide domestic and musical needs for Monticello; he wanted a "court band." This was eventually accomplished as an enlargement of the Marine Band in Washington. A legend tells of Jefferson asking Colonel Burrows to enlist some musicians in Italy as marines and bring them to America. This eventually occurred, and the group of sixteen Sicilian musicians arrived in 1805. They contributed much to the quality and history of the president's own band.

According to musicologist Elise Kirk, Jefferson also must have enjoyed vocal soloists since on 4 July 1806 at a White House reception, a "Mr. Cutting" sang a song set to the tune of "Anacreon in Heaven."[23] Evidently this was the first hearing in the White House of the music that became our national anthem. The tune itself was written in 1780 by John Stafford Smith, a loyal Englishman from London. He disapproved of lawyer Francis Scott Key's lyrics to his melody. However, in 1814, Baltimore actor Ferdinand Durang first sang the text "Defense of Fort McHenry," the name given by Key to the original lyrical poem. This popular tune was thus immortalized as "The Star-Spangled Banner" even though it did not officially become the national anthem until 1931.

President Jefferson enjoyed and performed music regularly, but we know little about musical activities during his eight years in the White House. Though there was no official "First Lady," Jefferson's two daughters and Dolley Madison, wife of secretary of state James Madison, served as hostesses from time to time. Both of Jefferson's sons-in-law were senators. We do know that Jefferson officially dropped the title "Presidential Palace" when he took office. He informed the citizens that his home was to be known as the "President's House."

As for Jefferson's use of hymns, in a bound copy of music at Charlottesville, there is a manuscript of "Variations on the Sicilian Hymn 'Life Let Us Cherish.'" The family letters of Thomas Jefferson indicate that musician Gaetano Carusi may have "filled in as flautist or violinist, topping off a relaxing evening with a Sicilian hymn or folksong for the president."[24] Since Jefferson often worked thirteen hours a day at his desk, he was usually tired in the evening. Music for him was a "companion to divert, delight and sweeten many hours," and there is little doubt that he was familiar with many hymns and psalm settings.

Douglas Snow states that the government of Rhode Island was set up under distinctives fashioned on the model of a Baptist church. He further notes, "Thomas Jefferson was not a Baptist but his father, sister, and favorite aunt were, so he frequently attended a Baptist Church near Monticello, Virginia, and was much impressed with their democratic way of doing things and he concluded that their plan of government would be the best possible one for the American colonies."[25] During these visits he also would hear some hymns probably "lined-out" by a precentor (song leader). There is no mention of these in his writings, maybe because the congregational hymn singing was not very musical.

In 1784 the General Association of Connecticut commissioned poet Joel Barlow to make an official revision of Isaac Watts's 1719 psalter, titled *Psalms of David Imitated.* These psalm settings were used extensively in churches but needed to be updated to exclude references to Britain. The American Revolution had changed the colonies so radically that this revision seemed necessary. Barlow went too far in his revision, not only making changes in political language, but also in grammar, style, and theology. His 1785 publication was too radical for the pastors in Connecticut; nevertheless, Barlow's revision of Watts's psalter continued to be printed as late as 1813. When Barlow became a supporter of Thomas Jefferson and was appointed ambassador to France after the French Revolution, the pastors took exception to his work. France had come to symbolize godlessness and chaos to the established churches of New England. Jefferson symbolized disestablishment of the same churches. Suddenly, Barlow's revisions were viewed in a different light; seeds of "heresy" were discovered in his texts. A new revision was demanded immediately. The association of ministers in Connecticut called upon the most orthodox scholar to do it: Timothy Dwight, president of Yale.[26]

Dwight's edition of 1801 restored much of Watts's language and gave new interpretation to other psalm settings. Most notably for hymnody, this is the first appearance of Dwight's version of Psalm 137—"I Love Thy Kingdom, Lord," a psalm that Watts had chosen not to paraphrase. The edition supplanted Barlow's in most New England churches, becoming known as "Dwight's Watts." From Barlow, Jefferson must have become familiar with these events and perhaps with the psalm settings themselves.

Jefferson corresponded with John Adams about hymns during their retirement. From Monticello on 12 October 1813 he discussed the English psalm settings, both Sternhold's "Old Version" of 1562 and Tate and Brady's "New Version" of 1696: "Indeed bad is the best of the English versions; not a ray of poetical genius having ever been employed on them."[27] He concludes by discussing the poetic merits of David, who wrote many of the original psalms. He uses as examples Psalm 15 and Psalm 148.[28]

President Jefferson is known more for his writings than for his love and performance of music. However, it is notable that his words have often been set to music. The most enduring is Randall Thompson's choral work for men's voices and orchestra called *The Testament of Freedom* (1943). This exciting work was composed in honor of the 200th anniversary of Jefferson's birth with texts drawn from his own writings. It has also been edited for use with mixed voices and today is a standard choral work.

Thomas Jefferson's favorite Christmas carol was "O Come, All Ye Faithful" (ADESTE FIDELIS), but his favored hymn was "Hark, the Glad Sound, the Saviour Comes," written by Philip Doddridge in 1735. The first stanza of this hymn definitely fits into the Advent category and serves as a prelude to "Adeste Fidelis," which was popular during Jefferson's election to his first presidential term in 1800. Doddridge, born in 1702, came from a family of dissenters with beliefs similar to those of Isaac Watts. Young Philip learned scriptures from his mother, who had hung Dutch tiles of biblical characters in her home. He became an orphan at thirteen but grew spiritually because of his mother's early influence. At seventeen he felt the call to the ministry but turned down the opportunity to attend college to be an Anglican minister. Instead, he attended Kibworth Academy and remained as pastor of the Kibworth Congregationalist Church from 1723 to 1729.

On the advice of his close friend Isaac Watts, Doddridge opened his own academy in North Hampton. John Julian, a noted hymnologist, said that of the 200 students who studied under his tutorship, 120 entered the ministry.[29] With the aging Watts, Doddridge co-authored one of the most useful books in the eighteenth century. After Watts had written the outline, Doddridge wrote the text of *The Rise and Progress of the Soul,* which was published under his name and widely circulated and printed in many languages. The book was very helpful to William Wilberforce, John Wesley, and George Whitefield. Whitefield may have brought it to the colonies in 1739 when he came to aid Jonathan Edwards in the revival services that became "the Great Awakening." We do know that Whitefield brought with him many of Watts's hymns as well as Wesley's *Hymns and Sacred Poems* of 1739 and encouraged their use in his services. It is possible that he also brought Doddridge's "Hark, the Glad Sound," which Jefferson may have heard sung as a child or young person.

Doddridge's nearly 400 hymns were undoubtedly influenced by Watts. As was the practice, he based his hymns on sermons he delivered. Doddridge's hymns excelled Watts's in simplicity, serenity, and tenderness. The manuscript of "Hark, the Glad Sound" indicates that it was first sung 28 December 1735.[30] The heading is "Christ's Message from Luke 14:18–19,"

Hark, the Glad Sound, the Saviour Comes

Words: Philip Doddridge, 1735
Music: John Randall, 1715-1799

C.M.
CAMBRIDGE

1. Hark, the glad sound, the Sav-iour comes, The Sav-iour
prom-ised long Let ev-'ry heart pre-pare a
throne, And ev-'ry voice a song, And ev-'ry voice a
song, And ev-'ry voice a song.

2. He comes, the pri-soners to re-lease In Sa-tan's
bond-age held; The gates of brass be-fore him
burst, The i-ron fet-ters yield, The i-ron fet-ters
yield, The i-ron fet-ters yield.

3. Our glad ho-san-nas, Prince of Peace, Thy wel-come
shall pro-claim, And heaven's e-ter-nal arch-es
ring With thy be-lov-ed name, With thy be-lov-ed
name, With thy be-lov-ed name. A - men.

but in reality it is about Isaiah 61:1–2 and is the scripture Jesus read at Nazareth in the Luke passage. Because they were used as sermon summaries, all of Doddridge's hymns have strong biblical content; some are simply para-phrases of scripture. Collections printed in America of some of Doddridge's hymns were published in 1783 in a hymnal of 166 selections called *A Collection of Hymns,* edited by Simeon Howard in 1795, and in a book called

Sacred Poetry, edited by Jeremy Belknap. "Hark, the Glad Sound" is notably much more than an Advent hymn. Editors often omit at least three of the original seven stanzas of the hymn. One stanza, which reads "He comes, the prisoners to release in Satan's bondage held," could have influenced both Jefferson and the British statesman William Wilberforce in their feelings about slavery. Perhaps this important phrase was thus embedded in the mind of the author of the Declaration of Independence.

"Hark, the Glad Sound" was first officially sanctioned and used by the Church of Scotland in 1745. Since 1755 all of the leading hymnals of varying denominations (except the Methodists) have included this hymn in their collections. It has been used extensively in America since that time, but has also been translated into many languages. In popular usage it is the most widely known of all of Doddridge's hymns, along with "O Happy Day That Fixed My Choice." In 1866, Lord Selborne said of "Hark, the Glad Sound," "A more sweet, vigorous, and perfect composition is not to be found even in the whole body of ancient hymns."[31] Its stellar poetry may have been a reason for Jefferson's admiration of the hymn.

The music of "Hark, the Glad Sound" was composed by John Randall, an English composer. Having graduated from Cambridge in 1744, he was an organist for several notable churches and later became a music professor. Randall edited a collection of psalm and hymn tunes, including several of his own. CAMBRIDGE first appeared as a hymn tune in 1794. Being in common meter, this text could be sung to any number of tunes; however, the text by Doddridge is wedded to the tune by Randall. After the *fermata* (long-held note) on the third line, the succeeding lines of each stanza receive a contrasting melodic and harmonic treatment. The perfection of both text and music certainly would have appealed to Jefferson, a well-trained musician. Interestingly, the subject of hymns was contained in correspondence between Jefferson and John Adams after both retired from public service.

"Hark, the Glad Sound" may have been sung in any number of congregational services Jefferson may have attended. It was in the hymn repertoire of both established and separate church denominations during Jefferson's administration. Its simple but "classic" music and its well-written text make it a good choice as a favored hymn of Thomas Jefferson.

JAMES MADISON

1751–1836

Fourth President (1809–1817)

Great achievement at a relatively young age can be either a tremendous burden or an incredible blessing. In the case of James Madison, it probably became both. As a young man, leading Americans recognized Madison's important role in the Constitutional Convention, and his friends regarded him as a leading candidate for higher office. By the end of his political career, however, his two terms as president had been a bitter disappointment.

Born in 1751, the son of a Virginia planter, Madison attended the College of New Jersey (Princeton University). A diligent student and brilliant scholar, Madison became intricately involved in Virginia politics as the Revolutionary War began. At the age of twenty-five, he participated in the development of the Virginia state constitution. Virginia voters also elected him to the Continental

Congress. His involvement in Virginia and colonial politics led to his lifelong friendship with fellow Virginian Thomas Jefferson.

Once the colonies achieved their independence in 1783, the unity that had bound the thirteen states together began to disintegrate. Madison and a young New Yorker, Alexander Hamilton, were among those whom this disunity greatly disturbed. Subsequently, Madison and Hamilton were influential in calling what became the Constitutional Convention in 1787 and persuaded the hero of the Revolution, George Washington, to attend and serve as the presiding officer.

The Constitution that the convention produced was not the work of Madison alone, but if there was one individual who contributed the most, it was the young Virginian. Because of this document, he would later widely be regarded as the "Father of the Constitution." This did not complete Madison's work, however. In the months that followed, he worked tirelessly to ensure that the various states ratified the document. Among the agreements that Madison made to assure ratification was his promise to add a bill of rights to the Constitution through congressional amendments. He also produced many of the essays that those known as "Federalists" published in support of the Constitution.

After ratification, his home district elected Madison to represent them in the House of Representatives. Serving as representative throughout Washington's two terms, Madison found himself involved in some of the most important issues in American history. He fulfilled his promise to secure passage of the Bill of Rights. He agreed to a compromise by which the first Bank of the United States was chartered in exchange for the location of a permanent national capital in what was named Washington, District of Columbia. He served as an important constitutional consultant for President Washington and combated Alexander Hamilton's policies that he felt overexpanded the power of the central government. He and Jefferson formed a political party known as the Democratic-Republicans to serve as a counterweight to the Federalist Party led by Hamilton and John Adams. During the Adams presidency, Madison served as the true leader of this new party and engineered Jefferson's victory in 1800.

When the House of Representatives decided the election in Jefferson's favor, Madison immediately went to work as Jefferson's secretary of state. His voluptuous and vivacious wife, Dolley, served as the widower Jefferson's hostess in the White House. She became famous for her work as a hostess that carried over into her own time as First Lady. Madison and Jefferson found themselves embroiled in tense foreign affairs throughout his two terms in office, and Jefferson leaned heavily on his friend in those years. Most notably, Madison dealt with ongoing problems with Barbary Coast pirates and with wars in Europe between France and Britain. As a result of the European conflict, the United States found itself embroiled in a vicious trade war. When Jefferson stepped aside after two terms as president, the voters selected Madison as his successor. President Madison found himself dealing with many of the same problems as his predecessor.

Ultimately, this ongoing trade war, as well as violation of US concepts of freedom of the seas, a US desire for British Canada, and continued British support of Native American resistance on the US frontier led to war between the United States and Great Britain. Vastly unpopular in New England, the war's critics derisively mocked the conflict as "Mr. Madison's War." Despite the war's unpopularity in the Northeast, Madison won a second a term in the midst of the war. Madison also dealt with a myriad of problems as the poorly prepared country struggled to win the war. In an ultimate embarrassment, a British raid defeated a ragtag American army and forced Madison to flee. Dolley Madison won everlasting fame as she managed to gather several irreplaceable items, including a famous portrait of George Washington, saving them when the British burned the capital's public buildings, including the White House.

Fortunately for the nation, heroes like Andrew Jackson, William Henry Harrison, and Oliver Perry won enough victories to maintain the status quo, and after intense negotiations, the British agreed to a peace treaty at Ghent late in 1814. The remainder of Madison's administration was largely insignificant. He retired to Virginia, where he engaged in the life of a country-gentleman scholar until his death in 1836. For the remainder of his life he defended his precious Union from increasing attacks by states' rights advocates.

Madison's religious views were somewhat similar to those of Adams and Jefferson. He never completely rejected the early teachings he had received at Princeton but could not be described as an evangelical. Perhaps more than any other president, he was most concerned about the preservation of religious liberty. As his famous "Memorial and Remonstrance" argues, religion is a matter of "reason and conviction" and cannot be directed by "force or violence." He believed that failure to protect freedom of worship and failure to protect all citizens from government infringement upon religious freedom endangered all freedoms. His alliance with religious dissenters, most notably Baptists, was essential to the establishment of separation of church and state and the creation of religious liberty in the United States.[32]

Since the Madisons were the first presidential family to live in the White House long enough to make it a home and a place for entertaining, they definitely set some social precedents. Historian Elise Kirk states that Dolley Madison "managed to maintain an oasis of civilization in a lonely city that was only beginning to acknowledge its social needs."[33] Having assisted Jefferson with his entertaining when her husband served as secretary of state, Dolley added to the informal style of Jefferson her own flair, imagination, and touch of pomp.

Jefferson usually dominated the conversation in the partisan social events he held at the White House. Under Madison, with the First Lady's insistence on considering not only the needs of her husband's career but also the needs of their guests, the weekly series of "drawing room" events were open to all, rather than just for invited guests. Dolley's leadership in this area endeared her to the public; these social gatherings provided an occasion for the exchange of ideas in an informal setting. Dressed in fine French attire with elaborate headdresses, she became known as "Queen Dolley." In her entertaining, she was often assisted by her "master of ceremonies," John Pierre Sioussat, a polished Frenchman.

Although neither James nor Dolley played the piano, music in Madison's administration became a vital element in their hospitality. Both the Marine Band and invited guests provided musical numbers at these social events, described by frequent guest Washington Irving as evenings of "blazing splendor." Musical performers were mostly ladies playing the *pianoforte* in the true American tradition of the time. The Madisons purchased the first piano specifically for use in the White House. In 1809 a *pianoforte* was bought for $450; unfortunately, it was burned by the British in 1814 along with the other furniture. Dolley was not long in obtaining another. In only a few months she had purchased a used *pianoforte* for use in their temporary living quarters.

Shortly after the introduction of the new European dance craze—"the waltz"—into America, it was performed at the White House. Having evidently suppressed her strict heritage as a Quaker, Dolley enjoyed the glamour of this new dance movement. Kirk states, "Dolley Madison's light steps were delightfully immortalized in the earliest piece of music dedicated to a first lady—'Mrs. Madison's Waltz,' published by Willig in Philadelphia between 1810 and 1812."[34] Another purchase made by the First Lady was a fascinating collection of musical scores, an act revealing again the importance of the role of music in the Madison administration. Perhaps being influenced by Jefferson's extensive collection of music, these scores are in the Library of Congress. With the title *Journal of Musick of Italian, French and Italian Songs, romances and duets, and of overtures, rondos, etc. for the Forte Piano*, these were published in Philadelphia by subscription beginning in January 1810. Two volumes appeared each month for two years, each having several musical selections. These were edited by Mme. Le Pelletier, who was undoubtedly from a small French colony in Philadelphia. This collection probably provided the scores for some of the guest pianists.

As for the usage of hymns by the Madisons, there is no information concerning their use at the White House on any occasion. However, through extensive research by John Merrill in 1933, it was determined that James Madison especially appreciated the hymn "O God, My Strength and Fortitude," written by Thomas Sternhold in 1561.[35] This hymn, a metrical version of Psalm 18, first appeared in the Sternhold-Hopkins collection later termed the "Old Version." This psalter was in extensive use in Britain and America in Madison's time, although there were some alterations made in certain stanzas. Madison, if he attended some of the more formal church services, probably had often sung this hymn.

Thomas Sternhold was the groom of robes for Henry VIII of England when he began to write sacred ballads for the court to replace their amorous songs. He is the author of forty versions of various psalms with nearly all being in common meter. His work as a poet who put psalms in English meter is often compared with Clement Marot, who as valet to the bedchamber of Francis I of France originated the French metrical psalter. The primary difference is that the French used 110 different meters for their psalm settings. It is interesting that both psalters were completed in the same year, 1562. Some say that Sternhold retained his position under Edward VI because of his setting psalms to rhyme and meter. An interesting event in 1549 occurred when the eleven-year-old King Edward heard Sternhold composing and singing some poetry based on the Psalms. Edward enjoyed them very much, and eventually, when Sternhold had versified nineteen psalms, the dedication made to the twelve-year-old king was made with these words: "Albeit I cannot give your majesty great loaves or bring into the Lord's barn full handfuls…. I am bold to present a few crumbs which I have picked from under my Lord's board."[36]

The completed "Old Version" in 1562, with John Hopkins as the editor, contained not only thirty-six texts by Sternhold but also versifications of eleven other authors. The tune to "O God, My Strength and Fortitude" was written by Jeremiah Clarke in 1707.[37] It first appeared three years following Clarke's death in Henry Playford's *Divine Companion*. Playford was a music publisher concerned with improving psalm singing. Up to this time, tunes generally were anonymous; composers were more associated with the harmonizations than with melodies. Clarke has been called the "inventor of the modern English hymn tune." The ST. MAGNUS tune that was sung to

O God, My Strength and Fortitude

Words: Thomas Sternhold, 1561
Music: Jeremiah Clark, 1709

C.M.
ST. MAGNUS

1. O God, my strength and for - ti - tude Of
2. My God, my rock, in whom I trust; The
3. I sore be - set with pain and grief, Did
4. The Lord de - scend - ed from a - bove, And
5. On che - rub and on cher - u - bim Full
6. He brought me forth to o - pen place, That
7. Thou teach - est me thy sav - ing health, Thy

force I must love thee; Thou art my cas - tle
wor - ker of my wealth; My re - fuge, buck - ler,
pray to God for grace; And he forth - with heard
bowed the heav - ens high; And un - der - neath his
roy - al - ly he rode, And on the wings of
so I might be free; And kept me safe, be -
right hand is my tower; Thy love and gen - tle -

and de - fence In my ne - ces - si - ty.
and my shield, The horn of all my health!
my com - plaint Out of his ho - ly place.
feet he cast The dark - ness of the sky.
migh - ty winds Came fly - ing all a - broad.
cause he had A fa - vor un - to me.
ness al - so Do still in - crease my power. A - men.

Sternhold's text is noted as looking both backward and forward. It is related to earlier psalm tunes but is also "modern," being in a major key without any hint of the modal. It also has the bold octave leap to begin the last phrase. Clarke's innovation works because it has been properly prepared by the preceding use of the extreme melodic notes.

The text of this hymn could be compared with Luther's "A Mighty Fortress" but quickly moves to a positive stance. After using such words for God as "strength," "rock," "refuge," "buckler," and "shield," stanza three is a plea for grace. Referring to a God of nature, stanzas four and five recognize that God is in control of all things. The first two stanzas are certainly personal, as they acknowledge free will, providential care, love, and gentleness as aids to power which God bestows.

This hymn certainly could have comforted Madison in many critical decisions, especially those concerning war situations during his two terms as president. In any event, the hymn was well loved by several denominations of his day. It provided a prayer and a promise for a young nation and perhaps reinforced strong beliefs of complete religious freedom, which Madison championed.

JAMES MONROE

1758–1831

Fifth President (1817–1825)

Many American presidents acquire lasting fame because they serve during times of great national tragedy or for important events that occur during their administration. Some acquire lasting fame because of outstanding personalities or tremendous leadership skills. A very few are known because of an important policy that is named after them. James Monroe is one of the latter.

James Monroe was born in Westmoreland County, Virginia, toward the end of the colonial period. Westmoreland County, the birthplace of both George Washington and James Madison, was one of the oldest counties in Virginia and therefore in the colonies. While Washington was born a generation earlier and Madison was Monroe's elder by seven years, Monroe's career would be closely linked with both. Like another Virginian with whom he would be linked, Thomas Jefferson, Monroe attended the College of William and Mary, the institution typically attended by wealthy Virginians. However, when the American Revolution erupted, Monroe enlisted in the Virginia military. Monroe served with distinction, being severely wounded at Washington's famous victory at Trenton in December 1776 and suffering through the many travails of the infamous winter at Valley Forge. Toward the end of the Revolution, he worked closely with Governor Thomas Jefferson, whom he served as an aide.

After the Revolution ended, Monroe attached himself closely to Jefferson and James Madison, Jefferson's closest political ally. In the years that followed, Monroe served with some distinction in the early Congress of the United States as well as the Virginia legislature. In the 1790s, he joined the new political party formed by Jefferson and Madison, the Democratic-Republicans, where he rose quickly due to his support of their policies. The Virginia legislature selected him to represent the state as a US senator in 1790, where he served until President Washington selected him as minister to France. Afterward, Virginia elected Monroe as governor, where he completed three terms.

As the new republic continued to grow, Jefferson called upon Monroe to travel to France to engage in negotiations that ultimately resulted in the Louisiana Purchase. After almost three years in the White House, President James Madison called upon his fellow Virginian, Monroe, to serve as his secretary of state. Monroe functioned in this capacity during the period leading up to and during the War of 1812 until Madison chose him to serve as secretary of war. When Madison stepped down after two terms, he recommended that Democratic-Republicans choose Monroe as their nominee. Monroe defeated the dying Federalist Party's candidate. Subsequently, when the next presidential election occurred in 1820, the Electoral College elected Monroe virtually unanimously for a second term.

In 1817 a newspaper labeled Monroe's presidency as "the Era of Good Feelings." While Monroe's eight years in office were certainly not without problems, Monroe sought to achieve this type of political climate in the aftermath of the controversial War of 1812. He undertook public tours of much of the country to create goodwill, and he appointed a capable cabinet representative of diverse political elements that included John C. Calhoun and John Quincy Adams. During his administration, the country settled the difficult "Missouri Question" with the Missouri Compromise of 1820 and pacified conflict with Spain over Florida and various boundary questions with the Florida Purchase agreement. He also led the country during a time of recovery from the Panic of 1819 and, though somewhat reluctantly, supported the expansion of internal improvements known as the "American System." He stressed nationalism and unity during a time when sectionalism and slavery began to emerge as critical national issues.

Perhaps the greatest achievement of Monroe's presidency came from an address he delivered to Congress in 1823. With the disintegration of the Spanish Empire, Monroe and Secretary of State Adams issued a response to Congress concerning the fears of European meddling in the New World. Later known as the Monroe Doctrine, this address stated that the United States would not tolerate European intervention in the Western Hemisphere. The Monroe Doctrine became a cornerstone of American foreign policy. Upon his retirement from the White House in 1825, Monroe lived a relatively quiet and uneventful life until his death in 1831.

James Monroe was a practicing Episcopalian who worshiped regularly on Sundays in Washington, DC. He was both married and buried through the Episcopal Church; other than that, however, little is known of his religious beliefs. Franklin Steiner has stated that Monroe was one of the least religious presidents. However, given Monroe's close relationship with Thomas Jefferson, his early support from Virginia Baptists, and his support for the cause of religious liberty, it is quite possible that he regarded religious matters a personal issue. Unlike Jefferson and others of the era who tended toward unorthodox views, there never seems to have been criticism that Monroe held heretical or controversial religious ideas.[38]

Very little is known about Monroe's views and usage of music, but on 4 March 1817, he became the first president to be honored by an inaugural concert. This may have been due to First Lady Elizabeth Monroe having acquired French sensibilities when her husband served as ambassador to France under Washington. This also may have accounted for the Monroes being the first presidential couple to attend the theater in Washington.

Since the White House had been burned by the British during the War of 1812, the Monroes did not move into that residence until nine months after the election. On New Year's Day, 1818, President and Mrs. Monroe held a public reception on its reopening. This must have been a festive occasion since the Marine Band was using Turkish-influenced instruments, which were in vogue at the time. In addition to oboes, clarinets, bassoons, and horns, they added a bass drum, bugle horn, cymbals, and a predecessor of the bass tuba, the serpent. The Monroes purchased a fine *pianoforte* for the White House in 1818. It was "a French piano made by the Erard Brothers, decorated with bronze, having three legs and four pedals."[39]

Because of Elizabeth Monroe's chronic illness, the elder daughter, Eliza, who studied harp and other cultural subjects in France, took her place as hostess at the White House. Had it not been for the Marine Band and the fine Erard piano, the White House would have been a stiff, formal residence. Interestingly enough, during Monroe's two terms as president, "Washingtonians were deprived of the two most popular activities of city parties: dancing and cards."[40] However, during Monroe's second term, the weekly "drawing room" parties were crowded with invited guests, including secretaries, senators, foreign ministers, and consuls. The Monroes were even entertained by Pawnee chieftains, who staged an elaborate ceremonial dance on the White House lawn. An audience of 3,000 gazed in awe and amazement at the spectacle. Since Monroe insisted on court etiquette at the White House events, this was an unusual program. Elizabeth and Eliza had followed the President's wishes in establishing protocol.[41] These rules were strictly observed for weekly entertainment. No mention has been found concerning any hymns either played or sung during Monroe's administration. However, Merrill's research has determined that the most favored hymn of President Monroe was "O Lord, I Would Delight in Thee."

Written by John Ryland, Jr., in 1777, this hymn is representative of the ninety-nine hymn texts by Ryland from age sixteen until his death in 1825. Today, approximately thirteen of Ryland's hymns are in common use. In his time there were few names more honored among Baptists than Ryland. Since Monroe was a lifelong Episcopalian, it is interesting that a hymn written by a leading Baptist pastor would be selected. Probably Monroe's support of Virginia Baptists' desire for religious liberty, along with the influence of his mentor Jefferson, caused the fifth president to choose this hymn.

John Ryland, Jr., was the son of the pastor of the Baptist congregation at Warwick, England.[42] The elder Ryland, an effective mentor and scholar, taught Hebrew to young John at the age of five and Greek by the age of nine. From his mother, John received scriptural instruction, learning Bible verses from Dutch tiles mounted around the fireplace. He was converted and baptized at fourteen in the river Nen near Northampton.

In recognition of his progress and calling, his father's church made John assistant minister. In 1781 he was ordained and appointed as co-pastor of the congregation. When his father moved to London five years later, John succeeded him as pastor. Subsequently, Ryland accepted the presidency of the Baptist College in Bristol in 1793, concurrently becoming the pastor of Broadmead Church. He continued his duties for both of these institutions until his death.

John Ryland was a man of considerable literary culture. He was awarded the Doctor of Divinity degree from Brown University in Providence, Rhode Island, in 1792. He was also one of the founders of the Baptist Missionary

O Lord, I Would Delight in Thee

Words: John Ryland, 1771
Music: Thomas Haweis, 1792

C.M.
CHESTERFIELD

1. O Lord, I would de - light in thee, And on thy care de - pend; To thee in ev - 'ry trou - ble flee, My best, my on - ly friend.
2. When all cre - a - ted streams are dried, Thy ful - ness is the same; May I with this be sa - tis - fied, And glo - ry in thy name.
3. No good in crea - tures can be found, But may be found in thee; I must have all things and a - bound, While God is God to me.
4. He that has made my heaven se - cure, Will here all good pro - vide; While Christ is rich, can I be poor? What can I want be - side?
5. O Lord, I cast my care on thee; I tri - umph and a - dore: Hence - forth my great con - cern shall be To love and please thee more. A - men.

Society in England. It is quite interesting that Ryland had the privilege of baptizing William Carey in 1783 in the same river in which he himself had been immersed fifteen years earlier. Carey was the first English Baptist missionary sent out by the society.

After Ryland's death, two volumes of discourses written by him were published. Attached to these works are many of his hymns and the date of their composition. John Ryland's original manuscript to "O Lord, I Would Delight in Thee" contains this comment: "I recollect deeper feelings of mind in composing this hymn than perhaps I felt in making any other."[43] This hymn is a reflection of the writer's heart as well as a perfect selection for James Monroe, who was conspicuous by his silence on religious beliefs. He is quoted as saying, "Religion is a matter between our Maker and ourselves."[44] He seldom mentioned the Lord at all; perhaps this hymn said it all for the fifth president.

The hymn tune CHESTERFIELD was composed by Thomas Haweis in 1792.[45] This name was selected to honor Lord Chesterfield, statesman and author, who frequently visited Selina, Countess of Huntingdon, while the composer was chaplain to her chapel in Bath, England. It has also been called RICHMOND when the Haweiss's tune is adapted by Samuel Webbe the Younger.[46] This common-meter tune has been used with texts by a number of authors: Philip Doddridge, Charles Wesley, Samuel Johnson, Frederick Hosmer, and Isaac Watts (notably, Watts's "Joy to the World" and "Come, Let Us Join Our Cheerful Songs").

The tune covers an octave plus one note and initially outlines the key with an arpeggio. The marriage with Ryland's text, "O Lord, I Would Delight in Thee," is an excellent one; the music reflects the mood of the words. Haweis was himself an accomplished hymn writer, but his main occupation was that of a physician. However, after taking holy orders, he held several positions in the Church of England. This hymn tune appeared in 1792 in the hymnal *Carmina Christo (Hymns to the Savior).*

This hymn is a sincere prayer of gratefulness for the friendship of Christ. The words are scripturally based and meaningful for all Christians. The first stanza is very clear in stating a dependence on the Lord. Stanza two ends with giving glory to the Lord of life. Stanza three climaxes in the unique phrase "while God is God to me."

The confidence and faith of the believer is clearly outlined in stanza four, ending with the question, "What can I want beside?" The fifth stanza again comes from scripture—"casting my care on Thee" (1 Peter 5:7) and climaxes with the beautiful thought "to love and please Thee more."

There is little doubt that "O Lord, I Would Delight in Thee" reflects the presidency of James Monroe, considering that his administration was labeled as "the Era of Good Feelings." It seems to instill positive thoughts to go along with the accomplishments of our fifth president.

JOHN QUINCY ADAMS

1767–1848

Sixth President (1825–1829)

Being the child of an extremely successful parent is never an easy burden to bear. Being the child of a US president must be especially difficult. Being the son of one of the founding fathers of the nation must have carried with it an inconceivable pressure. In the case of John Quincy Adams, he responded by not only dealing with the pressure but by developing into a great man himself and becoming, with his father, the first father-son presidents in American history, something that did not occur again for almost 200 years.

John Quincy Adams was born in 1767 in Braintree, Massachusetts, the second child and first son of John Adams, a prominent young colonial attorney, and his wife, Abigail. From the beginning, he was known as Johnny to distinguish him from his father. Early in life, he set himself apart by signing his letters and other writing as JQA. In the years of his early life, John Quincy also distinguished himself by his decidedly quick mind and his capacity to learn foreign languages. He also was noted for his strict devotion to learning and his exacting Puritan upbringing. His father was rising quickly in political ranks in the crisis that resulted in American independence, and young John Quincy, by both aptitude and upbringing, seemed determined to live up to his father's name. When John Adams traveled to Europe on behalf of the fledgling nation, his eldest son accompanied him to continue his studies and to serve as his father's personal secretary. At the age of fourteen, John Quincy served as the personal secretary and translator for the American ambassador to Russia.

From that point forward, John Quincy Adams was destined for greatness as a public servant. He returned to Harvard to complete his education and then studied law. At the age of twenty-six, President George Washington chose him to serve as ambassador to the Netherlands, one of only five of the new nation's ministerial posts. The years that followed saw him become his country's most distinguished diplomat while also serving a term in the US Senate. When James Monroe was inaugurated president in 1817, he chose John Quincy Adams for the most significant cabinet post, secretary of state.

As secretary of state, John Quincy Adams made his greatest contributions to the United States. He settled leftover disputes from the War of 1812 with Great Britain that threatened to disrupt the peace and laid foundations for a lasting peace between two nations who had been bitter enemies but ultimately became the best of friends. He negotiated a peaceful resolution to a conflict that emerged with Spain over Florida. These negotiations with Spain led to the US purchase of Florida and also to the settlement of Louisiana's western boundary and California's northern and eastern boundary. He led the nation's recognition of new republics developing in Latin America and forged friendships with those new nations. He hammered out a policy that ultimately became known as the Monroe Doctrine even though he served as its primary author. In the years that followed, the Monroe Doctrine became the cornerstone of American foreign policy.

In 1824, as President Monroe completed his second presidential term, John Quincy Adams became the frontrunner for the presidential nomination due to his service as secretary of state, generally regarded as the stepping stone to the presidency, as it had been for Presidents Jefferson, Madison, and Monroe. Lacking a real party system, however, the nation stumbled into a situation in which four major candidates emerged—William Crawford, Henry Clay, and Andrew Jackson being the other three. When no candidate won a deciding majority in the Electoral College, the election was thrown to the

House of Representatives. In one of the most controversial elections in American history, the House of Representatives chose John Quincy Adams as the sixth president of the United States.

It was a difficult presidency. Supporters of Andrew Jackson harassed Adams before his administration began with charges of a "corrupt bargain" between him and Henry Clay. Clay, who had swayed the congressional vote in Adams's favor, benefited from Adams's appointment as secretary of state, and was a mortal enemy of Andrew Jackson. Unfortunately for Adams, conflict with Jackson's supporters riddled his entire presidential administration, and his presidency created little in the way of lasting change and enduring contributions. Jackson's congressional supporters and other enemies of Adams thwarted every piece of major domestic legislation and foreign policy modification proposed by Adams and his supporters. It came as no surprise when Andrew Jackson handily defeated Adams in his reelection bid in 1828.

After recovering from the bitterness of his defeat, John Quincy Adams decided to continue his career in public service. He took the unusual step of running to represent Massachusetts in the US House of Representatives. Elected in 1831, he served with distinction until his death in 1848, frequently taking a stance against slavery as the nation sped toward division over that issue.

John Quincy Adams was one of the most brilliant of US presidents. He was certainly one of the most religious presidents as well. He acknowledged that he read the Bible each morning for an hour throughout his life. Typically, he alternated the language in which he read the Bible. He also regularly attended worship services, first as a Congregationalist and later as a Unitarian. He also sampled other denominations as occasion permitted. Throughout his life he indicated a deep interest in spiritual matters, although his speculation frequently fell outside of accepted evangelical norms.[47]

Because of his extensive service in various cultures, both John Quincy and his wife, Louisa Catherine, had a broader knowledge of European heritage than some of his presidential predecessors. As a result, he had particular views about the status of American culture. Historian Elise Kirk quoted him as saying that American genius was very much addicted to painting, but that we had neither cultivated nor were attached much to music.[48] This was possibly true for him because America did not produce any stirring patriotic tunes during and after the Revolution while the French enjoyed rousing patriotic music during their fight for liberty. However, Adams was evidently very fond of music. He had learned to play the flute as a young boy and delighted in studying poetry. His English-born wife grew up in a musical family, played the harp and piano, and had a fine singing voice. These activities no doubt influenced John Quincy's attitude toward music.

An interesting fact is that John Quincy and Louisa often performed together even during their courtship. One of their favorite pieces was the aria "Angels Ever Bright and Fair" from Handel's oratorio *Theodora.* When John Quincy became secretary of state under Monroe, he opened his home for small ensemble concerts for entertainment. The Adamses' house was second only to the White House for such events.

Louisa was strongly influenced by the Irish poet Thomas Moore, who once said that "melancholy is the soul of music." The First Lady had an 1808 edition of his plaintive songs. She also wrote some words for which the little-known Italian composer Gaetano Carusi wrote music, calling it simply, "Hymn." The text was perhaps indicative of her mental condition as she sang them mournfully: "Lord, listen to my great distress, / Oh hear my feckle plaint. / Could language all my grief express, / Those words that griefs could paint." This manuscript is dated 21 April 1828, shortly before her sensitive, tormented son, George Washington Adams, committed suicide.[49]

John Quincy Adams was also a hymn writer, the only president known to write verse as hymns. In addition, he paraphrased all of the Psalms into meter that could be sung. All of his versions of the 150 psalms were written in rhyme and meter so that they could be performed congregationally or devotionally.[50] It should come as no surprise that his most favored hymn is one of his own compositions: "Send Forth, O God, Thy Light and Truth." This is actually a setting of Psalm 43. Adams studied poetry as a young man, read the Bible daily, and regularly wrote poetry throughout his life. He wrote both long and short poems, on both secular and sacred subjects. A collection of Adams's *Poems of Religion and Society* was published in 1848 and widely reprinted. Even though he did not officially join a church until 1826, he was a regular participant at the First Parish (Unitarian) Church in his hometown of Quincy, Massachusetts. Since he was a man of faith who had poetic gifts, it is no surprise that he became a hymn writer.

According to hymnologist David Music, Adams wrote versifications of all the Psalms no later than 1832. This is his most significant musical accomplishment, particularly the twenty-two selections printed by his pastor, William Lunt, in *The Christian Psalter: A Collection of Psalms and Hymns for Social and Private Worship* (1841).[51] Included in this text were seventeen psalms of Adams's as well as five hymns. Very few of these were recent poems. Some were written as early as 1816 and as late as 1839. The freely composed poems were probably written as devotional material while the psalm settings were designed for congregational song.

The music of the tune-books by later American composers included psalm tunes, fuging-tunes, anthems, and set pieces "designed for the use of singing schools, music societies, and churches."[52] Thus, the same music served the secular as well as the religious needs of the people and was a part of everyday life. As to the music used for the hymn "Send Forth, O God, Thy Light and Truth," there are few records of any specific tune suggested for this text. Since this hymn is in common meter, the meter used for most of the *Bay Psalm Book* (1640) and the *Sternhold and Hopkins Psalter* (1562), there were many tunes that would fit the 8.6.8.6 pattern of syllables.

However, a specific musical setting of Adams's "Send Forth, O God, Thy Light and Truth" has been found that was not discovered by John Merrill when he compiled his book on the presidents' hymns in 1933. Interestingly, the tune is titled HOLDEN and was composed by Thomas Whittemore the same year the text appeared—1841.[53] Whittemore was a clergyman, author, and composer who also edited a magazine for thirty-three years called *Trumpet and Universalist*. He compiled a series of hymnbooks, including *Songs of Zion* (1837) and *The Gospel Harmonist* (1841).[54] It was in this latter hymnal that the Adams setting of Psalm 43 appeared. The hymn was included in thirteen publications from 1841–1956, second only to another Adams hymn "Alas, How Swift the Moments Fly," which was published twenty-four times between 1841 and 1894.

As is readily seen, the continuous four-part texture of this common-meter doubled tune is relieved by a two-bar duet for soprano and alto marked *piano* at the beginning of the second half of the tune. This is similar to the two-part section in Oliver Holden's CORONATION tune set to Edward Peronet's "All Hail the Power of Jesus' Name" composed in 1779.

The text of the hymn certainly expresses the humble faith reflected in the political life of John Quincy Adams as diplomat, president, and congressman. The first stanza is a plea for divine guidance from God for "light and truth" (wisdom) as Adams attempts to always do "right" (make the correct decisions) with the help of God. Reading some of his diary and knowing that he read his Bible consistently, it comes as no urprise that he would write such a stanza.

The second stanza of the hymn is a statement of having reached the pinnacle of God's "holy hill." The words reflect joyful thanksgiving and gratitude for guidance thus far. This stanza reveals true reliance on God in each endeavor, which Adams made in the service of his country. The third stanza indicates that there were times of distress in Adams's life. Perhaps this refers to his defeat by Andrew Jackson for reelection. Yet a positive outlook is evident in the last line, where Adams states that these times

Send Forth, O God, Thy Light and Truth

Words: John Quincy Adams, 1841
Music: Thomas Whittemore, 1841

C.M.D.
HOLDEN

1. Send forth, O God, thy light and truth, And let them lead me still, Un-daunt-ed, in the paths of right, Up to thy ho-ly hill. Then to thy al-tar will I spring, And in my God re-joice; And praise shall tune the trem-bling string, And grat-i-tude my voice.

2. O why, my soul, are thou cast down? With-in me why dis-tressed? Thy hopes the God of grace shall crown; He yet shall make thee blessed. To him, my nev-er-fail-ing Friend, I bow, and kiss the rod; To him shall thanks and praise as-cend, My Sav-iour and my God.

will become "blessed of God." Indeed, he said that his tenure as congressman was more satisfying to him than even his presidency.

There is no doubt that John Quincy Adams was one of the most humble and spiritually minded presidents. In his inaugural address, he quoted Psalm 127: "Knowing that 'except the Lord keep the city, the watchman waketh but in vain,' with fervent supplications for His favor, to His overruling providence I commit with humble but fearless confidence my own fate and the future destinies of my country."

Adams was as dedicated a hymn writer as he was president. In 1845 his diary records his feelings when his version of Psalm 65 was sung in church: "Were it possible to compress into one pulsation of the heart the pleasure which, in the whole period of my life, I have enjoyed in praise from the lips of mortal man, it would not weigh a straw to balance the ecstasy of delight which streamed from my eyes as the organ pealed and the choir of voices sung the praise of Almighty God from the soul of David, adapted to my native tongue by me."[55]

John Quincy Adams was a hymn-writing president who read his Bible through in the course of every year. He also penned a series of letters to his son about the Bible's importance, encouraging him to read his Bible regularly. These letters were published by the *New York Tribune*. In addition, he was truly admired by another great hymn writer, Fanny Crosby. Edith Blumhofer states that in 1844 there were sixteen selected students from the New York Institute for the Blind who gave a program for Congress at the Capitol in Washington, DC. In the audience were some of the decade's most famous Americans. Crosby's part in the program was the recitation of an original thirteen-stanza poetical address, which drew calls for an encore. She was rewarded by a handshake from John Quincy Adams. During another visit she heard the aging Adams argue on behalf of the Smithsonian Institute. She cherished those memories for the rest of her life.[56] John Quincy Adams's pastor, Reverend William Lunt, made this statement at the interment of his parishioner in 1848 in Boston: "He who had occupied the throne of the people was, like the Hebrew monarch, also a Psalmist in our Israel."[57] What a lasting tribute.

ANDREW JACKSON

1767–1845

Seventh President (1829–1837)

American history is filled with colorful characters. Some have achieved almost mythological status. Some of them have gone on to be president of the United States. One such colorful character, dubbed "Old Hickory" during his military career, rose from the most humble of origins to become one of the most controversial and influential chief executives ever to serve the United States.

Born on the edge of the South Carolina frontier in 1767, Andrew Jackson and his background gave little indication of the heights to which he would rise. His Scotch-Irish parents left Northern Ireland only two years before his birth, and his father died while his mother was still pregnant with Andrew. Due to these circumstances and to the beginnings of the American Revolution, Andrew experienced a difficult childhood. As a teenager, he watched as rampaging British Tories burned and destroyed the property of rebels. He also began to fight against the British as a guerilla fighter alongside his two older brothers. Capturing Jackson at his aunt's home, a British officer wounded the young man with his sword while his men destroyed the family's belongings. Subsequently, all three members of Jackson's immediate family died as a result of the war's ravages. Smallpox also infected Jackson, but he managed to survive.

Essentially orphaned by the war, Jackson chose to move west across the Appalachian Mountains into the newly settled areas of Tennessee. There, he studied law and became involved in the state militia and frontier politics. He also acquired a reputation as a brawler and duelist. On more than one occasion, men wounded Jackson in duels, at least once very seriously. He fell in love with Rachel Donelson Robards, the abandoned wife of Lewis Robards. Eventually, when they believed Robards had divorced Rachel, she and Jackson were married in 1794. The marriage lasted until her death in 1828. Unfortunately, the circumstances surrounding the divorce and their marriage resulted in damage to both their reputations.

Jackson managed to continue his climb in Tennessee politics. Tennessee elected Jackson as its first representative to the US House of Representatives, and he served briefly in the US Senate. He also acquired the property and standing of a Tennessee planter, including substantial numbers of slaves. Still, it was the War of 1812 that made Andrew Jackson a national hero. Leading Tennessee volunteers and American army regulars, he put down the rebellion of the Creek Indians in Alabama, captured Pensacola from the British, and then held New Orleans against a vastly superior British force. The Battle of New Orleans catapulted Jackson to national prominence. In the years that followed, he led an invasion of Florida that ultimately resulted in the United States purchasing that Spanish territory in 1819. Tennessee elected him governor, and westerners began to endorse him as a presidential candidate.

In the presidential election of 1824, Jackson ran against fellow westerner and Speaker of the House Henry Clay, secretary of the treasury William Crawford, and secretary of state John Quincy Adams. In one of the most controversial elections in American history, no candidate won a majority in the Electoral College. This threw the election into the House of Representatives. Since Clay had finished fourth and he and Jackson were enemies, Clay threw his support behind Adams, even though Jackson had received the most popular and electoral votes. In the following four years, Jackson's supporters rallied behind him, and in 1828, Americans elected Jackson president over Adams by a substantial margin in one of the dirtiest campaigns in US history. Amidst the mudslinging that occurred, accusations about Jackson's rough past arose, and accusations about his marriage surfaced that ultimately may have contributed to Rachel's death after the election and before Jackson's presidential inauguration.

Jackson's two terms in office proved to be equally tumultuous. Believing that the people of the United States had given him a mandate to act in their behalf, Jackson refused to let Congress dictate policy and utilized the presidential veto more than all other previous US presidents combined. He unsuccessfully recommended the elimination of the Electoral College, as he considered it undemocratic. He successfully destroyed the Second Bank of the United States and managed to avoid civil war during the nullification crisis with South Carolina. He also strongly supported the removal of the remaining eastern tribes of Native Americans to the area west of the Mississippi River known as the Indian Territory. He also clandestinely supported the Texas Revolution led by his former protégé Sam Houston, although he refused to annex Texas to the United States. As a strong leader, he polarized American politics in such a way that it led to the division of the Democratic Party that had served as the only national party for more than a decade. Those who opposed Jackson ultimately developed what they named the Whig Party. After two terms, Jackson retired to his plantation, the Hermitage, near Nashville, where he remained interested in the American republic until his death in 1845.

Jackson's mother raised him as a devout Presbyterian. As a young man, however, he showed little interest in religion. His wife, Rachel, exhibited a deep and abiding Christian faith, and gradually Jackson, too, began walking in the faith of his forebears. Partially due to a later re-emergence of his faith and partially due to his belief in separation of church and state, Jackson did not join the Presbyterian Church until after he left the White House. By the end of his life, apparently Jackson had become increasingly interested in his faith.[58]

Since Rachel Jackson died on Christmas Eve before her husband's inauguration, Mrs. Jackson's niece, Emily Donelson, and later Andrew Jackson's daughter-in-law, Sarah Yorke Jackson, served as hostesses in the White House. Food, music, and congeniality were abundant. On his first Fourth of July reception, Jackson treated his guests to a 1,400-pound "mammoth cheese" while the Marine Band played the president's favorite tune "Auld Lang Syne."[59] Even though Jackson was welcomed into his presidency with the normal dedicatory marches, gala parades, and balls for "Old Hickory," his presidency was unique. At his inauguration on 4 March 1829 there was an "elegant comedy" performance of *Belle's Strategem* (one of George Washington's favorite plays). In addition, a "Jackson Overture" was composed and performed by orchestra conductor Henry Dielman in honor of the new president.

Music was enjoyed informally during these years. Sarah Jackson often played the guitar for various events. On 21 November 1831 a new rosewood *pianoforte* with six octaves was purchased. This keyboard replaced the old Erard piano of the Monroe presidency. It appears that music and pretty ladies were evident during Jackson's administration. Some women played the piano; others danced. During Jackson's years, one ballerina, Fanny Elssler, was so popular that when she was in town, Congress would meet only on the days when she was not dancing.[60] It is easy to understand that even the name of the residence began to change. The former terms "President's Palace" and "President's House" gradually became simply the "White House." Because of the open-door policies and public receptions, it was clearly a place for the people to meet and enjoy themselves. Even so, "White House" did not become the official name for the residence until Theodore Roosevelt's presidency.

It is difficult to ascertain what might have been Andrew Jackson's first choice of hymns. With his election, a new native vitality entered the presidency. This resulted in the Marine Band playing Christmas music and children throwing candy snowballs at each other in the White House. The period also marked the beginning of American-composed Christmas music. The most typical and best known was "Shout the Glad Tidings" by the Reverend William Augustus Muklenberg. This hymn was first performed at Trinity Church in Manhattan on Christmas Day, 1826.[61] It appeared in hymnals as late as 1940.

According to journalist Clint Bonner, the favorite hymn of Jackson's wife became the president's most favored hymn. Jackson, in the course of a conversation at the Hermitage in September 1843, remarked, "There is a beautiful hymn on the subject of the exceeding great and precious promises of God to his people. It was a favorite hymn of my dear wife till the day of her death. It commences thus: 'How firm a foundation, ye saints of the Lord.' I wish you would sing it now."[62] Some hymnologists assume that this became his favored hymn. Andrew Jackson asked that it be sung at his bedside as he died in 1845.

However, the anonymous poem "Come, Thou Almighty King" was determined by John Merrill to be Jackson's favored hymn. Since Jackson had a deep appreciation for Holy Scripture, either of the aforementioned hymns is possible. In his diary he recorded that it was his custom to read three to five chapters from the Bible each day. According to McCollister, Jackson wrote to one of his sons-in-law, "Go read the scriptures, the joyful promises it contains will be a balsam to all your troubles."[63]

"Come, Thou Almighty King" first appeared in a tract published by George Whitefield in 1757. Since Whitefield was such a close colleague of the Wesleys, the text had been attributed to Charles Wesley for a hundred years. The hymn's original title was "A Hymn to the Trinity," and it certainly proclaims Trinitarian doctrine. Whoever wrote the text, God has used an especially effective poet in writing these words. Later research leads one to believe that the hymn was an imitation of the English national anthem "God Save Our Gracious King," which appeared fifteen years earlier. This hymn appeared in print the second time in 1763 set to the "God Save the King" tune. Perhaps because of possible reprisal, the author chose to remain anonymous. Partially because the text uses a unique meter, which Wesley had never used, most hymnologists conclude that there is no conclusive evidence that Wesley wrote the text.

Many writers relate the story of the use of this hymn in defiance during the Revolutionary War. This incident involved the British interrupting a worship service of colonists on Long Island. The American patriots were ordered to sing "God Save the King." They complied at gunpoint but substituted the words of "Come, Thou Almighty King" to the tune of the English national anthem. The congregation confidently sang the complete hymn, including "Help us thy name to sing."[64] This event certainly was in character with "Old Hickory."

This hymn has found its place in the hymnals of all branches of the Christian church. Today it is exclusively sung to another tune. Even though this tune has sometimes been called TRINITY and MOSCOW, its most enduring title is ITALIAN HYMN. Its composer was Felice Giardini, a popular Italian violinist who resided in London for thirty-four years. He began his musical career as a choirboy in Italy at Milan's cathedral. After intense study in singing, composition, harpsichord, and violin, he made his debut in London in 1750 as a concert violinist. He spent his later years in Russia as a conductor of opera, dying in Moscow at the age of eighty. This tune has a hint of Russian vigor, ruggedness, and open chords. In its original form it was even more evident than in the present Italianized form.[65]

Even though Giardini was a successful opera conductor who received huge sums of money, he apparently was always poor due to his spendthrift lifestyle. We have inspiring music today wedded to this classic text as a result of his desire for some ready cash. Because Giardini needed the money, he contributed several tunes to a hymn collection compiled by Martin Madan. This hymnbook was printed in 1769 and titled *The Collection of Psalm and*

Come, Thou Almighty King

Words: Anonymous
Music: Felice de Giardini, 1769

6.6.4.6.6.6.4
ITALIAN HYMN

Hymn Tunes Sung at the Chapel of the Lock Hospital in London. The music that Giardini wrote specifically for "Come, Thou Almighty King" is the only surviving tune used today from this hymnal.

The hymn itself is one of the most frequently used opening hymns for congregational worship. Of more than usual importance is the first word "Come," which invites, even demands, everyone to promptly and vigorously enter the worship experience. The natural expression of awe and sublimity of adoration and praise sometimes demands a slow tempo in performance. It could even be sung with a subdued tone after the proclamation of the invitation to "come" from each member of the Trinity. In accordance with the prevalent eighteenth-century hymn writers, the petitions of the last stanza are concerned with the future life. The worshiper looks forward to the joy of ceaseless praise in the hereafter.

This scripturally based hymn could be termed an outline of Andrew Jackson's life. Known as being flamboyant, he still recognized the sovereignty of God in later life; he knew that the "Father!…[was]…all victorious." Stanza two brings in the offensive battle symbol the "sword of the spirit." The sword's success is dependent upon God's holiness descending on the participants in the conflict. Stanza three follows with the Holy Comforter, who is ruling in every warrior's heart. The concluding stanza brings the Trinitarian concept into focus as leading the combatants to victory. The final phrase, "Love and adore," is a concept of submission, which is the result of life's tribulations. The powerful message of this text is evident in the skillful way the author uses biblical metaphors for God—"almighty King," "Ancient of Days," and "incarnate Word."

Relating this hymn to the seventh president's administration, especially to his preparation for the job as a victorious general, is obvious. This should inspire believers as they corporately worship through Andrew Jackson's favored hymn.

MARTIN VAN BUREN

1782–1862

Eighth President (1837–1841)

In the early years of the Republic, an inner circle of individuals generally selected the next presidential nominee. In the years immediately after Thomas Jefferson's election, tight control of presidential politics continued. The rise of Andrew Jackson in the 1820s and the more popular style of rough-and-tumble presidential politics changed all that. A New York politician was at the heart of that transition and best prepared to capitalize upon it. In doing so, he earned the nickname the "Little Magician" and essentially transformed the American political system in ways unforeseen by the founding fathers.

Martin Van Buren was born in the small village of Kinderhook, New York, in the Hudson River Valley, at the very end of the American Revolution. Like his friend and colleague Andrew Jackson and later successors Abraham Lincoln and Andrew Johnson, Van Buren came from humble origins. His immediate family roots originated in the hardy Dutch settlers of New York. Unlike later presidents with Dutch ancestors, Theodore Roosevelt and Franklin Roosevelt, however, Van Buren's life was far from one of privilege. His schooling was quite limited until he had the opportunity to work in the office of a local attorney. Beginning with menial tasks, he gradually availed himself of opportunities to study law until he became an attorney as well. He succeeded in his law practice, married, and began a family. It was, however, in the New York political scene that he flourished.

Van Buren recognized that the Federalist Party was dying in New York and affiliated with the Democratic-Republican, or Republican, Party. His home district elected him to the state senate in 1812. He mastered New York state politics and became one of the "movers and shakers" in the rough-and-tumble politics of the 1820s. Increasingly he sought to bring party order out of the tumultuous political scene. When Andrew Jackson emerged as a national candidate in the presidential election of 1824, Van Buren quickly assessed Old Hickory's prospects and threw his support behind him. He became one of Jackson's closest political allies, and though elected New York governor in 1828, he moved to Washington, DC, to become the nation's secretary of state. Throughout Jackson's two terms, Van Buren loyally supported Jackson. In 1832, the Democrats selected him as Jackson's running mate. When Jackson stepped aside after his traditional two terms, he handpicked Van Buren to be his successor. Martin Van Buren became the nation's eighth president.

Unfortunately, Van Buren had barely assumed office when the Panic of 1837 plunged the nation into a deep economic depression. The ensuing crisis led to hundreds of bank and business failures. Thousands of farmers lost their land. Van Buren's own beliefs about government did little to soften the crisis. An adherent of the Jeffersonian-Jacksonian concepts of limited government, Van Buren was ill equipped to face the crisis. In fact, in his third annual message to Congress in 1840 he stated, "All communities are apt to look to government for too much."[66] He also continued Jackson's policy of removal of the eastern tribes of Native Americans to lands west of the Mississippi River. He dealt ineffectively with the controversial case of the slave ship *Amistad* that ultimately ended in the Supreme Court. Fortunately, Van Buren did deal effectively with a border crisis between the state of New York and British Canada.

All these issues led to a dynamic political campaign for the presidency in 1840. The Democrats chose Van Buren for reelection, while the Whigs took a page from the Democrats' and Van Buren's political textbooks and chose war hero William Henry Harrison as their candidate. The campaign that followed typified the concepts that Van Buren had advocated. Unfortunately for Van Buren, the voters rejected Van Buren and chose Harrison as president.

Van Buren had been a widower for many years. He returned to his home near Kinderhook and devoted himself to improving his home, farm, the orchards that he named Lindenwald, and also his relationships with his sons and their children. He continued to be active in Democratic Party and national politics, however. Democrats considered him as their presidential candidate in 1844 but chose James Polk instead. In 1848 a broad coalition of political participants formed the Free-Soil Party and selected the "Little Magician" as their candidate. Not expected to win the election, they hoped to garner enough support to throw the election into the House of Representatives. Instead, Van Buren found only enough support to shift votes in the state of New York, probably costing Democrat Lewis Cass the election and making Zachary Taylor president. He endorsed a reunion of the Democratic Party and remained supportive of Democratic candidates in the years that followed. He remained a strong Unionist and supported Abraham Lincoln as Lincoln called for troops to put down the rebellion. Not long after the beginning of the Civil War, his feeble health began to decline. He died in July 1862.

Like many Democrats of the nineteenth century, Martin Van Buren believed that religion should remain a private matter for public figures. He was reared in the Dutch Reformed Church as a boy, and it was at this church in Kinderhook that his funeral service was held. Since there was no Dutch Reformed Church in Washington, DC, Van Buren worshiped in the Episcopal Church and occasionally attended a Presbyterian church when he was in New York City. Despite his critics' accusations, Van Buren appears to have been a moral man and was known to have sung hymns lustily when he attended church.[67]

As far as music heard during Van Buren's administration, there are only scant references. Some opponents branded Van Buren's White House as an "Asiatic Mansion," containing imported carpets, exotic artificial flowers, and even a bathtub! However, Van Buren did have an elegant gilt-mounted *pianoforte* with damask satin-covered music stools.[68] The Marine Band often played music of well-known and admired national airs.

Among the songs heard was "Hail to the Chief." Even though this tune had been in the band's repertoire since John Quincy Adams, we do not know exactly when it became closely identified with the presidency. But newspaperman Benjamin Poore wrote that it was just another "hum-drum" melody heard at social events during Van Buren's administration. Poore criticized the president's use of the Marine Band: "As the people's cash, and not his own, pays for all the services of the Marine Band, its employment at the palace does not conflict with the peculiar views of the president in regard to the obvious differences between public and private economy."[69] It appears that Van Buren acquired an attitude of "royalty" during his term, which became the subject of satire and song during the 1840 campaign. Perhaps this view was enhanced by a statement made by dancer Fanny Elssler, who, after being invited and visiting the president at the executive mansion, said, "I think his demeanor is very easy, very frank and very royal."[70]

Martin Van Buren never sacrificed his integrity for political gain. Andrew Jackson referred to his trusted friend and advisor as "a true man with no guile." Van Buren evidently was not ashamed to express himself in congregational song. In the Kinderhook church, even as a young man, Van Buren's voice carried above the rest, especially when the hymn "O God, Our Help in Ages Past" was sung.[71] This was considered his favorite hymn at this time. However, Merrill's research discovered that Van Buren also loved to sing Joseph Hart's "Come, Holy Spirit, Come."

Hart, born in London in 1712 to parents who probably attended George Whitefield's services, had an intense interest in classical studies. Having learned Greek and Hebrew, he eventually desired to be a teacher of languages. Beginning at age twenty-one, Hart went through an extended period of doubt about his spiritual condition. It was not until 1757 that he finally realized a permanent change. His conversion occurred after hearing a sermon on Revelation 3:10 at the London Moravian Chapel. During the two years following this experience, many of his most earnest and impassioned hymns were written. Hart had a true poetic gift with a style of unequaled power and terseness of expression. In his hymns he handles many aspects of Christian truth, but writes most effectively about Christ's sacrifice for man's sins. With his poetic talent in the hymn "Come, Holy Spirit, Come," Hart emphasizes the necessity to utilize the power of the third person of the Trinity. This text is as it appeared in the 1759 version. Even though August Toplady made some alterations in 1776, which many American compilers adopted, these are the stanzas most likely sung during Van Buren's presidency. The sincere prayer recognizes the comforting and guiding hand of the Holy Spirit that the Christian should utilize. This hymn is normally sung during Whitsuntide[72] in churches that follow the liturgical calendar.

Even though at one time Hart's hymns were widely used, especially by Calvinistic nonconformist churches, this hymn is little known today except in certain strict Baptist churches, mainly because it is too "experiential" for

Come, Holy Spirit, Come

Words: Joseph Hart, 1759
Music: Garret Wellesley, 1760

S.M.
MORNINGTON

modern Christians.[73] It is notable that Hart also wrote "Come, Ye Sinners, Poor and Wretched," a hymn that presents the gospel and epitomizes much of his bitter, long-lasting spiritual struggle. With this text, he sympathized with those who were "weary, heavy-laden bruised and broken by the fall." With Van Buren's defeats in later life, he may have identified with this hymn as well as "Come, Holy Spirit, Come."

After his authentic conversion experience, Hart wanted to be used in turning souls to God. He preached his first sermon at the Old Meeting House in St. John's Court, Bernondsey. In 1760 Hart became minister of

Jewin Street Independent Chapel and remained there until his death eight years later.

The music for "Come, Holy Spirit, Come" was composed by Garrett Wellesley, the father of the Duke of Wellington. Having the title of first Earl of Mornington in 1760, he named the tune MORNINGTON. Wellesley wrote a chant for use in the Dublin, Ireland, cathedral, and this hymn tune was arranged from that chant.[74] Although other standard meter tunes, such as BELLA and HALSTEAD, were suggested to be used with this text in the 1861 hymnal *Hymns Ancient and Modern,* it is almost certain that MORNINGTON was sung during Van Buren's day.

As a presidential favorite, "Come, Holy Spirit, Come" reflects the seriousness of President Van Buren's faith. As with other of Hart's hymns, this one is unashamedly evangelical with experience-oriented language. Even as Hart stresses feeling, Van Buren needed such assurance as he faced decisions concerning changing political processes and siding with Lincoln on calling for troops in preparation for the coming Civil War. Since the hymn text is also a prayer for a revival of faith and a removal of doubt, it also reflects a prayer that Van Buren must have felt often. In the words for a "new creation" in stanza three, this hymn precisely describes a "man with no guile" as Jackson had stated concerning Van Buren's character. Stanza four, being a plea for the Holy Spirit to dwell in the heart so that all would "praise and love, the Father, Son and Thee," can be seen in Van Buren's actual singing in church "lustily" as a testimony of his praise.

"Come, Holy Spirit, Come" and Isaac Watts's "O God, Our Help in Ages Past" are truly fitted as Martin Van Buren's most esteemed hymns. (A discussion of Watts's hymn is included in the chapter on President Gerald Ford.) At President Martin Van Buren's funeral on 24 July 1862, the congregation of the Kinderhook church gathered to pay their final respects to their native son, and they sang in his honor "O God, our help in ages past, our hope for years to come," a prayer suitable for all presidents.

WILLIAM HENRY HARRISON

1773–1841

Ninth President (1841)

With the Federalist Party's death after the War of 1812, essentially a one-party system governed the United States for more than two decades. By 1836, however, opposition to Andrew Jackson and his protégé Martin Van Buren coalesced to form the Whig Party. Unfortunately for the Whigs, Van Buren won the presidency in 1836. The Panic of 1837, however, created a golden opportunity for the Whig Party. Rather than nominate their perennial standard bearer, Henry Clay, the Whigs chose to "out-Jackson" the Democrats by nominating their own war hero, William Henry Harrison. They also sought to cast him in the frontier mold similar to Andrew Jackson. Although successful in the election, Harrison ultimately gained tragic distinction by becoming the first US president to die in office. He also held office for the shortest presidential term ever.

Despite later presidential campaign slogans, William Henry Harrison was born in 1773 into planter aristocracy in Virginia. His father, Benjamin Harrison, signed the Declaration of Independence as a representative from Virginia when William was only three. William received a college education and studied to be a physician, but when he was eighteen, he joined the army. Commissioned as an officer, he served with some distinction in fighting Native Americans on the frontier in the 1790s. He left the military but served the national government in territorial administration of the Northwest Territory. After Congress separated the Indiana Territory from the remainder of the Northwest, he served as governor of the new territory for twelve years. As governor he forced continued cession of Indian lands to land-hungry whites, antagonizing the Native Americans and being forced to defend white settlers from Indian attacks.

Ultimately, Harrison's greatest challenge came from Shawnee war leader Tecumseh and his brother, Tenskwatawa, whom whites called "the Prophet," who urged Native Americans to reject the ways of the whites and resist US incursions into hereditary lands. Tecumseh lobbied with diverse Indian nations, forging an alliance to resist the whites, and also allied his coalition with British Canadians seeking to limit US expansion. Opportunistically, Harrison seized the initiative when he found Tecumseh away drumming up support among other Native Americans and lured Tenskwatawa into an attack. Harrison's forces defeated Tenskwatawa's warriors and burned their villages. Though this battle of Tippecanoe catapulted Harrison to national prominence and forced the Native Americans to withdraw, when Tecumseh returned, Indian reprisals continued. Eventually, this Indian War of 1811 and perceived British support of Tecumseh became key causes of the War of 1812. President Madison appointed Harrison the commanding general in the Northwest, and Harrison defeated British and Native American forces in the southern edge of Canada just north of Lake Erie at the Battle of Thames River. Tecumseh was killed in the fighting, and his Indian alliance subsequently collapsed. Harrison, like Jackson, emerged from the War of 1812 as one of a handful of legitimate American war heroes and returned to public life.

In 1840 the relatively new Whig Party rejected their perennial candidate, Henry Clay, and chose Harrison as their presidential nominee with Virginian John Tyler as his running mate. In many ways, historians have regarded the election of 1840 as the first modern election. Whigs used the campaign slogan "Tippecanoe and Tyler Too" to remind voters of Harrison's military heroics and turned a critical statement by Democrats into a promise that their candidate was a man of "hard cider and log cabins" despite the fact of his privileged upbringing. The campaign succeeded by the slim margin of only about 150,000 popular votes. However, due to the intricacies of the Electoral College, Harrison won by a substantial number of electoral votes, becoming the oldest man (until Ronald Reagan) to be elected US president. Inauguration Day 1841 dawned cold, dreary, and wet, but attempting to demonstrate his vigor, Harrison refused to wear an overcoat or a top hat. He then delivered the longest presidential inaugural address in American history, nearly two hours long; consequently, he caught cold, which developed into pneumonia. Unfortunately, Harrison died after only four weeks in office.

Little is known about Harrison's religious beliefs. He attended the Episcopal Church on occasions when he worshiped and was observed reading his Bible. His inaugural address referenced God, but in a rather impersonal way, similar to earlier leaders who referred to divine providence or some other rationalistic term to denote God. Still, at his funeral, the Episcopal priest claimed that Harrison had intended to be baptized while other traditions indicate that he was baptized as an Episcopalian earlier in life, though no documentation has been located that verifies this claim.[75]

To counteract the feeling that Martin Van Buren had made the presidential palace "his marble hall," William Henry Harrison restored the White House to its rightful position as the people's house.[76] In the 1840 presidential election there was a persuasive outburst of song and singing. The campaign by the Whigs in their desire to elect Harrison and Tyler had an energizing effect on the country. With the catchy slogan of "Tippecanoe and Tyler Too" set as a melody, not only was this music played by brass bands at rallies, but it became a spirited and popular song for glee clubs. However, after only one month, "overnight the joyous bursts of song changed to mournful dirges."[77]

While we do not know what specific music was performed at Harrison's funeral, we do know that the music was excellent. The 13 April 1841 edition of *National Intelligencer* reported that the president-elect said that for him during the past twenty years, Bible reading had become a pleasure, not a duty.[78] On his deathbed, Harrison asked that Psalm 103 be read: "Bless the Lord, O my soul, and all that is within me, bless his holy name."

According to John Merrill's 1933 study, "Lord, It Belongs Not to My Care" was Harrison's most admired hymn. This unique hymn was written by Richard Baxter in 1681 as an expansion of Philippians 1:21: "For me to live is Christ and to die is gain." This verse seems strangely appropriate for a president who died after only thirty days in office.

There are some unusual parallels in the lives of Baxter and Harrison. Both Baxter and his father became Christians through reading of the scripture. At fifteen, Baxter said, "Without any means but books, God was pleased to resolve me for Himself."[79] Perhaps this also occurred in the life of William Henry Harrison, since he regularly read his Bible. Baxter was forced to exhibit his faith since he experienced the anguish of the English Civil War. Harrison, a hero of the Indian Territorial conflicts, had also experienced the horrors of war; his faith comforted him in difficulties.

Richard Baxter, ordained in the Anglican Church in 1640, served twenty years as curate of Kidderminster. He had served as chaplain to a regiment of Cromwell's army. Later, because of ill health, he was forced to rest; thus, he wrote his famous book *The Saints Everlasting Rest.* On his return to Kidderminster, Baxter changed a very immoral congregation into one known for its godliness. He did this partially through the witness of self-denial as well as through earnest biblical preaching. Teaching the doctrines of the faith, the sounds of praise and prayer were consistently heard in the households of his church members. A man of independent thought, his contemporaries said that he grew "too Puritan for the Bishops and he was too Episcopalian for the Presbyterians."[80]

Baxter retired in 1673 as an Anglican minister, becoming a nonconformist minister. He soon was imprisoned for six months for preaching in his own house. This was only one of many instances of suffering that he endured. There were many occasions when Baxter was persecuted for his preaching, theological publication, and hymn writing. One time he was imprisoned, given a large fine, and, with the sale of his own books, ordered to pay for his bail.[81] Baxter wrote three extended poems from which his hymns are taken. "Lord, It Belongs Not to My Care" was extracted from the longer poem "The Covenant and Confidence of Faith." Hymnologist John Julian notes that Baxter attached this statement to the poem: "This covenant, my dear wife, in her former sickness subscribed with a cheerful will,"[82] referring to his sick wife of nineteen years, who died in 1681. He wrote that "when we next sing this hymn let us remember that it came out of much tribulation." Baxter's poems consisted of accounts of his religious experience in verse. Not being limited to paraphrases of the Psalms, his hymns prepared the way for Isaac Watts's freely composed verses.

There are two tunes suggested for "Lord, It Belongs Not to My Care" in the 1862 *Hymns Ancient and Modern,* a common-meter text. Even though the WACHUSETT tune, which first appeared in the *Congregational Harmonist* in 1828, fits the text well, the other tune, ST. HUGH, seems to work better. ST.HUGH was arranged by Edward J. Hopkins from an English traditional melody, based on the ballad air "Little Sir William." Hopkins, organist at the Temple Church in London from 1843 to 1898, edited several hymnals and harmonized tunes for the Methodists, Presbyterians, and Congregationalists.

Lord, It Belongs Not to My Care

Words: Richard Baxter, 1681
Music: E. J. Hopkins, 1814

C.M.
RESIGNATION

1. Lord, it be-longs not to my care Whe-ther I die or live; To love and serve Thee is my share, And this Thy grace must give.
2. If life be long, oh make me glad The long-er to o-bey; If short, no la-bour-er is sad To end his toil-some day.
3. Christ leads me through no dark-er rooms Than He went through be-fore; He that un-to God's king-dom comes Must en-ter by this door.
4. Come, Lord, when grace hath made me meet Thy bles-sed Face to see: For if Thy work on earth be sweet, What will Thy glo-ry be!
5. Then I shall end my sad com-plaints And wea-ry sin-ful days, And join with the tri-um-phant Saints That sing my Sav-iour's praise.
6. My know-ledge of that life is small, The eye of faith is dim; But 'tis e-nough that Christ knows all, And I shall be with Him. A-men.

The legend of St. Hugh of Lincoln concerns a lad named Hugh who was put to death by the Jews in 1225; the story is found in Chaucer's *Canterbury Tales.* Eighteen wealthy Jews were hanged because of the incident and Hugh was given a state burial and the title of saint.[83] Perhaps the most satisfying tune for these words was RESIGNATION, mentioned by Julian. It appeared first in 1814 in Pittsburgh and in 1836 was set to Watts's "My Shepherd Will Supply My Need" in Winchester. The tune also was printed in William Walker's *Southern Harmony* in 1835. This beautiful common-meter text could very well have been sung to any of these tunes by President Harrison while attending Episcopal services.

Interestingly, a text that appeared in *Mercer's Cluster* in 1810 seems to capsulize Harrison's career. Set to a tune called WAR DEPARTMENT, it provides a unique glimpse of the warrior himself.[84] One stanza reads, "No more shall the war-whoop be heard. / The tomahawks buried, shall rest in the ground, / The ambush and slaughter no longer be fear'd / And peace and good-will to nations abound."

While hymn writer Fanny Crosby did not write the words of the above stanza, she heartily supported Harrison for president. Even though she considered herself a Democrat, she held war heroes in high esteem. After being moved to excitement by the 1840 election, she joined the nation in mourning Harrison's death. According to hymnologist Edith Blumhofer, Crosby wrote a poem of lament in her private grief.[85]

The hymn "Lord, It Belongs Not to My Care" is an example of Puritan covenant theology.[86] The stanzas enact an encounter between God and the inner self. Some versions add a "Now" at the beginning, bringing one to an immediate decision. Stanza one leads the singer to a point of service. Perhaps this duty as president is what Harrison felt as his promise to God and his country. Stanza two presents the idea of obeying God even though one's life may be short. Was this an anticipation of the coming days? Stanza three emphasizes the fact of Christ's crucifixion, leading to stanza four and the glory received from serving in Christ's name. Stanza five briefly introduces the end of life on earth followed by the knowledge that being with Christ is reward enough.

This hymn is certainly a worthy one for all Christians and especially for a president who had the shortest term of all those in that position. It breathes a gentle faith in God's leadership and implicit trust that what God says is good. The example of Christ and looking forward to joining him is the crowning joy of serving him here below.

JOHN TYLER

1790–1862

Tenth President (1841–1845)

When elected, John Tyler was known by most Americans only as the second half of a campaign slogan. By the end of his time in office, many regarded him as a man without a political party. Despite being nicknamed "his Accidency," John Tyler ultimately led the country into critical decisions that affected the future of the United States.

John Tyler was born in the "home of presidents," Virginia, in 1790. Educated at the College of William and Mary, Tyler studied law and committed himself to a life of public service. His home district elected him to the House of Representatives in the aftermath of the War of 1812. After serving three terms, Virginia elected him to two terms as governor and then selected him for the US Senate. Despite some concerns, he supported the presidential candidacy of Andrew Jackson in 1828, but the new Whig Party quickly drew him in as his opposition to Jackson's strong nationalism arose. The Whigs were strong nationalists also, but Tyler's dislike of Jackson and his successor, Martin Van Buren, was so strong that when Whigs nominated William Henry Harrison as their presidential candidate, Tyler agreed to run as his vice-presidential candidate in hope of attracting anti-Jackson Democrats to the fold. Most historians agree that Whig Party leaders Daniel Webster and Henry Clay hoped to manipulate the aging Harrison behind the scenes to control his administration. Harrison and Tyler were elected in November 1840 and inaugurated in March 1841. Unfortunately for Whigs, Harrison died shortly after assuming office.

The United States had never faced a similar situation. No US president had ever died in office. While the Constitution provided for vice-presidential succession to the presidency, some perceived a lack of clarity regarding the permanency of the arrangement or the degree of Tyler's powers. Despite the debate, Tyler assumed full powers of the presidency. Due to his difference with the Whigs over many policies, he quickly alienated many Whigs, including Henry Clay. All the members of his cabinet resigned except for Daniel Webster, who was engaged in ticklish negotiations with Britain over the Maine boundary question. Eventually, the Whig Party voted Tyler out of their party. Tyler appointed Southerners and Democrats amenable to his ideas and proceeded to govern. His policies reflected both Whig and Democrat concepts, but both parties often distrusted him. His veto of a Whig tariff bill resulted in the first impeachment resolution ever brought before the US Congress, charging that he had abused the presidential veto despite the fact that his predecessor, Andrew Jackson, had utilized the veto more than all prior US presidents combined. Though the resolution failed, it further soured Tyler's relations with congressional Whigs.

Despite being a president without a party, Tyler's administration accomplished many positive things. He signed a revised tariff into law that protected American manufacturing in its infancy, and Webster successfully negotiated the Webster-Ashburton Treaty, which settled boundary disputes. He also signed a law that permitted pioneers to settle farmland in the West at a relatively low cost. This law, called the "Log-Cabin Bill," anticipated the later and better known Homestead Act passed during the Civil War.

As the Whig Party and Democrats drifted further apart in 1844, neither party nominated Tyler as their presidential candidate. However, when James Polk was elected on a platform that included the annexation of Texas, Tyler viewed Polk's election as a public mandate for annexation despite opposition from Northern abolitionists and the threat of war with Mexico. He successfully led Congress to annex Texas by joint resolution before leaving office.

Tyler retired to Virginia. When the Civil War loomed in 1861, Tyler sought to work out a compromise between North and South. When his efforts failed, Tyler chose to remain loyal to his home state and his principles regarding states' rights and was elected as a member of the Confederate Congress. He died in 1862 without seeing either the Confederacy win its independence or the Union restored.

Tyler's church membership was listed as Episcopalian, but some historians have regarded him a Deist. Franklin Steiner lists him as a president whose "religious views were doubtful," and one of his key biographers questions the denominational nature of his faith. John McCollister, however, cites both Tyler and a contemporary who stated that orthodox Christianity was a part of Tyler's life. Like most Democrats in that day, Tyler was a strong believer in separation of church and state.[87]

Tyler was a fine musician, having inherited his love for music from his father. As a boy, he enjoyed playing the violin, much like Thomas Jefferson had. However, young John played reels, hornpipes, and breakdowns on his violin rather than the more serious music that Jefferson performed. Tyler also wrote poetry, some of which was set to music. His talented second wife, Julia, composed the music for a poem written by John especially for her during their courtship. This musical score is extinct, but the verses of "Sweet Lady Awake" still exist in Tyler's own handwriting.[88]

Julia, the queenly "Mrs. Presidentess," has been credited with beginning the tradition of playing "Hail to the Chief" with the appearance of the president. She persuaded the Marine Band to do this for her husband on various occasions. It grew to be the official custom until the present.[89] During the Tyler administration, the White House was very active socially. When Congress was in session, there were twice-weekly dinner parties and informal "drawing room" events every evening. In addition to special holiday events, there were numerous balls. These climaxed with an elaborate masquerade "Farewell Ball" for the Tylers' grandchildren in 1845. The new dance craze, "the polka," was introduced at this event.

The Marine Band contributed much to the entertainment events with weekly outdoor concerts that were open to the public. Their director, Francis Scala, began his service in 1842 and served for nine presidents until 1871. Often leading the band with his clarinet and stamping his feet to direct the drummer who could not read music, Scala's main contribution was the expansion of arrangements of operatic selections for the band's repertoire. Since America was just beginning to enjoy European opera, the "president's own" band ended up with about one-third opera-related selections under Scala.

Tyler purchased two pianos for the White House: one concert grand piano, especially for noted pianists, and one elegant Scherr piano for vocal and ensemble groups. "America's Beethoven," Anton Philip Heinrich, played a concert of his own music called *Jubilee* for President Tyler but was upset when in the middle of the performance Tyler asked Heinrich, "That may all be very fine, sir, but can't you play us a good old Virginia reel?" Obviously, this ended the piano recital when the composer exclaimed (in his German accent), "No, sir; I never plays [*sic*] dance music!"[90]

Because of the popularity and influence of such musical groups as the Christy Minstrels (1842) and the Virginia Minstrels (1843), vocal music ensembles became very important beginning in the 1840s. These groups became the vehicle for making strong social statements to the nation. Other popular ensembles included the Rainers (also called the "Tyrolese Minstrels"), who in 1839 introduced "Silent Night" to America in New York City.

With messages concerning reform, humanitarianism, rugged nationalism, and idealistic sentiment ringing loud and clear, these groups had much influence on public opinion. Probably the most notable family group was the Hutchinson Family Singers, who first appeared in the White House on 30 January 1844. The Hutchinsons became a stirring symbol of the Yankee spirit in music. With rich harmonization and clear diction, "the Hutchinsons expressed their genuine concern for human misery and social reform in subjects involving woman's suffrage, alcohol, war, prisons, and especially slavery."[91] Some historians go so far as to say the Hutchinsons' music hastened the confrontation and conflicts that led to the Civil War. It is thus notable that the Hutchinson family sang for seven presidents.

Interestingly, this family quartet (which sometimes had five singers) would always open or close their program with their signature song, "The Old Granite State," in antiphonal style—alternating with solo and chorus in echo fashion—which became characteristic of later gospel hymnody. No mention has been noted of these groups singing any hymns, although there were many patriotic songs.

With both a musical father and mother, it was not difficult for the Tylers to form their own singing ensemble. There were fifteen children in the family, eight by Tyler's first wife, Letitia, who died in 1842, and seven by Julia, whom John married a few months before he left office in 1844. According to Letty, his daughter, Tyler turned to music to escape from all the environments of political and social cares and duties. The *Washington Evening Star* quotes her as saying, "In spite of the comparatively quiet life at the White House, my father's time was rarely ever his own. 'Now sing, Letty,' he would say when we found ourselves far from the maddening crowd enjoying the quiet of some country road. And then I would sing his favorite songs, the old Scotch ballads we loved so well."[92]

The Tylers formed their family musical group at Sherwood Forest following his presidency. Tyler practiced on his new violin, purchased in 1848, and it is noted that in 1855 he was still "fiddling away every evening for the little children, black and white to dance."[93] The family patterned their group after the Virginia Minstrels: John played violin, with Julia on guitar, son-in-law William on banjo, and young Tazewell on the bone castanets. Julia termed this a true "minstrel troupe," which reflected America's joy in this spirited art form that was prevalent in this era.

Blumhofer noted that when President John Tyler visited Manhattan, hymn writer Fanny Crosby recited a poem of welcome for him, including these lines: "And the glad song of our nation shall be, Hurrah for John Tyler and liberty tree."[94] It is quite notable that both Jefferson and Tyler played the violin. It is also significant that Philip Doddridge wrote the favorite hymn of these two presidents. (Since the life of Doddridge has been covered in the chapter on Thomas Jefferson, this discussion will be about Tyler's favorite hymn rather than the life of Philip Doddridge.)

"O Happy Day That Fixed My Choice," one of the most frequently sung hymns of Doddridge, is often used for personal devotion as well as congregational singing. John Merrill lists this well-known hymn as John Tyler's favorite. Its simple yet powerful words have been loved by many generations of Christians. The text is full of words that suggest abundance and happiness. It is a perfect example of what James Montgomery spoke of in the preface to his *The Christian Psalmist* as he wrote of this hymn having "the piety of Watts, the ardor of Wesley, and the tenderness of Doddridge." These adjectives identify the distinctive qualities of these three hymn writers. Doddridge was a strong believer in the evidence of God's providence in national and religious affairs. Some say his literary sensibility in word and image is related to Shakespeare. The result is a hymnody unusual in range, accessibility, and seriousness. Doddridge's hymns proved to be very useful as supplements to Watts's collections, but only a few of the 400 he penned are found in today's hymnals.

As was the custom, Doddridge's hymns were based on the sermon of the day. When published, his hymns were listed chronologically from Genesis to Revelation. "O Happy Day" is based on 2 Chronicles 15:15.[95] It expresses the human side of the salvation experience, using the words "my choice," "my vow," "my love," and "I followed." Stanza one is a statement of the salvation commitment to the Savior, which is followed by joy on the journey to heaven in stanza two. Stanza three states the assurance of salvation in the

O Happy Day That Fixed My Choice

Words: Philip Doddridge, 1755
Music: John Hatton, 1793

L.M.
DUKE STREET

1. O hap - py day that fixed my choice
2. O hap - py bond that seals my vows
3. 'Tis done, the great trans - ac - tion's done;
4. High heaven, that heard the sol - emn vow,

On thee, my Sav - iour and my God!
To him who mer - its all my love!
I am my Lord's, and he is mine;
That vow re - newed shall dai - ly hear;

Well may this glow - ing heart re - joice,
Let cheer - ful an - thems fill his house
He drew me, and I fol - lowed on,
Till in life's lat - est hour I bow,

And tell its rap - tures all a - broad.
While to that sa - cred shrine I move.
Charmed to con - fess the voice di - vine.
And bless in death a bond so dear. A - men.

"great transaction," after which, in stanza four, a solemn vow is made and daily renewed.

The tune DUKE STREET has been used with many texts but perfectly fits with Doddridge's "O Happy Day." Written by John Hatton, who died in 1793, the tune is named after the street in Lancashire where the composer resided.[96] The tune first appeared in 1793 as music for Joseph Addison's version of Psalm 19—"The Spacious Firmament on High." In more recent settings DUKE STREET has been matched with Watts's paraphrase of Psalm 72—"Jesus Shall Reign." The melody, utilizing only one octave with mostly step-wise motion, is very usable for congregational singing.

The hymn "O Happy Day" appears to reinforce the possibility that President John Tyler was a Christian in spirit if not in action. The positive tone of the text expresses a sense of joy in a personal relationship with God. If the selection of this hymn as Tyler's most favored one is true—the premise of this book, that the presidential hymns were most significant to each man—then the acceptance of orthodox Christianity by John Tyler must be concluded.

JAMES K. POLK

1795–1849

Eleventh President (1845–1849)

The president's job is a twenty-four-hour occupation. Vacationing presidents frequently have found themselves summoned back to Washington, DC, in response to various crises, and even while on vacation, US presidents receive regular briefings. Even in the nineteenth century, presidents were challenged by what Thomas Jefferson called "the splendid misery of the presidency."[97] One president who embraced the challenging nature of round-the-clock service was James K. Polk, who in today's terminology would have been labeled a "workaholic."

James Polk was born in North Carolina in 1795, but his family moved to Tennessee when Polk was ten. A diligent student, Polk excelled in his studies, and the University of North Carolina admitted him even though he had completed only about two years of formal schooling. He graduated with honors and returned to Tennessee to study law with prominent attorney Felix Grundy. He later established his own thriving law practice in Columbia and turned his attention to state politics. His district's voters elected him to the state legislature when he was only twenty-seven years old. He married the daughter of a wealthy Tennessean. His wife, Sarah, not only provided a social promotion for Polk, but also was a lifelong friend and a valuable asset in his political career.

In 1824 Polk rode the crest of rising Jacksonian democracy and was elected to his first term in the US House of Representatives. He served for fourteen years prior to and throughout Jackson's presidency, rising to become Speaker of the House and becoming a major advocate of Jackson's congressional policies. He left the House of Representatives in 1839 when Tennessee voters elected him governor. Unfortunately for Polk, growing Whig power in Tennessee and voter disenchantment with Democrats in the aftermath of the Panic of 1837 led to his being defeated in his reelection bid and to subsequent defeat in his attempt to regain the governorship two years later. Despite these defeats, Polk remained active in Democratic politics at both the state and national level.

In 1844 Polk became the frontrunner for the vice-presidential nomination prior to the Democratic National Convention. However, his aging mentor, Jackson, correctly surmised the growing national spirit of Manifest Destiny and encouraged his protégé to adopt an aggressive position of expansionism. When the convention was unable to agree upon either former president Martin Van Buren, Lewis Cass, or John Calhoun, they turned to Polk as their nominee. For this reason, historians have often referred to Polk as the first "dark horse" presidential candidate. In the presidential campaign that followed, Polk and his partisans loudly touted their aggressive territorial ambitions, including the controversial annexation of Texas and the acquisition of the entirety of the Oregon Country. His slogan "54' 40' or Fight"[98] became one of the best-known campaign slogans of the nineteenth century. American voters captured that spirit and chose Polk as the nation's eleventh president.

Before Polk's inauguration, however, the outgoing president, John Tyler, viewed the election results as a referendum on the annexation of Texas. Avoiding a controversial floor fight, Tyler shrewdly proposed that Texas be annexed via joint resolution of Congress. The resolution passed, thus accomplishing one of Polk's primary campaign goals. Unfortunately, Polk also realized that this annexation might lead to war with Mexico. Mellowing in his approach to Great Britain over joint occupation of the Oregon Country,

Polk's administration agreed to a compromise line of the 49' latitudinal line, roughly dividing the Oregon Country in half.

As potential war with Mexico loomed, Polk continued his aggressive expansionist pursuits. He sent an emissary to Mexico, offering the purchase of the California and New Mexico Territories for twenty million dollars plus the settlement of American citizens' claims against Mexico. When Mexico refused to bargain with the nation it believed had "stolen" Texas, Polk took matters into his own hands. He ordered General Zachary Taylor to begin patrolling disputed territory across the Nueces River in Texas, certainly knowing that this would provoke Mexico. When some of Taylor's men were killed and wounded in this region, Polk used the fighting as a pretext for a controversial declaration of war. In truth, both nations were spoiling for a fight. Congress granted the declaration, and the United States was at war for the first time since 1814.

In the months that followed, Polk managed the Mexican-American War from his office in the White House. Small armies quickly defeated Mexican forces in New Mexico and California while General Taylor won several victories in northern Mexico. When Mexico failed to sue for peace, Polk authorized another invasion force under General Winfield Scott that landed in Vera Cruz and, in a brilliant campaign that followed stiff resistance, captured Mexico City and ended the war. The Treaty of Guadalupe Hidalgo that followed recognized the annexation of Texas and ceded all of California and New Mexico to the United States while the United States paid Mexico fifteen million dollars and assumed the claims of US citizens against Mexico.

The remainder of Polk's presidency was relatively uneventful. While the war and Polk's administration were extremely controversial, and abolitionists and other anti-slavery advocates charged that Polk, a slaveholder himself, had fought the war to expand slave territory, it is also true that Polk avoided war with Britain and peacefully settled the Oregon question and expanded US territory by more than 800,000 square miles. In doing so, Polk fulfilled some of his predecessors' dreams of stretching the nation from sea to sea.

Polk kept his campaign promise and refused to run for a second term. He returned to Tennessee via a rather circuitous but triumphant route. Exhausted due to his incessant workaholic lifestyle, especially while in the White House, and an obligation to respond to the plaudits of the crowds that met him along the way, Polk fell ill while en route and became tragically sick shortly after returning to Nashville. Experiencing the shortest retirement of any president and dying at an age younger than any president not assassinated, Polk died in June 1849. He was only fifty-three.

Polk's mother raised him in a devout Presbyterian home and was said to be a direct descendent of the reformer John Knox. Polk's wife was also a devout Presbyterian and would not allow either dancing or card-playing in the White House. Polk regularly attended church with both his mother and wife but never joined a church. In keeping with Democratic Party tradition, he made few public pronouncements about faith but continued a rigid defense of religious liberty. He did attend a moving Methodist camp meeting revival while in Congress and afterward identified himself more as a Methodist than a Presbyterian. While on his deathbed, he requested and received Methodist baptism and professed his faith.[99]

James Polk described his mother's chief joys as "the Bible, the Confession of Faith, the Psalms, and Watts' Hymns."[100] Evidently, her love of hymns had little effect on James, and even his appreciation of music was not strong. Francis Scala, conductor of the Marine Band, recalled that Polk did not care much for music, resulting in the president's lack of attention shown to that select musical group. Polk considered music as "a mystical language that fortified the spirits of those who knew no other means of communication."[101] The president noted in his diary on 30 April 1846 that thirty blind and deaf children demonstrated their skills for him, including their music. He wrote, "One of the females performed on the piano, one of the males on the violin, and several of them sung very well."[102]

Since the Polks had no children, Sarah devoted her undivided attention to her husband and his position. She was regarded as a capable White House hostess, famous for her intelligence and wit, and highly respected even by her husband's political foes. The most unique entertainment she allowed at her glittering parties, receptions, and open houses was juggling; there was certainly no dancing to the music performed.

There were some notable social events during Polk's term in Washington. The Polks inaugurated the tradition of Thanksgiving dinner in the White House. Since Sarah had been given an Astor *pianoforte* by her father as a young girl, she studied music and the arts at the Moravian Female Academy in Salem, North Carolina. These studies prepared her to redecorate the White House and even compose music while serving as the First Lady.

A typical musical program during Polk's time in the White House was by ballad singer William Dempster. Dempster, a very popular balladeer of that time, sang songs of a similar message as the Hutchinson family but with less urgency. Polk recorded in his diary a brief mention of an event on 7 March 1846 when "Dempster, a celebrated musician, entertained the company by singing and playing on the piano."[103] The music he performed was mainly sentimental Scottish and Irish tunes, climaxing with Dempster's own solo cantata "The May Queen."

No records have been found of any hymns being sung in the White House during Polk's administration. However, when President Polk and his staff made an official visit to the Institute for the Blind in New York City in 1845, he met songwriter Fanny Crosby. As usual, Fanny was drafted to recite a poem of welcome. She made a poetical address, "praising republican government."[104]

In 1846 when Fanny Crosby traveled to Washington, DC, to advocate support for the education of the blind in Boston, Philadelphia, and New York, she spoke to Congress and to a special subcommittee. Bernard Ruffin states that the president remembered Fanny from the former visit. Afterward, at the White House, he asked, "Well, Miss Crosby, have you made any poetry since I saw you last year?" She responded, "Yes, I have composed a song and dedicated it to you."[105] President Polk was in disbelief, but after dinner, he escorted her to the music room where Fanny gave an impromptu recital, accompanying herself on the piano. Among other songs, she sang for him these words, "Our President! We humbly turn to thee—Are not the blind the objects of thy care?" On her second trip, Fanny met Polk again and, for her first and only time, his wife. She was deeply impressed with the First Lady.

In 1848 Crosby again met President Polk when he made a summer visit to the institute. Being in ill health, he had already decided not to run for reelection, but he simply needed a rest. Remembering the tranquil beauty of the school, he went there for his rest. He didn't want an official reception. Since he was already well acquainted with Fanny, she accompanied him as he leisurely strolled around the grounds. President Polk died in the summer of the following year.

From the research of John Merrill, we learn that James Polk's most favored hymn was "All Hail the Power of Jesus' Name." Since Polk attended both Presbyterian and Methodist services, and since this hymn ranks near the top among hymns most frequently printed in America, it was certainly well known and loved by evangelicals during the 1840s. It became extremely popular when in 1793 American composer Oliver Holden wrote the tune CORONATION to the powerful words. It has been sung to this tune in America ever since, even though Englishmen prefer its first musical setting, the MILES LANE tune.

Edward Perronet, who wrote the words of the hymn, was a protégé of John Wesley, serving for some time as one of his itinerant preachers. Coming from a family of French Huguenot refugees, Edward's father was actively associated with the Wesleys, George Whitefield, and the English evangelical movement within the Church of England. First educated at home, Edward had a brilliant mind and great poetic talent. He was also very independent and often critical of the Anglican Church. Eventually, he left the Methodist movement, becoming a Dissenter and pastoring an independent church in Canterbury, where he was buried in the Anglican Cathedral in 1792.[106]

Perronet's hymns were published anonymously in successive volumes. The most important volume was *Occasional Verses, Moral and Sacred.* The third hymn in this collection is titled "On the Resurrection," which is known today as "All Hail the Power of Jesus' Name." The fact that it has survived for over 200 years is testimony to its worth. Interestingly, 126 years passed before it was finally proven that this hymn was penned by Perronet. On examining *Occasional Verses*, hymnologist Louis Benson discovered a poem, "On Sleep," in which the first letter of each line spells out Edward Perronet. This is the same book where "All Hail the Power of Jesus' Name" is found.[107]

The first stanza of President Polk's favorite hymn appeared alone in the *Gospel Magazine* in 1779, set to the British-preferred MILES LANE tune, composed by nineteen-year-old London organist William Shrubsole. English composer Edward Elgar pronounced this music the finest tune in English hymnody. Shrubsole is most remembered for this hymn tune. In 1780, "All Hail the Power of Jesus' Name" appeared in complete form with eight stanzas under the title "On the Resurrection, the Lord Is King." It was revised by Baptist pastor John Rippon in 1787 when he included the hymn in his *Selections of Hymns from the Best Authors.* Rippon rewrote some verses, eliminated three, and added two of his own. His climaxing last stanza is printed in almost all hymnals today.

The tune most used in America for this text is CORONATION, composed by Massachusetts native and self-taught musician Oliver Holden in 1793. Holden was a carpenter from Charlestown who became a wealthy storeowner and eventually a member of the Massachusetts House of Representatives. Having only two months of instruction in a singing school in 1783, he became a music teacher, composer, compiler of music collections, and even a choral conductor. CORONATION first appeared in his hymnal *Union Harmony*, printed in Boston in 1793.[108] The tune was first sung to Baptist minister John Rippon's version of the text in four voice parts. Having studied some of William Billings's music, Holden has the melody migrating briefly from tenor to soprano, becoming a quasi-fuging tune. The tune name comes from the phrase "crown Him Lord of all." It is significant that Holden's CORONATION is the oldest American hymn tune still widely sung.

It is almost certain that Holden also wrote original music for the text "Ode to Columbia's Favorite Son" in 1789 for the visit to Boston by

All Hail the Power of Jesus' Name

Words: Edward Perronet, 1779
Music: Oliver Holden, 1793

C.M.
CORONATION

1. All hail the pow'r of Jesus' name! Let angels prostrate fall; Bring forth the royal diadem, And crown him Lord of all. Bring forth the royal diadem, And crown him Lord of all.
2. Crown him, ye martyrs of our God, Who from his altar call; Extol the stem of Jesse's rod, And crown him Lord of all. Extol the stem of Jesse's rod, And crown him Lord of all.
3. Ye seed of Israel's chosen race, Ye ransomed of the fall; Hail him, who saves you by his grace, And crown him Lord of all. Hail him, who saves you by his grace, And crown him Lord of all.
4. Sinners whose love can ne'er forget The wormwood and the gall, Go, spread your trophies at his feet, And crown him Lord of all. Go, spread your trophies at his feet, And crown him Lord of all.
5. Let every kindred, every tribe, On this terrestrial ball, To him all majesty ascribe, And crown him Lord of all. To him all majesty ascribe, And crown him Lord of all.
6. O that, with yonder sacred throng, We at his feet may fall; We'll join the everlasting song, And crown him Lord of all. We'll join the everlasting song, And crown him Lord of all. A-men.

President George Washington. In addition, he wrote the music for the Charlestown observance of the death of Washington in 1799.

The grand design of "All Hail the Power of Jesus' Name" is the positive message that it presents of the kingship of Christ. Regardless of the tune choice or stanzas chosen by a hymnal editor, all Christians ascribe royal honors to Jesus' name as they "crown Him Lord of all." The hymn had meaning to President Polk as he carried out the task of expansion of territories during his administration. He was constantly reminded of the extreme importance of this aspect not only for the strength of the nation, but also the well-being of those already in the land.

After the setting of stanza one, which is based on Matthew 28:18 and Revelation 19:16, stanzas two and three refer to the Christian church as the "new Israel." In Galatians 3:29 Paul clearly teaches this position. Stanza four is an all-inclusive prayer for sinners to remember Christ's atoning death; this statement is from Lamentations 3:19. The message becomes clear for every tribe in stanza five; these words are for all people on our globe (terrestrial ball). A scripture passage that substantiates these truths is Revelation 7:9–10. The climaxing words in the last stanza are beautifully stated in Philippians 2:10–11, which tells us that someday "every tongue shall confess that Jesus Christ is Lord, to the glory of God the Father."

Even though President Polk, in following his party's tradition, said little about his personal beliefs during his administration, perhaps this hymn said it for him. "All Hail the Power of Jesus' Name," a powerful hymn of praise and adoration, has been loved and sung by generations of Christians.

ZACHARY TAYLOR

1784–1850

Twelfth President (1849–1850)

When the Whig Party began to coalesce in opposition to Andrew Jackson and the Democrats, politically attuned Americans generally expected prominent Whigs Henry Clay or Daniel Webster to be the first Whig president. Despite this, however, American voters chose only two Whig presidents in the party's short-lived history. In both cases, their choices were war heroes, similar to Jackson in many ways. In 1840 voters elected William Henry Harrison as the first Whig president, but Harrison's presidency was the shortest in American history as he became the first president to die in office. The second, Zachary Taylor, had a slightly longer tenure, but like Harrison, he also died in office.

Zachary Taylor was born in Virginia. While an infant, however, Taylor's family moved to Kentucky, and Taylor always identified himself as a Kentuckian. Probably inspired by his Revolutionary War hero father, Taylor enlisted in the US Army and was commissioned an officer. He served with distinction in the War of 1812, where he served at times under the command of Harrison. He spent the next thirty years of his career as an officer in the army. Throughout much of his career, Taylor put down Native American uprisings as the United States expanded ever westward. His most significant military experience in these years came in Florida in the infamous Seminole Wars.

Taylor rose to command in the old American Southwest. When the United States annexed Texas in 1845, President Polk sent Taylor to defend the Texas border with Mexico. After Polk ordered Taylor to send troops into disputed territory across the Nueces River, war erupted with the southern neighbor. Polk placed Taylor in command of the US forces that invaded Mexico. Soon afterward, Taylor defeated Mexican forces at Palo Alto and Resaca de la Palma. In the weeks that followed, Taylor won even more impressive victories at Buena Vista and Monterrey. Quickly, "Old Rough and Ready," as he was nicknamed, became a national hero.

Becoming increasingly jealous of Taylor's popularity, fearing Taylor's Whig sentiments and possible presidential aspirations, and disagreeing with the general on several war issues, Polk transferred many of Taylor's troops away and shifted the war's focus to an invasion of Mexico via Vera Cruz on the central Mexican coast. Polk ignored Taylor and chose General Winfield Scott to lead the successful invasion that captured Mexico City and ended the war. Despite Polk's political tactics, Taylor's immense popularity due to his victories, his strong nationalist sentiments, and his status as a slaveholder in Louisiana made him an attractive presidential candidate in 1848. Even though Taylor was a slaveholder, he never defended sectionalism or slavery, and he never defined his position on key issues in the presidential campaign. The Whigs simply promoted him on the basis of his war record. The emergence of a third party, the Free-Soil Party, which rejected both Taylor, as a slaveholding southern Whig, and Lewis Cass, as a northern Democrat favoring popular sovereignty, swayed enough votes in the critical state of New York to give Taylor a close victory.

Despite his Whig background, President Taylor did not become a puppet for more experienced Whig leaders like Clay and Webster. Some political observers and Washington insiders criticized his roughhewn ways and charged that he was simpleminded. Others argued that Taylor simply viewed himself above politics. When crisis loomed in 1850 regarding the admission of California as a free state, Taylor stood up to Southerners who threatened secession much in the same way that Jackson had nearly two decades before. However, before either a confrontation occurred or a compromise was completed, Taylor suddenly fell ill after a Fourth of July celebration where he reportedly overindulged in chilled cherries and milk and died a few days later. Some historians suspect that he fell as a victim of a cholera outbreak that occurred that summer.

Taylor is generally regarded as one of the least religious US presidents. He enthusiastically chewed tobacco and used rough language frequently associated with military life. His wife was a devout Episcopalian, however, and Taylor did attend church with her occasionally while he was president. He is never known to have made a profession of faith of any kind, although his youngest daughter did claim that he regularly read the Bible.[109]

Even though Marine bandmaster Francis Scala said that President Taylor was rather gruff and fond of older martial music, because of Taylor's military feats, he became America's idol. Music publishers capitalized on his heroic status with numerous songs and even piano pieces appearing soon after the general became commander in chief.

The White House curator has three volumes of music from the estate of Taylor's youngest daughter, Betty, who served as hostess in place of her semi-invalid mother during the family's brief stay in the mansion. Elise Kirk states that "it is uncertain whether the music was used at the White House or whether it was merely a part of the family collection over the years."[110] Most of the music is from the 1840s, but some was published in the 1820s. One composition is obviously related to Taylor's military service. Written in 1847 and titled "The Battle of Buena Vista," it is a musical salute to a victory won by General Taylor.

On 24 April 1849 the Baker family presented a program of popular songs for the Taylor White House. Even though there were no hymns sung, the press indicated that the family's entertainment was an inspiring and positive experience, saying that the program had moral influence. Singing in a style reminiscent of the Hutchinson family, the group sang four-part harmony of moralizing verses that bore more sentimental feeling than social commentary. Included in their concert were "The Death of Washington," "Happiest Time Is Now," and "Is There No Comfort for the Sorrowing Heart."

After stating that those who heard the Bakers' concert would become better persons, the *National Intelligencer* on 30 April 1849 indicated that something else was emerging. This was a statement of approaching danger voiced by Ralph Waldo Emerson when he wrote that there was "a war between intellect and affection, a crack in Nature which split every church in Christendom. The key to the period appeared to be that the mind had become aware of itself—The young men were born with knives in their brains."[111] This seems to be an analysis of the national situation of the country.

America's first popular Christmas carol was written during the same year as Taylor's inauguration. The hymn "It Came upon a Midnight Clear" by the Unitarian minister Edmund Sears has been studied by hymnologists as a reflection of the times. The minister Ernest Emurian's study concluded that the carol is partially a restatement of Sears's 1834 hymn "Calm on the Listening Ear," especially in the use of the phrase "Peace on earth, good will to men."[112] Others believe that its doleful words about war refer to the Mexican-American conflict of 1846–1848, perhaps the country's most unpopular military intervention up to that time. "It Came upon a Midnight Clear" was not published until 29 December 1849 when it appeared in the *Christian Register*. In 1850 Richard Willis composed the music CAROL, the tune to which it is sung today. Since President Taylor died on 9 July 1850, he may have never heard the hymn. Insightfully, hymnologist William Reynolds states that the hymn had evidence of implications of a social gospel since the third stanza definitely makes a comment that is almost a prediction of the festering Civil War.[113] The stanza, omitted by most hymnals, includes the phrase in referring to the song of the angels: "And man, at war with man, hears not / The love song which they sing."

While there is no record that Fanny Crosby ever met Zachary Taylor, she joined the country in mourning his death by writing these lines: "A wail is in the capital, A wail of anguish deep / That startles with a fearful sound, The night wind from its sleep. / The brave old oak hath bowed his head, A victim to the blast. / Death holds within his conquering arms The conqueror at last."[114]

According to John Merrill's extensive research, President Taylor's choice of a favored hymn was "Great God, How Infinite Art Thou" by Isaac Watts. Watts was one of the most important figures in hymnody since he "christianized" the Psalms and succeeded in writing excellent, freely composed hymns for worship. For these and other reasons, he is often called the "father of English hymnody."[115]

Born in England in 1674, young Isaac was a brilliant child, having learned Latin by age four and mastered Hebrew, Greek, and French before age fourteen. Since his father opposed the Anglican Church, Isaac's family was termed "dissenters." Therefore, Isaac chose not to attend Oxford or Cambridge although he was academically qualified. His first poetic effort to be published was *Honrae Lyricae*, which included Latin poems, poems on divine love, four psalm versions, and twenty-two devotional poems. The work included his initial experiments in hymn writing. The hymn "Great God, How Infinite Art Thou" first appeared in this poetry book in 1705.

It seems that a large number of Watts's hymns and psalm paraphrases have no personal history beyond their date of publication. This hymn is listed under the subject of "God's Eternal Dominion" with the subtitle "Thy Throne Eternal Ages Stood." In the preface to the 1709 edition of *Honrae Lyricae*, Watts states that his intention was to demonstrate that poetry was "supremely fitted to celebrate the truth of the Christian religion…the proper station of poetry was in the temple of God."[116] Watts deplored the absence of poetry in Puritan worship and criticized those who steadfastly held onto solely psalm paraphrases in their worship.

It wasn't long before Watts realized that hymns should be simple to serve the common man in worship. In his next attempt he purposely avoided complicated metrical structures, limiting his hymns to the three standard meters—common, long, and short. This decision partially accounted for the success of his 1707 collection called *Hymns and Spiritual Songs*. He retained "Great God, How Infinite Art Thou" in that hymnal.

In his lifetime, Watts wrote about 650 hymns, but he also devised a theory on congregational praise. Because of his language skills he was able to paraphrase psalms in meter by 1719. Titled *Psalms of David Imitated,* several of his psalm settings are sung even today: "Joy to the World" is a setting of Psalm 98, while "O God, Our Help in Ages Past" is Watts's versification of Psalm 90. Watts was well known and respected by English evangelicals, including Countess Lady Huntingdon, a distant relative of George Washington, who subsidized many pastors and hymn writers in chapels she built in the eighteenth century. John Wesley introduced Watts's hymns to America in Georgia in 1737; George Whitefield used Watts's hymns in revivals in New England in 1739. Benjamin Franklin's first book printed on his press in 1729 was Watts's *Psalms of David Imitated,* and in 1741 Franklin reprinted Watts's *Hymns and Spiritual Songs.*

The tune for Watts's lyrics "Great God, How Infinite Art Thou" was composed in four-part harmony by French Protestant musician Guillaume Franc, who left Geneva in 1545 to serve as cantor in Lausanne, France. While there, he collected and harmonized melodies that became the *Lausanne Psalter* of 1565. Having been the first music editor for the *Genevan Psalter* working during 1542–1543, Franc developed the "French style" of tune writing as distinct from the German and later English hymn tunes. Combining both plain song and folksong with many borrowed melodies, he also composed some original music. Waldo Pratt states that through editorial shaping, Franc was quite successful in fitting the music to the texts of the

Great God, How Infinite Art Thou

Words: Isaac Watts, 1707
Music: Guillaume Franc, 1615

C.M.
DUNDEE

day.[117] The completed *Psalter*, which Franc edited, introduced forty-six new tunes, of which twenty-six were composed by Franc himself, while twenty came from other sources. They were not widely accepted at that time because harmonized music was forbidden in public worship.[118]

The tune DUNDEE by Guillaume Franc first appeared in *The Scottish Psalter* in 1615 but was used with other texts besides Watts's "Great God, How Infinite Art Thou." In 1621 it was found in Thomas Ravenscroft's *Whole Book of Psalms*; in 1736 the tune was used with Philip Doddridge's "O God of Bethel, By Whose Hand"; in 1759 it was sung to Charles Wesley's

"Let Saints on Earth in Concert Sing." DUNDEE is one of twelve common-meter tunes in *The Scottish Psalter*, where it is called FRENCH TUNE. In most English and American books of psalmody, DUNDEE is the same as WINDSOR and COLESHILL. The tune contains some similarity to those of the *Genevan Psalter* of 1562 primarily because Franc was so familiar with Genevan principles of tune writing. Blume points out, "The special Lausanne tradition of the earlier editions lived on in the melodic repertory of 1565."[119]

DUNDEE may seem simple; it has sometimes been described as a "gracious little tune." While being very different from the older music preferred by President Taylor, it was an ideal contrast for worship music for which it was intended. For a president, there are times when such changes are necessary for survival in the position.

Based on Lamentations 5:19, this hymn has five stanzas; often the first stanza is repeated as the last stanza. The lyrics clearly and simply state in poetry the omnipotence of God. Such words of assurance probably helped President Taylor reach a higher plane than his critics. In times of decision, following the text of this hymn, Christians are encouraged by knowing that God is in control of man's affairs. The hymn exemplifies Watts's leaning toward Calvinism while praising God wholly. ·

Being similar in thought to the modern hymn "How Great Thou Art," a hymn that has been a favorite song of at least three US presidents, it should not be surprising that one of the least religious presidents, as was Zachary Taylor, would choose such a lofty thought as the "God of infinity." The phrase "Great God, there's nothing new" is a positive statement that God, having made all, continues to be in control of creation. This is confirmed in the phrase "Thou art the ever living God." What tremendous thoughts for the president of a country founded in part on Christian principles.

MILLARD FILLMORE

1800–1874

Thirteenth President (1850–1853)

His name has sometimes become a punch line in presidential humor and American history. In fact, many Americans have never even heard of him. While he stepped into the breach at a crucial time in American politics after the unexpected death of President Zachary Taylor, when the Whig Party died a few years later his political career essentially died with it, even though he was still a relatively young man. Unfortunately, Millard Fillmore also became associated with a political party that marred his name.

Millard Fillmore was born in the Finger Lakes region of New York in 1800. Like the more famous Abraham Lincoln, Fillmore's parents reared their family in a log cabin. Also like Lincoln, Fillmore studied law. He rose to wealth and prominence as an attorney in Buffalo. His district's voters elected him to the state legislature, where he served for approximately three years. He affiliated himself with the new Whig Party and allied himself with the New York political boss Thurlow Weed. New York voters subsequently elected him to the House of Representatives from 1833–1835 and again from 1837–1845. Afterward, he served as the state comptroller, probably owing to his relationship with Weed.

In 1848 the Whigs decided to nominate the Mexican War hero Zachary Taylor as their presidential nominee. Because most Whigs regarded Taylor a political novice and a Southerner, even though Taylor had served most of his life in the US military, they sought to balance the ticket with a more experienced politician and Northerner as his running mate. With Weed's backing, Fillmore became their choice for vice president, and he and Taylor were elected in 1848.

Fillmore found himself presiding over the tumultuous Senate during its debates concerning various aspects of the Compromise of 1850 and the admission of California. For a time it looked as if the Union might dissolve. Throughout the deliberations Fillmore maintained a fair and even hand in his moderation of Senate sessions, not revealing his feelings regarding the compromise to anyone except President Taylor. Surprisingly, a short time later, Taylor took ill and died unexpectedly, thrusting the little-known Fillmore into the presidency. With Fillmore's diligent support and backing, the various measures that made up the Compromise of 1850 passed Congress, and he signed them into law.

Unfortunately for Fillmore, the more radical wing of the northern Whigs viewed Fillmore as a traitor. This came back to haunt him in 1852 when he sought the Whig presidential nomination. As a result, the Whig Party chose General Winfield Scott as their presidential nominee. Franklin Pierce defeated Scott in the election. Fillmore probably would have passed into obscurity as the Whig Party divided and then splintered in the aftermath of the election of 1852 as he refused to join the new Republican Party to which many northern Whigs fled. Instead, another new political party, the American Party, drafted Fillmore as their presidential nominee in 1856. The American Party, better known as the "Know-Nothings," was a loose political movement that opposed easy immigration into the United States and wanted to prevent Roman Catholics from holding political office. Fillmore and the party were defeated, and he retired from public office. When the Civil War began, Fillmore supported the Union but was often critical of President Lincoln. Because of this criticism, he sank further into obscurity. He died in 1874 and was largely forgotten after being a somewhat prominent Whig in the 1840s and 1850s.

Millard Fillmore, like Taylor, is generally regarded as one of our least religious presidents. He is never known to have read the Bible and rarely mentioned God or religion in his public pronouncements, something that was especially unusual at that time, especially for Whigs. As far as is known, any church attendance was infrequent, though he did affiliate with the Unitarian Church in 1831 and may have attended various Unitarian congregations.[120]

Fillmore was raised in a Methodist environment by a father who owned only two books—a Bible and a hymnbook. Even though there is a hymn tune called FILLMORE, supposedly written by American composer Jeremiah Ingalls, it did not appear in his *Christian Harmony* of 1805. The earliest publication of this tune did not occur until 1869 in Philadelphia when it was printed in a collection compiled by William G. Fischer called *Joyful Songs*. The tune was arranged by Fischer, as sung by Chaplain C. C. McCabe, according to hymnologist Robert McCutchan, who suggests that the tune was named after President Fillmore.[121]

Other than this reference to a tune named after him, there is little known about Fillmore's appreciation or interest in music. However, his wife, Abigail, was a great lover of music, and Mary, their only child, was a pianist who also played the harp and guitar. During the Fillmore administration, there was an increasing interest in opera in America. Elise Kirk states that in 1852, two of the nineteenth-century prima donnas sang in Washington, DC, within five days of each other. President Fillmore and his family were in attendance at both Maria Alboni's and Henrietta Sontag's vocal recitals.[122]

Perhaps the most exciting musical event for the first family occurred in 1850 when the world-famous singer Jenny Lind visited the capital city. Having just retired from opera because of its "immoral and evil roles," in which she had sung over 700 times, Lind performed two very successful concerts at the Washington National Theater. Accompanied by a sixty-piece orchestra, she thrilled the audience with numerous arias and popular ballads of the era. The 18 December 1850 playbill shows that Lind sang "Home Sweet Home" and closed her program with the popular "Hail Columbia."[123]

After her concert, the Fillmores invited the diva to the White House. Even though she did not perform there, her biographer wrote that the singer was impressed with the down-to-earth conversation she experienced with America's first family. There were some special programs at the White House, however. Occasionally even the president would join in singing as Mary would accompany a group gathered in the great room for a "sing-along." Fillmore especially enjoyed a new tune by Stephen Foster called "Old Folks at Home." No hymns were noted as being sung at these events.

There are no hymns in five volumes of music bound in the Fillmore collection, which is comprised of piano pieces or vocal solos accompanied by the piano. This treasured collection is a fine representation of the tastes of an artistic and educated American family during the 1830s and 1840s, containing Scottish and Irish airs, operatic transcriptions, patriotic songs, and battle pieces. This family collection does not necessarily mean that the music was performed at the White House for special programs.

Since the First Lady was a Baptist and Fillmore had a cousin who was a Methodist minister, it is surprising that the future president joined Buffalo's Unitarian church. However, because he associated with Unitarians, this relationship likely contributed to the research John Merrill made concerning Fillmore's most favored hymn being the Unitarian one, "While Thee I Seek, Protecting Power" by Helen Maria Williams.

This unique hymn came from the 1786 book of poetry by Williams, which contained only two religious poems. When used as hymn lyrics, "Trust and Providence" became known by the first line of text. The words are especially effective because they are expressions of personal experience. One of the most brilliant women of the eighteenth century, Helen Williams, born in 1762, was the daughter of a British army officer. After obtaining an excellent education, she published her first book at age twenty. In her life she wrote on varied subjects such as fiction, science, and poetry as well as her specialty—the French Revolution.

Following her sister, who married a French Protestant, Williams spent most of her life in Paris. Having an intense interest in the politics of this tumultuous period in which she sympathized with the French republicans, she was eventually imprisoned for her beliefs. The lyrics of the hymn "While Thee I Seek, Protecting Power" represent her deepest spiritual feelings. It is the only piece out of her many writings that has survived in common usage. Written while she was in prison, Samuel Rogal says, "It has clear references to a particular spiritual mood that may in turn, identify specific conclusions and discoveries. She identifies and speaks for herself!"[124]

Williams's hymn first appeared in 1790 in a Unitarian hymnal titled *Psalms and Hymns for the Use of the New Meeting in Birmingham,* edited by Joseph Priestly. In 1795 this hymnal was reprinted by four Presbyterians who leaned toward Unitarianism. Their book contained 690 hymns and psalm paraphrases by more than fifty poets.[125] Following this, "While Thee I Seek, Protecting Power" appeared in a Unitarian hymnal yearly for forty-five years. There were at least twenty American hymnals from ten different denominations—including Episcopal, Methodist, and Baptist—published between 1854 and 1957 that have included the Williams hymn.

While Thee I Seek, Protecting Power

Words: Helen M. Williams, 1786
Music: Ignaz J. Pleyel, 1791

C.M.
PLEYEL'S HYMN

1. While Thee I seek, pro-tect-ing Pow'r, Be my vain wish - es stilled, And may this con - se - crat - ed hour With bet - ter hopes be filled. Thy love the pow'r of tho't be-stowed, To Thee my tho'ts would soar; Thy mer - cy o'er my life has flowed, That mer - cy I a - dore.

2. In each e - vent of life, how clear Thy rul - ing hand I see! Each bless - ing to my soul more dear, Be - cause con - ferred by Thee. In ev - 'ry joy that crowns my days, In ev - 'ry pain I bear, My heart shall find de - light in praise, Or seek re - lief in prayer.

3. When glad - ness wings my fa - vored hour, Thy love my tho'ts shall fill; Re - signed when storms of sor - row lower, My soul shall meet Thy will. My lift - ed eye, with-out a tear, The gath - 'ring storm shall see; My stead-fast heart shall know no fear; That heart shall rest on Thee.

The music for Helen Williams's text was composed by Ignaz J. Pleyel in 1791. In the *Sacred Harp* collections, beginning in 1844, the tune has been called PLEYEL'S HYMN, but several other tune names have been connected with the lyrics including BRATTLE STREET, CONDOLENCE, GERMAN HYMN, SILOAM, and VIENNA.[126] Obviously the first tune name comes from the composer, while the other names derive either from Pleyel's teacher, Franz Joseph Haydn in Vienna, or some editor's experience with the music. The hymn is still sung with Pleyel's music in several fa-sol-la books, including *The Missouri Harmony* and *The New Harp of Columbia*.

Pleyel worked in Austria, Italy, England, and France, founding a music publishing firm and a piano company. He wrote forty-five symphonies as well as numerous other compositions, including hymn tunes. Since this tune is in common meter, the lyrics could fit any number of tunes. One other alternate tune suggested is SIMPSON, arranged from Louis Spohr, a noted European composer.

It is notable that President Fillmore spoke more of what he was against than what he stood for. As a state assemblyman, he fought unsuccessfully to abolish a law requiring witnesses in court to swear belief in God. Fillmore never felt comfortable expressing his religious beliefs in public, but obviously preferred the intellectual stance of Unitarians. Eventually, he fellowshipped with Episcopalians and Baptists, although not regularly. It may be that Fillmore heard this hymn in an Episcopal church, since in 1808 the Trinity Church, Boston, in preparing their own hymnal, relied heavily on a book edited by Jeremy Belknap in 1795 called *Sacred Poetry: Consisting of Psalms and Hymns Adapted to Christian Devotion*, which contained "While Thee I Seek, Protecting Power." According to hymnologist Henry Foote, the Unitarians in general had already been using Belknap's hymnal for forty years.[127]

The text of the hymn regarded as Fillmore's favorite is one of true submission to God's will. Whether he followed the substance of these lyrics honestly is difficult to ascertain. But in the opening stanza, the author quickly disposes of a common dilemma: human vanity succumbs to the protection and power of God. After that realization, Helen Williams pours forth her own religious enthusiasm. In stanza two she emphasizes the importance of mercy in the believer's life, and follows this with thankfulness for the blessing of life and its events. Continuing this thought of praise, Williams leads the singer to his knees in prayer. The essence of stanza three is that gladness is contained in a person's love and desire to follow God's will. This may be interpreted as a "praise of total trust by directing the singer's thought not toward her own mind or soul, but in the direction of her own rebirth."[128]

Such honest thought of submission to God's will may have been comforting to Fillmore toward the end of his term and even in his unsuccessful attempt to regain the White House for a second term. His support of the Union, even in disagreement with Lincoln's policies, demonstrates his stand for principles dear to him. It is not difficult to say that this hymn could have been a factor in accepting defeats and providing guidance in his life as president.

FRANKLIN PIERCE

1804–1869

Fourteenth President (1853–1857)

In the tumultuous days leading up to the Civil War, Americans increasingly found themselves forced to choose sides between pro- and anti-slavery forces. The growing conflict centered upon the political parties. Southerners and slavery's advocates often dominated the Democratic Party. While in the 1850s Democrats nominated Northern politicians for the presidency, they also selected Northerners who generally were proslavery or pro-Southern candidates. One such candidate was Franklin Pierce.

Franklin Pierce was born in Hillsborough, New Hampshire. He attended Bowdoin College in Maine and then studied law. Voters from his home district elected him to the New Hampshire state legislature when he was only twenty-four. He distinguished himself so much that his fellow legislators chose him as Speaker of the New

Hampshire House of Representatives at the age of twenty-six. Only a few years later, New Hampshire voters elected him to the US House of Representatives. In 1837, at the age of thirty-three, the New Hampshire legislature chose Pierce as one of New Hampshire's US senators. Pierce accomplished little of note as a US senator, generally holding the traditional Democratic Party line and also opposing rising abolitionism.

Pierce's wife disliked life in Washington, DC, and Pierce was known to engage occasionally in excessive alcohol consumption. The Pierces also experienced the deaths of their two oldest sons. They returned to New Hampshire, where Pierce pursued his law practice. In 1845, President Polk appointed him to a federal attorney's position. With the outbreak of the Mexican War, Pierce volunteered for the New Hampshire militia. Enlisting as a private, he was quickly promoted to colonel and then brigadier-general. He served in combat at Churubusco, where he was injured by a fall from his horse.

His war record and thriving law practice combined with his experience in Congress attracted attention to Pierce as the presidential campaign of 1852 drew near. Democrats hoped to regain the White House after the presidencies of Taylor and Fillmore, and New Englanders hoped to nominate Pierce as a favorite son candidate. In the Democratic nominating convention, no clear frontrunner emerged and no prominent candidate could gain a majority of votes. After almost fifty ballots, Democrats turned to Pierce as their candidate. Pierce won an overwhelming victory in the presidential election over the Whig Party nominee Winfield Scott, mainly due to divisions between Northern and Southern Whigs. Unfortunately, before the inauguration, Pierce and his wife witnessed the tragic death of their surviving son in a train accident while the family was traveling. Benjamin was only eleven, and his death devastated both Pierces.

Pierce began his presidency in 1853 during a period of relative prosperity and domestic tranquility in the aftermath of the Compromise of 1850. An ardent expansionist, Pierce dispatched an emissary to purchase land from Mexico for a proposed southern route for a transcontinental railroad. This agreement, known as the Gadsden Purchase, added significant land to present-day New Mexico and Arizona. Pierce also attempted to purchase Cuba from Spain, in hopes of expanding not only US borders but specifically land for further expansion of slavery, and tried unsuccessfully to acquire Alaska and Hawaii as well. During Pierce's administration, Commodore Matthew Perry opened Japan to the West after years of diplomatic isolationism by that country.

While Pierce was unsuccessful in his attempts to acquire Cuba, abolitionists recognized Pierce as a proslavery Northerner who appointed Southerners to key cabinet and other governmental positions. For example, Pierce selected Jefferson Davis as his secretary of war. Davis subsequently selected several Southern officers for key military commands.

The greatest problem Pierce faced in his presidency was the crisis over the Kansas-Nebraska Act. His support of this controversial legislation led to his vilification by abolitionists. As the situation worsened, Pierce's popularity dropped, which probably was the reason that he was denied the Democratic nomination in 1856, despite his desire to be reelected. He returned to New Hampshire and died in 1869.

Pierce grew up in a strict Puritan family. Most historians acknowledge that Pierce had a significant drinking problem that went directly against his Puritan upbringing. Even his friend Nathaniel Hawthorne recognized Pierce's issues with sobriety. While president, he sometimes attended Presbyterian churches in Washington, DC, hoping that church attendance, quiet Sabbaths, and sharing in prayer with his wife might assuage her terrible grief and help him deal with his struggle with alcohol. After his wife's death in 1863, Pierce apparently decided that he could not overcome his problems. However, he was baptized in the Episcopalian Church four years before his death. Some have suggested that this may have provided Pierce some solace without pressure to cease his drinking and helped him deal with his grief.[129]

Having been influenced by the faith of his upbringing, Franklin Pierce remembered and practiced his beliefs even in college; he knelt nightly in prayer with his roommate. However, his faith was threatened and tested on every hand, especially when he entered politics. After the tragic experience of losing his remaining son in a train accident only weeks before his inauguration, Pierce's grief turned him closer to God. This was reflected by regular church attendance, saying grace at mealtimes, and refusing to even read his mail on Sunday in observance of the Sabbath as a day of rest.

Naturally, the First Lady, Jane Pierce, entered the White House with a troubled heart. Both she and the president felt that eleven-year-old Benjamin's death was related to his election to the high office. Therefore, there was a somber overcast in the mansion at the beginning of Pierce's term. Mrs. Pierce wore black and did not take up duties as hostess until New Year's Day 1855. The Pierce administration was socially very quiet. While there were some public receptions and dinners, there were no flashy entertainment programs. But some of the senators, cabinet members, and wealthy citizens of the city helped to take up the slack by hosting some social events. The outdoor Marine Band concerts continued to draw large crowds. A former attaché of the White House said, "The most fashionable gatherings in Pierce's administration occurred during these concerts."[130]

The indoor weekly receptions also continued with the "president's own" band furnishing music, primarily that of new arrangements by bandmaster Francis Scala. The *Washington Weekly Star* reported that on 26 April 1856 when there was "a delegation of Seminole Indians present…they stationed themselves as near as possible to the Marine Band, were oblivious to naught else but the music, for the entire evening."[131] However, there is little information available concerning Pierce's concept and use of music: "But the irrepressible [Fanny] Crosby could not resist noting the Democrat Franklin Pierce's victory with the lines 'The election's past and I'm pierced at last: the locos have gained the day.' (New York Democrats were popularly known as locos)."[132]

The detailed research of John Merrill revealed that President Pierce's most esteemed hymn was one that reflects his life in many ways. The writing of "When All Thy Mercies, O My God" in 1712 by Englishman Joseph Addison was sparked by the appearance of Isaac Watts's collection *Hymns and Spiritual Songs* of 1707. Addison only wrote five hymns, but he did this in a two-month period; the hymns were printed in *The Spectator*, beginning with the 9 August 1712 issue.

Born in 1672 into a family steeped in Christianity, Addison seemed destined to serve in some ministry position since his father was the Dean of Litchfield and his mother was the sister of the bishop of Bristol. But at Oxford, Joseph preferred to study law and politics; upon graduation, he entered government service. When he was named chief secretary of Ireland, he gained a pension from King William III. Marrying Charlotte, Countess of Warwick, in 1716, he came to an untimely death from asthma in 1719. When Addison was dying he asked for his stepson, Lord Warwick; when the young man, who had strayed from his faith, arrived, Addison said, "See in what peace a Christian can die."[133] His real ministry and the outlet for his literary works was the founding of *The Spectator* and four other weekly papers, which became the forerunners of today's magazines.

Becoming the bright star of early eighteenth-century literature, Addison was a man of unblemished character. Writer Amos Wells said that Addison wrote a "series of wonderful essays in the purist English, full of wit and wisdom papers that have never been surpassed."[134] "When All Thy Mercies, O My God" was written after an escape from a shipwreck and "How Are Thy Servants Blessed, O Lord," often called the traveler's hymn, was penned after his return from the same voyage. "The Spacious Firmament on High" is Addison's finest hymn and one of the best in the English language.

When All Thy Mercies, O My God

Words: Joseph Addison, 1712

Music: William Gardiner, 1812

C.M.

BELMONT

1. When all thy mer - cies, O my God, My ris - ing
2. Un - num - bered com - forts to my soul Thy ten - der
3. When in the slip - pery paths of youth With heed - less
4. When worn with sick - ness, oft hast thou With health re -
5. Ten thou - sand thou - sand pre - cious gifts My dai - ly
6. Through ev - ery pe - riod of my life Thy good - ness
7. Through all e - ter - ni - ty, to thee A joy - ful

soul sur - veys, Trans - port - ed with the view, I'm
care be - stowed, Be - fore my in - fant heart con -
steps I ran, Thine arm un - seen con - veyed me
newed my face; And, when in sins and sor - rows
thanks em - ploy; Nor is the least a cheer - ful
I'll pur - sue; And af - ter death, in dis - tant
song I'll raise; For, O, e - ter - ni - ty's too

lost In won - der, love and praise.
ceived From whom those com - forts flowed.
safe, And led me up to man.
sunk, Re - vived my soul with grace.
heart That tastes those gifts with joy.
worlds, The glo - rious theme re - new.
short To ut - ter all thy praise! A - men.

The tune BELMONT, which is usually sung to "When All Thy Mercies, O My God," was composed by William Gardiner in 1815. Gardiner was a vio- list in the Leicester, England, orchestra and a minor composer who sang in the 100-voice choir for the 1838 coronation of Queen Victoria.[135] BELMONT was published in 1854 in his own collection, *Sacred Melodies*; it is the only tune from that book to survive. Gardiner was the first to make adaptations of instrumental music classics for hymn tunes. This practice is an extension of using melodies from *The Messiah* for hymn tunes. There are several alternate tunes for the Addison text, including TALLIS' ORDINAL, BELGRAVE, CONTEMPLA-TION, and ST. PETER (composed in 1836 by Alexander Reinagle, who was the music teacher for George Washington's step-granddaughter, Nelly Custis). The merits of these arrangements should be assessed solely by their success as hymn tunes for their respective lyrics. Written in common meter with four lines for each stanza, this original hymn contained thirteen stanzas.

Addison attached each of his five hymns to a related essay he wrote in his paper; thus, an essay on "gratitude" preceded "When All Thy Mercies, O My God." The phrase "my rising soul" indicates that this is a morning hymn of thanksgiving. In the lyrics, the author perceives life as an upward journey, traveling from childhood ("infant heart"), to young person ("paths of youth"), leading to manhood ("up to man"), proceeding through sickness and health. Often this pattern is interpreted as going from ignorance into God's presence and being transformed from the unseen to a full consciousness of his providence.[136] These stages sum up every period of life as the Christian reaches maturity, which is the full perception of God. In the hymn, Addison recognizes that one can escape from the physical and spiritual dangers of vice only by the providence of God: "By lengthening out the time elements, Addison strengthens the feeling of long-continued goodness of God.... He believes that God is good and just."[137] Because this is true, the Christian also must be good. Springing from the attitude toward God called "natural religion," this hymn is usable to all sects, even for most non-Christian groups.

This hymn must have ministered and comforted President Pierce, particularly in times of turmoil as an alcoholic, in the almost unbearable tragic experience in the loss of his sons, in his disappointing career, and in the sadness following the death of his wife. Whether or not this led Pierce to baptism in the Episcopal Church, this hymn certainly leads to God. Perhaps the statement Franklin Pierce wrote would confirm his feelings: "My mind has long been impressed with the fact that if our present life is not probationary in its character, if we are not placed here, as the blessed word of God teaches, to prepare for another and more exalted state of being, we are destined to waste our energies upon things that are unsubstantial, fleeting, passing away and that can bring no permanent peace—can give no calm hope that is an anchor to the soul."[138]

JAMES BUCHANAN

1791–1868

Fifteenth President (1857–1861)

Discussions evaluating the abilities and quality of US presidents typically take two directions. One question asks, "Who were the greatest presidents?" Usually this discussion evolves to a second question: "Who were the worst presidents?" In virtually every discussion of the second question, most historians will agree that James Buchanan was one of, if not *the* worst US president ever to serve. A look at his record prior to becoming president would have given the casual observer little hint of such ignominy.

James Buchanan was born in Pennsylvania in 1791. Some accounts claim that he was born in a log cabin, but if that was the case, his family apparently prospered later. Some accounts also state that his modest origins contributed to a romantic breakup that ultimately contributed to the young woman's death. Regardless of his socioeconomic background, Buchanan did receive a college education at Dickinson College, despite an early expulsion due to his conduct. While at Dickinson he acquired a reputation as a debater and student of law.

After a successful law career, Pennsylvania voters elected him to the US House of Representatives. During Jackson's presidency, Buchanan had a distinguished career as ambassador to Russia, where he negotiated a successful commercial treaty. Returning home, the Pennsylvania legislature selected him for the US Senate, where he served for ten years. During the Polk administration, he served as secretary of state and successfully negotiated a treaty with Great Britain over the Oregon Country. After defeating Buchanan for the Democratic presidential nomination and winning the election of 1852, President Pierce appointed Buchanan as ambassador to Great Britain.

Despite Buchanan's insistence that he was not a presidential candidate in 1856, his absence from the United States during the bitter debates over Kansas worked in his favor. In their 1856 nominating convention, Democrats chose Buchanan as their presidential nominee. Buchanan and the Democrats defeated the upstart Republican Party and the short-lived American Party to make Buchanan the fifteenth president.

In the years that followed, Buchanan took a decidedly pro-Southern stance, despite his Northern background. He did not approve of slavery but believed that abolitionists were tearing the country apart. He urged that Kansas be admitted as a slave state despite the fraudulent vote on slavery there. He split with Democratic congressional leader Stephen Douglas, thus fracturing the party. When Republicans gained control of the House of Representatives in 1858, Buchanan liberally used his veto power to counteract their influence. He made few efforts to bring about a reconciliation of any kind. In fact, the abilities to compromise that Buchanan exhibited throughout his career failed him and the country when the country needed those abilities the most.

The sectional crisis exploded in 1860 when Republicans elected Abraham Lincoln and defeated the divided Democrats. When South Carolina seceded, followed by the other Deep South states, Buchanan rejected the constitutionality of secession but responded meekly. When a feeble attempt to resupply Fort Sumter failed, Buchanan hoped for compromise but quietly faded away as the crisis deepened. When Lincoln was inaugurated in March 1861, Buchanan quietly retired to his home in Pennsylvania. He died there in 1868, largely ignored by a country that recognized his shortcomings as president.

Buchanan never married and hence is the only US president to be a bachelor. His niece, Harriet Lane, became quite well known as the White

House hostess during his presidency. Some biographers opine that he apparently struggled with a deep-seated guilt related to his failed romance early in life. Though his brother was a minister and Buchanan demonstrated an interest in the Christian faith, Buchanan had difficulty accepting faith until after he left the White House. He attempted to profess his faith and join the Northern Presbyterian Church during the war, but the church initially rejected him because of its abolitionist stance and Buchanan's earlier hostility toward abolitionism. Eventually, the church allowed him to profess his faith, and he joined the Presbyterian Church a few years before his death.[139]

A revival of social and musical activities in the White House occurred during President James Buchanan's administration. This was partially due to the contrasting family situation to his predecessor, but also because of the twenty-seven-year-old, vivacious Harriet Lane, Buchanan's orphaned niece who was his ward, and who became the hostess for the presidential mansion. Under her direction, some of the more brilliant receptions during the nineteenth century were held at the White House. Not only did the Marine Band's outdoor concerts draw well, but the indoor events were held to overflow crowds. In addition, opera stars and concert artists occasionally appeared at the White House, even though the president was not noted as being musical.

Harriet enjoyed playing the piano; a large volume of her music is contained at the Wheatland home in Lancaster, Pennsylvania. This collection, with her name imprinted in gold on the cover, is comprised mainly of piano arrangements of Italian opera arias and overtures dating from Buchanan's presidential period. There were some pianists who played in the White House, the most unusual being Thomas Greene Buthune, a ten-year-old blind slave. One of his acts was listening to a piano piece played for the first time and performing it shortly afterward as a selection on his recital. On a program for President Buchanan, "Blind Tom" played a twenty-page piano selection in this manner. Not long after his White House performance, piano manufacturer William Knabe gave Thomas a grand piano with a plaque inscribed with "a tribute to genius."[140]

A most significant musical event occurred in 1859 when William Bradbury, a pupil of America's first music educator, Lowell Mason, was conducting a choir at a weeklong music convention in Washington, DC. Singing choruses from Handel's oratorio music, the choir made an appearance before President Buchanan in the East Room on 22 April. After personally conducting the group on a White House tour, the president invited them to sing an encore. Kirk speculates that they may have sung the hymn "The God of Love Will Sure Indulge," which appeared in *The Mendelssohn Collection* edited by Bradbury and Thomas Hastings in 1849. WOODWORTH was the tune Bradbury had written for that popular hymn.[141]

Being a good writer of evangelistic and Sunday school songs, Bradbury's tune WOODWORTH was selected in 1875 by Ira Sankey and used in the D. L. Moody campaigns in England but with the lyrics of Charlotte Elliott's "Just as I Am Without One Plea." In the twentieth century it has been very effectively used as the invitation hymn by Cliff Barrows in the Billy Graham crusades. Bradbury's most popular musical setting was for the well known "Jesus Loves Me." His collection of songs, *The Golden Chain* of 1861, sold 2,000,000 copies. In addition, he founded the Bradbury Piano Company, which began a unique association with US presidents for forty years. His was the first company to furnish pianos for the White House, starting with Grant's term and continuing through McKinley's administration.

In October 1860 for a visit of the Prince of Wales, who became King Edward VII, the Marine Band played an arrangement of "Listen to the Mockingbird," written by a Negro barber noted for his whistling and guitar playing. Bandmaster Scala dedicated this music to Harriet Lane in appreciation for her serving as White House hostess.

Even though there is no mention of hymns being sung in the White House during Buchanan's time in the White House, with the possible exception of Bradbury's tune, it is John Merrill's research that names Buchanan's most cherished hymn as William Cowper's "God Moves in a Mysterious Way." This hymn certainly is a reflection of his struggles in life, not just as president, but also in his spiritual journey.

Cowper was born in England in 1731, the son of a clergyman. His mother, whom he dearly loved, died when William was six years old; in his youth, the boy was distressed by mental attacks. In boarding school, he faced loneliness, insecurity, and bullying, so at the age of nine, he transferred to Westminster School, where he excelled in languages. But after several years of depression caused by the death of both his father and stepmother, combined with the drowning of his closest friend, he had cause for a possible mental breakdown, which was brought to a climax by the anxiety of preparing for an examination for a position as clerk in the House of Lords.

Eventually, William was committed to a home for the insane, where Nathaniel Cotton, an evangelical, led Cowper to conversion based on Romans 3:25.[142] After this experience in 1764, William was overwhelmed with love and wonder that Christ's atonement was for him. After his release from the institution at age thirty-three, Cowper settled in Huntingdon, near Cambridge, as a boarder with the Unwin family. It was providential that upon the accidental death of the Reverend Unwin, the Reverend John

Newton of Olney called upon the family to offer sympathy. At Newton's insistence, Cowper moved to Olney in a house near the vicarage, where he assisted Newton in ministry. For a special weeknight service the two friends wrote hymns for a collection called *Olney Hymns*, printed in 1779.[143] The last hymn Cowper wrote for this hymnal was "God Moves in a Mysterious Way."

According to writer Noel Davidson, this poem was penned on New Year's Day 1773 when Cowper returned from a walk alone in the mid-winter gloom at Olney. Feeling a growing premonition of the return of mental illness, on his arrival at his house, Cowper "transcribed into verse, the words and thoughts that had been tumbling around in his mind during the walk."[144] The result is the hymn loved by President Buchanan, who had been having contradictory feelings about his spiritual condition for much of his life. Newton received word on 2 January 1773 that William Cowper had again lapsed into insanity.

Originally, Cowper's poem was titled "Conflict: Light Shining out of Darkness" because it describes storms that threaten a person, contrasting this scene with assurance of the reliance on God and his divine purpose in the life of the believer; later, the hymn acquired its title from the first phrase of the text.

MANOAH (who was the father of Samson) is the name of the tune traditionally sung to Cowper's text; it appeared in Boston in 1851 in Henry W. Greatorex's *Church Music* collection. This tune has been attributed to several composers, so David Music, a professor of hymnology, made an investigation of its true origin. After stating that the tune first appeared in an English book called *The Weigh House Congregational Tune Book* in 1843, edited by T.F. Travers, he paints this scenario: "Rossini, in composing *L'Italiana in Algeri*, borrowed the outline of the theme of 'Languis per una bella' from Haydn's trio 'Von deinem Segensmahle' in the *Seasons*; a later tunebook editor (Travers?) discovered Rossini's theme and reworked the hymn tune, attributing it to the Italian composer."[145] David Music concluded that whatever its origin, MANOAH is a fine tune and well deserves a place in our hymnals. Other tunes used for this common-meter hymn have been DUNDEE, BELMONT, LONDON NEW, and ST. ANNE.

The first line of this hymn is so well known that it appears in colloquial speech. The *Oxford Dictionary of Quotations* gives six quotations from the lyrics, embodying the entire hymn except for two lines. This proves that the verses are significant, easy to remember, and very quotable. Generally regarded the most sublime hymn ever written on divine providence, "God Moves in a Mysterious Way" teaches the believer to respond to the doctrine with the proper attitude of trust.

God Moves in a Mysterious Way

Words: William Cowper, 1779
Music: Anonymous, 1843

C.M.
MANOAH

1. God moves in a mys - te - rious way His wond - ers
2. Ye fear - ful saints, fresh cou - rage take; The clouds ye
3. Judge not the Lord, by fee - ble sense, But trust Him

to per - form; He plants His foot - steps in the
so much dread Are big with mer - cy, and shall
for His grace; Be - hind a frown - ing pro - vi -

sea, And rides up - on the storm.
break With bles - sing on your head.
dence He hides a smil - ing face. A - men.

Susan Wise Bauer gives an outline of the hymn as follows: stanza one presents God's sovereign power in nature; stanza two tells of carrying out God's will; stanza three addresses the redeemed man and the preservation of God's people, which is reinforced by stanzas four and five; and stanza six gives an interpretation of God's own work.[146] There are other interpretations of the hymn, such as Madeleine Forell Marshall's, who clearly states that stanza one gives "pictures of God," stanza two says God is "unfathomable," stanza three "comforts the saints," stanza four warns to "not judge God," stanza five gives God's purpose as "fruit," and stanza six "confirms our unbelief."[147]

This is a rare hymn because it attempts to describe God's mystery in poetry, a difficult task even in prose. Cowper achieves this by talking about God in positive terms instead of negative ones. His use of terms like "bright designs" and God's "generous mercy and grace" illustrates this well.[148] The main thesis of the hymn expresses the Christian attitude toward disaster in the world, not only natural disaster, but also war, which Buchanan was facing in his term. God has directed the course of events toward his own ends, not known by the believer. In these lyrics, Cowper preserves the grandeur of God while maintaining the personal concern of the Christian Father.

While eventually becoming a Presbyterian, Buchanan was seeking salvation during much of his adult life. He wrote to his brother from Russia where he was ambassador in 1832: "I can say sincerely for myself that I desire to be a Christian." While stating that he sometimes almost persuaded himself that he was a Christian, he admitted that he was often haunted by skepticism and doubt. He wrote that on many occasions his feeling was "Lord, I would believe; help my unbelief."[149]

His doubts persisted for many years until in August 1860 he poured out his misgivings for the Reverend William Paxton of New York City's First Presbyterian Church. For more than two hours, Buchanan questioned the pastor on religious matters. This event led to Buchanan's full acceptance of Christ's promises as outlined in his most favored hymn. This president's life was really not too different from modern-day Christians in America who are active church members, say daily prayers, and read their Bibles regularly. Hopefully these Christians will also sing such hymns as "God Moves in a Mysterious Way" to reinforce their faith in times of fear and doubt.

ABRAHAM LINCOLN

1809–1865

Sixteenth President (1861–1865)

"With malice toward none, with charity for all, with firmness in the right as God gives us to see the right, let us strive to finish the work we are in, to bind up the nation's wounds, to care for him who shall have borne the battle and for his widow and his orphan, to do all which may achieve and cherish a just and lasting peace among ourselves and with all nations." With these beautiful words, Abraham Lincoln closed his second inaugural address. Only a little more than a month later, even as the greatest cataclysm ever faced by the United States came to an end, Lincoln himself would become one of the last casualties of the great Civil War, "testing whether that nation or any nation so conceived and so dedicated [could] long endure."

Born on the Kentucky frontier in the most humble of origins in 1809, Abraham Lincoln would rise to become perhaps the greatest president the United States has ever known. His father, Thomas Lincoln, was a struggling farmer who moved his family to Indiana when Abraham was seven. Two years later, Abraham's mother, Nancy, died. Never having a really positive relationship with his semiliterate father, Abraham's life dramatically changed when his father remarried. Sarah Lincoln became the most influential person in Abraham Lincoln's early life, encouraging him in his limited schooling and providing a nurturing environment. Sarah Lincoln also tolerated the fact that the teenage Abraham rejected his father's Baptist religious views.

Reaching his later teenage years, Lincoln moved out on his own. The following years saw Lincoln drift from Indiana to Illinois and from one occupation to the next, trying his hand at odd jobs, storekeeping, management of local businesses, postmaster, and even a brief service in the short-lived Black Hawk War. He also became interested in politics. Despite frequent disappointments, Lincoln continued to run for political office as a Whig, studied law, and eventually became one of the most successful attorneys in antebellum Illinois. He briefly served in the state legislature and served one term in the US House of Representatives, opposing the Mexican War even though he knew that it would probably cost him reelection. Eventually, he married Mary Todd, the daughter of a prominent Kentuckian, and fathered four sons.

A keen observer of national politics, Lincoln became intensely interested as events accelerated toward a conflict over states' rights and slavery. When the Whig Party dissolved, Lincoln and others founded the Illinois Republican Party in 1856. Subsequently, the Republican Party nominated him to run against incumbent Democrat US senator Stephen Douglas. The contest launched a series of five statewide debates in which Lincoln earned his political stripes and established himself as a national political force. When the Republican Party met in 1860 to nominate its presidential candidate, they selected Lincoln on the third ballot. When the Democratic Party divided and the popular and electoral votes were split four ways in the presidential election, the nation elected Lincoln its sixteenth president.

In response to Lincoln's election, seven Southern states seceded from the Union, and after Fort Sumter was fired upon by Confederate troops, four other slave states joined the Confederacy as the nation was plunged into a bloody Civil War. The following four years saw Lincoln grapple with the difficulties of trying to preserve the Union, end the terrible blight of slavery in the South, and fight a victorious war against the secessionist states. At many times, it seemed as if only Lincoln's belief in the Union and his desire to preserve it kept the Union war effort going. He also suffered the death of a second son and his wife's plunge into mental illness at a time when the war itself seemed headed toward a dismal outcome. Through it all, Lincoln himself struggled with personal depression but managed to grow as a political leader and, as the civilian head of the military, demonstrated tremendous insights into constitutional government, military strategy, and an irrepressible sense of humor.

In 1862–1863, Lincoln issued one of the important documents in US history, the Emancipation Proclamation. The Emancipation Proclamation transformed the war from a conflict to preserve the Union into a war to free the slaves and fulfill the promise of the Declaration of Independence. In November 1863 he defined the war in one of the most outstanding speeches in all of US history, the Gettysburg Address. His perseverance was essential throughout 1862 and 1863 when many thought the Union could not survive. He struggled with poor congressional and state election results, conflicts with the Supreme Court, with Congress, and within his own cabinet. Finally, after many battlefield defeats and much public opposition, the war began to take a positive turn and Lincoln was reelected by a landslide in fall 1864. When Union victories accelerated late in 1864 and 1865 and victory seemed inevitable, Lincoln turned his attention to rebuilding the shattered Union. Only a few days after Robert E. Lee's surrender to Ulysses S. Grant at Appomattox, and with the end of the war clearly in sight, Lincoln's efforts to complete the restoration of the Union were tragically cut short when he was shot by John Wilkes Booth. President Lincoln died on 15 April 1865.

Lincoln "never joined a church nor ever made a clear profession of standard Christian beliefs," writes Mark Noll. Indeed, as a young man, Lincoln frequently identified himself as a religious skeptic. However, the war and his own personal tragedies forced him to consider deep questions of faith. Noll adds, "Lincoln's speeches and conversation revealed a spiritual perception far above the ordinary. It is one of the great ironies of the history of Christianity in America that the most profoundly religious analysis of the nation's trauma came not from a clergyman or a theologian but from a politician.... The source of Lincoln's Christian perception will probably always remain a mystery, but the unusual depth of that perception none can doubt."[150]

Lincoln grew up with music in his home since his mother regularly sang folksongs to him and his sister. He had been responsive to music from his early boyhood days. He learned to play the harmonica to entertain himself through music. Often the children would stay home from church while his parents attended. When he was about fifteen, Abe would organize a home service; he would read a Bible verse, line out a hymn to sing, and then give a message, ending with a chorus of tears.[151] As a boy, the hymns that he loved must have had an influence on him. Some of those mentioned are "When

Adam Was Created," "There Is a Fountain," "Alas, and Did My Savior Bleed," and "Am I a Soldier of the Cross?" Author Carl Sandburg wrote that Abraham and his sweetheart, Ann Rutledge, often sang from the shape-note tune book *The Missouri Harmony* at her father's tavern in New Salem, Illinois.[152] From this experience he probably learned at least two hymns that he loved his entire life. This collection of psalms and hymns was the 1816 collection edited by Allen D. Cardin and was very popular in the Midwest. It contained "How Tedious and Tasteless the Hours," set to the GREENFIELDS tune, which became one of his favorites. It also contained "When I Can Read My Title Clear," set to the PISGAH tune, which also was a favored hymn of the future president.

While neither Abraham nor Mary Todd Lincoln could read music or play an instrument, we should not assume that music did not play a role in the Lincoln presidency. His musical tastes were simple and uncultivated; he loved old airs, songs and ballads, and spirited banjo tunes. The Lincolns saw to it that both Willie and Tad had piano lessons. Historian Elise Kirk states that "the music that made its way to the White House during the Lincoln's tenure...reflected the spirit of the times more than it did during any other period in American history."[153] During this era, the emotional aspect of the years was reflected in musical tones with various expressions. The music ranged from sad, tense, and sentimental songs to jubilant, tense, courageous choruses, sung and performed in all manner of situations. Music seemed to serve to sustain and divert the nation's spirit during this time of national struggle. Lincoln, like all Americans during this chaotic time, became absorbed in the music fitted to every occasion and mood: "[Lincoln] felt its strength and realized its power and influence. More than once he had been thrilled and moved to tears by [music]."[154]

Lincoln also loved opera; he attended nineteen grand opera performances as president and was the only president to have an opera performed during his inauguration events. He was very adamant in replying to criticism concerning his attendance at operas during the Civil War. He retorted, "The truth is I must have a change of some sort or die." Lincoln also enjoyed concerts by the popular New Orleans-born pianist and composer Louis Gottschalk, who wrote the hymn tune MERCY, which was set to the text "Holy Ghost, with Light Divine." There is no doubt of Lincoln's seriousness concerning music during these turbulent years. He especially enjoyed hymns and spirituals. Often the popular Methodist singing evangelist and hymn writer Philip Phillips was requested by President Lincoln to sing. Lincoln jump-started Phillips's career when this relatively unknown singer rendered the song "Your Mission" at a mass anniversary meeting for the Christian

Commission in Washington, DC. Lincoln was so moved that he scribbled a note asking Phillips to repeat the song again at the close of the meeting.[155]

Thousands of African Americans sang spirituals on the White House lawn on 4 July 1864. Various hymns, including Julia Ward Howe's "The Battle Hymn of the Republic" and Dan Emmett's "Dixie," were sung for the president on 27 January 1865. Implying that both the North and South would find unity and fellowship in these common musical expressions, Lincoln exclaimed after each was sung, "Let's have it again! It's our tune now!"[156]

It should be no surprise that Abraham Lincoln had many favorite hymns. Research reveals that two stand out as a reflection of his spirituality and service to his country. The deeply moving "Lead, Kindly Light" by John Henry Newman (1833) was particularly meaningful to Lincoln, as well as the universal short hymn of praise "The Doxology" by Thomas Ken (1709). "We Three Kings of Orient Are" was written in 1857 by John H. Hopkins, rector of Christ Church at Williamsport, Pennsylvania. The hymn quickly became popular, and Lincoln must have heard it even before he became president. Since he was a deeply religious man, Lincoln made regular appearances at midweek prayer meetings at the New York Avenue Presbyterian Church in Washington. However, two other hymns seem to have been his strongly favored hymns.

John Newton, the author of "Amazing Grace," wrote the hymn "How Tedious and Tasteless the Hours," which Lincoln loved dearly. Written sometime before the 1779 publication of the *Olney Hymns,* it appeared in that collection with the subtitle "Fellowship with Christ."[157] Based on Psalm 73:25, "none upon earth I desire beside thee," this text clearly points out the joy of having Christ in one's heart during the dark and dreary days of life. Newton addresses all the senses with poetry related to a beautiful day in spring or summer. In the subsequent stanzas, he writes of the music in the soul when one finds Christ. Stanza three deals with the pleasures of fellowship with Christ in whatever circumstances one finds himself, even in prison. The last stanza may contain a reminder of the dreadful war during Lincoln's presidency. The cry of the singer in the phrase, "Oh, drive these dark clouds from my sky; thy soul-cheering presence restore; Or take me unto thee on high, where winter and clouds are no more," certainly seems significant comfort as a prayer for peace in the war-torn country.

The tune used for this text acquired several names. This early American melody is often called DEFLEURY because the tune is often attributed to Maria de Fleury. Others state that Lewis Edson, a chorister from Massachusetts,[158] wrote the music, while some say the melody was taken from the secular song

How Tedious and Tasteless the Hours

Words: John Newton, 1779
Music: Lewis Edson, 1782

L.M.D.
DE FLEURY

1. How te-dious and taste-less the hours When Je-sus no lon-ger I
2. His name yields the rich-est per-fume, And sweet-er than mu-sic His
3. Con-tent with be-hold-ing His face, My all to His pleas-ure re-
4. Dear Lord, if in-deed I am Thine, If Thou art my sun and my

see! Sweet prospects,sweet birds,and sweet flowers,Have all lost their sweetness to
voice; His pres-ence dis-pers-es my gloom, And makes all with-in me resigned,No chang-es of sea-son or place Would make an-y change in my
song. Say, why do I lan-guish and pine, And why are my win-ters so

me. The mid-sum-mer sun shines but dim; The fields strive in vain to look
joice: I should,were He al-ways thus nigh, Have noth-ing to wish or to
mind: While blest with a sense of His love, A pal-ace a toy would ap-
long? Oh drive these dark clouds from my sky; Thy soul-cheer-ing pres-ence re-

gay; But when I am hap-py with Him, De-cem-ber's as pleas-ant as May.
fear; No mor-tal so hap-py as I; My sum-mer would last all the year.
pear; And pris-ons would pal-a-ces prove, If Je-sus would dwell with me there.
store;Or take me un-to Thee on high, Where win-ter and clouds are no more.

"Farewell, Ye Green Fields and Sweet Groves." For this reason it has also been called GREENFIELDS. It has even been called NEWTON because of the author of the text. In any event, the lilting melody certainly reflects the words of the hymn and the joy of fellowship with Christ. It would be interesting to hear the sermon that Newton delivered that this hymn summarizes.

Another cherished hymn of President Lincoln was "When I Can Read My Title Clear," according to the research done by hymnologist Don Hustad.[159] Isaac Watts published this text in his 1707 *Hymns and Spiritual Songs* with the title "The Hope of Heaven Our Support under Trials on Earth." The message of the text is that Christians will have a "clear title" when they arrive in heaven. Since the words emphasize the "paid in full" theological doctrine, meaning that Christ paid the complete cost for our sins, the first line says it all. Christians have the promise of a dwelling place for all eternity (John 14:1–3). Gone are the nagging fears of economic demands, job security, and stacks of unpaid bills. The Christian has reached the last mortgage payment. This would be a happy day for those surviving the terrible Civil War that was raging.

Isaac Watts knew firsthand about troubles and trials, having come from a nonconformist home in a country that was controlled by the Church of England. He held to Separatist views, causing him to be limited in educational opportunities and professional appointments. In addition, his physical appearance repelled the only woman he desired to marry. (She fell in love with his poetry.) Well might he look beyond present trials to future joy! The words could account for the selection by Lincoln as a meaningful hymn. He undoubtedly longed for peace in a nation that was so divided by internal war.

The tune for "When I Can Read My Title Clear" is called PISGAH after a mountain near Mount Nebo near the Dead Sea. From this view, Moses looked over to the Promised Land of Canaan. Typical of the religious folk tunes of the South during the early nineteenth century, this music first appeared in 1816 in *Kentucky Harmony*, a collection of shape-note music. This tune book credited J. C. Lowry as the composer.[160] However, in 1819 it was printed in *Tennessee Harmony* with Alexander Johnson as the writer of the music. Some have even called it an American variant of an English folk tune. Regardless of the composer, the melody is very singable with moderate range and enough repetition to illustrate the text. It makes an inspiring and joyful congregational hymn.

The selection of these hymns as Lincoln's favorites seem to verify the hope of salvation and the look to better days in the future, both for him individually and for his beloved nation. Lincoln's actions and vital decisions certainly were consistent with this hope. Even though Lincoln never joined a specific church, he worshiped regularly with Presbyterian congregations. Evidently, the hymns that he learned and appreciated had an impact on his life. Many scholars agree that Lincoln was one of the most spiritually insightful presidents. His choice of hymns certainly verifies this belief.

ANDREW JOHNSON

1808–1875

Seventeenth President (1865–1869)

Some American presidents, including Thomas Jefferson, Theodore Roosevelt, Franklin Roosevelt, and John Kennedy, have come from privileged backgrounds. Others, such as Andrew Jackson, Abraham Lincoln, and Bill Clinton, came from very humble origins. Few, if any, have come from a background as humble as Andrew Johnson. Unfortunately, during his presidency, Johnson found himself unable to capitalize on those origins to identify with the common people who make up the United States. Because of this, the time period in which he served, and his own personal quirks, Johnson may be identified as one of the least effective American presidents.

Andrew Johnson was born in North Carolina in 1808. His parents were most likely virtually illiterate and impoverished. Orphaned at ten and apprenticed to a tailor, he ran away but later became a tailor himself in Tennessee. He married, and his wife, Eliza, became a significant influence upon him, aiding and encouraging him in his self-education. As a young man, he identified with fellow Tennessean Andrew Jackson and became a Jacksonian Democrat. Despite his lack of education, Johnson became actively involved in local politics. His fellow east Tennesseans appreciated his identification with their upbringings and his ability as a popular speaker in local and state politics. They also allied with Johnson in his criticisms of low-country planters, who controlled much of the South's politics. Due to this identification, they elected him to serve eight years in the state legislature.

In 1843, voters in his home district chose Johnson as their US congressman. He held that seat for ten years until Tennessee voters elected him as governor in 1852 with the collapse of the Whig Party's national structure. After four years as governor, the Democratic-controlled legislature chose Johnson as US senator. However, when Tennessee seceded from the Union in 1861, Johnson opposed secession and remained in the US Senate, believing that the state's secession was unconstitutional. Many Southerners vilified Johnson as a traitor to the South and Tennessee. In east Tennessee, however, many Tennesseans also opposed secession, resisted Confederate control, and viewed Johnson as a hero. Northerners also hailed him as a Unionist patriot. When Union forces gained control of large sections of Tennessee, including Nashville, President Lincoln appointed Johnson as military governor.

In 1864, Lincoln sought to reach out to the War Democrats, who had supported the Union cause. Republicans renamed their party the National Union Party. Lincoln dropped vice president Hamlin from his ticket and invited Johnson to be his running mate. Lincoln and Republicans hoped that nominating the loyalist Johnson would help to bind the nation's wounds. Unfortunately, they also never anticipated that Lincoln would be assassinated. Also unfortunately, Johnson fell ill with typhoid prior to his inauguration. Though he recovered, he was still weak. Even though Johnson rarely drank alcoholic beverages, someone recommended that he take a strong drink of whiskey to bolster him. Instead, he appeared drunk at the inauguration, slurring his words, slumping in his chair, and generally embarrassing his party, Lincoln, and himself.

Only about a month later, Johnson found himself president upon Lincoln's assassination. Johnson ordered a vigorous pursuit and prosecution of the assassins. Knowing his previous record, Radical Republicans thought they had found a ready ally to their plans to reconstruct the South as conquered territories. Instead, increasingly, Johnson allied himself with poor whites and other Unionists in the South who had wanted to end slavery and preserve the Union but had no intention of granting equal rights to African Americans. In the eyes of the Radical Republicans, Johnson moved too quickly to accept the South's self-Reconstruction and was far too conservative in doing so. The final straws came when Southern states began to legislate "black codes," which appeared virtually to return the freedmen to a status much like slavery, and when Southern voters elected numerous former Confederate officials and military officers whom Johnson had pardoned to Congress in fall 1865. The Radicals moved quickly to counteract Johnson's Reconstruction, but Johnson stymied their efforts by a liberal use of his presidential veto.

Increasingly, moderate Republicans and Northerners found themselves pushed into the Radical camp while Johnson gradually aligned himself more closely with the Southerners he once so despised. Johnson genuinely regarded the Radicals' programs unconstitutional and feared Congress's growing powers at the expense of the presidency. Advocating his more conservative policies for Reconstruction, Johnson campaigned on behalf of supportive congressional candidates in the elections of 1866. Heckled unmercifully by crowds, Johnson repeatedly lost his temper and appeared un-presidential. Radical Republicans also reminded voters of Johnson's inauguration and raised the specter of drunkenness. Johnson and his supporters were crushed, and Radicals passed a plan for Reconstruction much more protective of the former slaves and policies that granted them equal rights. They also restricted Johnson's presidential powers. Johnson regarded these restrictions unconstitutional. When he broke one of them, the Radical-controlled Congress sought impeachment. The House of Representatives voted for impeachment, but the Senate failed to remove him from office by a single vote.

Johnson stood no chance of reelection in 1868. However, Tennessee did select him for the US Senate in 1875. Unfortunately, he died a few months later. At his request, he was buried with a copy of the Constitution. Years later, the Supreme Court vindicated Johnson by ruling unconstitutional the Tenure of Office Act that had served as grounds for impeachment. The most notable achievement of his administration was the treaty with Russia that resulted in the purchase of Alaska.

Johnson never joined a church or denomination. He may have had some religious upbringing as a child, and he occasionally attended a Methodist church with his wife. He also is known to have visited a Catholic church as well, and on occasion, he did state a belief in the Bible but is never known to have made a profession of faith of any kind.[161]

The mood of the music of America changed rather drastically after the Civil War. Because of the influx of immigrants from European countries with a constant stream settling in the western states, some cultural aspects, especially music, began to be reflected in these new citizens. As they became homesteaders, much was expected of women on the frontier. As they prospered, many homes even had pianos. Alistaire Cooke states, "It was the mother who accompanied the family hymn singing…[the musical] culture belonged to the women."[162] German immigrants were in the majority, but other European cultures had their enclaves. As free men, blacks joined other ethnic groups in the enrichment of musical culture as never before had happened. All genres of music, from opera and formal concerts, to popular and folk music, made their contribution. Native Americans, however, played a lesser role in the process with their music either being Westernized or incorporated into other developments.

The music of the postwar period became nostalgic rather than stirring and patriotic. Music historian Charles Hamm explains it this way: "In deliberately turning away from contemporary issues, our song writers made popular song something it had never been before—escapism."[163] As a result, music in Andrew Johnson's White House was very entertaining, appealing to youth and even children. This was a natural fit for the first family because there were eleven residents in the mansion with the oldest grandchild being only ten years old. There were many music and dance lessons given. President Johnson cared so much for the ladies in his family and their joy of music that he purchased each of his daughters a fine Steinway square *pianoforte.*

Martha Johnson Patterson, wife of Senator David Patterson, took over most of the hostess duties for her ailing mother. Dancing soon returned to the White House after a twenty-year absence. Guest musical groups who performed included the Pauls from England and the following American families: the Peakes, Alleghanians, Bakers, Bergers, and Barkers. Often, family groups would combine with other acts to put on a better "show." The Peake and Berger families performed with the P. T. Barnum-sponsored "Swiss Bell Ringers" on 21 January 1867. In reality these were the "Lancashire Ringers" from Liverpool, England, dressed in Swiss costumes.[164] There were twenty-five performers, including two solo bell ringers, on this program with a total of 280 silver handbells on tables. Bell-ringing shows remained popular to the end of the century. It is most probable that there were no hymns played because these concerts were for entertainment and not for worship. However, in 1923 the Beacon Hill Ringers was organized in Boston. This eventually led to the chartering of the American Guild of English Handbell Ringers, which today has more than 80,000 members worldwide who often perform religious programs, utilizing many hymn arrangements.

Through the research efforts of Merrill, it was determined that Andrew Johnson's most admired hymn was "O for a Closer Walk with God" by William Cowper. (Since this same author wrote "God Moves in a Mysterious Way," the reader will find Cowper's life story under the section on President Buchanan.) Johnson's hymn was written by Cowper during the serious illness of his close friend and caretaker, Mary Unwin, which began in December 1767. The hymn, based on Genesis 5:24, "And Enoch walked with God: and he was not; for God took him," was originally titled "Walking with God."

The text has some of the most poignant lyrics in hymnody. While expressing some phases of the spiritual life common to all, it was penned during a period of struggle concerning the health of a dear friend. Cowper wrote, "She is the chief of blessings I have met with in my journey since the Lord was pleased to call me.... I began to compose the verses yesterday morning before daybreak but fell asleep at the end of the first two lines; when I awakened again, the third and fourth were whispered to my heart in a way which I have often experienced."[165] The hymn is somewhat autobiographical since it recalls Cowper's life both before and after his conversion. It also includes lyrics that refer to his time in the asylum and his being willing to rid himself of any "idol" he had, even if this included Mary, in order to meet God sincerely and truthfully. This deeply moving prayer as a hymn was answered with the restoration of Mary Unwin's health.

Susan Bauer, writer, terms this a narrative hymn with clearly delineated elements. She analyzes stanza one as the thesis: a desire for greater nearness to God, leading to an elaboration of the problem in stanzas three and four— once he was nearer than he now is. Following is an encounter with a member of the Trinity: "O holy dove." Stanza five begins a transition to a new state of being, climaxed by the sixth stanza, which ends in an improved state of mind in the believer's standing with God. This final stanza is faith's beautiful return to former blessedness; the longing for peace becomes a definite assurance that the light will grow stronger and the goal surer.[166] President Johnson may have come to know and love this hymn while visiting various churches; it may have even been sung by his family in the White House. If he followed the steps of the text, it could have led him to belief in a divine being, which he spoke of near his death.

The tune sung for "O for a Closer Walk with God" during Johnson's presidency is named MARTYRDOM even though it has also been called AVON and FENWICK. According to hymnologist Paul Westermeyer, the original melody may have been an eighteenth-century folksong that Hugh Wilson, a shoemaker and music leader of a Scottish Secessionist church, arranged in duple meter sometime before 1800.[167] Robert McCutchen suggests that

O For a Closer Walk With God

Words: William Cowper, 1779
Music: Hugh Wilson, 1768

C.M.
AVON

1. O for a clos - er walk with God, A
2. Where is the bless - ed - ness I knew When
3. What peace - ful hours I then en - joyed! How
4. Re - turn, O Ho - ly Dove, re - turn, Sweet

calm and heav'n - ly frame, A light to shine up -
first I saw the Lord? Where is the soul - re -
sweet their mem - 'ry still! But they have left an
Mess - en - ger of rest; I hate the sins that

on the road That leads me to the Lamb!
fresh - ing view Of Je - sus and His word?
ach - ing void The world can ne - ver fill.
made Thee mourn, And drove Thee from my breast. A - men.

when R. A. Smith used the tune for his book *Sacred Music* in 1825, he didn't know that Wilson had been born in Fenwick, and assumed that the tune was in honor of James Fenwick, the martyred Covenanter. When Smith changed the tune to triple meter, he renamed it MARTYRDOM in honor of all martyred Covenanters.[168] The title AVON refers to "rivers" in general so is inadequate for this hymn tune name. The tune utilizes a pentatonic melody, which is most appropriate for Cowper's lyrics. As is true of all common-meter hymns, it may have been sung to numerous tunes.

The final words uttered by Andrew Johnson on 31 July 1875 are quite revealing concerning his spirituality: "I have performed my duty to my God, my country, and my family. I have nothing to fear in approaching death. To me it is the mere shadow of God's protecting wing.... Here I will rest in quiet and peace beyond the reach of calumny's poisoned shaft, the influence of envy and jealous enemies, where treason and traitors or State backsliders and hypocrites in church can have no peace."[169] Many people have talked to or about God on their deathbeds just moments before meeting him face to face. There is both confidence and bitterness in Johnson's last words. He could have quoted Cowper's hymn "O for a Closer Walk with God," which would have been just as appropriate. Perhaps he was subconsciously thinking of the powerful words of this hymn in his final moments and adding his own feelings of retribution.

ULYSSES S. GRANT

1822–1885

Eighteenth President (1869–1877)

Historically, Americans have loved war heroes. Beginning with George Washington, through Andrew Jackson, Theodore Roosevelt, and John F. Kennedy, and as recently as George H. W. Bush, Americans have loved war heroes enough to elect them as president of the United States. Perhaps one of the greatest war heroes ever elected began the Civil War as an unknown officer. However, eight years later, he occupied the highest office in the land. That man was Ulysses S. Grant.

Grant was born in Ohio in 1822, the son of a tanner. In those days the job of tanning was one of the dirtiest and nastiest jobs imaginable. This only makes his later accomplishments more extraordinary. Grant proved to be an excellent horseman and throughout his life exhibited great care for and interest in horses.

He received an appointment to West Point despite his disdain for a military career. With the outbreak of war with Mexico, Grant distinguished himself while fighting under General Zachary Taylor in northern Mexico. With the end of war he found himself stationed in isolated frontier outposts where rumors of his drinking brought about his resignation from the army. He returned to work in his father's leather store and was working as a clerk there when the Civil War began. He volunteered and served initially as an enlistment officer.

Once he began to serve in combat, Grant again distinguished himself. Despite being forced to retreat in an early skirmish, Grant clearly showed that he knew how to command men. Then, early in 1862, he became one of the Union's first war heroes when he utilized the combined forces of the US Navy with his division to capture the key strategic Forts Henry and Donelson, which controlled the Tennessee and Cumberland Rivers and provided entrance to central Tennessee. After the capture of Fort Donelson, Nashville quickly fell. Subsequently, Confederate forces surprised Grant's army at Shiloh in southern Tennessee and seemed to be winning an overwhelming victory. On the second day of fighting, however, the tenacious Grant received reinforcements and went on to carry the field. Temporarily deposed because he had been surprised and also because of swirling rumors that he was drinking again, Grant was tempted to quit the army. However, his friend William Tecumseh Sherman persuaded him to stay on. President Lincoln also believed in him, reputedly saying, "I can't spare that man. He fights."

Lincoln and Sherman's confidence proved merited when Grant, in a brilliant campaign of combined forces, maneuver, combat, and siege, captured the key fortress of Vicksburg on the Mississippi River in July 1863. Later, Lincoln placed Grant in command of Union forces in the West, and Grant lifted the Confederate siege of Chattanooga and opened the interior of Georgia to invasion. Afterward, Lincoln transferred Grant back east to serve as overall Union commander.

Grant placed Sherman in command of the forces in Georgia and unleashed him upon Georgia's interior. Grant chose to command the Army of the Potomac and engaged in one of the epic campaigns of American history. Beginning in the Wilderness of Virginia in May 1864 and throughout bloody battles at Spotsylvania Courthouse, Cold Harbor, and outside of Petersburg, Virginia, Grant slugged it out with Confederate general Robert E. Lee. After months of siege that ran through the winter and early spring of 1864–1865, Grant gradually wore down and outmaneuvered Lee's army until he forced the Confederates out of Richmond and into surrender at

Appomattox Court House. Granting generous surrender terms as Lincoln wished, Grant went a long way toward restoring peace in the country. After the war, Grant continued to serve as general of the army.

As the presidential campaign of 1868 approached, Grant, despite having no political experience and having been completely unknown seven years before, became the frontrunner for the presidency. American voters elected him the nation's eighteenth president. Grant's urgent plea to the public was symbolic. "Let us have peace," he urged, as reports became widespread of racial violence and white resistance to Reconstruction in the South.

Grant inherited a nation still deeply divided. While many historians have criticized Grant for the terrible corruption that plagued his two terms, no one has charged that he was dishonest. However, these same historians have generally charged that Grant was one of the least effective US presidents. On the other hand, recent historians have begun to appraise Grant differently, despite disgraces like the "Whiskey Ring Scandal," the "Belknap Scandal," and the "Credit Mobilier Scandal." They acknowledge the problems encountered by Grant, such as these scandals and the Panic of 1873, and insist that the Grant administration did accomplish some significant things, including settlement of the *Alabama* claims from the Civil War and strong attempts to enforce Radical Republican reforms in the South. Though unsuccessful in the latter, historian Stephen Ambrose concludes that Grant did more to help African Americans than any other president until Lyndon Johnson.

After leaving the White House, Grant invested in a New York financial firm. Mismanagement plagued the firm and it ultimately went bankrupt, forcing Grant and his family into bankruptcy. About the same time, doctors diagnosed Grant with terminal throat cancer. Determined to eliminate his debts and provide for his family after his death, Grant began writing his memoirs of the Civil War. Completed only a few days before his death, they were a smashing success and eventually cleared almost a half million dollars. Only a few days after completing the book, Grant died in 1885.

Grant's parents reared him with strict morals, and he sometimes attended a Methodist church when he was young. He disliked West Point's chapel attendance requirement but attended a Methodist church with Julia, his wife. While she joined, he never did. He was baptized on his deathbed but expressed surprise at this event. He later indicated that "he didn't care how much praying went on if it comforted his wife and children." He said nothing about the prayers comforting him.[170]

Following the Civil War and the difficulties involved in Reconstruction, the country was ready for a grand celebration when General Ulysses Grant was inaugurated on 4 March 1869. This event, with its gala parades and brilliant balls, was the grandest of all up to date. During his two terms, the Grants held dinners and receptions that were almost as lavish as the inauguration. However, ex-General Grant, like most military heroes, preferred military and patriotic music to artistic performances. This resulted in the Marine Band's participation in most events. Perhaps the most elaborate social occasion was the marriage of Grant's daughter, Nellie, when the band played a major role. At concerts, the forty-piece band often played for encores a piece that would eventually become the "Marine's Hymn." The music was called "The Duet of the Queen's Guards" and was sung by two men in Jacques Offenbach's 1859 comic opera *Genevieve de Brabant.*[171] Most scholars believe that the melody originally came from a century-old Spanish folksong. While the operatic piece and the "Marine's Hymn" share the same spirit, the duet and the service theme song are certainly different textually. The words for the service song were written by an anonymous author (or authors), but it is really not a "hymn."

Since Grant had a "tin ear" and little appreciation for artistic music, there were only a few recitals at the White House. Perhaps he was the first president to fit the quip of noted pianist Louis Gottschalk, a favorite of Lincoln, that Grant knew only two tunes—"One was 'Yankee Doodle' and the other isn't." The president openly avoided grand opera and the theater. Notable pianists certainly would have enjoyed playing recitals on the new piano that William Bradbury donated to the mansion in 1871, which was especially designed for Julia Grant. Even Gottschalk commented on Bradbury pianos as very superior instruments: "I have especially remarked their thorough workmanship and the power, purity, richness and quality of their tone."[172]

President Grant, however, certainly seemed to enjoy the Hutchinson family in their numerous concerts in the capital, most of which were held at the Metropolitan Methodist Episcopal Church. Records indicate that the program for these concerts probably contained some hymns. The book *Story of the Hutchinsons* states, "We were somewhat restricted in our selections when singing in this church, as the trustees objected to anything of a secular nature. Our entertainments were therefore sacred concerts."[173] They must have sung Grant's favorite hymn, perhaps by request.

The "Washington Sangerbund," a German men's chorus that had sung at Grant's inauguration, performed at the East Room on 16 July 1870. They did not include any German hymns (chorales) in their program. But during Grant's administration, since he had rented a pew at the Methodist church, he could hardly avoid hearing music of the newly published and popular hymns. One of these hymns was "O Little Town of Bethlehem" by the Reverend Phillip Brooks of Trinity Church in Philadelphia. After returning from a trip to the Holy Land, Brooks penned the lyrics as his impression of the visit. While the first three stanzas reflect his feelings about the Bethlehem event of Christ's birth, the fourth stanza expresses his dismay at the problems being created by the approaching Industrial Revolution.[174] Brooks, being an outstanding orator who loved his country, had spoken at Lincoln's funeral. Printed in cheap leaflet form with his organist Lewis Redner's inspiring music, "O Little Town of Bethlehem" was an instant hit. Before long, almost every church was singing it during the Christmas season. By the time of Brooks's death in 1893, it had become a worldwide favorite.

One of the most significant musical events during Grant's term in the White House was a concert by the Fisk University "Jubilee Singers" of Nashville, Tennessee. This choir, sponsored by a university established in 1866 as a school of higher education designed to serve the needs of emancipated slaves, had become a well-known choral group. After appearing by invitation at the Boston World Peace Jubilee in 1872, the ensemble came to Washington, DC, to sing in Lincoln Hall. The president, vice president, and many members of Congress turned aside from their regular public duties to give the Jubilee Singers an audience at the White House.[175] President Grant personally assured the choir of interest in their work of raising money for the financially troubled school. Quoting a clergyman, David W. Stowe wrote that the Jubilee Singers "sang the most touching of Christian melodies, full of Jesus, and of Heaven; the most wild plantation melodies, full of sorrow and aspirations for freedom."[176] Of course they were singing, for the first time in public, the secret music of the African Americans' slave songs. Many of these very songs, in time, were included in hymnals of most Christian denominations and sung by all races. These comments echo Henry Wadsworth Longfellow's poem about a slave singing at night: "And the voice of his devotion, Filled my soul with strange emotion; For its tones by turn were glad, Sweetly solemn, wildly sad." The Fisk Jubilee Singers made a very successful European tour, followed by a worldwide trip. During their seven years of touring, they raised millions of dollars; they not only saved their school financially but also introduced the power of the spirituals to the world.

After receiving information from President Grant's grandson, Lieutenant Colonel U. S. Grant III, John Merrill determined that Grant's favorite hymn was "God Is My Strong Salvation" by James Montgomery. This hymn is not to be confused with Paul Gerhardt's chorale translated from German by John Jacobi with the same English title.

Montgomery was born in Scotland in 1771, where his father was a Moravian minister. In 1776 the family moved to Northern Ireland, but when James was twelve years old, he was sent to the Moravian Seminary in Yorkshire, England. In 1783 his parents went to the West Indies as missionaries, where they both died. James had begun to write poetry at the age of ten, having been influenced by Moravian hymnody. With the tragic death of his parents, he became a very unsettled young person. After flunking out of school at fourteen and running away to London at age sixteen, he sold a poem that covered his expenses until he landed a job in Sheffield, England. In 1796 James was hired by the radical weekly paper the *Sheffield Register.* Soon he took over the paper and changed its name to *Iris.* He served as publisher and editor for thirty-one years. Becoming a fearless social leader, he reprinted a song that celebrated the fall of the Bastille. Consequently, he was imprisoned but took advantage of his time by writing poetry while in jail. In 1825 Montgomery left the paper to devote his full time to writing poetry and lecturing. His social work earned him the honor of Sheffield's first citizen, followed by a royal government pension in 1833. Montgomery learned tolerance among religious groups by doing some "free thinking" while visiting worship services in Anglican, Independent, Baptist, and Methodist congregations; he even cordially cooperated with Catholics, Unitarians, and Quakers. Nevertheless, he returned to his Moravian moorings at age forty-three.[177]

Montgomery wrote 400 hymns, edited and published three hymn books, but his 1825 *The Christian Psalmist,* containing 562 hymns, was his most important. In this collection, 103 of his own hymns were included, and in this book most of Montgomery's hymns sung today originated. In the "Introductory Essay," we have the first English writing on hymnology. Montgomery gives a broad outline of a good hymn when he "calls for unity in hymns, graduation and mutual dependence in the thoughts, a conscious progress, and at the end a sense of completeness.... Hymns ought to be easy to understand."[178] Montgomery's hymns testify to this definition; being a product of a skilled hand, they bear traces of the writer's maturity as a poet and as a Christian. Their simple poetic expressions are ideal for congregational singing. Montgomery's poetic genius is of the highest order. With a vast knowledge of scripture, combined with the faith of a strong personality, he was still able to write with the simplicity of a child—a true genius with a sanctified heart.[179]

There have been many tunes used for the text "God Is My Strong Salvation." John Merrill recommended CHENIES, composed by Timothy R. Matthews in 1855. Since Matthews was tutor for the family of Lord Russell, who was cannon of Windsor and rector of Chenies, one can easily see the

God Is My Strong Salvation

Words: James Montgomery, 1822
Music: Timothy R. Matthews, 1855

7.6.7.6.D
CHENIES

1. God is my strong sal - va - tion: What foe have I to fear? In
2. Place on the Lord re - li - ance, My soul with cour-age wait, His

dark-ness and temp - ta - tion, My light, my help, is near. Though
truth be thine af - fi - ance, When faint and des - o - late. His

hosts en-camp a - round me, Firm to the fight I stand. What
might thine heart shall strength - en, His love thy joy in - crease, Mer -

ter-ror can con-found me With God at my right hand?
cy thy days shall length - en, The Lord will give thee peace. A - men.

reason for its title. A very stately tune with a quite singable melody, it is not difficult to understand why it was sung in the Methodist Church during Grant's time. However, the same could be said of AURELIA, which was composed by Samuel S. Wesley in 1864 and was placed in the hymnal *Selection of Psalms and Hymns*. The same thoughts apply to WEDLOCK, a tune that was in the 1844 collection of *Sacred Harp*, edited by Benjamin Franklin White. Furthermore, some musicians have even used the tune VULPIUS, composed by Melchior Vulpius in 1609, to accompany these words. VULPIUS has also been called CHRISTUS, DER IS MEIN LEBEN, coming from the German hymn beginning with the words "Christ is my life."[180]

"God Is My Strong Salvation," based on Psalm 27, first appeared in Montgomery's 1822 *Songs of Zion, Being Imitations of Psalms.* It begins with an ideal statement of confidence, which can be viewed as a reflection of Grant's military service as general. Sounding similar to "marching orders" from a higher command, these phrases reveal reasons why Lincoln stood behind his decision to promote Grant to the highest military position in the Union forces. Each stanza has relevance to Grant's life of service with his troops and eventually to his commander in chief position.

Stanza one is comprised of a free paraphrase of Psalm 27:1–3. In direct and well-chosen words, the text is clearly a fine-tuned modulation of the inspiring thought of confidence. The lyrics do not include any wavering of a position; Grant, as general, always stood by his decision to hold his ground. Stanza two emphasizes reliance of the Christian on God, following the final phrase of the preceding thought "with God at my right hand." "His truth will be my Sustenance" sounds strikingly similar to "His truth is marching on" from the immortal "The Battle Hymn of the Republic." The strengthening of the heart, leading to the increase of joy, and climaxing with the promise of a long and peaceful life is a prophecy of the life of Grant. Could Grant have been influenced by this hymn, as the words seem to be a fulfillment of David's words?

Fanny Crosby remarked that there was a warm spot in her heart for President Grant. It is notable that some hymnologists say that "Safe in the Arms of Jesus" was the Crosby hymn her generation preferred to all others.[181] Written in haste for William Doane's music to be used at a Sunday school convention, the hymn enjoyed immediate and immense acclaim. The *New York Times* in the 1890s reported that "no modern hymn ha[d] circumnavigated the religious globe more thoroughly than this one or been translated into more modern tongues."[182] These statements can be justified, as "Safe in the Arms of Jesus" was sung and played during the mourning of the death of both Presidents Garfield and Grant. This is also verification that President Grant himself expressed many times his belief in God, the Bible, and heaven. This was the feeling of the country at his demise.

RUTHERFORD B. HAYES

1822–1893

Nineteenth President (1877–1881)

In fall 2000, the uncertainty surrounding the outcome of the presidential election dismayed most Americans. Only after the state of Florida invested substantial time, effort, and money in recounting the votes, and only after the US Supreme Court upheld the recount, did Republican George W. Bush receive the confirmation as the next president of the United States. Bush won the election through a five-vote majority in the Electoral College despite receiving a minority of the popular vote. What many people did not realize was that more than a century before, even greater uncertainty surrounded the outcome of a presidential election. For a time, there was even some talk that the nation might divide again over the controversy. The votes from Florida were among those disputed, and in this case also, the Republican nominee, Rutherford B. Hayes, won that election by only one vote in the Electoral College despite receiving a minority of the popular vote.

Rutherford Hayes's background and early life gave little indication that he would someday become controversial or that he would achieve his nation's highest office. Hayes came from humble origins, and when he was young, his father died. Supported largely by a bachelor uncle who became a surrogate father, Hayes was offered the opportunity of an excellent education in his home state of Ohio. When he was only sixteen, he began his college education at Kenyon College, where he graduated as valedictorian. Afterward, he read law for a time before attending Harvard Law School for three semesters upon the insistence and with the support of his uncle. Subsequently, he returned to Ohio to establish law practice and met and married Lucy Webb.

As his law practice began to thrive, Hayes began to get involved in politics, first with the Whig Party and then with the new Republican Party. When the Civil War erupted, like many men, Hayes volunteered and, due to his age, political involvement, and education, became an officer. During the course of the war he served with some distinction, was seriously wounded at the battle of South Mountain, and rose to the temporary rank of major general in the Union army. While he was still serving in the army, Ohio Republicans nominated Hayes for a seat in the US House of Representatives. Despite the fact that he refused to take a furlough and campaign for himself, his district's voters elected him. After brief service in Congress, he served an unprecedented three terms as Ohio's governor.

As the presidential election of 1876 neared, Hayes began to be recognized as a dark horse candidate, mainly due to his record as governor and the fact that both parties recognized Ohio as a key electoral state. The national nominating convention eventually chose Hayes as a compromise nominee when various rivals could not win a clear-cut majority. The Democrats chose as their nominee New York governor Samuel Tilden, best known as the reformer who broke the Tammany Hall ring in New York City.

The campaign that resulted was a heated one. When the election returns came in, it appeared initially that Tilden had won. In fact, Tilden had a majority of popular votes. Four states, Louisiana, South Carolina, Oregon, and Florida, all had disputed election returns, however, thus throwing the deciding electoral votes into question. Essentially, the controversy revolved around the dispute as to whether Republican or Democratic sets of votes would be counted. For weeks, the controversy hovered, and there was even talk of another civil war. Finally, Republicans and Democrats agreed upon a compromise by which the last Union troops would be removed from the South, officially ending Reconstruction, while Hayes received the White

House. Ultimately, this compromise led to the resumption of a South controlled by white Democrats and the establishment of laws that were prejudiced against African Americans.

Unfortunately, the election controversy overshadowed Hayes's entire presidency. Despite this, Hayes won the respect of many with his dignity and honesty in the aftermath of the corrupt years of the Grant presidency. He sought some reform of the patronage system and was forced to deal with labor unrest and with conflict over Chinese immigration. As promised, he refused to run for a second term. He retired to Ohio for the remaining twelve years of his life.

Rutherford Hayes was one of the nation's most outspoken Christians. While he never joined the Methodist Church, he regularly attended with his wife and clearly professed his faith as a Christian. His genuinely ethical behavior was consistent with the norms of evangelical Christianity of that day. He and Lucy were committed proponents of the temperance movement, and he banned alcohol from the White House during his presidency. Pundits thus nicknamed his wife "Lemonade Lucy." The Hayes family also instituted the forerunner of the Easter egg hunt that has become a part of White House tradition.[183]

From a letter to his daughter Fanny, we learn that Rutherford Hayes loved music. He wrote on 24 January 1886, "Music, you know, is the pet of both your mother and father." Elise Kirk, historian, said that Rutherford Hayes and his wife, Lucy, appeared to enjoy music and America's new cultural image more than any other first family of the century.[184] This is evident in the nearly fifty musical programs at the White House during his 1877–1881 term. The Hayeses were the pioneers in inaugurating the "musicale," a term denoting a private concert for social entertainment. Being informal and homelike, these gatherings were special to invited friends, often including congressmen, the presidential cabinet, distinguished guests, and even foreign dignitaries.

President Hayes and his First Lady realized the need to have a presidential impresario, a practice followed by most succeeding presidents. Their first choice was Professor Frederick Widdows, a virtuoso organist, especially on the chimes, at the Metropolitan Episcopal Church. He actually composed music for the text "Rock of Ages, Cleft for Me," which Hayes enjoyed hearing. However, this is not to be confused with the tune by Thomas Hastings, which, when set to the lyrics of Augustus Toplady, became the favorite hymn of Hayes.

Other musical accomplishments of the Hayes presidency include the appointment of the twenty-six-year-old John Philip Sousa as the director of the Marine Band. Sousa, the first American-born conductor, met the challenge of developing a new image for this already storied organization. Since the former directors took their music scores with them, he had to start from scratch. However, he was quite capable of composing and arranging music specifically for certain events, resulting in a renewed polish to the group. For instance, he limited some robust-sounding instruments in selections that required quieter and softer sounding instruments such as woodwinds and even strings. This resulted in a Marine orchestra. Sousa maintained a high standard for the band, expanded it, took them on a national tour, and wrote many marches for the ensemble. He became the "march king," and his "Stars and Stripes Forever" eventually became the official march for America.[185]

Pianos had always been an important White House furnishing. During Hayes's administration some piano manufacturers began the marketing tool of donating their pianos for use in the presidential mansion. It was considered a great honor, but also guaranteed fine pianos for the presidential residence. In addition, Hayes was active in promoting outstanding black performers for the White House musicales. This practice continues even today.

Besides the musicales, which represented the finest in American tastes in music during the Hayes years, Sunday evenings also had a unique character all their own. Quite often, intimate friends were invited to dinner at the White House, after which they would participate in a White House hymn-singing session. This was compatible with the love that Rutherford had for his wife. He wrote to her before they married, "With no musical taste or cultivation myself, I am yet so fond of simple airs that I have often thought I could never love a woman who did not sing them." At times, Lucy even accompanied the hymn-sing as the group would gather around the piano and harmonize. From the diary of Hayes, we learn that "hymn books were distributed and with someone at the piano, one favorite hymn after another would be sung in one of the parlors."[186] The Hayeses were convinced that hymns could accomplish miracles by satisfying social, recreational, and religious leanings, according to Kirk. It mattered little that President Hayes could not sing well. The *Ohio State Journal* wrote, "Hayes can't sing any more than a canal-boat."

The following hymns were among others sung at a Sunday evening hymn-sing in 1887: "Jesus, Lover of My Soul," "Nearer, My God, to Thee," and "Tell Me the Old, Old Story." Author John McCollister notes that on another date with congressmen, the cabinet, and Vice President Wheeler in attendance, they also included the hymn "Blest Be the Tie That Binds,"[187] as well as "Majestic Sweetness Sits Enthroned." For these occasions the hymns were selected from the hymnbook *Songs for the Sanctuary*, published by

Barnes of New York in 1872. Lucy's own copy is housed in the Hayes Center at Freemont, Ohio.

Because of the Hayeses' love of hymns, on several occasions guest soloists or ensembles would include hymns during their programs. In April 1879 Guiseppe Operti, "*Celebrated Chef d'Orchestra,*" and other members of the Hess English Opera Company sang at a musicale program. According to the *New York Times,* they "sang a few hymn tunes to the delight of the Executive household in the library upstairs." Among the singers in this group was the popular prima donna Emma Abbott. Later she formed her own opera company and was noted for interposing hymns, such as "Nearer, My God, to Thee," within an actual opera performance. This obviously brought her much criticism.

Rutherford Hayes's most loved hymn was "Rock of Ages, Cleft for Me," written by Augustus Toplady, an Englishman born in 1740. His father, Major Toplady, was killed in battle in Columbia while his son was only months old. Young Augustus was converted in a barn while listening to a Methodist preacher in Ireland. After training for the ministry and holding a short pastorate at Broadhembury, Toplady went to London and associated himself with the Countess of Huntingdon, an ardent Calvinist and a distant relative of George Washington. She inherited her wealth at age thirty-nine and began building chapels all over England to evangelize the country. By subsidizing interim preachers, she gave them the status of her private chaplains. She also edited and printed hymnals for use in the chapel congregational services. However, the Church of England, through the force of law, eventually forced her to secede from the established church and organize her chapels into an independent "connection."[188]

Toplady often preached to multitudes of people in open fields. At Leicester Fields, it is documented that 1,300 horses were turned loose in an adjoining field to disturb his services. John and Charles Wesley also had similar experiences. Being contemporary with the Wesleys, however, didn't ensure him a good relationship. John on one occasion said, "Mr. Augustus Toplady I know well, but I do not fight with chimney sweeps; he is too dirty for me to meddle with."[189] The uneasy feelings between the two men occurred because of the strong Calvinistic leanings that Toplady held to, in contrast to the equally strong Arminian theology held by John Wesley. However, both of these Anglican ministers were very familiar with Dr. Daniel Brevint's manual dealing with Holy Communion. Wesley included long extracts from this work in his *Hymns on the Lord's Supper.* Toplady also received inspiration in writing "Rock of Ages" from Brevint. That this prayer of Brevint closely parallels Toplady's hymn can't be ignored: "O Rock of

Rock of Ages, Cleft for Me

Words: Augustus M. Toplady, 1776
Music: Thomas Hastings, 1830

7.7.7.7.7.7.
TOPLADY

1. Rock of A - ges, cleft for me, Let me hide my - self in
2. Not the la - bor of my hands Can ful - fill Thy law's de -
3. No - thing in my hand I bring, Sim - ply to Thy cross I
4. While I draw this fleet - ing breath, When my eye - lids close in

Thee; Let the wa - ter and the blood, From Thy
mands; Could my zeal no res - pite know, Could my
cling; Na - ked, come to Thee for dress; Help - less,
death, When I rise to worlds un - known, See Thee

side a heal - ing flood, Be of sin the doub - le
tears for - ev - er flow, All for sin could not a -
look to Thee for grace, Vile, I to the foun - tain
on Thy judg - ment throne, Rock of A - ges, cleft for

cure, Save from wrath and make me pure.
tone; Thou must save, and Thou a - lone.
fly, Wash me, Sa - vior, or I die.
me, Let me hide my - self in Thee. A - men.

Israel, Rock of Salvation, Rock struck and cleft for me, let those two streams of blood and water, which once gushed out of thy side, bring down pardon and holiness into my soul. And let me thirst after them now, as if I stood upon the mount whence sprung this water, and near the cleft of that Rock, the wounds of my Lord, which gushed this sacred blood."[190] Toplady wrote this hymn during a two-year period when his mind was active but his body was weak with consumption. "Rock of Ages" has been termed by some as the greatest hymn in the English language.

The hymn was first published in 1776 in the *Gospel Magazine*, a periodical edited by Toplady himself. The original title was "A Living and Dying Prayer for the Holiest Believer in the World." The lyrics pointed toward a doctrine of "sinless perfection," which Toplady mistakenly thought was being proposed by Wesley. The hymn is asserting that however good or holy a person may be, he is still a sinner and is always in need of God's mercy and forgiveness. Therefore, this prayer is one suited for the greatest saint as well as the worst sinner.

"Rock of Ages" found its way into almost every hymnal in the past 200 plus years and has been sung by Christians of all persuasions. The secret of the hymn's popularity is its vivid and passionate language, matched by its equally emotional music. Thomas Hastings, the composer of the TOPLADY tune, was born in 1784 in Connecticut. He received training under Boston music educator Lowell Mason and began his career as a music teacher and also edited the *Recorder* newspaper in Utica, New York, in 1823. During his lifetime he composed almost 1,000 tunes and 600 hymn texts.[191]

The TOPLADY tune was first included in *Spiritual Songs for Social Worship* in 1832. Even though the proper tempo for the music has been difficult to standardize, the music has been successfully used since its composition. Twentieth-century hymnologist Eric Routley described "Rock of Ages" as "the only popular and universal hymn about sin." Reinforcing Hayes's deeply committed Christian life, this hymn must have meant much to him. During the time of the difficult compromise agreed upon in his election, he was probably reassured by this hymn's serious message. Rutherford B. Hayes's ethical behavior as a dedicated Christian spoke louder than any words delivered by him as president of his country. Or maybe the hymn-sings in the White House worked miracles for this president during trying times.

JAMES A. GARFIELD

1831–1881

Twentieth President (1881)

When John Wilkes Booth assassinated Abraham Lincoln in 1865, Americans were shocked. No president had ever been assassinated. As time passed, people viewed Lincoln as a martyr and as a last casualty of the terrible Civil War. Despite the assassination, subsequent presidents moved about freely without any increase in security, and people came and went into the White House with little obstruction. In 1881, things began to change. While James Garfield held the presidency for the shortest term of any president other than William Henry Harrison, his assassination resulted in lasting changes.

Garfield was born in Ohio in 1831, the last US president to be born in a log cabin. Orphaned at the age of two, Garfield quickly learned to be self-sufficient. He raised enough money to attend college in Ohio at Western Reserve Eclectic Institute, and then to attend Williams College in the East. He was such an accomplished student that he graduated with honors and returned to Western Reserve to teach and then to serve as the school's president. He also began to get involved in Republican politics. Fervently opposed to slavery, he became an effective public speaker. In 1859, though he was only twenty-eight years old, Ohio voters elected him to the state senate, where he proved to be an effective legislator. When the Civil War came, Garfield volunteered for service. Commissioned as a colonel, he led his troops to victory in a minor skirmish in Kentucky and achieved great notoriety in the press. As a result, he received promotion to brigadier-general. He also used the publicity to be elected to the US House of Representatives at the age of thirty-one. Since he was not scheduled to begin in Congress until December 1863, he continued to serve in the army. The War Department ordered him to report to the Army of the Cumberland in Tennessee, where he served as the chief of staff for General William Rosecrans. He served with distinction in that position until he left to assume his congressional position.

Garfield served in the House of Representatives for seventeen years and became one of the leading Republicans in Congress. He supported the radical wing of the Republican Party throughout the remainder of the war and through the Reconstruction era. He survived some minor scandals during a time when scandals were widespread in American politics. He also served on the electoral commission that settled the controversial presidential election of 1876. In 1880, with the Republican Party divided, President Hayes chose not to run for reelection. When the Republican nominating convention deadlocked, the delegates turned to Garfield and nominated him for president on the thirty-sixth ballot. Garfield, in an effort to unify the party, agreed to take Chester Arthur, the protégé of corrupt New York Republican boss Senator Roscoe Conkling, as his vice-presidential running mate. In a hard-fought campaign, Garfield defeated Democratic nominee and war hero Winfield S. Hancock for the presidency.

Garfield was determined to reform the government's civil service and bring about change to the so-called "spoils system" that had dominated government appointments since the 1830s. He met significant resistance from Conkling and Arthur. His stated position led to his shooting by a disappointed office seeker, Charles Guiteau, in a Washington, DC, railroad station. Simple security probably would have prevented the attempt. For modern medicine, Garfield's wounds would not have been fatal. Unfortunately, without x-rays, the attending physicians could not locate the bullet and misdiagnosed his wound. Studies in antiseptics and microbiology were still not widely accepted in the medical community, and the physicians also used unwashed hands and surgical instruments to examine the stricken president. After lingering painfully for more than two months, Garfield died dreadfully. His death led to changes in the civil service system, presidential security, and medical treatment. The trial of his assassin also led to changes in the legal system.

Garfield was a devout Christian. A member of the Disciples of Christ, as a young man he preached and held revival meetings. Despite some alleged infidelity early in his marriage, his marriage survived, and Garfield remained a dedicated Christian. As the father of seven children, five of whom survived to adulthood, he was a committed family man. When it became apparent that he might run for president, he vacillated due to the strain that it would place on his private life. Even though he apparently was a strong Christian, he refused to use his religious faith as an object of political promotion and vigorously defended freedom of religion and separation of church and state.[192]

Music was very important to James Garfield. As a lover of literature, languages, and fine arts, the congenial Garfield liked to make up tunes to his favorite poems by Tennyson and Longfellow.[193] He and his future wife, Lucretia, had studied Greek and Hebrew, music, art, and religion as classmates at the Eclectic Institute in 1850. This school, founded by the Disciples of Christ denomination in Hiram, Ohio, provided the backdrop for their courtship, which began in 1853. Later, Garfield became a lay preacher while a student at Williams College in New York. Because of his belief in a literal interpretation of the Scriptures, he concluded that the only course for a Christian was to make his faith a personal matter of constant practice. The experience of addressing large crowds by preaching greatly aided his confidence. Garfield was outspoken on both war and slavery, relating them to scripture. He said, "Where the Bible is silent, there we are silent; where the Bible speaks, there we speak."[194]

The Garfields made certain that their daughter, Mollie, and four sons all had music lessons. Hal, their eldest son, became a gifted pianist by the age of seventeen. The president often would go to the Oval Room to listen to his son play on the Bradbury upright piano. There are many hymn references noted during the short term of President Garfield. From his diary we read his personal testimony: "Thanks be to God for his goodness. By the help of God, I'll praise my Maker while I've breath." This last phrase is a direct quotation from a hymn written by English hymn writer Isaac Watts in 1719 as a paraphrase of Psalm 146. While nearing death, he seemed to temporarily rally and was allowed to sit near a window. His wife began to sing the William Williams hymn of 1745 "Guide Me, O Thou Great Jehovah." Listening intently to her, Garfield began to cry: "To his doctor, William Bliss, he said 'Glorious, Bliss, isn't it?'"[195]

At the mourning of his death from an assassin's bullet, the hymn "Peace! Be Still" by Mary Ann Baker was heard at funeral services held in his honor. While his body lay in state, newspapers reported that a ten-year-old relative of Garfield died with "Safe in the Arms of Jesus" on her lips.[196] This Fanny Crosby hymn was also played by the Marine Band on 25 September 1881 for throngs of people gathered in Cleveland in remembrance of President Garfield. "Nearer, My God, to Thee," by Sarah Frances Adams, was played at the interment of Garfield at Lakeview Cemetery in Cleveland.

According to John Merrill's research, President James Garfield's most favored hymn was the moving "Holy Ghost, with Light Divine," written in 1817 by Andrew Reed. Textually similar to Samuel Longfellow's 1864 text "Holy Spirit, Truth Divine," Garfield may have been familiar with both poems. Reed, born in London in 1787, was a Congregationalist minister trained at Hackney College. After serving as pastor of three successful churches, he began establishing community projects, utilizing his outstanding organizational skills. While devoted to the evangelical movement, he founded six notable welfare institutions, raising more than $500,000 for his philanthropic enterprises. His humble Christian belief can be capsulized in the statement that appears as his epitaph: "I was born yesterday, I shall die tomorrow and I must not spend today in telling what I have done, but in doing what I may for Him who has done all for me." Yale University conferred the Doctor of Divinity degree on him in 1834 in recognition of his many achievements.

Andrew Reed is most remembered for his literary achievements, particularly for writing the hymn "Holy Ghost, with Light Divine," which first appeared under the title "Prayer to the Holy Spirit" in Reed's collection *Supplement to Watts' Psalms and Hymns* of 1817. The hymn has often been titled "Holy Ghost Thou Light Divine" or "Holy Spirit, Light Divine."[197] Even though he wrote only twenty-one hymns, Reed greatly enlarged his collection in 1825 and 1842. Hymns from these collections have subsequently been printed in numerous hymnals. After his death in 1862, Reed's wife republished the collection in 1872, calling it *Wycliffe Supplement* after the last and largest congregation where Reed served, Wycliffe Chapel.

The composer of the tune MERCY, Louis Moreau Gottschalk, was born in New Orleans in 1829. He became America's first concert pianist of note and a prolific composer whose work was recognized on both sides of the Atlantic. The son of an English father and French mother, Gottschalk studied piano at an early age. At the age of three, he played a melody on the piano

Holy Ghost, with Light Divine

Words: Andrew Reed, 1817
Music: Louis M. Gottschalk, 1854

7.7.7.7.
GOTTSCHALK

1. Ho - ly Ghost, with light di - vine, Shine up - on this
2. Ho - ly Ghost, with power di - vine, Cleanse this guilt - y
3. Ho - ly Ghost, with joy di - vine, Cheer this sad - dened
4. Ho - ly Spi - rit, all di - vine, Dwell with - in this

heart of mine; Chase the shades of night a -
heart of mine; Long has sin, with - out con -
heart of mine; Bid my man - y woes de -
heart of mine, Cast down ev - ery i - dol -

way, Turn my dark - ness in - to day.
trol, Held do - min - ion o'er my soul.
part, Heal my wound - ed, bleed - ing heart.
throne; Reign su - preme, and reign a - lone. A - men.

from memory that he had heard his mother sing one morning.[198] His father wasted no time in arranging lessons for his son. At the age of twelve he was sent to a French boarding school to further his music education. The young boy made highly successful concert tours of France, Switzerland, and Spain while in Europe. When he returned to New Orleans, he played many piano recitals and directed orchestral concerts. He also began to blend classical music with popular music in his compositions. This set a precedent followed by other American composers like Charles Ives and George Gershwin. It was natural for Gottschalk, who grew up hearing a rich mixture of French and Italian opera, Creole folksongs, and minstrel show music.

Gottschalk, having assumed the financial responsibility of his family because of the death of his father, began to tailor his programs to the tastes of his audiences. In 1862–1863 he gave 1,100 programs in the United States and Canada. An ardent patriot and supporter of the Union, Gottschalk sought to foster a distinctive American musical culture. His 1862 musical medley "The Union" consisted of a fantasy in the style of Franz Liszt on "The Star-Spangled Banner," "Hail, Columbia," and "Yankee Doodle." It was played for a delighted Abraham Lincoln at the White House in 1864.[199]

Gottschalk's most successful music compositions were a pair of salon pieces titled "The Last Hope" (1854) and "The Dying Poet" (1864). These simplified versions of Chopin nocturnes could be enjoyed by musically naïve listeners and executed with ease by amateur pianists. While "The Dying Poet" became a standard silent movie piano selection, "The Last Hope" provided the music for the hymn "Holy Ghost, with Light Divine." The tune's name, MERCY, is a result of the music's early association with Charles Wesley's hymn "Depth of Mercy."[200] GOTTSCHALK is also used for the tune name. The music itself is very expressive of the text and is dearly loved when used with these lyrics. Gottschalk made a quite successful tour of South America and, after contracting yellow fever, eventually died from exhaustion in Rio de Janeiro in 1869.

"Holy Ghost, with Light Divine" is based on Romans 8:4, which in part says, "We can do nothing worthwhile for God without the energizing Holy Spirit's power." This verse reflects the process that Garfield used in making presidential decisions. His focus was ultimately on the source of his guidance, God. He would listen to advisors and counselors but rely on God as the ultimate source of wisdom. His inauguration address clearly states his desire and support of Almighty God.

This hymn has been Christianity's most eloquent expression of the ministry of the Holy Spirit. The first stanza is an invocation to allow the Holy Spirit to come into a life in order to cleanse sins that would dim the light—shine the Light into the soul. The second stanza is a reminder of the need for the power of the Holy Spirit for Christians to live pure lives. Stanza three is a promise that a man will have joy when he yields to the Holy Spirit to control his emotions. Stanza four climaxes the thought with the all-controlling Holy Spirit requiring total commitment by conformity to God's will.

Garfield's choice of his most favored hymn emphasizes the practical, consistent vigil that Christians should exhibit in living. The Holy Spirit is available in times of difficulty and doubt, but man must yield his desires to God's will. This message must have meant much to President Garfield since his reforming the "spoils" practice became crucial to the development of the modern-day civil service system. Even his choice of inauguration scripture relates to his future decision to put the country in God's hand as president. He wisely chose Proverbs 21:1, which says, "The king's heart is in the hand of Jehovah as the water courses: He turneth it withersoever he will."

CHESTER A. ARTHUR

1830–1886

Twenty-First President (1881–1885)

For most of the nineteenth century, the "spoils system" created one of the great problems of the US political structure. The spoils system rewarded supporters of candidates from the presidency down to local elections with government jobs. This patronage created an arrangement in which victors swept aside all government employees, regardless of their level of competence, and replaced them on the basis of political involvement rather than merit. Incredibly inefficient and, in some cases, notoriously corrupt, the spoils system ruled in US politics until after the Civil War when reformers vowed to replace it with a merit system, laying the groundwork for the current civil service. One product of the spoils system was Chester Arthur. Ironically, he rejected his political background and led the nation into reform.

Chester Arthur's father emigrated from Northern Ireland in the early nineteenth century. Chester Arthur was born in Vermont in 1830. Educated at Union College, he taught school for a time and studied law. Upon his admission to the New York bar, he practiced law in New York City. The son of an abolitionist Baptist preacher, Arthur became active in Republican Party politics. When the Civil War began, Arthur served as the quartermaster general of New York, being responsible for supplying state troops and militia. Remaining active in Republican politics, he became a protégé of notorious New York senator Roscoe Conkling. In 1871, President Grant rewarded Arthur for his loyalty by appointing him to the prestigious and lucrative position of collector of the Port of New York, normally a patronage position from which much personal gain could be skimmed. Arthur, however, remained personally incorruptible. He did pack the Custom House with "Stalwarts," as supporters of Conkling's faction in the state were known, including more employees than were actually warranted.

In an 1878 attempt to initiate reform, President Rutherford Hayes replaced Arthur. In response, Conkling's supporters sought to nominate former president Grant for a third term in 1880. Reformers blocked this effort by successfully nominating reformer James Garfield for the presidency. As a compromise with the Stalwarts, Arthur received the nomination as vice president. In the early days of his administration, Garfield placed a reformer in the lucrative New York customs position despite Arthur's opposition. This decision led to a dramatic decline in Conkling's influence. When Garfield was shot by a disgruntled office-seeking Stalwart months later, despite his worsening condition, he refused to receive Arthur because of Arthur's continued support of Conkling. However, when Garfield died and Arthur became president, Arthur renounced Conkling and continued Garfield's reforms. Much to the chagrin of the Stalwarts, Arthur and Congress used the public outcry against Garfield's assassination to pass the Pendleton Act. This act initiated the Civil Service Commission, which created the current merit system.

Arthur also attempted to lower tariff rates in order to reduce the tax burden on southerners and westerners and decrease the federal budget surplus (yes, there was a budget surplus then!), despite the fact that Republicans favored high tariffs. Arthur's administration also enacted the first national immigration law.

An immaculate dresser in his personal attire, Arthur found the dilapidated condition of the White House and its furniture appalling. His enthusiastic redecoration of the presidential mansion became legendary when he hired Louis Comfort Tiffany, the nation's best-known designer, for the project. Despite the fact that his beloved wife had died before he entered the White House, Arthur became recognized for his elaborate parties in which he sometimes showed off his children. Most Americans regarded him especially "presidential" in his looks and manners and nicknamed him "Elegant Arthur." Unfortunately, during his presidency, doctors diagnosed him with a terminal kidney disease. With this in mind, he did not actively seek reelection and was not nominated by Republicans. He died only two years after leaving the White House. Despite this fact, Arthur served as president at a key moment in US history and is a major transitional figure in the Gilded Age.

Arthur's minister father reared him as a devout Baptist, but Chester Arthur never affiliated with any church. His wife, Ellen, was a faithful Episcopalian, and he regularly attended services with her. After her death, he continued to attend Episcopalian services. Though not a church member, Arthur was widely regarded for his personal integrity despite his political connections. As one contemporary noted, "No man ever entered the Presidency so profoundly and widely distrusted, and no one ever retired…more generally respected."[201]

Chester Arthur's life was consumed with the memory of his dear wife, who died a year before he took office. On taking the presidential oath, he opened the Bible to Psalm 31:1–3 because the opening verses reminded him of the hymn "Te Deum," which his wife frequently sang in the Episcopal choir. President Arthur loved music, especially vocal music, since Ellen Arthur had a fine contralto voice and had been an active member of the Mendelssohn Glee Club of New York City, which sang at her funeral. The president donated a stained-glass window in her honor to St. John's Episcopal Church, where he attended. He ordered fresh flowers placed daily before her White House portrait.

While Arthur was president, there were many operatic recitals given in the White House. After the Canadian soprano Emma Albani sang, it is probable that the president requested her to sing his favorite song, "Robin Adair." Elise Kirk wrote, "His late wife Ellen had sung the popular Irish ballad often before they were married, and time and again, he had asked her to sing the song. Albani's interpretation…must have conjured up memories for the lonely president."[202] One of the most moving music programs during Arthur's term was an appearance by the Jubilee Singers of Fisk University from Nashville, Tennessee. This ensemble of black singers had presented a concert when Grant was president, but returned on 17 February 1882 to sing their distinctive music for President Arthur.

While touring, the Jubilee Singers had absorbed some European harmonic concepts and combined these with native African idioms, including blues notes, rhythmic vitality, and "call and response" patterns, creating a unique, plaintive, yet emotionally powerful music. Hymnologist Eric Routely stated, "Their moving words and haunting airs had captured the imagination of many distinguished European musicians…[with their spirituals becoming] the real American hymn…songs of Christian experience from indigenous Americans."[203] Many of these songs became hymns and are included in most hymnals today. For President Arthur, the Jubilee Singers sang mostly spirituals but also included Fanny Crosby's "Safe in the Arms of Jesus," bringing the president to tears. Their leader, Reverend Rankin, said, "I never saw a man so deeply moved." The president apologized to the group, confessing that he had never before been guilty of so impulsive an exhibition of his feelings.[204]

Even though Arthur's youngest sister, Mary McElroy, was the White House hostess, the president made most of the decisions on musical performances. Often he was quite frank in his opinions. After John Philip Sousa complained that "Hail to the Chief" was unsuitable for use as presidential music, President Arthur ordered him to change it. The bandmaster noted in his diary, "I wrote the 'Presidential Polonaise' for White House indoor affairs, and the 'Semper Fidelis' march for review purposes outdoors." "Semper Fidelis" became very popular, but "Hail to the Chief" is still played. Because of John Merrill's study, we learn that Henry Francis Lyte's "Abide with Me" was President Arthur's favorite hymn. Considered by many as one of the finest in the English language, this hymn was a natural for Arthur's choice.

Born in 1793 in Scotland, Henry Lyte's poetic talent surfaced early in life under the guidance of his godly mother. He won a prize for composing the best English poem while a student at Trinity College in Dublin, Ireland. After his sincere conversion by reading the Scriptures with a pastor, he decided to become a minister. He lived a busy life in spite of his chronic health problems. Marrying a Methodist minister's daughter, he accepted the "perpetual curacy" at Brixham, England. He became a power for good in this seaside town noted for immorality, and he labored there for almost twenty-five years while his health steadily deteriorated.[205]

Lyte wrote several hymns after paraphrasing the Psalms in meter. His setting of Psalm 103 became the well-known "Praise, My Soul, the King of Heaven." In 1847 he preached his last sermon at Brixham after being urged by his family not to speak because of his ill health. He justified his action by stating, "It is better to wear out than to rust out." He was to travel to Italy for recuperation after that Sunday service. But in September 1847, Lyte walked

Abide with Me

Words: Henry F. Lyte, 1847
Music: William H. Monk, 1861

10.10.10.10.
EVENTIDE

1. A - bide with me! fast falls the e - ven - tide;
2. Swift to its close ebbs out life's lit - tle day;
3. I need thy pre - sence ev - ery pass - ing hour;
4. Hold thou thy cross be - fore my clos - ing eyes,

The dark - ness deep - ens, Lord with me a - bide!
Earth's joys grow dim, its glo - ries pass a - way;
What but thy grace can foil the tempt - er's power?
Shine through the gloom, and point me to the skies:

When oth - er help - ers fail, and com - forts flee,
Change and de - cay in all a - round I see;
Who like thy - self my guide and stay can be?
Heaven's morn - ing breaks, and earth's vain shad - ows flee;

Help of the help - less, O a - bide with me!
O thou who chang - est not, a - bide with me!
Through cloud and sun - shine, O a - bide with me!
In life and death, O Lord, a - bide with me! A - men.

on the seashore at sunset; on returning home, he stayed in his study for an hour. Afterward, he gave his daughter the manuscript to "Abide with Me," a hymn based on Luke 24:29, which reads, "Abide with us, for it is toward evening, the day is far spent." Lyte died in Nice, France, in November of the same year.

With the words of this hymn, Lyte had produced the imagery of eventide linked with low tide of death. "Abide with Me" soon became the favorite hymn of Christians during times of sorrow and deep distress. Its first appearance in America was in Henry Ward Beecher's *Plymouth Collection* of 1855 with the note that it is to be read and not sung. Later, William Monk, an organist and champion of congregational song, who was the music editor for *Hymns Ancient and Modern,* discovered the text. In less than thirty minutes he composed a tune for the lyrics and named it EVENTIDE. Monk did not so name the tune because he wanted it to be sung at evening services of worship; rather, the hymn deals with the evening of life. The solemn beauty of the music matches the text perfectly, although some say it tends to be sentimental. Since its appearance in 1861, "Abide with Me" has comforted and inspired countless people, being printed in almost all English-language hymnals. Because some American hymnists wanted to give a unique voice to their new country, even if it meant rewriting some of England's finest hymns, hymn writer Harriett Beecher Stowe rewrote a version of Lyte's hymn.[206]

Chester Arthur's choice of scripture at his inauguration must have bolstered his life as president. From Psalm 31 we find, "Be thou to me a strong rock, a house of defense to save me. For thou art my rock and my fortress; therefore for thy name's sake lead me and guide me." These words were certainly meaningful to him as Arthur continued Garfield's reforms, leading to the current merit system in civil service policies. The hymn served the same purpose in Arthur's dealing with his grief over the loss of his wife. The metaphors of "falling eventide," "deepening darkness," "growing dimness," and "fading glories" are apt descriptions of "ebbing life" in stanzas one and two. Stanza three is a call for spiritual help in critical hours, claiming the promises of God's presence in this time of need. The triumphant hope of salvation through the cross, which heralds heaven's morning, climaxes the hymn's fourth stanza. Lyte's final spoken words contain these same thoughts: "It is my desire to induce you to prepare for the solemn hour which must come to all, by the timely appreciation and dependence on the death of Christ." Each stanza ends with the common prayer for God to constantly "abide with me." In life and death, President Arthur sought God's presence in his choice of both scripture and hymn.

GROVER CLEVELAND

1837–1908

Twenty-Second President (1885–1889)
&
Twenty-Fourth President (1893–1897)

In the years following the Civil War, the party of Lincoln dominated presidential politics as no subsequent party in American history has. Rallying its constituency with the reminder that the Republican Party had "saved the Union," American voters elected Republican candidates in every presidential election except two between 1860 and 1912. A New York Democrat provided the sole exception to this pattern. In doing so, Grover Cleveland also became the only US president to hold two non-consecutive presidential terms.

Grover Cleveland, born in 1837 in New Jersey at the peak of Jacksonian democracy, was one of nine children born to a Presbyterian minister. His family moved to upstate New York when he was only four, raising him in the small village of Fayetteville, about 120 miles northwest of the very town where Martin Van Buren had been born and lived at this time. Though Cleveland never received a college education, he studied law with a prestigious firm in Buffalo where President Millard Fillmore had once been an attorney. Admitted to the bar, he became an assistant district attorney in 1863. As he contributed the primary support for his widowed mother and sisters, Cleveland legally paid a Polish immigrant as his substitute in the Union army and thus avoided the draft. However, other prominent Americans of draft age, such as John D. Rockefeller, Andrew Carnegie, and Theodore Roosevelt, Sr., did the same without any disgrace, and Cleveland proudly had two younger brothers who served in the army. His avoidance of the draft apparently had nothing to do with his political convictions. As an attorney his contemporaries recognized in him a tremendous ability to focus on whatever case or assignment he had at a given time. Throughout the next several years he alternated time in public service as district attorney and county sheriff with his law practice.

When he was forty-four, stirrings of reform ultimately coalesced in both the Populist and Progressive movements. Living in Buffalo, New York, Cleveland ran on a reform platform and was elected the city's mayor. Democrats regarded him so successful that they nominated him for governor in 1882. New York elected Cleveland, despite his lack of notoriety, by a landslide. During his two years in office he loudly advocated civil service reform, one of the key public issues in the 1880s. His record as a reform governor served him well in the following years. Even reform-minded Republicans such as the young legislator Theodore Roosevelt, Jr., appreciated Cleveland's efforts.

In 1884, Democrats at the national level sought someone to lead them in the presidential election. Americans had elected Republicans to the White House in every presidential election between 1860 and 1880 (Andrew Johnson, while a Democrat, was elected as vice president on the Union ticket in 1864, assuming the White House upon Lincoln's assassination). As governor of the nation's most populous state and with a reputation for reform, Cleveland became an attractive candidate and the Democratic nominee. Republicans nominated veteran politician James G. Blaine to oppose him. Democrats delighted in dredging up questionable facets of Blaine's reputation, and many reform Republicans, nicknamed "Mugwumps," deserted the party to support Cleveland. Unfortunately for Cleveland's reputation, Republicans issued an accusation that Cleveland, at the age of thirty-four, had fathered an illegitimate son and for many years had quietly supported him. Distasteful facts emerged in their investigation and report and led to rowdy Republicans campaigning for Blaine, chanting, "Ma, Ma, where's my Pa?" Cleveland supporters frequently chanted back, "Gone to the White House, Ha, Ha, Ha!" Cleveland never admitted that he fathered the boy, and a recent biographer suggests that he may have supported him to protect a deceased friend. Ultimately, Blaine's scandalous financial reputation and the desertion of the Mugwumps outweighed Cleveland's possible indiscretion, and Americans chose Cleveland by a narrow margin.

Cleveland pursued some reforms as promised. He sought to lower protective tariffs and utilized the presidential veto to stop benefits to special-interest groups. He launched a critical investigation of the railroads and ordered various railroads to return more than eighty million acres to the federal government that had been awarded to them. He also signed the Interstate Commerce Act, which created the Interstate Commerce Commission, the first attempt at the national level to regulate the powerful railroad lobby. He also became the first president to marry while in the White House when he married a young woman less than half his age. A daughter, Ruth, was born to the couple during his first term.

In 1888, Cleveland ran for reelection, but despite garnering a slight margin in popular votes, he lost because Benjamin Harrison achieved a majority in the Electoral College. Re-nominated again by Democrats in 1892, Cleveland became the first president to hold non-consecutive terms when he defeated Harrison. Unfortunately for Cleveland, the Panic of 1893 plunged the nation into a deep financial crisis that Cleveland dealt with his entire second administration. Addressing the financial crisis in a largely conservative fashion, Cleveland received no small measure of criticism from the rapidly growing Populist movement. He also faced pressure from a march on Washington, DC, by "Coxey's Army." Though popular with big business, Cleveland also received much criticism for his use of federal troops to break a railroad strike. He dealt effectively with a diplomatic crisis with Great Britain over Venezuela.

After leaving the White House, Cleveland moved to Princeton, New Jersey, where he died in 1908. Cleveland was reared a Presbyterian and especially treasured a Bible given to him by his mother. In keeping with Democratic tradition from the antebellum period, he said little about his personal religious faith. Some biographers have insisted that his Presbyterian roots affected his presidential decisions, but others argue that they had little effect on his policies. He did apparently draw upon his faith during another moment of crisis in 1904 when his precious daughter, Ruth, died.[207]

The White House was a fairly somber place under Grover Cleveland, especially during his first term. Being a very serious man, he seemed to have a distaste for the glitter of social life. This was the case in spite of the mania that swept the nation at the time—the Gilbert and Sullivan rage. However, he soon came to enjoy the theater. According to the 1885 *Washington Post,* "He is said to enjoy comedies and farces and to like a minstrel troupe or comic opera better than grand opera or oratorio." After the 1878 Boston premier of *H.M.S. Pinafore,* Gilbert and Sullivan operettas became extremely popular. During Cleveland's first term, 163 performances of *Mikado* were performed in Boston alone.[208] It was difficult to ignore the catchy tunes of these productions since the Marine Band played them often, even at Cleveland's wedding.

Grover Cleveland was the only president who married in the White House. The ceremony was on 2 June 1886 when President Cleveland wed the daughter of his former law partner, Oscar Folsom. Frances became a charming First Lady, devoted wife, and mother. Hoping for a simple private ceremony, the couple soon realized it had to be more public. Since the Marine Band provided the music for the event, John Philip Sousa had to refuse bribes to let some come in as band members. However, one account said that there were at least 150 men in red coats disguised as Marine Band members.[209]

The music at the wedding included the tune "And He's Going to Marry Yum Yum," as well as other *Mikado* melodies. There was also music by Felix Mendelssohn and Richard Wagner. Because of the popularity of the Gilbert and Sullivan operettas, which were satirical of English royalty, journalists, cartoonists, and even performers used this craze to satirize current American politics. Cleveland became "Grover Pooh-Bah" from an episode in the *Mikado* in an 1892 *Washington Post* cartoon. While neither the president nor Frances were known to play the piano, a Steinway grand piano was presented to them as a wedding gift in 1886 by William Steinway, the head of the firm. He was a close Democratic friend of Cleveland. Similar to other first ladies, Frances Cleveland was an active supporter of young artists and musical organizations. Frances was particularly helpful to working women, including women who were performing artists. Both she and the president were members of the Washington Choral Society.

Even though there is no record of hymns being sung in the White House, Cleveland was unique among presidents because he was a close friend of the blind Fanny Crosby—the most prolific American hymn writer of the nineteenth century. Being the son of a Presbyterian minister, it is certain that Cleveland was familiar with many great hymns. Because of his father's death in the early 1850s, Grover and his older brother, William, had to help support the family. In 1853, Grover joined his sibling, who was a teacher at the

Institute for the Blind in New York City. Grover was hired as a teacher of writing, reading, and arithmetic as well as secretary to the administrator. Crosby, who was a teacher as well as dean of students, was assigned to help the seventeen-year-old new employee, Grover Cleveland.[210] Some long conversations apparently cemented a bond between them. Grover often took dictation of Crosby's poetry. Since she had become a Christian in 1850 at a revival service during the singing of Isaac Watts's "Alas, and Did My Savior Bleed," many of the poems Grover wrote down may have become hymns. The two spent many hours together after the day's work was done. This friendship continued until Cleveland's death in 1908, although they didn't have close contact or correspondence for several years during Cleveland's rise to fame.

Later, Crosby professed to have recognized in the teenage lad that he would go on to bigger and better things. Hymnologist Douglas Snow said that Fanny knew all of the presidents who served during her lifetime.[211] This is unlikely during her early years but is probably true from 1846 until her death in 1915. Crosby's autobiography, which appeared in 1906, carried a recommendation from President Cleveland. In March 1908, just before his death, Fanny went to New Jersey to visit Cleveland for the last time. For more than fifty years he had been interested in her life and work. On learning of his death she told a reporter, "Yes...I can give him up, for I have learned to know 'Thy will be done.'" According to Crosby's biographer Bernard Ruffin, "She hailed Cleveland as a 'lovely, noble character,' and a 'noble, faithful Christian gentleman.'"[212] Following President Cleveland's passing, Fanny was asked to write a poem to be read at the dedication of his birthplace, which was being made into a national shrine.

"Guide Me, O Thou Great Jehovah" was the most favored hymn of President Grover Cleveland, according to information provided by Mrs. Frances Cleveland Preston from the research Merrill made public for his 1933 book on the presidential hymns. Written in 1745 in the Welsh language by William Williams, the "sweet singer of Wales," this hymn is not only full of scriptural allusions but serves as a prayer for all Christian leaders.[213] While studying for the medical profession, Williams had come under the spell of Howell Harris, the leader of the Welsh evangelical movement. By 1741, great crowds of people were being converted. Williams was among the converts who, with the initial intent to scoff at Harris's preaching, remained to pray and dedicated his life to Christ's service. After this "Damascus road" experience, he trained for ministry in the Anglican Church. Soon, his bishop took exception to Williams's evangelical views and refused to ordain him as a priest.

Guide Me, O Thou Great Jehovah

Words: William Williams, 1745   87.87.87.
Music: Henry Smart, 1867   REGENT SQUARE

1. Guide me, O thou great Je - ho - vah, Pil - grim thro' this
2. O - pen now the crys - tal foun - tain, Whence the heal - ing
3. When I tread the verge of Jor - dan, Bid my anx - ious

bar - ren land; I am weak but thou art might - y,
stream doth flow, Let the fire and cloud - y pil - lar
fears sub - side: Death of deaths, and hell's de - struc - tion,

Hold me with thy power - ful hand; Bread of heav - en,
Lead me all my jour - ney through, Strong De - liv - er - er,
Land me safe on Ca - naan's side. Songs of prai - ses,

bread of heav - en, Feed me till I want no more.
strong De - liv - er - er, Be thou still my strength and shield.
songs of prai - ses, I will ev - er give to thee. A - men.

Williams then joined Harris's movement, becoming a dissenting preacher. For forty-eight years he took all of Wales as his parish. During his ministry, Harris had some difficulty because there was a lack of good evangelical hymns in the Welsh language. Since the Welsh people were especially good singers, when they became believers they wanted to express the joy of their salvation in song. Harris searched for a person among the itinerant evangelists he had trained until he found God's man for this task—William Williams. While Williams was a great preacher, he was an even greater poet. Eventually he was called the "poet laureate" of the Welsh revival. Hymnologist Frank Colquhoun said that Williams's more than 800 Welsh hymns had a profound influence on the spiritual life of the nation. Elvert Lewis wrote in his *Sweet Singers of Wales,* "What Paul Gerhardt has been to Germany, what Isaac Watts has been to England, that and more William Williams has been to the little principality of Wales. His hymns have both stirred and soothed a whole nation for more than a hundred years; they have helped to fashion a nation's character and to deepen a nation's piety."[214]

"Guide Me, O Thou Great Jehovah" is the best and one of only a few hymns that has been successfully translated into English from the Welsh language. Even though Williams wrote 123 hymns in English, the first English version of this hymn was not made until 1771. Translated by Peter Williams (no relation), it consisted of three of the original five stanzas in Welsh. William Williams was satisfied with the first stanza, but considerably revised the second and completely rewrote the third. The completed hymn in English was printed in 1772 in the form of a leaflet with the heading that it was sung by Lady Huntingdon's Young Collegians. While the students of Trevecca College, to whom this dedication was made, may have sung this hymn when the college opened in 1768, the English version was not available until four years later. Trevecca College, founded and financed by the Countess Huntingdon to train young preachers of the gospel, became Cheshunt College, Cambridge. This great hymn is "a genuine heart song"; the citizens of Wales love it dearly since the song is a true prayer of the heart and has always been sung to vigorous tunes especially suitable for congregational singing.

The tune REGENT SQUARE, which was sung to the text by Williams during Cleveland's presidency, was originally written for Horatius Bonar's hymn "Glory Be to God the Father." The tune was first used in the English Presbyterian Church's *Psalms and Hymns for Divine Worship* in 1867, edited by James Hamilton. He named the tune since he was the minister of Regent Square Church in London at the time.

Henry Smart, the blind composer of REGENT SQUARE, was organist at the "Presbyterian Cathedral," and this tune was included in the same hymnal as his other popular tune LANCASHIRE. Hymnologist Paul Westermeyer said, "Smart was regarded very highly in his time. He composed a number of other tunes…but none [appear] so extensively as LANCASHIRE or REGENT SQUARE." This same tune often has been used for James Montgomery's 1816 Christmas hymn "Angels from the Realms of Glory."[215] American composer Thomas Hastings wrote the tune ZION for use with Williams's text in 1830, and it appeared in hymnals as late as 1956. Following the composition of CWM RHONDDA in 1903 by John Hughes for the annual Baptist *Gymnfa Ganu* (Singing Festival) in Wales, this musical setting has been the most used for "Guide Me, O Thou Great Jehovah."[216] Because it is an inspiring congregational tune, CWM RHONDDA has also been used quite frequently for Harry Emerson Fosdick's text "God of Grace and God of Glory" of 1930.

The imagery of the hymn is drawn from the Exodus story of the Israelites' journey to the Promised Land. Its original title was "Strength to Pass through the Wilderness." The allusions are obvious, but one should note that the entire hymn is a prayer. It's fairly certain that this text was especially meaningful to Cleveland during his second term because of the nation's financial crisis of 1893. The first stanza's last phrase could be better understood as "Feed me till I am no more in need, till the hunger of my soul is satisfied." The second stanza, while coming from Exodus 17, clearly refers to 1 Corinthians 10:4, where Paul boldly declares, "The Rock was Christ." It is from Christ that the "healing stream" flows. This stanza may have been helpful to the president as he dealt with the railroad strike and his use of federal troops in his first term, as well as during the stress related to the diplomatic crisis that he negotiated.

The final stanza may symbolize the physical problems Cleveland encountered, more specifically his cancer. This must also have been a valued prayer during his moment of crisis in 1904 when his beloved daughter passed away. Thus, his life ended as he must have concluded with the hymn writer, "Songs of praises, I will ever give to thee." These songs are not just for a time, but forever in eternity. President Cleveland chose wisely in selecting this positive prayer hymn of comfort to his soul.

BENJAMIN HARRISON

1833–1901

Twenty-Third President (1889–1893)

Mark Twain derisively labeled the era between the Civil War and 1900 the "Gilded Age" due to the attitudes and actions displayed. Others have called it the "Era of Forgettable Presidents" since it seemed as if the best leaders were in business rather than politics. When teaching about the "forgettable presidents," some instructors have chosen to use "tags" or notable facts about each to help their students remember them. Benjamin Harrison is almost always identified as the only grandson of a president to also serve as president.

Benjamin Harrison was born into a prestigious family in Ohio in 1833. He grew up on the family farm near Cincinnati and attended Miami University in Ohio. He studied law in Cincinnati and then moved to Indianapolis, where he began his law practice.

He married his wife, Caroline, in 1853 and, due to his abolitionist leanings, became active in Republican Party politics when that party organized in the mid–1850s. When the Civil War came, he served in the Indiana Volunteers with some distinction. He rose to the temporary rank of brigadier-general and participated in battles in Kentucky and Tennessee, Sherman's campaign on Atlanta, and George Thomas's successful defense of Nashville in 1864. He returned home with a stellar war record and re-immersed himself in his law practice and Republican politics. He held office as reporter of the Indiana Supreme Court and unsuccessfully ran for governor of Indiana. In 1880 Harrison took an active role in campaigning for James Garfield, and he himself was elected to the US Senate. He advocated veterans' pensions and high tariffs, in keeping with party policy, as well as civil service reform. While in the Senate, he also supported the modernization of the US Navy and protection of Native Americans rights.

After the Republicans lost the presidency for the first time in decades in 1884, they sought to regain the White House in 1888. They returned to the Midwest for a candidate since Lincoln, Grant, Hayes, and Garfield had all been Midwesterners. They also sought a war hero once again. Harrison, bolstered by his historic family name, became the party's nominee on its eighth ballot. He ousted the incumbent, President Grover Cleveland, despite the fact that Cleveland actually polled more popular votes mainly because Harrison carried the larger industrial states of the Northeast and Midwest with their larger numbers of electoral votes.

Inaugurated in 1889, Benjamin Harrison pursued the most aggressive foreign policy in decades. He hosted the Pan-American Congress in Washington, DC, signed commercial agreements with numerous foreign powers, resolved disputes with Chile, Great Britain, and Germany, and negotiated the annexation of the Hawaiian Islands, although this particular treaty was later withdrawn when Harrison left the presidency. In domestic affairs he continued to promote veterans' pensions, high tariffs, elimination of the national debt, and the enlargement of the US Navy. He was a powerful speaker, but outsiders generally regarded Harrison as cold and aloof. Though re-nominated by Republicans in 1892, he failed in his bid for a second term when Democrat Grover Cleveland, the previous incumbent, was reelected.

Harrison retired to Indianapolis, where he assumed the role of elder statesman. Though he supported the Spanish-American War, he quickly opposed the rising colonialism advocated by many Republicans. He died in 1901.

Benjamin Harrison was one of the most devout Christians among American presidents. An active Presbyterian, he supported several bills with religious undertones during his presidency. One bill proposed was a "National Sunday Rest Bill," and another was an "Educational Amendment" to the Constitution, which advocated teaching children "the principles of Christian religion." The failure of these efforts undoubtedly disappointed Harrison despite the fact that each violated the First Amendment clauses about religious liberty and separation of church and state. Nevertheless, Harrison's orthodox Christian beliefs were well known by Americans.[217]

During Harrison's term in the White House there was a potpourri of serious musical programs in the mansion. Since the First Lady, Caroline Harrison, was a professional musician, having taught piano in the music department at Oxford Female Institute (now Miami University of Ohio), the variety of musical events was excellent. She initiated the first concerts with printed programs, a practice that continues to the present day. The Harrisons' son gave his mother a Fisher piano as a Christmas present in 1889. Their daughter, Mary McKee, was also a pianist and often played in the White House.[218]

Most of the performers were chosen by Mrs. Harrison. The Harrisons were fascinated by the music of Louis Gottschalk, particularly his popular piano solo "The Last Hope." The First Lady had taught this piece to many students. The hymn tune MERCY is based on a portion of Gottschalk's score. The only hymns sung at the White House that were noted were sung at the funeral of secretary of the navy Benjamin Tracy's wife and daughter. Both having perished in a house fire, the double funeral was held in 1890 in the East Room. The St. John's Episcopal Church choir sang "Lead, Kindly Light" and "Abide with Me" for the service. President Harrison was deeply moved as he supported his colleague with tears rolling down his cheeks. As with most funerals, this is an account of the power of music on the human spirit in a time of stress and grief.

A popular waltz dance called *The German* was in vogue during President Harrison's term. He received considerable criticism for allowing this dance to be performed at the mansion. *The Inland* newspaper reported that it was a dance of depravity, un-Christian, and should be banned.[219] Two typical concerts presented at the White House during President Harrison's administration involved vocalists of contrasting characters. The former prima donna Laura Schirmer-Mapelson gave her "soiree musicale" in the East Room in October 1891. The formal program consisted of operatic arias but concluded with Stephen Foster's "Old Folks at Home." The recital was followed by a state dinner, after which the guests returned for more music. Then, in February 1892 Sissieretta Jones, called "Black Patti," presented a less formal program in the Blue Room, where she also sang operatic arias, some with costume and scenery, concluding with Foster's "Swanee River" and Henry Bishop's "Home, Sweet Home." Later, she sang for William McKinley and Theodore Roosevelt, but she never realized her true ambition of singing on the operatic stage. The *Detroit Tribune* reported that she said, "My color is against me."[220]

From emotionally moving music at funerals to operatic arias, music in the White House provides a unique experience like no other art form. Hymns, in particular, unite Americans in different ways. The choice of President Harrison's most favored hymn—"I Love Thy Kingdom, Lord," by Timothy Dwight—is a reflection of his unfailing belief in the church. Harrison's upbringing was full of Bible reading, family prayers, and hymn singing. The local church provided not only religious activities but also social life for the Harrisons. As a college student, Benjamin made a Christian decision at a revival meeting and considered going into the ministry. During his adult life, he was active in his church, serving as deacon, elder, and Sunday school teacher; he also organized Bible classes for the YMCA. He even addressed the General Assembly of the Presbyterian Church. Being a strong believer in prayer, he once advised his son Russell that "prayer steadies one when he is walking in slippery places."[221] President Harrison refused to do government business on Sunday and held a pew at Washington's Presbyterian Church of the Covenant. The president's life was a testimony of his love for the local church.

Timothy Dwight, who wrote the lyrics to "I Love Thy Kingdom, Lord," was born in 1752 in Northampton, Massachusetts, the grandson of noted evangelist Jonathan Edwards. Young Timothy could read the Bible at age four, taught himself Latin as a preteen, and entered Yale College at thirteen. Graduating from Yale at seventeen, Dwight became a tutor at his alma mater in 1769. He served as a chaplain under George Washington during the Revolutionary War, and his sermons proved to be very inspirational to his regiment. He even wrote songs for the men. When Dwight returned from military service in 1778, he became a successful farmer, a Congregational minister at Greenfield, Connecticut, a state legislator, and a member of the faculty at Yale.

Dwight was named president of Yale in 1795. He not only raised academic standards but also began a spiritual emphasis at the college. Since most of the students had been infected with the "free thought" of Thomas Paine and Jacques Rousseau, when Dwight became president there were only five professing Christians on campus. Under his dynamic leadership, a spiritual revival was ignited at Yale, which spread to other institutions in New England.

I Love Thy Kingdom, Lord

Words: Timothy Dwight, 1800   S.M.
Music: Aaron Williams, 1763   ST. THOMAS

1. I love Thy king-dom, Lord, The house of Thine a-
2. I love Thy church, O God; Her walls be-fore Thee
3. For her my tears shall fall, For her my prayers a-
4. Be-yond my high-est joy I prize her heav-'nly
5. Sure as Thy truth shall last, To Zi-on shall be

bode, The church our blest Re - deem - er saved With
stand, Dear as the ap - ple of Thine eye, And
scend; To her my cares and toils be giv'n, Till
ways, Her sweet com - mu - nion, sol - emn vows, Her
giv'n The bright - est glo - ries earth can yield, And

His own pre - cious blood.
grav - en on Thy hand.
toils and cares shall end.
hymns of love and praise.
bright - er bliss of heav'n. A - men.

In 1797 Dwight was asked to rewrite Isaac Watts's *Psalms and Hymns.* His revision of 1801 restored much of Watts's language but also included thirty-three texts written by Dwight, including his paraphrase of Psalm 137, which Watts had chosen not to versify. This became the hymn "I Love Thy Kingdom, Lord." Dwight's revision, termed *Dwight's Watts,* was so successful that it was used in many Congregational and Presbyterian churches in New England for over thirty years. "I Love Thy Kingdom, Lord" is the oldest hymn by an American writer in continuous use, being found in practically all hymnals even today. Hymnologist Augustine Smith said that Dwight wrote the hymn "doubtless with memories of his twelve years of pastoral service at Greenfield in mind. Dr. Dwight here condenses into twenty lines the ripe scholarship of years, the fire of that poetical genius...and that deep, earnest love for the church which led him to serve in every possible way."[222]

Aaron Williams—a Welsh composer, singing teacher, and engraver of music—wrote the tune most commonly used today for Timothy Dwight's paraphrase "I Love Thy Kingdom, Lord." Williams named this tune ST. THOMAS after Thomas the apostle. Having published several church music collections "for country choirs," this tune appeared in 1763 in his *The Universal Psalmodist*. ST. THOMAS was originally one-fourth of the longer English tune HOLBORN. It was reprinted in New England in *The American Harmony*, a book very popular in the nineteenth century. ST. THOMAS has been sung to Wesley's "Soldiers of Christ Arise," as well as Merrill's "Rise Up, O Men of God" and Watts's "Come, We That Love the Lord." Some scholars speculate that it was an adaptation from a work by George F. Handel.

In the hymn, "kingdom of God" and "Zion" refer to the church. An analysis of the five stanzas reveals why this hymn has held a secure place in church hymnody. The first stanza emphasizes the Redeemer's role of atonement in dying for the church, followed by the second stanza, which states that the church was made and loved by God. The emotional third stanza begins, "For her my tears shall fall, for her my prayers ascend," which leads to the church's shepherd role: "To her my cares and toils be giv'n." The heavenly vision is presented in stanza four, ending with the joy of singing "her hymns of love and praise." The last stanza's reference to "Zion" leads to the "bliss of heaven."

Writer William Hart said, "Deep in the affections of thousands of Christians there dwells this love for the church of the living Christ. Therefore, through the decades since this hymn was written, Christians have assembled in their various places of worship, and have meaningfully and happily sung [these powerful lyrics]."[223] He adds that Christians cannot afford to neglect the church. President Harrison strongly believed in the supremacy of the church over the state. The failure of the Sunday rest bill and the amendment to require the teachings of basic Christian principles to children did not diminish his backing for the church as stated in "I Love Thy Kingdom, Lord." Harrison's inaugural scripture was Psalm 121, termed by some as "the mountain psalm" because of its bold affirmation of faith; it underscores the strengths of the presidency of Benjamin Harrison.

WILLIAM McKINLEY

1843–1901

Twenty-Fifth President (1897–1901)

As the Gilded Age drew to a close, the American political structure continued to choose candidates who would be amenable to titans of big business. At the same time the rapid changes rushed the United States toward the twentieth century. This transition forced national leaders to be more readily equipped for public speaking and more mentally prepared to grasp the tremendous responsibility the nation's emerging power as an industrial giant brought to its people. Forced into this transitional role was a genuinely kind politician from Ohio, William McKinley.

William McKinley was born in Ohio in 1843. Raised by a devout Christian mother, McKinley originally planned to become a Methodist minister. As a young man he taught in a small country school until the Civil War erupted in 1861. He enlisted in the

Union army as a private and eventually served on the staff of future president and fellow Ohioan, Rutherford B. Hayes. McKinley witnessed some of the war's worst horrors and rose to the temporary rank of major by war's end. His life was forever changed by the Civil War, and after the war he chose to study law.

His experiences of the war and his law practice provided his entry into Ohio Republican politics. Hayes, his former commander and governor of Ohio, sponsored him in his political career, and McKinley's home district elected him to seven consecutive terms in the US House of Representatives. After serving fourteen years in Congress, McKinley was elected governor of Ohio for two terms of office. While he was generally conservative, some of his fellow congressmen regarded him somewhat progressive.

When the Panic of 1893 occurred, both Republicans and Democrats fell under attack by the rising tide of Populism. The Republican National Convention of 1896 recognized McKinley's popularity in the key electoral state of Ohio and chose him as its presidential nominee. McKinley chose to hold to tradition and not actively campaign for himself, largely conducting a "front porch" campaign from his home in Ohio, while Republicans campaigned on his behalf using the financial resources of conservative businessman and political mogul Mark Hanna. The Democrats chose popular orator and rising Populist William Jennings Bryan as their nominee. The campaign proved to be one of the fiercest presidential campaigns in American history with the key issue being monetary policy. McKinley's conservative reputation, Hanna's financial backing, and Republican tactics won the day.

McKinley benefited greatly from the fact that the economic crisis had essentially run its course and prosperity had returned for large segments of the American economy. However, he soon found the nation embroiled in a conflict with Spain over Cuba. Initially, McKinley tried to keep the country out of involvement with the Cuban revolt against Spain. Unfortunately, his efforts went for naught as a rising tide of imperialism, fueled by sensational journalistic tactics, captured the American public's attention. When the US battleship *Maine* exploded and sunk with the loss of 200 American lives, McKinley was forced to act, despite the fact that an investigation ruled that the explosion was accidental and not the result of Spanish sabotage. Ever sensitive to public opinion, under tremendous pressure, and after intense personal agony, McKinley asked for and received a declaration of war against Spain from Congress.

The Spanish-American War was what Theodore Roosevelt termed, "a splendid little war" in which the United States won a smashing victory and propelled the nation into international affairs. Later revelations uncovered that the nation was ill prepared militarily for the war, though the public attached little blame to President McKinley for the lack of preparedness. Fortunately, the superior US Navy and the poor quality of Spanish fighting forces sealed the United States' victory. Despite the objections of anti-imperialists, the United States established control over the former Spanish colonies in the Philippines, Guam, and Puerto Rico, while assuming a "protectorate" over Cuba. The United States also used the war to complete annexation of the Hawaiian Islands.

McKinley ran for reelection in 1900, once more against William Jennings Bryan. For this election, however, war hero Theodore Roosevelt was chosen as McKinley's running mate. Once again, McKinley remained above the fray while Roosevelt hammered Bryan and his policies, capitalizing on US success in the Spanish-American War while deflecting criticism of US rule and ongoing warfare with Filipino revolutionaries. Ultimately, McKinley won by a substantial margin in both popular and electoral votes. McKinley's second term came to an abrupt and unexpected end a few months after his second inauguration when an anarchist shot him while he was in Buffalo, New York, in a receiving line at the World Exposition. He died little more than a week later.

McKinley was one of the nation's most religious presidents. He regularly prayed and openly reflected upon his personal faith. He remained seriously devoted to his Methodist heritage. During his presidency, Christian mission enterprises fascinated him, and he often referred to his personal prayer life. While some of this may have been for public consumption, most Americans believed he was sincere.[224]

McKinley's close association with the Methodist Church is reinforced by the fact that he served as Sunday school director for the First Methodist Episcopal Church in Canton, Ohio, when he opened his law practice. He wrote in 1899, "My belief embraces the Divinity of Christ and a recognition of Christianity as the mightiest factor in the world's civilization."[225] McKinley embraced Christianity with a fervor few could equal. He was definitely a man of his word. The story is told of how Ida McKinley met the future president. Their paths crossed while walking to church in Canton; she attended Presbyterian services while he attended services at the Methodist church, having been converted and joining the church at the age of ten. Historian Jane Cook relates that "after passing each other several times, he suggested they attend the same church. They did for the rest of their lives."[226] They attended the Methodist Church.

As a result of the deaths of both of their young children, Ida had a nervous breakdown from which she never completely recovered. President

McKinley personally cared for his invalid wife for the rest of his life. First Lady Ida McKinley enjoyed hearing good music. The director of the Marine Band arranged a medley of her "beloved airs," calling it *Timely Thoughts*. She thoroughly enjoyed hearing this tribute to her favorite melodies. She also appreciated good vocalists, especially her niece, Mabel McKinley, a professional singer who appeared at the White House. The McKinleys, after reviewing past traditions, set the stage for the state dinner musicale pattern, which became the norm for modern White House entertainment events.[227] There were many pianos in the mansion by this time, and the McKinleys utilized them in a variety of ways. Also during the McKinley administration, the original American two-step dance was introduced on Valentine's Day 1901.

Since during the last decades of the nineteenth century Americans were caught up in the band craze, the "president's own" Marine Band became very important to McKinley. Realizing that there were many types of bands—for example, industrial bands, circus bands, Salvation Army Bands, and school bands—he signed a bill for the Marine Band that increased the players' pay and enlarged the group to sixty performers with a director and assistant. This was the greatest reorganization of the band in their history. The tradition of the fanfare "Ruffles and Flourishes" used by the colonists to honor high-ranking officials during the Revolutionary War began to be used for President McKinley. This English practice involved a short drum roll followed by a two-note bugle call.

A number of black musical performers appeared at the White House during McKinley's terms. Violinist Joseph Douglass, the grandson of orator and statesman Frederick Douglass, played for McKinley and, later, for President Taft. President McKinley was himself a fine musician. Growing up, he sang in the church choir on a regular basis. He had a fine bass singing voice, which often attracted attention during church congregational singing. Perhaps being influenced by his former army commander and president Rutherford Hayes, the McKinleys invited friends and members of Congress for Sunday evening hymn-sings at the White House. Participants at these gatherings probably sang from the Methodist hymnal used in their churches during the 1890s. The president and his family regularly attended the Metropolitan Methodist Church in Washington, DC.

It is logical that McKinley had many favorite hymns. While the beautiful hymn "Lead, Kindly Light," by John Henry Newman, was listed by John Merrill in 1933 as President McKinley's favorite, further research leads to a choice of the equally moving "Nearer, My God, to Thee," by Sarah Adams, as a more appropriate selection. In fact, the attending physician present when McKinley was on his deathbed from a bullet wound, is quoted

Nearer, My God, to Thee

Words: Sarah F. Adams, 1841
Music: Lowell Mason, 1856

64.64.6664.
BETHANY

1. Near - er, my God, to thee, near - er to thee!
2. Though like the wan - der - er, the sun gone down,
3. There let the way ap - pear, steps un - to heaven;
4. Then, with my wak - ing thoughts bright with thy praise,
5. Or if, on joy - ful wing cleav - ing the sky,

E'en though it be a cross that rais - eth me,
Dark - ness be o - ver me, my rest a stone;
All that thou send - est me, in mer - cy given;
Out of my ston - y griefs Beth - el I'll raise;
Sun, moon, and stars for - got, up - ward I fly,

Still all my song shall be, near - er, my God, to thee;
Yet in my dreams I'd be, near - er, my God, to thee;
An - gels to beck - on me near - er, my God, to thee;
So by my woes to be near - er, my God, to thee;
Still all my song shall be, near - er, my God, to thee;

Near - er, my God, to thee, near - er to thee!

as saying, "[The president] whispered softly 'Nearer, my God to Thee, nearer to Thee, E'en though it be a cross that raiseth me…this has been my constant prayer.'"[228] These were his last audible sounds in 1901 before lapsing into a final coma, the words of a hymn often sung at the White House during his presidency. At this time of mourning for the assassination of President McKinley, "Nearer, My God, to Thee" was sung in churches all over America. This hymn was also heard at the death of President Garfield in 1881. Interestingly, this same hymn was played by the ship's band as the *Titanic* sank in the North Atlantic in 1912.

William McKinley is the only president whose telegram inspired the writing of a hymn. When his mother became ill in winter 1897, he had her home in Canton, Ohio, connected by special wire to the White House. Keeping a train standing by under full steam, one night his mother called for her son. Attendants immediately wired, "Mr. President, we think you had better come." The answer from the White House flashed back, "Tell mother I'll be there." On 12 December 1897, Nancy McKinley died in the arms of her fifty-four-year-old son. Hymn writer Charles M. Fillmore, on hearing the story of McKinley's telegram, wrote a hymn titled "Tell Mother I'll Be There."[229]

The author of "Nearer, My God, to Thee," Sarah Flower Adams, was born in 1805 in Harlow, England. The daughter of a magazine editor, she lost her mother at age five, and her father died when she was twenty-four years old. Believing that moral truths could be taught from the stage as well as the pulpit, Sarah dreamed of being an actress. After realizing this dream in a dramatic triumph of playing Lady Macbeth, she became ill and was forced to give up the stage as a career.[230] Having been inspired by her poet friend Robert Browning, she turned to literature and became a frequent contributor to magazines. After writing a long poem called "Vivia Perpetua," based on the sufferings of early Christian martyrs, she realized how much their ideals had inspired her own life.

Sarah's closest friend, her own sister Eliza, composed music for the hymn texts that Sarah began to write. When Sarah married William Adams in 1834, Eliza moved to a place close to the Adams's London home. At their London church, the sisters helped their pastor compile a hymnbook, contributing thirteen texts and sixty-two tunes for the 1841 collection titled *Hymns and Anthems*. Her pastor asked Sarah to write a closing hymn for a sermon he was to preach about Jacob and Esau. After studying Genesis 28:11–17, where Jacob's dream of a ladder reaching to heaven occurs, she penned five stanzas. This hymn—"Nearer, My God, to Thee"—eventually became a favorite of Queen Victoria, Edward VII of England, and also the Prince of Wales. The lyrics were introduced to America in 1844.

The tune BETHANY, which is now sung to "Nearer, My God, to Thee" in America, was written in 1856 by Lowell Mason, sometimes referred to as the "father of American church music."[231] Born in Medfield, Massachusetts, in 1792, he began his musical experiences by leading a church choir as a young man. After spending fifteen years in Savannah, Georgia, he returned to Boston in 1827 to serve as president of the Handel and Haydn Society. His first collection of music had been published by that organization in 1822. Mason began his work in Boston by teaching children how to sing in local churches. Eventually, this led the Boston school district to include music in their curriculum. Thus, he also became the "father of American music education."

Hymnologist Robert McCutchan states that the word "Bethany," even though it is the name of a town often visited by Jesus during his ministry, has no particular significance for this text. Mason used BETHANY for various tunes that he wrote.[232] Although the lyrics came to America earlier, this tune did not appear until 1859 when it was published in the successful *Sabbath Hymn and Tune Book*, a collection of hymns by the professors of Andover Seminary. The BETHANY tune assured the popularity of "Nearer, My God, to Thee" among Americans.

As to the composing of the music for this text, Mason said, "One night, sometime after being awake in the dark, eyes wide open, through the stillness in the house, the melody came to me, and the next morning I wrote down the notes."[233] One of Mason's goals for church music was that it was to be good, often based on European models. Being the composer of OLIVET, the tune for Ray Palmer's "My Faith Looks Up to Thee," and of HAMBURG, the tune for Isaac Watts's immortal "When I Survey the Wondrous Cross," he obviously succeeded in upgrading the composition of church music of his era. Mason composed over 1,600 religious works, including many worshipful hymns. He also established music schools and trained other composers in his ideals, including William Bradbury, George Root, and Thomas Hastings. These, among others, became very successful hymn writers during their times.

"Nearer, My God, to Thee" should be read and sung with the scripture text fresh in the mind. In application, perhaps the "cross that raiseth me" in the first stanza was for Sarah Adams the closed door to her life ambition. For President McKinley, it could have been his invalid wife's continual bouts with epilepsy. Stanza two speaks of "the darkness be over me," which may refer to McKinley's difficult decision to go to war with Spain. In stanza three, the reference to Jacob's vision of "steps unto heaven" may be symbolic that the war lasted only 113 days and America's mission was accomplished. "In mercy given" could refer to the faith of trusting in God during this time. Perhaps the phrase "out of my stony griefs," in stanza four, indicates that the country had learned from the war; this is certainly true when one considers the phrase "Bethel I'll raise" as a reminder of God's goodness and grace. The triumphal last stanza reveals the continuing song as "upward I'll fly." Since William McKinley was very musically aware and a good singer, it may be assumed that "Still all my song shall be" was the theme of McKinley's life. This hymn is a fitting tribute to President McKinley's life of service to his country.

THEODORE ROOSEVELT

1858–1919

Twenty-Sixth President (1901–1909)

As a young boy, Theodore Rooselvelt watched Abraham Lincoln's funeral procession from a window in his family's New York home. The child of a privileged background, he experienced and overcame terrible personal tragedy as a young man. Following the great national tragedy of presidential assassination, he became the nation's youngest president in its history to that point. As president, his dynamic, energetic, and bold leadership launched the nation onto the world stage and instituted progressive reforms in domestic policy. Bombastic, creative, opinionated, and sentimental were all adjectives used to describe him. Of all the unique individuals to serve as president of the United States, perhaps Theodore Roosevelt was the most unique.

Theodore Roosevelt, Jr., was born in New York in 1858, the son of a prominent New York businessman, Theodore Roosevelt, Sr., and a genuine Southern belle, Martha Bulloch. When the Civil War erupted, young Theodore's earliest memories were of the tension that resulted in his household, as his father was a loyal Unionist while his mother had brothers and other family members serving the Confederacy. Despite this tension, the marriage was a strong one, and Roosevelt spent his childhood and adolescence wrapped tightly in a strong family life. This care was especially important since he suffered from severe problems with asthma. His illness and wealthy family encouraged a precocious interest in science, and he was essentially home-schooled. The most outstanding figure in his youth was his father. Theodore, Sr., served as a civic leader and philanthropist, and his son worshiped him. His father also challenged him to "remake" himself physically to overcome his physical challenge. Young Theodore embraced this challenge and spent the rest of his life in constant activity.

His beloved father died while Roosevelt was in college, but Roosevelt overcame this setback and graduated from Harvard. He published his first book and launched a lifelong career as an author, generally writing history or about adventures in nature. Roosevelt chose a life of public service. New Yorkers elected him to the state legislature while he was still in his twenties, where he quickly gained a reputation as a reformer. Unfortunately, his mother and his wife died within a few hours of one another, only a short time after his wife delivered his first child. For a time, Roosevelt went west to the Dakota Badlands, where he worked as a rancher and hunted big game. After about two years he returned to New York and shortly thereafter married his childhood friend, Edith Carow. He immersed himself in New York City and state politics, again gaining a reputation as a reformer and continuing to write.

When William McKinley was elected president in 1896, he appointed Roosevelt as assistant secretary of the navy due to Roosevelt's vigorous campaigning and his well-known advocacy of a strong navy. When the United States declared war against Spain in 1898, it was largely due to Roosevelt's initiative that Admiral George Dewey launched a surprise attack upon the Spanish-held Philippine Islands. An ardent imperialist, Roosevelt resigned from the Navy Department and volunteered to serve in the Spanish-American War. He organized a volunteer unit called the Rough Riders and led them in their famous charge up San Juan Hill in Cuba, winning immortal fame for himself and his men. After the war ended, he returned to a hero's welcome and capitalized upon his fame by winning the New York governorship, despite the opposition of New York state Republican Party bosses who resented his reformist impulses. Seeking to rid themselves of Roosevelt, they nominated him as McKinley's vice-presidential candidate in the election of 1900. Little did they know that only a few months after McKinley's reelection, President McKinley would be assassinated by an anarchist in Buffalo, New York, catapulting Roosevelt to the presidency. He became the youngest president in US history at that point.

Despite his relative youth, Roosevelt quickly became one of the nation's most dynamic leaders. He was easily reelected in 1904, and his young family charmed the nation. He launched a moderately progressive series of reforms, "The Square Deal," which sought "control of corporations," "consumer protection," and "conservation of natural resources." Despite great controversy and questionable methods, he initiated the separation of Panama from Columbia and signed the agreement that gave the United States control over what became the Panama Canal Zone. While construction on the canal was not completed until 1913, four years after he left the White House, the Panama Canal ranks as his greatest achievement, despite its controversial origins. He also built the US Navy into one of the most powerful in the world and launched the United States into international affairs. He was awarded the Nobel Peace Prize for his mediation in ending the Russo-Japanese War.

Roosevelt chose not to run for reelection in 1908, supporting his close friend William H. Taft as his successor and leaving for an extended safari in Africa. Upon his return, however, Roosevelt believed that Taft had departed from his reforms, so he sought the Republican presidential nomination in 1912. Rebuffed by the party machinery but embraced by Republican progressives, Roosevelt created the short-lived Progressive Party and ran as their presidential nominee. Despite Roosevelt's still enormous public popularity, Woodrow Wilson defeated both him and Taft.

Despite declining health, Roosevelt remained active in national politics and actively advocated American entry in World War I. Republicans might have seriously considered him as their presidential nominee in 1920; unfortunately, Roosevelt died at the still relatively young age of sixty-one.

Roosevelt grew up in the Dutch Reformed Church but apparently also was a member of the Episcopal Church with his wife Edith. As a college student he served in a Congregational church. He was outspoken in his faith, and although he had some associations with the Unitarian Church through his first wife, his faith appears to have been orthodox. Many of his ideas and associations reflected the social gospel among many Progressives. He was one of the most visible US presidents with regard to his personal faith. He also enjoyed singing hymns and, like so many other things in his life, did so without inhibition and with great gusto.[234]

The love of singing hymns was a sincere reflection of the energetic, enriching, and diversified music heard at the White House during Theodore Roosevelt's terms. When the unique and gracious hostess Edith combined with the entertainment talents of Theodore, music events became a major, regularly scheduled feature of the mansion's social scene.[235] Even though neither was especially musically talented, the first family was very conscious of America's diverse culture. This can easily be seen in the eight musicales presented annually. Thus Irish, Welsh, and Dutch folksongs were heard along with ragtime, opera, and concert pianists of varying heritage. The president was particularly supportive of research done in American music, and the First Lady kept this in mind as the programs were planned. The Roosevelts also enjoyed Victor Herbert operettas in vogue at this time. However, much serious and sophisticated music was heard at the White House, including a string of "firsts": the first single opera, the first full concert of a noted pianist, and the first recital on a clavichord. A string quartet played a composition by Johann Sebastian Bach, the first one heard at the presidential mansion. Both instrumental and choral musical groups increased in number.

The president liked the singing of the great tenor Enrico Caruso. He commented once that "there have been many presidents but only one Caruso." As to Roosevelt's singing ability, Archibald Butt, his personal aide, wrote in a 1908 letter that the president "had a poor idea about music for while he sang all the choral parts of the service, he was usually an octave lower than the choir on the hymns." Interestingly, Roosevelt's favorite battle music was "Dixie," although he also appreciated "The Battle Hymn of the Republic." One day while riding horseback with Captain Butt, the president voiced his opinion about the text written by Julia Ward Howe: "The line 'as he died to make men holy, let us die to make men free' is universal, catholic and true a hundred years ago as it is now, equally true of Anglo-Saxon or Hindu. Yes, that hymn ought to be our national hymn but how can we bring it about?… Would it not be fine to have a hymn that this great country could sing in unison?"[236]

As for the president's choice of hymns, he confided in his military aide that one day his favorite would be "Abide with Me" while on another it might be "The Son of God Goes Forth to War." He also declared that he loved a translation of a Latin hymn "Christ Is Made the Sure Foundation," "Holy, Holy, Holy," as well as "Jerusalem, the Golden." On 27 July 1908, following the morning service at the Episcopal Church in Oyster Bay, New York, Captain Butt referred to the difference in hymns sung in the South from those sung in the North. Butt said, "I think the South likes strong, sentimental hymns while every one which was sung at Oyster Bay had some poetic value."[237] That did not seem to matter to Roosevelt, who sang all hymns with zest and enjoyed a great variety of hymns as this lists indicates. He often sang hymns from memory even after he left the White House. In 1912 when Roosevelt was running to regain the presidency, he spent a weekend in Emporia, Kansas. The plan was to take the former president to the Congregational church on Sunday morning, but the guest asked to attend a German Lutheran church. His host was delighted to note that Roosevelt stood and sang the hymns without looking at a hymnal. Theodore showed no hesitation in singing three stanzas of "How Firm a Foundation" entirely by memory.[238]

Roosevelt even utilized a gospel hymn in this particular campaign. During the Billy Sunday evangelistic meeting in Wilkes-Barre, Pennsylvania, in 1913, song leader Homer Rodehaver introduced a new hymn to the congregation titled "Brighten the Corner Where You Are." He used it in every service of that revival effort. It became so well known because of the catchy tune and cheerful message that Roosevelt utilized the song to begin each of his political rallies.[239] It was the custom of the Roosevelt clan to celebrate Christmas at the family home in Sagamore. Theodore Roosevelt's daughter Alice Longworth remembered the family singing "Christmas on the Sea" after her father read the Christmas story.

After extensive research by John Merrill, including consultation with former First Lady Edith Roosevelt, one must assume that "How Firm a Foundation" was the favorite hymn of Theodore Roosevelt. This opinion has been verified by hymnologists William Reynolds and Ernest Emurian as well as other scholars. It is a good memory hymn, for its assurances are fitted to many situations and emergencies in life. Perhaps this helps account for "How Firm a Foundation" being a favorite hymn of Andrew Jackson, Woodrow Wilson, and Franklin Roosevelt; it was sung at the funeral of each of these.

Perhaps this hymn became the favored one for Theodore Roosevelt because it is all based on solid scriptural passages. Since Roosevelt knew the Bible well and often quoted favorite biblical verses, this could have been important to him. Each of the original seven stanzas is taken from various biblical promises. The original title was "Exceeding Great and Precious Promises." The president may have also known of an occasion when "How Firm a Foundation" was sung by the entire Seventh Army Corps when they were encamped on the hills above Havana, Cuba, on Christmas Eve 1898. Roosevelt had led his Rough Riders, a cavalry regiment of former college athletes and cowboys, to charge and capture San Juan Hill on 1 July 1898. Later, he claimed this as the "greatest day in my life." He was probably very impressed to hear of a whole army corps singing, "Fear not, I am with thee,

O be not dismayed" to the inspiring Christmas tune ADESTE FIDELES on that beautiful tropical night.[240]

The authorship of "How Firm a Foundation" has always been a hymnological mystery. Its first printing appeared in a 1789 hymnal called *Selection of Hymns from the Best Authors*, published by John Rippon, pastor for Carter's Lane Baptist Church in London. Being the pastor of this church for sixty-three years, he was one of the most influential dissenting ministers of his time. Dr. Rippon, although an ardent admirer of Isaac Watts's hymns, desired to print some newly written hymns. As the result of this publication, many hymns appeared for the first time and have been with us ever since. Rippon's *Selection* quickly became popular; before his death in 1836, eleven editions had already been published. In 1820 Philadelphia Baptists printed an edition.

"How Firm a Foundation" appeared anonymously in Rippon's collection with only the letter "K" as its author. Since the music director of Carter Lane's church was Robert Keene, it is now generally assumed that he penned the text of this seven-stanza hymn. As further proof, the hymn was originally sung to GEARD, a tune Keene wrote.[241]

Since the hymn's initial title was "Exceeding Great and Precious Promises," it would be instructive to note powerful Bible verses on which it is based: stanza one from 2 Peter 1:4; stanza two from Isaiah 41:10; stanza three from Isaiah 43:2; and stanza four from Isaiah 46:4. Other scriptures the hymn uses for assurance are 2 Corinthians 12:9 and Hebrews 13:5. This hymn certainly has the first ingredient of a great hymn: it is scripturally based. This may be the chief element accounting for the extreme popularity of this text.[242]

Another reason for this hymn's wide usage is the tune to which it has been wedded, whether it be ADESTE FIDELES, the tune sung soon after its first appearance, or FOUNDATION, one of the most widely used "gapped tunes," which first appeared in Joseph Funk's *Genuine Church Music* of 1832 with the lyrics of "How Firm a Foundation."[243] A "gapped scale (tune)" is a scale that contains at least one interval greater than a whole tone (for example, the pentatonic scale). FOUNDATION has been the setting most used in Baptist and Methodist hymnals, especially in the South. For these reasons, Theodore Roosevelt probably sang "How Firm a Foundation" to the ADESTE FIDELIS tune. Even though Roosevelt grew up in the Dutch Reformed Church, he often attended the Episcopal Church with Edith.

Ira Sankey, in his *Gospel Hymns* of 1896, named ADESTE FIDELES as his first tune for "How Firm a Foundation" with FOUNDATION as the second choice. The latter anonymous tune has also been called PROTECTION, BELLEVUE, and BRETHREN.

How Firm a Foundation

Words: "K" in John Rippon's "Selection of Hymns", 1787
Music: John Francis Wade, c. 1742

11.11.11.11.11.
ADESTE FIDELES

1. How firm a foun-da-tion, ye saints of the Lord, Is laid for your faith in His ex-cel-lent word! What more can he say than to you He hath said, To you who for ref-uge to Je-sus have fled? To you who for ref-uge to Je-sus have fled?

2. "Fear not, I am with thee; O be not dis-mayed! For I am thy God, and will still give thee aid; I'll strength-en thee, help thee, and cause thee to stand, Up-held by My right-eous, om-nip-o-tent hand, Up held by My right-eous, om-nip-o-tent hand!

3. "When thro' the deep wa-ters I call thee to go, The ri-vers of sor-row shall not o-ver-flow; For I will be with thee, thy trou-bles to bless, And sanc-ti-fy to thee thy deep-est dis-tress, And sanc-ti-fy to thee thy deep-est dis-tress.

4. "The soul that on Je-sus hath leaned for re-pose, I will not, I will not, de-sert to his foes; That soul, though all hell should en-deav-or to shake, I'll ne-ver, no, ne-ver, no ne-ver for-sake; I'll ne-ver, no, ne-ver, no ne-ver for-sake. A-men.

The music of ADESTE FIDELES was composed by John F. Wade,[244] who also translated the lyrics and Latin that are now sung to "O Come, All Ye Faithful." In 1745 Wade was caught up in a "holy war" between the Church of England and the Roman Catholic Church. To avoid prison or death, many English Catholics fled to France, settling in the town of Douay, which had been established by the king of Spain for Catholic refugees. Wade was a music teacher and noted music copyist who spent most of his creative life in France. Even though Wade was a serious music research scholar and excellent calligrapher, he also was a skilled musician. He not only reclaimed old hymns but also wrote new ones. He wrote ADESTE FIDELES somewhere between 1740 and 1744. It appeared in a manuscript at the English Roman Catholic College in Lisbon, Portugal, in 1750. Since the tune was performed in 1797 and following years at the Portuguese Embassy in London, the tune was named PORTUGUESE HYMN.

The music for the refrain follows the pattern of New England "fuging tunes"—tunes that contain one or more groups of contrapuntal voice entries involving textual overlap. The melody itself has been compared to Beethoven's classic tune in his Ninth Symphony. In any event, ADESTE FIDELES, with some alterations, is very effective with the lyrics of "How Firm a Foundation." Even though today FOUNDATION is the more common tune, in Theodore Roosevelt's time ADESTE FIDELES was just as thrilling. Since the president enjoyed singing so boisterously in church during his era, this joke circulated: "On T. R.'s first day in heaven, he told Saint Peter that the choir was quite weak and should be reorganized immediately. Saint Peter quickly assigned the task to T. R. 'Well,' said the former president. 'I need ten thousand sopranos, ten thousand altos, and ten thousand tenors.' 'But what about the basses?' inquired Saint Peter. 'Oh,' said T. R., 'I'll sing bass.'"[245]

"How Firm a Foundation" meant much to the life of President Roosevelt. He understood biblical Christianity as voiced in stanza one. This truth led directly to the Savior, Jesus Christ; the president himself lived with this blessed assurance. Stanza two reminded Roosevelt of the time when he had to build up his physical strength to overcome an asthmatic condition as well as his poor eyesight. Stanza three aided him for certain times as he strove to be strong in his outdoor activities. His extreme decisiveness and brave stand on issues important to his beliefs are reinforced by these words. The strong fourth stanza, with the repetition of the words "will not" and "never, no," even though being negative, illustrates well the positive administration established by this most unique president.

WILLIAM HOWARD TAFT

1857–1913

Twenty-Seventh President (1909–1913)

Despite the fact that Thomas Jefferson described the presidency as "splendid misery," scores of individuals have sought the land's highest office throughout our nation's history. In the case of John Tyler and Andrew Johnson, vice presidents found themselves thrust into office by assassination or unexpected illness and death. Others, such as Herbert Hoover and Richard Nixon, found the presidency the culmination of many years of public service. Few individuals have ever sought the presidency so reluctantly or found themselves so miserable once in office as William Howard Taft.

William Howard Taft was born in Ohio in 1857. Reared in the home of a distinguished judge, Taft's early life pointed him clearly in the direction of law. Among other positions, his father served as secretary of war and as attorney general in the Grant administration, and later served as ambassador to Russia. His father's experiences presaged his own experiences in many ways. Like his father and half-brother, he graduated from Yale. He studied at the University of Cincinnati in his hometown, where he practiced law and became active in Republican politics. Taft loved practicing law and thrived while serving as a judge in Ohio, as US solicitor general, and as a US circuit court judge. In those years, reaching the US Supreme Court became his highest aspiration. His wife, Helen ("Nellie"), had greater dreams, however, and encouraged her reluctant husband to involvement in Republican politics. When President McKinley designated Taft to serve as the governor general of the Philippines in an attempt to calm the Filipino rebellion against US rule, Taft agreed only after his advisors and wife pressured him to accept. Despite his reluctance, Taft proved to be an excellent administrator, sympathizing with the Filipinos while adhering to US policy. By the time he left the Philippines, he had successfully established a civilian government as a territory of the United States and ended the rebellion.

After leaving the Philippines, Taft proved to be an equally adept administrator in the War Department. He served as President Theodore Roosevelt's secretary of war from 1904 to 1908. During this time Roosevelt relied heavily upon Taft as an advisor and friend. When Roosevelt decided not to run for reelection in 1908, he persuaded Taft to run instead as his handpicked successor, despite Taft's reluctance. Taft's victory over William Jennings Bryan demonstrated the public's confidence in a continuation of Roosevelt's policies.

Taft proved to be ill equipped to follow in Theodore Roosevelt's footsteps. Although he exhibited a wonderful personality and sense of humor, Taft remained more comfortable with administering law than with exhibiting leadership. He basically continued Roosevelt's aggressive foreign policy, although he generally urged what he called "dollar diplomacy." He instituted a postal savings system and pushed the Interstate Commerce Commission to set railroad rates, a longtime Populist and Progressive goal.

Largely, however, Taft failed to continue Roosevelt's Progressive agenda. He attempted to lead Congress into tariff reform, but the conservative Congress balked. He upheld the secretary of interior's removal of the nation's director of forestry, thus appearing to renounce Roosevelt's earlier conservation reforms. While he actually proved more effective at breaking up monopolies, known as "trusts," than Roosevelt, he appeared to lose interest in "trust-busting" to control corporations after 1911, and he incurred Roosevelt's wrath for his attacks on United States Steel, which the former president viewed as a good trust. All these actions led progressives within the

Republican Party to renounce Taft and urge Roosevelt to run in 1912 for the presidency. Eventually, the two friends became bitter enemies. When the party machinery denied Roosevelt the nomination in 1912, Roosevelt led a Progressive walkout and formed a third party by the same name. This split in the Republican Party led to Woodrow Wilson's election, despite the fact that Wilson received only approximately forty percent of the popular vote.

Relieved of the burden of the presidency, Taft once again became the jovial person his friends and family enjoyed. Having struggled with his weight his whole life, which reached over 300 pounds while he served as president, Taft lost approximately eighty pounds after leaving the White House. He competed avidly in golf and tennis, and he loved baseball. Friends often remarked that Taft was an accomplished dancer. His alma mater, Yale University, appointed him as a law professor there. After eight years at Yale and upon the death of Supreme Court justice Edward Douglass White, Taft realized a lifelong dream when President Harding appointed Taft to that position. He thus became the only US president ever to serve as chief justice and the only American ever to serve as the head of both the executive and judicial branches. As chief justice, Taft distinguished himself as the responsibilities of the Supreme Court grew. He died in 1930 after years of notable service in that capacity.

Taft was a member of the Unitarian Church. He was generally regarded as a pleasant and moral man, but in keeping with Unitarian ideas, Taft openly questioned the divinity of Jesus Christ and other orthodox beliefs. For this, his presidential opponent in 1908, William Jennings Bryan, attacked him. He suffered little for this, however, when Roosevelt rallied to his side and defended separation of church and state. He also criticized any efforts to utilize religious beliefs for political gain.[246]

There is little information concerning President Taft's musical abilities, but he had a preference for classical music, probably due in part to the influence of his musically trained wife. After a visit to the Hayes White House as a seventeen-year-old, Helen "Nellie" Herron was determined to prepare herself to be a future First Lady. Her upbringing certainly aided her in this ambitious goal. Nellie grew up in Cincinnati, which, because of Germanic influence, provided exceptional musical training and performance opportunities for its citizenry. She benefited greatly from this musical presence, feeling that music, especially the piano, could be her life's work. She became a fine pianist and in the 1890s was the founder of the Cincinnati Orchestra Association. This is only one of many experiences that prepared her well for the position as White House hostess.[247]

As First Lady, Nellie Taft selected most of the musical artists for White House performances. She, along with the president, initiated the "Lenten Musicales," which were scheduled between February and April. These events became established as traditional for future presidents. Besides numerous women pianists who appeared at the mansion during Taft's term, Nellie arranged for a music room in the White House, and the president was assigned a corner where he listened to recorded music of his favorite operatic selections. He especially enjoyed Enrico Caruso. She even bought all the latest records for the president, saying that listening to music helped keep his mind off his troubles. President Taft sometimes chose classical music as encores following musicales. They hosted some choral groups at the White House, including the 210-voice Mormon Tabernacle Choir, which no doubt sang some hymns.

The most outstanding vocalists to sing were baritone Alexander Heinemann and soprano Johanna Gadski. It is interesting that when opera diva Lilla Ormand sang a recital of classical selections at the special request of the president in 1911, for encores he asked to hear "Home, Sweet Home," "Swanee River," and "Robin Adair." Rave reviews were evident when legendary pianist Josef Hofmann played. The *New York Times* reported that "nobody so made the piano sing."[248]

White House aid Archie Butt told the story of President Taft, who had spent the entire day listening to "brain-killing banalities" in his office. When [popular vocalist] O'Connor sang 'My Cousin Caruso' and 'A Warbling Rose' at a Gridiron Dinner, the whole room began to shake and President Taft's smile became an audible and vibrating laugh."[249] Remembering his time as governor in the Philippines, President Taft invited their Constabulary Band to play at his inauguration on 4 March 1909. In 1910 a quartet of Hawaiians performed a series of "melodious and mysterious songs" on their ukuleles.

Through consultation with President Taft's son Charles, John Merrill learned that Taft's favorite hymn was "Deal Gently with Us, Lord." Even though President Taft was a Unitarian, Charles became an avowed Christian and staunch member of the Episcopal Church. "Deal Gently with Us, Lord" was written by William Everett in 1866. This hymn writer also wrote "Almighty Father, Thou Didst Frame" for a 27 May 1869 Unitarian festival. Everett was born in Watertown, Massachusetts, in 1839. After graduating from Harvard he earned a master's degree from Trinity College in Cambridge, England. Becoming a Latin tutor at his alma mater, he was made assistant professor in 1873, after which he received his doctorate from Williams College. The American *Christian Register* printed the hymn

Deal Gently with Us, Lord

Words: William Everett, 1866　　　　　　　　　　　　　　　　　S.M.
Music: Henry J. Gauntlett, 1848　　　　　　　　　　　　　　ST. GEORGE

1. Deal gent- ly with us, Lord, The ways of sin are wide; O
2. Deal gent- ly with us, Lord, Our foes press thick and bold, O
3. Deal gent- ly with us, Lord, So shall we gen - tle be, And

take us by thy ten - der hand, And in thy path-way guide.
who shall fight the war - fare thro'; If thou thine arm with - hold?
like thee with our breth - ren deal In love and char - i - ty. A-men.

"Deal Gently with Us, Lord" in 1866. Six of William Everett's hymns were published in the collection *Singers and Songs* of 1874.[250]

English organist Henry J. Gauntlett was the composer of ST. GEORGE, the tune sung to the standard meter text "Deal Gently with Us, Lord." Born in England in 1805, Henry's father was the priest at Olney parish (of John Newton fame); from age ten to twenty, Henry was the organist there. Serving several churches as organist/choirmaster, Henry Gauntlett became well known as a performer, writer of church music, and organ designer. Having composed thousands of tunes, he was the creator of the four-part hymn tune. IRBY is the only surviving Gauntlett tune in wide circulation today. Set to the text of Cecil Alexander's "Once in Royal David's City," it has been used as the processional at the annual King's College, Cambridge, Christmas Festival since 1918.

While not as well known as IRBY, Gauntlett's ST. GEORGE fits the Everett text perfectly, matching the simplicity of the lyrics. Since Henry Gauntlett is the most prolific of all Victorian hymn composers, some call his tunes "dull" while others say he is the master of the commonplace. His tunes may not be exceptional, but they are always singable, the result of his writing for congregational usage. The great composer Felix Mendelssohn gave words of praise to Gauntlett's music. In 1846, Mendelssohn chose Gauntlett to play the organ for the Birmingham, England, performance of the oratorio *Elijah*. Henry played from the open score to the pleasure of the composer Mendelssohn.[251] Much of Gauntlett's music is found in *The Congregational Psalmist* of 1858, compiled by Union Chapel in Islington. His tunes aided in raising the level of congregational song in that church after many years of use. Since the original name of this tune caused confusion with ST. GEORGE'S WINDSOR, later some editors changed Gauntlett's tune name to ST. OLAVE because Henry Gauntlett was organist at that church in London for twenty years.[252]

President Taft's selection of 1 Kings 3:9–12 as his inauguration scripture was a clear indication of his true desire to attain wisdom to become part of America's highest judgeship, which he eventually attained. Verse twelve is Solomon's request for wisdom, which God granted him: "a wise and understanding heart." The three short stanzas of "Deal Gently with Us, Lord" comprise a direct and yet tender prayer for God's guidance and wisdom, much as is stated in Taft's scripture. Asking for help is in the second stanza as the lyrics implore the Lord to include his strong arm in support of the leader against his foes. With the third stanza's emphasis on gentle but tough love, the prayer ends with the petitioner asking for the same charity given to him by the Lord. What a profound thought not only for Taft as president but also for his role as chief justice of the Supreme Court of the land! In fact, many scholars believe that Taft distinguished himself as judge much more than as president.

WOODROW WILSON

1856–1924

Twenty-Eighth President (1913–1921)

When Woodrow Wilson was a young boy, William Tecumseh Sherman's army had marched through Georgia only miles away. Before the end of his life, Wilson led his nation through a cataclysmic world war, and he had ridden in automobiles and watched the first airplanes fly overhead. In many ways he spoke idealistically of his dreams for his nation and world, but he could also be sternly pragmatic. Viewed as a progressive and a visionary in many ways and for many of his ideas, Woodrow Wilson also demonstrated a lasting conservatism in many areas of his life. In many ways he became one of the most enigmatic of all US presidents.

Woodrow Wilson was born in the Blue Ridge Mountains of Staunton, Virginia, where his father served as a Presbyterian minister. When Wilson was only two years old, his father accepted a pastorate in Augusta, Georgia, and when the Civil War came, the elder Wilson served briefly in the Confederate army. Later, he accepted a seminary position in Columbia, South Carolina, and then a pastorate in North Carolina. Because of his early life in these locations, Wilson's roots in the Deep South would remain with him the rest of his life. The young Woodrow, or Tommy as he was called, struggled mightily in school. Today he would probably be diagnosed as dyslexic. With his and his family's persistence, however, Wilson overcame this disability in part because of extra tutoring he received from one of his father's fellow seminary professors. He also taught himself a form of shorthand that dramatically enhanced his learning abilities.

Having conquered this disability, Davidson College accepted Wilson. After attending Davidson for a year, he switched to the College of New Jersey, commonly known as Princeton. At both Davidson and Princeton, Wilson excelled in public speaking, writing, and history. He attempted to study law at the University of Virginia but eventually began graduate studies at the new Johns Hopkins University in Maryland. He studied constitutional government and completed his dissertation, which was subsequently published and received positive reviews. He began teaching at Bryn Mawr College and then taught at Connecticut's Wesleyan College. After the publication of his second book in 1889, he answered a call to teach at Princeton the following year. While continuing to teach at Princeton, he also taught at New York Law School and Johns Hopkins. By this time he was a nationally recognized scholar and public speaker. He turned down the presidencies of the University of Illinois and the University of Virginia before accepting the presidency of Princeton in 1902. As university president he sought to initiate significant reforms.

Wilson's reform mindset attracted the attention of Democratic Party leaders in New Jersey, who were seeking a gubernatorial candidate. The reform movement known as Progressivism was taking hold in the United States during the Roosevelt Administration, and Wilson's progressive ideas about government appealed greatly to reform elements on the national and state stages. Thinking that Wilson was simply an academic who could be controlled, Democratic Party bosses enlisted him to run for New Jersey governor. Progressives in that state responded enthusiastically to Wilson's candidacy and elected Wilson as governor in a landslide.

With this success behind him, Wilson's supporters began preparations to launch his candidacy for the presidency in 1912. With the Republicans fatally split between Theodore Roosevelt's Progressives and William Howard Taft's mainline Republicans, whoever received the Democratic nomination appeared to be the favorite. Wilson received his party's nomination and went on to win an overwhelming majority in the Electoral College despite the fact that he received only about forty percent of the popular vote.

Wilson aggressively pursued his reform agenda, supporting the Clayton Anti-Trust Act, the Underwood Tariff Bill, and the passage of the Sixteenth and Seventeenth Amendments to the Constitution, all of which were reforms promoted by many Progressives. He supported intervention in Mexico to protect American interests and opposed US entry into World War I when that conflagration exploded in 1914. He suffered immense personal tragedy when his first wife, Ellen Louise, died from Bright's disease in 1914. However, he remarried a widow, Edith Bolling Galt, a few months later and appeared to be a new man.

When a German U-Boat sank the British liner *Lusitania*, Wilson resisted public desire for US entry into the war. In 1916 American voters reelected Wilson with the campaign slogan, "He Kept Us Out of War." Unfortunately, though, when the Germans resumed unrestricted submarine warfare in a last-gasp effort to force British and French defeat, Wilson reluctantly asked Congress for a declaration of war. Seeking to fight the war on the basis of his idealistic "Fourteen Points," Wilson pledged to "make the world safe for democracy" in what he labeled "the war to end all wars." The insertion of hundreds of thousands of American troops into the European theater of the war in 1917 and 1918 tipped the balance of the war in favor of the Allies, and the German-led Central Powers were forced to ask for peace terms.

In an effort to enforce his Fourteen Points, Wilson traveled to Europe to negotiate the Paris Peace Treaties. Instead, however, Wilson found himself forced to compromise on many of his ideals in order to get participation in the new League of Nations. Unfortunately for Wilson, the United States was slipping into isolationism, and the US Senate threatened to reject the Paris Peace Treaties. Wilson took his case to the American people, but in a rigorous and overly demanding speaking tour, he collapsed and apparently suffered a stroke. His wife and closest advisors hid his medical condition from the nation. Despite his collapse, he refused to compromise, and the treaties were defeated in the Senate. In many ways, Mrs. Wilson served as *de facto* president in the remaining months of his term. Wilson retired from public life and died in 1924.

Wilson was reared a devout Presbyterian, and his policies were often dictated by his religious beliefs. His eschatology appears to have been post-millennial, and he apparently hoped that the ideals he promoted would help usher in a lasting era of peace and prosperity. While he was extremely stubborn and hard-headed, he appears to have been a moral man, except for a marital indiscretion during his first marriage. He publicly announced his strong Presbyterian beliefs, especially his predestinarianism. After his election, he reportedly announced, "God ordained that I should be the next President of the United States."[253]

Woodrow Wilson was one of our most musical presidents. Noted American baritone David Bispham said, "President Wilson is devoted to music and something of a singer himself with a tenor voice of considerable power and sweetness." Ignacy Paderewski viewed the president as an "all-around, highly educated man who recognized intellectually that music was a part of human progress."[254] Both Woodrow and his brother grew up playing violin, a practice Woodrow continued into his young adult years. He sang in the college quartet while at the University of Virginia and participated in the glee clubs at both Princeton and Johns Hopkins Universities, where he also sang in the Chapel Choir. His interest in music is evident when, during World War I, the president asserted, "Music now more than ever before, is a national need."

Wilson's first wife, Ellen, was a lady of refined tastes with a fondness for art and music. As First Lady she painted in a third-floor studio at the White House. The Wilsons' daughter, Margaret, after studying voice at Peabody Conservatory in Baltimore, sang three concerts at the mansion. Wilson's second wife, Edith, was also an accomplished musician. Margaret, together with her mother and stepmother, arranged most of the White House musical programs. The president enjoyed vaudeville and musical comedies, but also encouraged "sing-alongs." Often the family would gather around the piano and sing favorite hymns and popular songs.

One of the most significant musicales during Wilson's administration was the 1914 appearance of the Russian Cathedral Choir from New York's St. Nicholas Cathedral. Among the thirty-five men and boys who sang Russian *a cappella* music was young Peter Wilhousky, who later created the stirring concert arrangement of "The Battle Hymn of the Republic," which today is sung the world over. Music for the Wilsons had a therapeutic value. Not only did President and Mrs. Wilson listen to America's new voice—the Victrola— but sometimes Wilson relaxed by singing with harp accompaniment. As the storm clouds of World War I were gathering, following a diplomatic dinner, harpist Melville Clark recalls an incident when the president asked that they—the president and Clark—retire to the back portico of the White House. President Wilson requested Clark to play "Drink to Me Only with Thine Eyes"; soon the president began to sing in a clear, lyric tenor voice: "He then suggested one song after another—Scotch and Irish songs and those of Stephen Foster. He sang with faultless diction, and it was nearly midnight when he stood up. And now, it pleased me to note, he was amazingly buoyant, relaxed and unworried."[255]

One cannot talk about President Wilson and his life without discussing his faith. His deep Christian beliefs were nurtured by daily Bible reading; he argued that the Bible was the one supreme source of revelation of the meaning of life.[256] He said grace before meals, prayed morning and night, and often attended prayer meetings. The president preferred to exclude the word "Judeo" from the characterization of the nation's religious heritage. President Wilson's choice of Psalm 119:43–46 for his second inauguration proved to be a startling prediction of later peace conferences: "And take not the word of truth utterly out of my mouth. For I have hoped in thine ordinances. So shall I observe thy law continually for ever and ever. And I shall walk at liberty; for I have sought thy precepts. I will also speak of thy testimonies before kings and shall not be put to shame." This biblical injunction says that only when man observes the law of truth can he walk in liberty. Combined with Isaiah 32, which states that the ultimate result of righteousness is peace, one sees how the Bible guided the president toward his goal of world peace. Learning of the deceitfulness of the peace negotiators at Versailles, Wilson quickly realized that no abiding peace could be achieved without belief in truth and honesty. Christ said, "Ye shall know the truth and the truth shall make you free." With the grueling eighteen-hour meetings in Paris and strenuous travel dates in the United States to convince people of his proposals, the president gave his life for his Christian ideals.

Three hymns have been mentioned among President Wilson's most favored. "How Firm a Foundation," which boldly speaks of the faith of God's word as the ultimate truth, is certainly a fine choice. "Onward Christian Soldiers," which uses images of war and marching as metaphors for life and faith's journey, would have had great appeal for this president since Wilson brought our nation into war. However, President Wilson's greatest desire was for peace, which is emphasized in the hymn "It Is Well with My Soul," his third favorite. In his attempt to form the League of Nations based on his fourteen-point plan, which he tried to negotiate in the Paris peace conference, peace was his highest desire. Nevertheless, the resulting Treaty of Versailles combined with the rejecting of Congress to enter the League of Nations was very disappointing to the president. Theologian J. W. Storer said, "Ignoring the Son of God was the fatal weakness of the Treaty of Versailles; it would have been the fatal defect in Wilson's League of Nations had it been adopted by the United States. It is the fatal deficiency in any treaty."[257] In essence, peace is impossible as long as the truth of righteousness in Christ is ignored.

It Is Well with My Soul

Words: Horatio G. Spafford, 1873
Music: Philip P. Bliss, 1876

Irregular
VILLE DU HAVRE

1. When peace like a riv-er at-tend-eth my way, When
2. Tho' Sa-tan should buf-fet, tho' tri-als should come, Let
3. My sin — oh, the bliss of this glo-ri-ous tho't: My
4. And, Lord, haste the day when the faith shall be sight, The

sor-rows like sea-bil-lows roll, What-ev-er my lot, Thou hast
this blest as-sur-ance con-trol, That Christ hath re-gard-ed my
sin, not in part but the whole, Is nailed to His cross, and I
clouds be rolled back as a scroll, The trump shall re-sound, and the

taught me to say: "It is well, it is well with my soul."
help-less es-tate, And hath shed His own blood for my soul.
bear it no more; Praise the Lord, praise the Lord, O my soul!
Lord shall de-scend, "E-ven so," it is well with my soul.

It is

well with my soul, it is well, it is well with my soul!
It is well with my soul,

Many great hymns are born out of suffering and are often created following a tragic event in the life of the hymn writer. Suffering ignites creative expression, which eventually gives comfort to those in bereavement. Horatio Spafford, the author of "It Is Well with My Soul," was a successful lawyer and real estate investor in Chicago in the 1860s. An active Presbyterian layman, he was blessed with a loving wife and four young daughters. Being a deeply spiritual person, he was devoted to Bible study, giving liberally to missions and actively assisting in street ministries and food kitchens. As a businessman, he was the guiding force behind the construction of the first Young Men's Christian Association (YMCA). In addition, he was a major supporter of the evangelistic efforts of Dwight L. Moody. All four of his daughters made professions of faith under Moody.

However, the great Chicago fire of 1871 wiped out most of his real estate holdings, and the financial loss had a devastating effect on his wife's health. Since doctors recommended an extended vacation, Spafford took his entire family to New York to board a ship bound for Europe. The trip would also provide an opportunity for him to assist Moody in the London evangelistic campaign. But just before their departure, Horatio was notified of a business problem in Chicago; he updated the family's accommodations on the SS *Ville du Havre* and saw them off, promising to meet them in France by Christmas. Unfortunately, on 23 November 1873, their ship collided with a western-bound vessel and sank in twelve minutes, carrying 226 passengers to their watery grave. All four girls perished, but Mrs. Spafford was rescued at sea and taken to Wales. She immediately cabled Horatio two words, "Saved alone." Upon reading it he remarked, "I am glad to trust Christ when it cost me something." Quickly, he boarded a ship to cross the Atlantic; when the ship's captain pointed out the place where the tragedy occurred, Horatio was inspired to write the words that today bring comfort to many people.[258]

The composer of the music set to Spafford's words was Philip P. Bliss, a prolific writer of gospel songs. The music he wrote is the only music sung to Spafford's text. The harmony utilizes a series of seventh chords, supporting a sequential melody that sounds like gentle ripples of waves and swells of the ocean. In adding the short refrain, the calmness of Christian assurance is painted in each stanza's final statement, "It is well with my soul." The tune is named VILLE DU HAVRE, after the fatal ship. The completed hymn first appeared in G*ospel Hymns No. 2* in 1876, compiled by Ira Sankey and Philip Bliss.

Stanza one deals with being satisfied with one's situation in life while stanza two emphasizes that Christ is in control when trouble comes. Stanza three tells of one's sins being covered with Christ's shed blood. Stanza four assures us that with Christ's return, the Christian will find that it is well with his own soul. This hymn provides a capsule of President Wilson's life, particularly the last few years. Determined to hold on to the principles of world peace, he never wavered from his idealism. His theological stance aided him in holding onto his Christian faith as he faced his declining years. The peace that came to him is testimony that the same peace is available to all believers.

WARREN G. HARDING

1865–1923

Twenty-Ninth President (1921–1923)

Unfortunately, corruption sometimes goes hand-in-hand with political and governmental structures. President Warren G. Harding's administration became synonymous with political corruption even though no evidence exists that he personally benefited from the dishonesty. Ultimately, corruption cost Harding not only his historical reputation but also probably his life.

Born in Ohio in 1865, Harding gave little indication in his early years of his potential in politics. After graduating from the little known Ohio Central College, he became a newspaper editor and publisher and married an attractive young divorcee when he was twenty-six. He served as a trustee of his church, participated in fraternal orders and charitable organizations, serving on the boards of several, as well as local business organizations. He loved music and organized a civic band that played at town activities, and he boasted that he had played nearly every instrument in the band at one time or another. A loyal Republican, his support of party bosses and machinery led to his being elected to the Ohio state senate. After four years of service, Ohio voters elected him the state's lieutenant governor. As newspaper editor, Harding played a prominent role in the Republican nominating convention in 1912, nominating William Howard Taft for reelection despite the opposition of Roosevelt Progressives seeking to topple Taft. Two years later, Ohio elected Harding as one of its US senators.

In the 1920 Republican Convention, Republicans could not choose a consensus candidate, in part because of division within the party regarding the Treaty of Versailles and League of Nations. Nevertheless, Republicans also recognized that, due to Americans' dissatisfaction with Woodrow Wilson and the Democrats, they had a golden opportunity to recapture the White House. Essentially, they chose Harding because he had offended no one and some because they believed he could be easily controlled by the party machinery. One of his closest supporters said that he "looked like a president." Harding's campaign lacked any real substance. One Democrat described Harding's statements as "an army of pompous phrases moving across the landscape in search of an idea," and Harding himself admitted that his oratory was "bloviating." Despite this, Harding proved to be a marvelous candidate. In those years, Americans viewed Ohio as the home of presidents and Harding as a worthy successor to his Ohio predecessors— Hayes, Garfield, McKinley, and Taft. Rejecting Wilsonian internationalism, American voters elected Harding by a landslide.

As the Roaring Twenties began, Republicans slipped into isolationism and turned back progressive-style reforms initiated more than a decade earlier by Theodore Roosevelt and Woodrow Wilson. They dramatically cut taxes, concentrated on a balanced budget, and created a strict quota system, especially limiting immigrants from war-torn southern and eastern Europe. They also negotiated several disarmament treaties and drastically reduced the US armed services. Some of Harding's cabinet officials, especially Herbert Hoover and Charles Evans Hughes, were excellent. Unfortunately, however, some of Harding's closest friends and cabinet officers were notoriously corrupt. One instance, known as the "Teapot Dome Scandal," implicated the Department of the Interior, while other scandals rocked the Veteran's Affairs Bureau and implicated the nation's attorney general and an old crony of Harding, Harry Daugherty. Harding, though not corrupt himself, was heartbroken by the course of events. Touring the West Coast in an attempt to prop up his struggling administration, Harding suffered a heart attack and died in San Francisco.

Harding's religious beliefs and practices have been an enigma. In Ohio his neighbors generally viewed him as a pillar of the local Baptist church. Upon reaching Washington, DC, however, Harding's morals and attitudes often demonstrated a character inconsistent with traditional Baptist convictions of that era. He loved to play poker and gamble, and even though Prohibition was in effect, he consumed and served alcohol in the White House while president. He also fathered an illegitimate child, who was born in 1919, just one year before the presidential contest. At the same time, he issued public pronouncements stating that he believed Americans had deviated too far from traditional Christian values.[259]

The musical scene in America during the 1920s was one of fun and relaxed entertainment, a natural consequence following World War I. The development of stage shows combined with motion pictures began to put vaudeville out of business. With the development of radio, recordings, movies, and musical comedy combined with the crazy dance styles in the Roaring Twenties, there was a feeling of "happy times," at least until 1929.

When Warren Harding became president in 1921, it was obvious that he enjoyed concert band music since he could play all the instruments in a brass band except the trombone and E-flat coronet. At Ohio Central College he played in the Iberia Brass Band and later founded the Citizens' Coronet Band of Marion, Ohio. As president, Harding was known to pick up an instrument occasionally and play when the Marine Band rehearsed at the White House. Florence, Harding's wife, was a well-trained pianist, having studied at the Cincinnati Conservatory of Music; in fact, while in the White House, she was known to have practiced an hour daily. Earlier in her career she had even supported herself as a piano teacher before marrying Warren in 1891. She was particularly interested in young pianists, as shown by her having eleven-year-old Shura Cherkassy play a recital in the White House on 17 May 1923. The boy's mother was a protégé of the great Russian pianist and composer Sergei Rachmaninoff.

President Harding was a fan of amateur vocalist George O'Connor, a singer who entertained every president from Cleveland to Franklin D. Roosevelt. His favorite O'Connor selection was an Italian dialect song, "My Cousin Caruso." Since the 1920s was a dancing decade, President Harding also enjoyed the waltz even though there were many other dance crazes popular during his term. After the Marine Band's concert at Mrs. Harding's garden party on 1 June 1921, President and Mrs. Harding went to the East Room with their guests. The *New York Times* reported, "The [Strauss] 'Blue

Danube' [was] played by the Navy Yard Band which the President was unable to resist."[260] This was a new jazz band organized only two years earlier.

Perhaps the most significant musical event for the Hardings was a gala tribute to the president for his support of National Music Week on 3 June 1921. At the White House ellipse, five bands played while 50,000 children sang patriotic songs, including "My Country, 'Tis of Thee" and "The Star-Spangled Banner." The president responded, "I have heard…the great choruses with their trained voices, the great bands and orchestras, but I have never heard such music from the sparkling voices of children of the capital city. It is the supreme music of all my life."[261]

There was a revival of musicales, garden parties, state dinners, and other social functions beginning with the Hardings. The season from 1921–1922 lists four state dinners, five receptions, and a resumption of the outdoor Marine Band concerts. Because of Mrs. Harding's illness, the first part of 1923 was socially quiet. President Harding died that summer of a heart attack.

Although there is no record of any hymns sung at the White House during Harding's administration, it is certain that President Harding was familiar with many hymns. Growing up, he attended his mother's Seventh-Day Adventist Church, and as president he regularly worshiped at the Calvary Baptist Church in Washington, DC. Through the assistance of the Harding Memorial Association, John Merrill determined in 1933 that Harding's favorite hymn was "Lead, Kindly Light," written by John Henry Newman. This unique hymn was also a favorite of Presidents William McKinley and Dwight D. Eisenhower.

The son of a banker, Newman was born in London in 1801 and was converted at the age of fifteen. An ardent student of the Bible and church doctrine, he graduated from Oxford at nineteen and in 1824 was ordained by the Church of England. An interesting comparison can be made between the ministries of John Newman and John Wesley. Both were ordained by the Anglican Church but were staunch evangelicals. Both were eloquent preachers, had magnetic personalities, drew large crowds, and influenced many listeners. Where the two Johns differed was in the manner in which they wanted to revitalize the Church of England. Wesley's approach was to take the gospel to the masses with the message of personal salvation and for-giveness. Newman, however, "became increasingly opposed to this evangelical emphasis, expressing concern that it lacked appropriate dignity and rever-ence. He claimed that a true religious experience could only be attained through proper church forms and rituals."[262]

In order to receive a new perspective on his religious beliefs, Newman scheduled a trip to Rome, where he talked with a cardinal of the Catholic

Church. This discussion still left his heart in conflict. He went on to Sicily, where he had a wretched, miserable stay, contracting the dreaded Sicilian fever and nearly dying. When strong enough, he began his journey back to England on a small boat loaded with oranges going to France. On the Mediterranean Sea, Newman had great physical, emotional, and spiritual despair; in his condition, he could only pray and hope for "light in the darkness" of his life. On 16 June 1833, he penned the words of a hymn, pleading for God's guidance.[263] Newman partially based this poem on Exodus 13:21–22, and he named it "The Pillar of the Cloud." First published in March 1834 in *The British Magazine*, it had the heading "Faith—Heavenly Leadings." Two years later, Newman printed it with "Light in the Darkness" as its title. This poem was eventually named "Lead, Kindly Light."

After his arrival in England, Newman became the dynamic leader of the Anglican High Church emphasis called the Oxford movement. This group of scholars and theologians sought to call attention to three things: apostolic succession; the administration of the sacraments in obtaining salvation; and a return to the ancient forms of worship, including Latin and Greek hymns. An eventual product of the movement was *Hymns Ancient and Modern* in 1861. Newman preached his last sermon as an Anglican in 1843. He became a leader in England's Catholic Church and was made cardinal in 1879. Among his many accomplishments, he is best remembered as the author of "Lead, Kindly Light." Hymnologist H. Augustine Smith says this is because of the hymn's depiction of an intense spiritual struggle, the mood of a fervent and humble prayer, a description of trials and hardships, and the sublime confidence in the final "dawn."[264] Perhaps these are also some of the reasons why this hymn was so meaningful to President Harding during his presidential service.

The composer of the music for "Lead, Kindly Light" was John Bacchus Dykes, one of the leading church musicians of the nineteenth century. An Anglican clergyman, Dykes was well known as an organist and composer of hymn tunes. A church organist from ten years of age, he served for some time as precentor at Durham Cathedral. For fourteen years Dykes was vicar at St. Oswald's, where he often played new tunes for his family and friends, welcoming suggestions. Composing nearly 300 tunes, they are notable for their "singableness." Even Newman admitted that it was not his words that made "Lead, Kindly Light" so meaningful; rather, the tune caused Christians everywhere to treasure the hymn.

Even though the tune is sometimes called ST. OSWALD, it is known more often as LUX BENIGNA, which is Latin for "kindly light." The tune is a perfect match for the text, according to most scholars. Interestingly, while the words were written when the author was on the calm quietness of the sea, the

Lead, Kindly Light

Words: John H. Newman, 1833
Music: John B. Dykes, 1867

10.4.10.4.10.10.
LUX BENIGNA

1. Lead kind-ly Light a-mid th'en-cir-cling gloom   Lead   Thou me
2. I   was not ev - er thus nor prayed that Thou   Shouldst lead me
3. So   long Thy pow'r hath blest me, sure it still   Will   lead me

on;   The night is dark, and I am far from home;   Lead Thou me
on;   I   loved to choose and see my path; but now   Lead Thou me
on   O'er moor and fen, o'er crag and tor-rent, till   The night is

on;   Keep Thou my   feet;   I   do not ask   to   see
on.   I   loved the   gar - ish day, and spite   of   fears,
gone;   And with the   morn those an-gel fac - es   smile,

The   dis-tant   scene, one step e-nough   for me.
Pride ruled my   will: re-mem-ber not   past years.
Which I have   loved long since, and lost   a-while.   A - men.

melody came from the roar of London traffic in 1867. Nevertheless, the union of the two is quite harmonious. Paul Westermeyer states, "Dykes was clearly a Romantic, as LUX BENIGNA demonstrates…[but] he did not escape one of the Romantic snares that [Erik] Routley isolated so well, writing 'listener's music'…better performed by a choral group than a congregation."[265] Quoting Routley again, Westermeyer says that Dykes's music evidences restraint, which may be the reason for its "lovable" quality. Many churches and hymnal editors have approved of its soothing melody and lush harmony in spite of some other contrary opinions.

Stanza one of "Lead, Kindly Light" begins with a solemn and humble prayer for guidance, indicating the unworthiness of the singer in the path set for him to follow. President Harding often felt at a loss on how to handle the situations in which he found himself. In his reliance too much on others, he often lost control. In stanza two, the author reminds one of pride in position and prays resolutely for help in spite of fears. The confidence in stanza three may have offered encouragement to President Harding in the realization that things would work out for the best as the "dawn" approaches. The dawn of the light is the recurring theme of the entire hymn.

CALVIN COOLIDGE

1872–1933

Thirtieth President (1923–1929)

American presidents have generally been colorful characters. Indeed, it has often been a vibrant public persona that has contributed significantly to the election of presidential candidates. Some, the electorate has given recognized nicknames like "Old Hickory" or "Honest Abe." Others, like Ulysses S. Grant, Theodore Roosevelt, and Dwight Eisenhower have been elected because of well-known war records that made them recognizable to the US public. On the other hand, some American presidents have been elected despite the fact that they have been little known before they were elected or had little to distinguish them from their competitors. One such president was Calvin Coolidge.

Calvin Coolidge was born in Vermont in 1872. His father was a shopkeeper and notary public. Coolidge graduated from Amherst

College and studied law. Later, he became involved in Republican politics. Voters in Northampton, Massachusetts, where Coolidge practiced law, elected him city councilman. After five years in local offices, he served a term in the state legislature and then was elected as Northampton mayor. After four years back in the state legislature, Massachusetts voters elected him lieutenant governor and, in 1918, governor. After two years as governor, he received the Republican Party's nomination for vice president and was elected in 1920.

Coolidge kept a low profile during the first two years of Harding's administration. Known for his honesty and frugality, the corruption and excesses of the Harding years must have appalled him. When Coolidge received word of Harding's sudden death, he took the oath of office upon the family Bible as his notary public father administered the oath of office. A man of few words, Coolidge earned the nickname "Silent Cal." His main success as president was, as 1928 Democratic presidential nominee Al Smith stated, "to restore the dignity and prestige of the Presidency when it had reached the lowest ebb in our history…in a time of extravagance and waste." Smith also acknowledged that Coolidge was "distinguished for character more than for heroic achievement."

Americans admired Coolidge's character and returned him to the White House in 1924. In fact, it is quite possible that had he chosen to run again in 1928, he would have been reelected. His conservative foreign policies represented the isolationism rampant in the United States in the aftermath of World War I, and he vetoed any congressional legislation that he believed endangered the prosperity of the Roaring Twenties. His vetoes included legislation that appeared to help farmers then suffering from an agricultural price crisis that presaged the Great Depression, despite the fact that this legislation was popular with many and probably was needed to soften the impact of declining prices in the aftermath of World War I. He simply believed that this legislation, and other similar legislation to help slumping industries not enjoying prosperity, created dangerous precedents and went against the Constitution.

Coolidge was known for being as frugal with his words as he was with the nation's budget. One of his most famous pronouncements, "The business of America is business," was ridiculed at the time but is probably truer than many would care to admit. He exhibited an amazingly dry sense of humor and, despite his rather stern visage and the perception of his having a puritanical and boring personality, proved to be one of the most accessible of all presidents, even allowing himself to be photographed in a feather war bonnet and in cowboy apparel. His dry wit is, in fact, legendary. In earlier years, while presiding over the Massachusetts senate, Coolidge witnessed a heated debate in which one senator told another that he "could go to hell." Too furious to respond, the insulted senator asked Coolidge to reply on his behalf. Coolidge calmly and dryly answered, "I've looked up the law, Senator, and you don't have to go there." On another occasion, a woman at a dinner party seated next to Coolidge told him that she had made a bet that she could get Coolidge to engage in at least three words of conversation with her. He never looked at her, but said quietly, "You lose."

In 1928, Coolidge decided not to run for reelection. He simply stated, "I choose not to run for president in 1928." He retired to New England, where he witnessed the unfolding of the Great Depression. He died at the height of the Depression in early 1933, clearly disillusioned by the course of events.

Coolidge's baptized name was John Calvin, after the great reformer, and his religious upbringing was significant. He attended church and Sunday school regularly while growing up. Late in life, he affiliated with the Congregationalist Church. He had held off on this decision because he doubted his ability to "set that example" he believed necessary. However, he defended religious liberty during his presidency while he also made statements that promoted the role of religion in the development and reforming of national character.[266]

The mid-1920s evidenced a growing awareness of the potential of the country's own musical life. During this prosperous time, the Coolidges' interest in American musical talent was reflected in the White House list of performers, in spite of the fact that neither President Coolidge nor his wife, Grace, had much musical ability. Even though Coolidge cared little for the theater or musical entertainment, he still wrote a lengthy article in September 1923 for *The Musician* magazine, stating, "Music is the art directly representative of democracy. If the best music is brought to the people, there need be no fear about their ability to appreciate it."[267] Mrs. Coolidge was not only a popular hostess, but also came from a background that fostered the love of music, through what she termed as the "family orchestra." She often attended musical concerts in Washington, evoking a comment from her husband: "I don't see why you have to go out to get your music. There are four pianos in the White House."

Grace Coolidge had a nice singing voice, according to the legendary Al Jolson, who was invited to the mansion in 1924 to help launch President Coolidge's election campaign. After telling a few presidential jokes, Jolson belted out in song, "Keep cool with Coolidge," and Grace joined in. Her clear soprano voice caught his attention; he invited her to continue, and they sang the song together several times.

When the president and his wife were aboard the presidential yacht *Mayflower* on a Sunday, they always held church services. Author Jane Hampton Cook points out that Mrs. Coolidge always sang the hymns lustily.[268] Grace's charm and vivacity proved a perfect complement to President Coolidge's reserved manner. Her image as an elegant and vibrant First Lady was the reason that the Secret Service nicknamed her "Sunshine." She loved to interact with people; she simply liked to make them feel right at home, just as her father had the people at his church.[269]

The Coolidges continued the Lenten musicales begun by President Taft. The performers for March 1924 were Sergei Rachmaninoff, Greta Torpadie, Marguerite D'Alvarez, John Barclay, John Charles Thomas, and Erica Morini. The presidential family also hosted more choirs than had ever before sung in the White House. They welcomed the 250-voice Bach choir from Bethlehem, Pennsylvania, university choirs from Missouri, Wisconsin, Furman, and also from the president's alma mater—Amherst College.[270] When George O'Connor performed, President Coolidge requested a 1916 Irvin Berlin hit called "Cohen Owes Me 79 Dollars." O'Connor thought that Coolidge liked this song because of his New England appreciation of thrift and frugality. The Coolidges also attended the openings of many theaters, with the most spectacular one being at the Fox when a fifty-piece orchestra played Victor Herbert's "American Fantasy" in 1927. With a replica of Fort McHenry as a backdrop, they performed "The Star-Spangled Banner," which was adopted in 1931 as the official national anthem.

Among concert artists, Rachmaninoff was the most popular, giving three programs at the White House for the Coolidges. Interestingly, there were many fine American artists who did not receive an invitation to perform. It was not until after the country recovered from the stock market crash that American composers and musicians became organized as a movement and began to make a real contribution to the nation's musical environment. Coolidge had his own sense of what music was appropriate. He felt that a program by the great black American bass Paul Roberson might offend some southerners. He also felt that it was inappropriate for the Marine Band to play American patriotic tunes when foreign guests were present.

The selection of President Coolidge's favorite hymn by John Merrill in 1933 was made in consultation with Mrs. Grace Coolidge. This was likely a joint decision made between the president and his wife because their selection was "O Love That Wilt Not Let Me Go," a hymn that seems to reflect some experiences that parallel those of the couple. There is no doubt that

O Love That Wilt Not Let Me Go

Words: George Matheson, 1882
Music: Albert L. Peace, 1884

Irregular
ST. MARGARET

1. O Love that wilt not let me   go,   I rest my wea - ry soul in
2. O Light that fol-l'west all my   way,   I yield my flick-'ring torch to
3. O   Joy that seek-est me through pain,   I can-not close my heart to
4. O Cross that lift - est up my head,   I dare not ask to hide from

Thee,   I   give   Thee back the   life   I   owe,   That
Thee;   My heart re - stores its bor - rowed ray,   That
Thee;   I   trace   the rain-bow through the   rain,   And
Thee;   I   lay   in dust life's glo - ry dead,   And

in Thine o - cean depths its flow May rich - er, full - er be.
in Thy sun-shine's glow its day May bright-er, fair - er be.
feel the pro - mise is   not vain That morn shall tear - less be.
from the ground there blos-soms red Life that shall end - less be.   A - men.

they were very much in love with each other, and going through a very traumatic experience in the loss of a son at age sixteen helped prove their love.
Grace's work with and love for the disabled and deaf are in some way
reflected in this beautiful hymn. After studying the hymn, its history as well
as its text, it would be difficult not to conclude a collaboration. One of the
finest hymns ever written, it came out of suffering and expresses Christianity
at its deepest and truest.

George Matheson, born in 1842 in Glasgow, Scotland, wrote the words
of this hymn. He became one of his country's outstanding preachers and
devotional writers.[271] In spite of his blindness, he graduated at the top of his

university class at age nineteen and was ordained by the Church of Scotland in 1866. Matheson never married since the one he loved could not accept his blindness. His family encouraged him in his intellectual pursuits, especially one sister, who literally gave her life to aid her brother. She learned Greek, Latin, and Hebrew, taking theological studies with George. She spent much time reading to him; thus, he leaned upon her heavily. His college essays are in her handwriting.

Despite strong opposition to having a blind pastor, George's first parish assignment was at Innellan. He soon won the hearts of the congregation, remaining there for eighteen years. His sister helped in all his pastoral duties, but especially in sermon preparation. George dictated his sermons in full to his sister, who read them back to him so he could preach them from memory; eventually, he preached from a memorized outline. During the summer, the church had to have two Sunday services because of the crowds. While at Innellan he was invited to preach at nearby Balmoral for Queen Victoria. After hearing Matheson, she was "immensely delighted with the sermon and prayers." It was said of his delivery, "Though his sight is eclipsed, he does see God, he does see into the hearts of his people. For forty minutes he preached. We were instructed, refreshed, inspired."[272]

Most of his "sacred songs" were written when George was a student while on family vacation, but his best hymn—"O Love That Wilt Not Let Me Go"—was written while at his first pastorate. In his own words, we have how he came to write this autobiographical poem, the only hymn of his sung today:

> My hymn was composed in the manse of Innellan, on the evening of June 6, 1882. I was at that time alone. It was the day of my sister's marriage, and the rest of the family were staying overnight in Glasgow. Something had happened to me, which was known only to myself, and which caused me the most severe mental suffering. The hymn was the fruit of that suffering. It was the quickest bit of work I ever did in my life. I had the impression rather of having it dictated to me by some inward voice than of working it out myself. I am quite sure that the whole work was completed in five minutes, and equally sure that it never received at my hands any retouching or correction.[273]

At the age of forty-four, Matheson was called to St. Bernard's Parish in Edinburgh, where he reached his zenith of influence. During his thirteen years there, he preached to large crowds and wrote many of his theological works. The 2,000-member congregation was consistently enriched with his sermons, which blended imagination with reason within a wide breadth of theology. He was especially helpful to the young men.

The composer of the tune ST. MARGARET, which is always and only sung to these lyrics, also had an unusual origin. Albert Lister Peace was organist at Glasgow Cathedral as well as music editor of *The Scottish Hymnal of 1885.* He normally carried with him the words of hymns that needed tunes for the hymnal. Smith relates the following story that happened in 1884: "Sitting one day on the sands of Arran, an island off the coast of Scotland, [Peace] read over the words of Dr. Matheson's hymn. Instantly the music came to him; the transcription of the tune, like the writing of the words, took only a few minutes."[274] However, being a church organist since the age of nine, Dr. Peace developed his musical ability early in life; he was evidently able to capture the complete essence of the hymn with a beautiful melody supported by effective harmony in minutes.

While there is direct information concerning the writing of the lyrics and the composition of the tune to "O Love That Wilt Not Let Me Go," there is no conclusive evidence about the tune name ST. MARGARET. Since the name "Margaret" is greatly revered in Scotland, there could be several possibilities. Hymnologist Robert McCutchan suggests that the name may have come from Margaret, Queen of Malcolm III, King of Scotland. She was canonized in 1251 because of her many benefactions to the church.[275] This is the most probable answer to the mystery.

The hymn is based on several scriptural passages. Among these are Jeremiah 31:3, John 12:32, and John 15:9–11. The theme is the twin parables of the lost sheep and the lost coin, which illustrate the pursuit of the human soul by the Spirit of God. In the lyrics, the Christian sings of his willingness to be found and to receive Christ's love, so he sings about the love that will not let go. He also sings about the light that sheds its rays on his path and the joy received from full acceptance of grace. The lyrics also express thankfulness for the cross, which ensures salvation. Each stanza has specific biblical references, which are necessary for a great hymn to have.

Strong symbols are mentioned in each of the four stanzas. The love of God, not human love, is emphasized in stanza one; love for spouses and children is given to us by God and is similar to God's own love, since he gave each human the capability of loving. President and Mrs. Coolidge truly loved each other, and they dearly loved their children. Stanza two emphasizes the symbol of light, a natural phrase for a blind author. This applies to the Coolidges, as they faced the sadness of not seeing Calvin, Jr., again in the present life. Even America was spiraling downward the last four years of the president's life. Stanza three calls attention to the joy received after experiencing pain. It is further illustrated by the existence of the rainbow following the rain. Since the joy is everlasting, it was more meaningful to the Coolidges. Stanza four begins with the cross symbol as a reminder of what Christ did for sinners. Old ambitions are buried at the foot of the cross, but the miracle is that "from the ground there blossoms red" (because of Christ's blood, which was spilled). This is a powerful symbol of the love of self-sacrifice, which blossoms in the splendor of immortality.

First Lady Grace Coolidge said that since she knew Calvin, Jr., had been converted, he would be waiting for her in heaven. She even penned a poem called *Open Door*, expressing her feelings at this time. This explains why the hymn "O Love That Wilt Not Let Me Go" was so significant to the Coolidge family.

HERBERT HOOVER

1874–1964

Thirty-First President (1929–1933)

Herbert Hoover entered office after years of being the Republican Party's rising star. He believed that the widespread prosperity in the United States heralded a day when poverty would be eliminated in the United States. He left office with his reputation tarnished by his inability to end the devastating Great Depression and with rampant poverty that had destroyed the optimism of previous years. Despite this tremendous disappointment, he lived for many years as a distinguished senior statesman in the Republican Party.

Hoover was the first American president born in Iowa. His parents both died before he was ten years old, and he spent the rest of his childhood and adolescence living with different family members. Finally, he resided in his teenage years with his uncle, who was a medical doctor in Oregon. He managed to receive some public education, although he never graduated from high school. Interested in engineering, he entered the first engineering class at the brand new Stanford University, eventually pursuing a career as a mining engineer. He spent almost twenty years working as a mining engineer primarily in Australia and China and amassing a fortune valued at approximately four million dollars. He also distinguished himself as one of the leaders in the expatriate community in China during the Boxer Rebellion.

When World War I began, Hoover was in London. He aided the American consul in organizing American citizens unable to get home due to the outbreak of war and assisting them in their travel. Later, he organized a humanitarian effort to relieve suffering in neutral Belgium, which had been attacked by Germany. Widely recognized for these efforts and for his administrative skills, President Woodrow Wilson selected Hoover as the chief executive of the Food Administration when the United States declared war on Germany and its allies in 1917. Hoover successfully directed a number of voluntary endeavors that enlisted American citizens in patriotic efforts to aid the war effort by voluntary rationing. The Food Administration promoted such initiatives as "Wheatless Wednesdays" and "Meatless Thursdays" in an effort to control prices and urged Americans to grow "victory gardens" in their yards. Highly successful, Hoover was regarded as one of the rising stars in US politics. His programs and values fit well with Hoover's Quaker religious background. After the war ended, Hoover created the Hoover Institute on War, Revolution, and Peace at his alma mater, Stanford.

Hoover also became increasingly involved in politics. When Republicans gained control of the White House in 1921, President Warren Harding appointed him secretary of commerce. Generally regarded a second-tier cabinet position, Hoover's diligence raised the prominence of the position during a time of unparalleled prosperity. Among his achievements were efforts to improve the Bureau of Fisheries, attempts to regulate the new media of radio, and the creation of an Aeronautics Board to supervise the developing field of aviation. He also supported the construction of the massive dam later named for him and expansion of commerce through the Great Lakes and Canada's Saint Lawrence Seaway. Due to these and other notable achievements, Republicans nominated him as their presidential candidate in 1928. Hoover won the election with an overwhelming majority in the Electoral College and nearly sixty percent of the popular vote.

Hoping to continue to build on the prosperity of the 1920s, Hoover's dreams were dashed with the collapse of the US stock market in fall 1929 and the onset of the Great Depression. A strong individualist, Hoover encouraged Americans to lift themselves by their own bootstraps rather than relying upon government aid. Unfortunately, the country slid further into an economic morass. Many Americans unfairly blamed Hoover for their predicament, giving shantytowns erected on public property the name of "Hoovervilles," calling newspapers "Hoover blankets," and coming up with other such similar nomenclatures. Torn between his belief in limited government and a genuine compassion for the growing poverty and distress in the country, eventually Hoover did come up with a plan for some forms of government assistance that anticipated the "New Deal" of Franklin Roosevelt's administration. Despite these efforts, the country slid further into depression. In 1932 American voters ousted Hoover in a landslide defeat at the hands of Roosevelt. After his defeat he became a leading critic of Roosevelt's policies, charging that President Roosevelt was leading the nation toward a socialistic style of government.

Hoover remained active in retirement. Recognizing his administrative skills, both President Truman and President Eisenhower enlisted Hoover's aid in reorganizing the executive branch of the government. In both cases, Hoover's advice was essential in substantial financial savings. He also wrote extensively, including a manuscript that he was writing at the time of his death in New York City in 1964.

Hoover's humanitarian tendencies were highly influenced by his Quaker faith, as was his strong predilection toward voluntarism. He recognized the tendency in the past toward governmental and ecclesiastical persecution of Quakers and stood strongly for separation of church and state. He was also outspoken on occasion about his personal belief in traditional Quaker concepts, such as the "divine spark," which Quakers teach resides in every human being.[276]

President Hoover's choice of his inaugural scripture reflects the confidence he had in the country's future. Proverbs 29:18, which reads, "Where there is no vision, the people perish," indicates Hoover's vision for our nation's greatness. Unfortunately, this was not realized during his term in office. But the social life of the Hoovers was remarkably elegant in spite of the nation's suffering. Often using his own funds for White House programs, the Hoovers climaxed the "Golden Age" of the musicales.[277]

Lou Hoover was a brilliant woman who spoke several languages, was interested in art, and became an outstanding White House hostess. Even though neither she nor the president had any notable musical talent, they approached the presidency as an opportunity for public service and a sacred duty. The newspaper society editors were thrilled because the First Lady was an experienced international hostess and took her ceremonial duties quite seriously. Lou Hoover was equally at home with royalty as with Girl Scouts.

She often led Christmas-caroling girls carrying lighted candles through the mansion; she strongly believed in the value of group singing. The First Lady was also intrigued with America's musical heritage. She even borrowed a 1799 *pianoforte* from the Smithsonian for a few years in an effort to capture a charming segment of early American musical ambience at the White House.[278]

During the Hoover era, musicales featured mainly American artists; the roster of performers reads like a Who's Who of emerging musical talent. Both the Hampton Institute and Tuskegee Institute choirs sang for the Hoovers, the first all-black choruses to sing at the White House since the Fisk Jubilee Singers. The musicales were mainly soloists, including Efren Zimbalist, Grace Moore, Jacha Heifetz, and Lawrence Tibbett. Sergei Rachmaninoff played so often he became a White House tradition, as did Ignacy Paderewski. When Paderewski—an old friend of the Hoovers—visited, he was often given the Rose Bedroom, which included a Steinway piano. In 1931 Vladimir Horowitz played his first concert in the mansion. After being instructed to say only "I am delighted" in the receiving line, in his broken English to each guest he clearly said, "I am delightful." Lou Hoover set a high standard for White House hostesses; some term her as the first "modern" First Lady.[279]

One of the most unusual groups to perform for the Hoovers was in July 1929 when sixty teenaged boys of the Philadelphia Harmonica Band played. Nicknamed the "Harmonica Wizards," they played sophisticated arrangements of Braham's "Hungarian Dances," Schubert's "Unfinished Symphony," and Sousa's "Stars and Stripes Forever." President and Mrs. Hoover were the first to invite an artist to play for a foreign head of state. In 1931 harpist Mildred Dilling performed for the king of Siam. On 3 March of that same year, the day before he left office, President Hoover signed the bill designating "The Star-Spangled Banner" as the official national anthem.

John Merrill contacted ex-president Hoover concerning his favorite hymn, "Faith of Our Fathers," written by Frederick W. Faber in 1849. It seems likely that Hoover loved this hymn because it reminded him of the persecution suffered by leaders of the Quaker faith. This unique group of Christians was given its name by Justice Bennet in 1650 as a nickname for founder George Fox because the latter bid the justice "to tremble at the Word of the Lord." The term "Friends," which Fox called his religious movement, came from Jesus' words found in John 15:24: "Ye are my friends if ye do whatsoever I command you." The Quaker faith powerfully influenced many people from all segments of society, often in the face of severe persecution. The group's stand against war, slavery, racial segregation, alcohol, gambling, and poverty has brought positive results in human reformation.[280] In 1682,

Faith of Our Fathers

Words: Frederick W. Faber, 1849
Music: Henri F. Hemy, 1864

8.8.8.8.8.8.
ST. CATHERINE

1. Faith of our fa - thers! liv - ing still In spite of dun-geon, fire and sword: O how our hearts beat high with joy When-e'er we hear that glo - rious word! Faith of our fa - thers, ho - ly faith! We will be true to thee till death!

2. Our fa-thers, chained in pri - sons dark, Were still in heart and con - science free: How sweet would be their child - ren's fate. If they, like them, could die for thee! Faith of our fa - thers, ho - ly faith! We will be true to thee till death!

3. Faith of our fa - thers! we will love Both friend and foe in all our strife: And preach thee, too, as love knows how, By kind - ly words and vir - tuous life: Faith of our fa - thers, ho - ly faith! We will be true to thee till death! A - men.

William Penn, a Quaker, founded the colony of Pennsylvania as a haven for persecuted Quakers who wished to emigrate to the New World. A constitution that guaranteed religious liberty was adopted. The colony had no militia until 1756, and little police protection was needed.

Having been raised a Quaker, Hoover had read the entire Bible by age ten. As president, he attended the Friends Meeting House in Washington, believing that the most important Quaker tenet was "individual faithfulness." He regarded war as morally justified only as a last resort when all attempts for peace had failed. Of all Christian bodies, many think the Friends have remained nearest to the teaching and example of Christ. Even though Hoover left the presidency as a rejected man, he was sustained by a faith that brought past generations of Quakers through untold troubles. Never losing his moral strength, he maintained his hope with courage. Historian John Bonnell said, "He lived to see the shadows lifted and himself esteemed, valued and beloved by a grateful nation."[281] His favorite hymn undoubtedly aided him enormously in this process of restoration. These are some hymns heard at his funeral: "Abide with Me," "Fight the Good Fight," "Lord, Thou Hast Been Our Dwelling Place," "The Battle Hymn of the Republic," "Now the Day Is Over," "America the Beautiful," and "The Light of God Is Falling."[282]

For Protestants, "Faith of Our Fathers" conjures up feelings expressed in the eleventh chapter of Hebrews, often termed "the great gallery of gallant Christian faith." Since the New Testament was written, there have been Christian martyrs in all centuries. In singing this hymn, believers can visualize the great "cloud of witnesses" of Hebrews 12:1. It is encouraging to be reminded of the rich heritage of those whose faith in God was counted more dear than life itself. However, the "faith of our fathers" noted in this particular hymn originally referred to the faith of martyred leaders of the Roman Catholic Church during the sixteenth century. Frederick Faber wrote these words with the hope of reversing the Protestant experiment and returning the British to their Catholic roots.

Faber, born in Yorkshire, England, in 1814, was raised in a strict Calvinist home by his father, who was an Anglican clergyman. Frederick became an Anglican minister after graduating from Oxford in 1843. However, within three years, and through the influence of John Henry Newman—a leader of the Oxford movement, which proposed a return to early Christian practice—Faber left the Anglicans and joined the Catholic fold. Noticing a great lack of congregational hymnody and remembering the singing in worship of his boyhood, he made it his life's mission to write hymns that promoted the history and teachings of his adopted church.[283] Of the 150 hymns he wrote (equal to the number of psalms), "Faith of Our Fathers" is his best known. This text first appeared in 1849 in Faber's *Jesus and Mary, or Catholic Hymns for Singing and Reading*. Non-Catholic hymnals eliminate stanza three, which clearly speaks of "Mary's prayers." Many Christian bodies sing some of Faber's other hymns, most notably "There Is a Wideness in God's Mercy." Faber's hymns have wide appeal because they possess the same power and quality of evangelical hymn writers John Newton, William Cowper, and Charles Wesley, who greatly influenced Frederick when he was an Anglican.

The composer of the music almost universally sung to "Faith of Our Fathers" was Henri F. Hemy, organist at St. Andrews Catholic Church in New Castle. The tune comes from the second part of Hemy's hymnal *Crown of Jesus Music* published in 1864. Since the music was first set to the text beginning, "Sweet Saint Catherine, maid most pure, teach us to meditate and pray," it was named ST. CATHERINE in honor of this fourth-century Christian martyr from Alexandria. The final eight measures of the hymn were added by James G. Walton in 1874 with the altered music appearing in his *Music for the Holy Communion Office.*[284] This version is sung today.

This hymn was evidently very significant for President Hoover. The "glorious word" of the Christian faith, as exemplified in the lives of Quakers, is echoed in stanza one. The second stanza clearly speaks of religious liberty with "heart and conscience free," even of those in prison. The possibility of children dying for their faith is also indicated in this verse. The last stanza outlines the love of "friend and foe," which undergirds a pacifist's view. It also includes the thought that love is not only taught in sermons, but also by the example of a "virtuous life." Each stanza concludes with Walton's addition, stating, "Faith of our fathers, holy faith! We will be true to thee till death!" St. Philip, who founded the Order of the Oratory in 1564 and whom Newman and Faber followed by establishing "oratorios" in England, said, "Only let a little love enter and the rest will follow."[285] For President Hoover, love was the "divine spark" that God gives to every human; it is presented in his most favored hymn.

FRANKLIN D. ROOSEVELT

1882–1945

Thirty-Second President (1933–1945)

All American presidents make multiple important decisions. Most American presidents face a national crisis of some kind. Presidents James Madison, Martin Van Buren, Abraham Lincoln, Grover Cleveland, Woodrow Wilson, and Herbert Hoover each confronted a major domestic or international crisis. Only one American president has had to face two of the most cataclysmic events in world history. Incidentally, that same individual is the only American president ever elected after being stricken with a normally debilitating disease. Yet, through it all, Franklin Delano Roosevelt maintained a spirit of optimism and a desire to make his nation and his world a better place.

Unlike some notable American presidents, such as Andrew Jackson and Abraham Lincoln, who came from the humblest of origins, Franklin Roosevelt was born into privilege. His family was one of the oldest and wealthiest families in the state of New York, and he was distantly related (a fifth cousin) to another president, Theodore Roosevelt. In fact, his godfather was Elliott Roosevelt, the older brother of Theodore Roosevelt. As a child and adolescent, young Franklin had the best of everything that an American patrician could experience in the last decades of the nineteenth century: life at the family mansion at Hyde Park, summers at Campobello in Maine, excellent tutoring, travel, books, exposure to culture and money, education at an exclusive private prep school, and the mark of a young American aristocrat, education at Harvard. Tall, handsome, patrician, well connected, well traveled, and with a fine education, he married a distant cousin, Eleanor, the niece of President Theodore Roosevelt, in 1905, and attended law school. Eleanor would bear Roosevelt five children who survived infancy and become a distinct asset to his growing political future.

After serving in the New York state legislature, Roosevelt went to Washington, DC, in the presidential administration of President Woodrow Wilson, serving as Wilson's assistant secretary of the navy prior to and during World War I. He was clearly a rising star in the political firmament of the Democratic Party, which selected him as its vice-presidential nominee in the election of 1920. After a defeat in which he distinguished himself, tragedy struck. While on vacation in Maine, Roosevelt contracted polio at the age of thirty-nine. Despite a painful illness and recovery that never allowed him the use of his legs, Roosevelt made a political comeback. After several years in private business, Roosevelt ran successfully for governor of New York and was reelected in 1930. As governor of the nation's most populous state at the beginning of the Great Depression, he gained a reputation as an executive who could "do something" about the Depression.

Elected by a landslide to the presidency in 1932, Roosevelt addressed the Great Depression after assuming office in March 1933. Utilizing a suave and calming personality, he spoke to the common people of the nation through a series of "fireside chats" in which he told Americans, "There is nothing to fear but fear itself." However, his programs were more than rhetoric. Utilizing assertive deficit spending and an "alphabet soup" of government programs known collectively as the "New Deal," FDR (as he came to be known) restored confidence in the US government and alleviated the worst elements of a depression that had led to twenty-five percent unemployment and severe underemployment that had spread worldwide. While his New Deal programs did not completely restore the American economy, they did bring enough relief, recovery, and reform to encourage Americans, and he won his reelection in 1936. Many of these changes, like the creation of the Social Security program, the Federal Deposit Insurance Corporation, and the Securities and Exchange Commission remain in place today and are accepted components of American life, playing a significant role in this nation's affairs.

In the closing years of the 1930s, Roosevelt's and the nation's attention increasingly focused upon the growing specter of war in Europe and Asia. Recognizing America's lack of preparation for war as World War II erupted, Roosevelt carefully negotiated support for Great Britain as Nazi Germany overran Europe and the United States remained locked in isolation. He also sought to limit militarist Japanese expansion in China. In 1940, Roosevelt chose to run for an unprecedented third term as president and was reelected.

After Japan's surprise attack on Pearl Harbor, Roosevelt rallied Americans to unparalleled heights as the United States became the arsenal of democracy and millions of American soldiers went to Asia and Europe to combat Japan, Germany, and Italy. He forged an alliance with such international leaders as Winston Churchill, Joseph Stalin, and Chiang Kai-Shek and oversaw an Allied war effort unlike any the world had ever seen. He worked with George Marshall to select Dwight Eisenhower to command the Allied war effort in Europe and led the United States in its secret development of the first atomic weapons. As the Allies moved toward victory in 1944, FDR was elected to a fourth term even though his declining health meant that he probably would not survive to serve the full term. Like his predecessor, Woodrow Wilson, he sought to establish an international organization that would secure peace around the world. He played a significant role in laying the groundwork for the formation of the United Nations. Unfortunately, on the virtual eve of victory in Europe, Roosevelt suffered a massive stroke and died on 12 April 1945. Almost an entire world grieved his death.

Roosevelt, despite documented moral failings, was a man who, as a recent biographer has concluded, held personal faith in God. This biographer, Kenneth S. Davis, writes that he was "an optimistic fatalist whose fatalism had a simple Christian definition." Of an early time in his life, Davis writes of FDR, "His religious belief, indeed, was of the simplest. He believed in a loving God who had created and now ruled a world...in Jesus Christ as the Son of God.... [His] faith was fused with the music and ritual and formal doctrine of the Episcopal Church.... He derived from worship an inner peace."[286]

Several presidents were musically inclined. John Quincy Adams was a hymn writer, Thomas Jefferson enjoyed playing the violin, Bill Clinton was a fine saxophone player, and Harry Truman and Richard Nixon both played the piano quite well. However, of all the presidents, Franklin Roosevelt was probably the most musical, having had more opportunities and experiences with music than the others. Having been born into a musical family who regularly gathered around the piano for evening "sings," the love of hymns and songs was a natural outgrowth of these enjoyable experiences. With Sara, Franklin's mother, as the capable accompanist, the love of music started early. When Franklin was a young teenager, Sara took him to opera performances and always properly prepared him for each musical experience.

Franklin reports how, as a student, he began a more serious study of music: "Today I got somewhat banged to pieces [at football] receiving a crack on the head, a wrench of the knee.… What do you think! I'm going to take singing lessons!… Singing should come before speaking so I have decided to take one lesson a week."[287] At the age of seventeen he began lessons, and while at Groton school he even played the small reed organ for some little neighborhood missions in the area. Young Franklin regularly sang in the Groton prep school choir until he graduated in 1900. Later on, much to his disappointment, he did not make the Harvard University Chorus but was active in the Harvard Glee Club and the Mandolin and Banjo Club, which often toured the Boston area. From these experiences he learned not only to love music, but also how important music was in people's lives.

Evidently the singing lessons paid off, because he sang very robustly in church. His eldest son, James, stated that the whole family participated in congregational singing. However, the children were often a little embarrassed that their father sang louder than anyone else. Franklin preferred hymns of various denominations. He sincerely enjoyed hearing and singing rousing Methodist and Baptist hymns and occasionally attended these churches for that reason. If he was criticized for deserting his own church's services and attending other denominational services, he would simply answer the critics by stating, "I love to sing with the Methodys!"[288]

As an adult, President Roosevelt loved songs that were expressive of the American spirit. His extensive collection of music on nautical themes reveals his interest in the sea, which may have been a contributing factor in his choice of "the navy hymn" as one of his favorite hymns. He had a real love of hymns, as reflected in his choice of music on several occasions. For a Thanksgiving Day service during his third term, he chose "Onward Christian Soldiers," "Faith of Our Fathers," "Eternal Father, Strong to Save," and "The Battle Hymn of the Republic." At this event, it is interesting to note that, while every other hymn had all the stanzas printed in the program, Roosevelt had decided to include only stanzas one, two, and five of the latter hymn. The president admitted that the South still objected to some of Julia Ward Howe's stanzas. He expressed the desire for new words to be substituted for stanzas three and four. At this same service, the presiding minister had instructed the Marine Band conductor to interpret the hymns as spirited songs of joy. After the service, the president reprimanded the director, saying, "Young man, why do you jazz up the hymns like that!?... Learn to play the hymns the way they were supposed to be played!"[289] Among other favorite hymns of FDR were "All Hail the Power of Jesus' Name," "O Master, Let Me Walk with Thee," and the relatively unfamiliar hymn "Be Strong," by Presbyterian minister Maltbie Babcock. Ironically, the words of this hymn are very close in meaning to those of a speech he was preparing just before he died: "The only limit to our realization of tomorrow will be our doubts of today. Let us move forward with strong and active faith." It is interesting to compare these words with a stanza of the hymn: "Be strong! We are not here to play, to dream, to drift. We have hard work to do and loads to lift. Shun not the struggle, face it, 'tis God's gift. Be strong!"

To President Roosevelt, American music meant Stephen Foster melodies, Sousa marches, and historical patriotic pieces such as "The Battle Hymn of the Republic." While being accompanied by the Marine Band, Roosevelt and Winston Churchill bellowed out this great hymn on the White House lawn 20 May 1943, when the prime minister was in the capital for the numerous war conferences—in the pouring rain.[290]

In the Roosevelt era, Eleanor was a very warm, thoughtful, and congenial hostess. Music at the White House included a wide variety of musical styles and performers with many notable operatic and concert artists appearing. There were a large number of black vocalists, choruses, and professional dancers as well as the first fully staged opera, *Hansel and Gretel.*

Mrs. Roosevelt was aided by social secretary Edith Helm and Henry Junge of the Steinway company. Beginning in 1935, because of the many requests, they increased the number of programs each year until the beginning of World War II. Todd Duncan, who had sung the role of Porgy in George Gershwin's *Porgy and Bess,* sang three times for the Roosevelts, while Marian Anderson appeared twice. Martha Graham, the legendary American dancer, opened a new era of modern dance with her White House performance of Aaron Copland's *Appalachian Spring,* composed especially for her in 1944. For President Roosevelt, folk music was very important. He felt that it was "a national fabric of beauty and strength," and he encouraged the country to "keep the original fabric so intact that the fineness of each will show in the completed handiwork."[291]

It is not at all surprising that many hymns were heard at various locales during the funeral and time of mourning for Roosevelt's passing. Besides the ones mentioned, other hymns included "Nearer, My God, to Thee," "Abide with Me," "The Old Rugged Cross," "In the Garden," "How Firm a Foundation," "God Is Working His Purpose Out," "O God, Our Help in Ages Past," "Rock of Ages, Cleft for Me," "Jesus, Lover of My Soul," "America the Beautiful," and "My Country, 'Tis of Thee." Any of these could be considered as Roosevelt's favorite; he simply loved hymns. However, it appears that a relatively obscure hymn today may have been his most loved.

"Art Thou Weary, Art Thou Languid" is considered by hymnologist Ernest Emurian to have been Franklin Roosevelt's favorite hymn. Written by Stephen the Sabaite in the seventh century, it is subtitled "the call of the religious life." The ancient Greek text was translated by John Mason Neale in or before 1862, but most scholars believe the lyric poem contains so little of Stephen's text that Neale's paraphrase would be more correctly called an original hymn.[292] Neale was one of the most capable translators of Greek and Latin hymns connected with the Oxford movement. This was a nineteenth-century attempt by certain Anglican leaders to revise the liturgy by enriching it with singing early church hymns in English. It is ironic that Neale was raised in an evangelical home and reacted strongly against the hymns he was

Art Thou Weary, Art Thou Languid

Words: John Mason Neale, 1851
Music: Henry W. Baker, 1861

8.5.8.3.
STEPHANOS

forced to learn as a child. As a twenty-two-year-old chaplain of Downing College, he wrote to a friend about his "general dislike of hymns." He felt that they encouraged dangerous emotionalism, especially those of Isaac Watts. This hostility inspired him to write a set of children's hymns "to free the poor children from the yoke of Watts."

Neale founded a society that became one of the main agencies for promoting the Oxford movement principles in local parishes. In 1851 he produced four volumes of English hymns based on ancient originals that were a main source for the monumental 1861 *Hymns Ancient and Modern*; this hymnbook was the primary result of the movement. Partially because of Neale, singing became an Anglo-Catholic as well as an evangelical passion in the Church of England. His "Christ Is Made the Sure Foundation" and "Of the Father's Love Begotten" are perhaps his greatest contributions.

However, the words of "Art Thou Weary, Art Thou Languid" clearly express the attitude Franklin Roosevelt may have felt after becoming immobilized at age thirty-nine. In this dialogue hymn, the words begin with Christ's promise of giving rest to one's soul. In the next two stanzas, Christ's anguish and suffering are recalled. Moving to a personalized application to earth's sorrows, the next two stanzas make the logical comparison of Roosevelt's condition to Christ's experience. The last two stanzas reassure the singer of those who have gone before on the same path that Christ traveled. In application to Roosevelt's physical state, the climatic seventh stanza reiterates his immense struggle to succeed even as his handicap seemed to dictate failure. How could Roosevelt not be inspired by this text: "Finding, following, keeping, struggling, Is He sure to bless? Saints, apostles, prophets, martyrs, answer yes"?

Henry W. Baker wrote the tune for "Art Thou Weary, Art Thou Languid" and named it STEPHANOS for Stephen the Sabaite.[293] Baker was a moving force behind the publication of the hymnal called *Hymns Ancient and Modern*. Even though he was the primary editor of the texts, he also contributed tunes and texts to this influential work. However, this tune was harmonized by the musical editor of the hymnal, William Henry Monk. To the simple singable melody, Monk wrote uncomplicated but not boring harmony. This music helps to guarantee the hymn's acceptance, particularly in times of sorrow and in need of solace.

Even though there were relatively few songs produced during World War II in comparison to previous wars, the Roosevelts certainly promoted music as a uniting factor in the nation. Eleanor Roosevelt reinforced her husband's feeling of the importance of music for the country. She said on one occasion, "People get together and understand each other while making music in a way that would be impossible were they doing anything else in the world. Music, when it is great, belongs to the world."[294]

There is no doubt that hymns strengthened Franklin Roosevelt's life and influenced many grave decisions he had to make as president. Not only as a peacetime administrator but most especially as commander in chief, hymns aided him in the formation of certain policies and in his decision making. It is certainly a truism that "you can tell the kind of man he was from the hymns he loved."[295] These words were spoken by the officiating minister at the funeral of Franklin Roosevelt on 15 April 1945 in Hyde Park, New York. Thus, one of the most musical of our presidents was laid to rest with the singing of the hymns he loved. As a result, the nation was for a while united by great hymns.

HARRY S. TRUMAN

1884–1972

Thirty-Third President (1945–1953)

No person has ever been totally prepared to assume the office of the president of the United States. A few, like John Adams, Martin Van Buren, Andrew Johnson, William Howard Taft, and John F. Kennedy, have had the responsibility of following either a living or recently deceased legend. Only a very few, Abraham Lincoln and Franklin D. Roosevelt among them, have had to deal with events of potential national disaster or world-changing events immediately as they assumed office. And perhaps only one US president, Harry Truman, has ever faced the challenges of all three of these situations. Yet, while Truman seemed little prepared when he assumed office and followed the recently deceased legend Franklin D. Roosevelt, and as the greatest world cataclysm ever known came to a climax, very few other US presidents have ever responded as capably as did he.

Like his predecessors Andrew Jackson and Abraham Lincoln, Harry Truman came from humble beginnings. Born in Missouri in 1884 to a farmer and livestock trader, young Truman developed into a precocious student and avid reader. He also pleased his mother by becoming an accomplished young pianist. As his father's business endeavors prospered, Truman had opportunities to expand his horizons. While mainly working on his father's farm, he acquired a reputation as a hard worker and a "joiner." Like his father, he became a Mason, and like his mother he became a Baptist, being selected as a deacon at his church. He fell in love with his future wife, Bess, and in 1900 attended his first Democratic National Convention with his father. Both these events shaped the future of his life. Unable to attend college due to financial considerations, the young man joined the Missouri National Guard for six years when the United States entered World War I. Though technically he was two years too old to be drafted and his eyesight too poor, he postponed his marriage to Bess and volunteered for the army. He served with some distinction as an artillery officer in France. This event demonstrated to Truman that he could be a leader.

After the war, Truman unsuccessfully tried his hand at business and then became involved in Democratic politics. As a result of an old army friendship, Truman found support from the powerful Pendergast political machine in Missouri. After a successful run for and service for eight years in the eastern district judge's position, Missourians elected Truman US senator in 1934 and reelected him for a second term in 1940. Chairmanship of an important committee to oversee the awarding of defense contracts in the rapid buildup for US entry into World War II catapulted Truman to national prominence. In 1944, sensing the need to replace the controversial and liberal vice president Henry Wallace, Democrats selected Truman as their vice-presidential nominee as President Franklin Roosevelt, despite increasingly poor health, ran for an unprecedented fourth term. When FDR was reelected by a somewhat narrow margin, Truman became vice president amidst concerns that President Roosevelt would never finish his fourth term.

These concerns proved correct when, after less than three months as vice-president, Truman became the nation's thirty-third president. Told gently by Mrs. Roosevelt that FDR had died, after a moment of speechlessness, Truman asked her courteously, "Is there anything I can do for you?" Mrs. Roosevelt responded, "Is there anything *we* can do for you, for you are the one in trouble now." Her words proved prophetic, for perhaps no president has faced what Truman faced at that moment.

Truman courageously led the nation through its time of grief and as it celebrated the end of the war in Europe less than a month later. A sign on his desk stated simply, "The Buck Stops Here." Truman lived up to this motto. Weeks after the war's end in Europe, Truman represented the nation in the postwar meetings in Germany with Soviet Communist dictator Joseph Stalin and British prime ministers Winston Churchill and Clement Atlee. He also made the momentous decision to use the world's first atomic weapons against the Japanese at Hiroshima and Nagasaki. Despite the controversy that followed, Truman always insisted that he made this decision in order to save lives.

The remainder of this term challenged Truman's international and domestic leadership in every way. He faced a brief economic recession, growing Communist and especially threatening Soviet aggression, and the challenge of what to do about the United States' position as the only great power not ravaged by the war. He also remained in FDR's lengthy shadow and faced a resurgent Republican Party. Under his leadership the United States developed the so-called Truman Doctrine, a policy for the containment of Communism, and the Marshall Plan, named after Secretary of State George Marshall, for the rebuilding of Europe's shattered economy. In 1948 he tackled the problem of the Soviet Union's blockade of Berlin by neither backing down and evacuating Berlin nor by attacking with military force, but with the successful airlift of millions of tons of supply. His dramatic decision forced the dictator Stalin to back down. That fall, he pulled off a stunning come-from-behind upset of the Republican presidential nominee, Thomas Dewey, to win his own term in the White House.

Unfortunately, the next four years proved to be equally challenging. He faced constant harassment from Republican congressmen seeking to expose real and supposed Communist sympathizers in the Democratic administration, tensions that were heightened when China became Communist in 1949. Furthermore, the Soviet Union developed its own nuclear weapons, and Communist North Korea invaded South Korea in 1950, beginning the Korean War. Mobilizing the United Nations and providing the bulk of UN forces, the US Army turned back the invasion under the leadership of the popular American general Douglas MacArthur. Unfortunately for Truman, he was forced to fire MacArthur after Communist China entered the war, resulting in a prolonged conflict and MacArthur's criticism of Truman's politics. This decision, along with other events, led to Truman's plummeting popularity and his choice not to run again in 1952. He retired to his humble home in Independence, Missouri; devoted himself to his beloved Bess and daughter, Margaret; and worked at his presidential library. He died on 26 December 1972 at the age of eighty-eight.

Harry Truman generally regarded himself as a Southern Baptist, although after he and Bess married he frequently attended Episcopalian churches with her. Many Southern Baptists claimed him reluctantly because of his rather colorful language and moderate enjoyment of alcohol. Otherwise, however, historians generally regard Truman as an ethical and moral individual. He was a devoted and loving father and husband. After becoming president, he regularly attended the First Baptist Church of Washington, DC, until its pastor criticized and opposed Truman's decision to appoint a US ambassador to the Vatican as a violation of separation of church and state. He also approved a congressional resolution for an annual day of prayer that would be selected by the president.[296]

Harry Truman ranks along with Thomas Jefferson in his love of music. Early in life, he considered a music vocation as a concert pianist. Truman's mother, having studied music at the Baptist Female College in Lexington, Missouri, was Harry's first piano teacher. She could play the piano very well. For young Harry, music and reading became very important. By the age of fourteen he had read the Bible through three times and had read all the books in the Independence Public Library.

Claiming it was pleasure and not work, Harry never had to be forced to practice his piano. He often rose at 5:00 A.M. to practice two hours before school. Grace White of Kansas City was his piano teacher from age eight to sixteen. With his usual spunk, Harry braved the jeers of boys as he carried his music to his lessons. However, he quit piano lessons at age sixteen, stating that he could not become a professional musician because he wasn't good enough. When further questioned, Harry explained that playing the piano wasn't a manly occupation: "It was a sissy thing to do, so I just stopped."[297]

However, Truman already had learned to love music, and that love remained with him for his entire life. His favorite compositions were Mozart's *Sonata No. 9 in A-major,* Beethoven's *Minuet in G,* Chopin's *Valse Opus 42 in A-flat major,* and Paderewski's *Minuet Opus 14, No. 1.* He also enjoyed some American music—for example, the songs of Stephen Foster and tunes from early musical theater. Contrary to legend, Harry intensely disliked the "Missouri Waltz," often refusing to play it.

Generally, his musical taste was conservative, meaning music with a nice melodic line, but he never became an opera buff. He once wrote to his wife Bess, "I haven't recovered from the siege of grand opera yet.… Perhaps if they had given me small doses I might have been trained because I do love music." His distaste of opera may have been a reflection of his vocal ability. On being asked if he sang tenor or baritone, he replied, "I never sing.… I'm saddest when I sing and so are those that listen to me."[298]

With five pianos in the White House, President Truman must have felt right at home. Even as another music-loving president, Thomas Jefferson, had a keyboard in his office, Truman had a piano by his desk. As Richard Nixon found it difficult to pass a piano anywhere without playing it for a minute or two, President Truman often unabashedly played the piano in public. He performed on various occasions for Joseph Stalin, Winston Churchill, John Kennedy, Lyndon Johnson, and other notable people. He was often photographed seated at a grand piano, once with the actress Lauren Bacall lounging on the lid. In 1945, at a county fair in Caruthersville, Missouri, Truman played for a group of women and winked at them as he said, "When I played this, Stalin signed the Potsdam Agreement." He played for the entire nation in 1952 during the televised tour of the newly renovated White House. After his presidential terms, he stated that he could take up playing the piano again and become the "Grandma Moses" of ex-presidents.

President Truman was very proud and protective of the musical talents of his only child, Margaret. When she became a professional singer, many critics admired her voice as being warm and lyric, soaring within a three-octave range, while others were less complimentary. Historian Elise Kirk gives a full account of the 1950 review of Margaret's Constitution Hall recital by *Washington Post* music critic Paul Hume.[299] In Hume's column he wrote, "Miss Truman cannot sing very well," along with other negative words. Bristling, the president dashed off a handwritten note to Hume, saying, "I hope to meet you.… When that happens you'll need a new nose, some beef steaks for black eyes." Much later, Hume and Truman talked about the incident at the Truman Library. The former president said to Hume, "I had a lot of fun out of you and General MacArthur over the years. I hope you don't mind."[300]

Truman, being infatuated with classical music, did not invite a mixture of artists and styles for music programs at the White House as his predecessor had. The planning of recitals was a family affair for the Trumans: the president chose the pianists, the First Lady chose the violinists, and Margaret chose the vocalists. The classical taste of the Trumans was evident since the artists had to perform at least one of the president's favorite pieces. Because of frugal finances during the postwar years, as well as the deteriorating condition of the White House, the Truman administration had only one series of concerts. These programs were held between November 1946 and February 1947, after which the first family moved to the Blair House for four years. Appearing were pianists Sylvania Zaremba and Oscar Levant, baritone Lawrence Tibbett, soprano Helen Traubel, tenor Frederick Jagel, and violinist Carroll Glenn with pianist Eugene List.

Truman was recognized for his intense love for good music by donations of many manuscripts and first editions of compositions. But his most distinguished gift was presented on 4 October 1951 when Salzburg, Austria, honored the president with the *Great Golden Mozart Medal*, "the highest award of the city for outstanding service in the field of music." Having played on Mozart's own *pianoforte* at his birthplace in Salzburg and having been entertained by a concert of Mozart's music, Truman wrote in his diary, "I've never attended a happier and more pleasing musical event."[301]

The Truman Library notes that in March 1969 President Richard Nixon paid Truman a visit in Independence, Missouri. Nixon presented to the library the White House piano that Truman had enjoyed while he was president. With their political differences forgotten, the two men seemed in good spirits. Nixon suggested that Truman play something, but when he declined, Nixon sat down and played the "Missouri Waltz" well enough to receive a warm applause from Truman.[302]

There is no record of Truman ever playing any hymns either in a Baptist church or the Presbyterian church where he sometimes attended with his mother in Independence. Truman, who was present at planning sessions for his funeral, chose not to have any hymns. Instead, he chose a variety of military and patriotic pieces. But the moving hymn "America the Beautiful" was included in the plans. The Memorial Service at the Washington Cathedral on 5 January 1973 included the congregational hymn "He Who Would Valiant Be," written by Baptist pastor John Bunyan in 1884 as a part of his classic book *Pilgrim's Progress*. The recessional was Isaac Watts's "O God, Our Help in Ages Past." From a September 1959 memo sent to the Salvation Army Tabernacle Band in Los Angeles, we know that Truman's favorite Christmas carol was "Silent Night."[303] Since President Truman had input in planning his own funeral, and those deliberations included "America the Beautiful," the conclusion is that this was his favorite hymn. No reference has been found to any other hymn in his writings, memos, newspaper clippings, or memoirs.

The author of "America the Beautiful," Katherine Lee Bates, was born in 1859 in Massachusetts. An 1880 graduate of Wellesley College, she returned to her alma mater, eventually becoming the head of the English department. Widely known as the author of many books, she is best remembered for writing this inspiring hymn. In 1893 she embarked on her first trip west with a group of colleagues headed for Colorado on a summer teaching assignment. On the way, they stopped at Niagara Falls, where she observed the majesty and power of cascading water. Then they visited the World's Columbian Exposition in Chicago, which had opened the preceding year.

America the Beautiful

Words: Katharine Lee Bates, 1893
Music: Samuel A. Ward, 1882 or 1885

C.M.D.
MATERNA

1. O beau-ti-ful for spa-cious skies, For am-ber waves of grain; For pur-ple moun-tain maj-es-ties A-bove the fruit-ed plain! A-mer-i-ca! A-mer-i-ca! God shed his grace on thee, And crown thy good with broth-er-hood From sea to shin-ing sea.

2. O beau-ti-ful for he-roes proved In lib-er-at-ing strife, Who more than self their coun-try love, And mer-cy more than life! A-mer-i-ca! A-mer-i-ca! May God thy gold re-fine, Till all suc-cess be no-ble-ness, And ev-ery gain di-vine.

3. O beau-ti-ful for pa-triot dream That sees be-yond the years Thine al-a-bas-ter cit-ies gleam, Un-dimmed by hu-man tears! A-mer-i-ca! A-mer-i-ca! God mend thine ev-ery flaw, Con-firm thy soul in self-con-trol, Thy lib-er-ty in law.

This fair was an event to celebrate the 400th anniversary of Columbus's discovery of America. With the festivities including 10,000 voices singing "My Country, 'Tis of Thee," Katherine was reminded of our country's greatness. Since the beautiful new fair buildings gleamed with a coat of whitewash, she was further inspired during this visit. After the teaching semester ended, the teachers ascended the 14,000-foot Pike's Peak near Colorado Springs. Here,

Katherine was so inspired by the vast beauty of America that she expressed these scenes by writing a poem with poetic descriptions that very evening.[304]

After keeping the poem in her notebook for two years, Katherine rediscovered it and sent it to a Boston publisher. Expecting a rejection, she was surprised that the *Congregationalist* magazine printed her lyrics in its 4 July 1895 issue. The poem attracted immediate attention. Many composers set the text to music, but none seemed to be right. Thus, she rewrote some words, simplifying the phraseology. This revised version was first printed in the *Boston Evening Transcript* on 19 November 1904.

There are two versions of how Samuel Ward, an amateur musician born in 1847, came to write the music to the version of "America the Beautiful" that is sung today. Some scholars say that one of the employers at Ward's music store in Newark, New Jersey, insisted that Ward composed the tune while crossing New York harbor after spending a day on Coney Island. The notes of the melody came to Ward so quickly that he jotted them down on the cuff of his shirt. However, Ward's own son-in-law said that the tune was written around 1883 in memory of Ward's oldest daughter. Both of these stories could be true.

By 1900 at least seventy-five tunes had been composed for Bates's poem.[305] However, in 1904, Baptist pastor Clarence Barbour, believed that the stanzas of the hymn were so spiritual that they could be wedded only to inspired music. After hours of searching in his library of Christian songbooks, he discovered Samuel Ward's tune for the hymn "O Mother Dear, Jerusalem," which Ward had named MATERNA, meaning "motherly." The composer himself was brought to tears on hearing a children's choir singing this hymn; this experience indicates its spiritual inspiration. Ace Collins, a hymnologist, states, "Barbour instantly realized he had discovered the soul mate to Bates's poem."

Later that year, the completed hymn was sung at Boston's Lake Avenue Baptist Church. But it was not until 1910 that Barbour printed this version in *Fellowship Hymns*. This printing predates Douglas Snow's findings when he wrote that the president of Massachusetts Agricultural College in 1912 asked the permission of Ward's widow to use MATERNA for Bates's words. Again, both stories could be true.

The hymn "America the Beautiful" is a great affirmation of the American story, a declaration of faith in God, in America, and in the brotherhood of man's common humanity. The hymn is not only a reminder of the noble past, beginning with the Pilgrims, but contains a prayer that God will be with America in the present and future. It should be no surprise that Truman agreed to have this hymn sung at his funeral. He was not only a great patriot, but a man of faith in God's hand on this country. Truman's actions agree with the four stanzas of this strong and sincere prayer. Even as Bates wrote of the nation's dependence upon God and God's love, so did Truman believe that America could not be great unless it was good.

"America the Beautiful" attained widespread popularity for the first time during World War I when Truman was in the military. This unique, sacred, patriotic hymn is a reminder that Americans cannot make "the dream that sees beyond the years" become a reality unless God "shed[s] His grace" on our nation. The hymn is a magnificent prayer, and it echoes Truman's hopes and dreams for the nation he served.

DWIGHT D. EISENHOWER

1890–1969

Thirty-Fourth President (1953–1961)

Dwight D. Eisenhower's foremost biographer describes him as "a great and good man" and "one of the outstanding leaders of the Western world of this century." Facing one of the greatest challenges of the twentieth century, the Allied landings in France, he earned the respect of friends and enemies alike. As president, even his detractors regarded him with admiration. To many Americans, he served as a genuine hero in two significant times of great uncertainty, World War II and the cold war.

Dwight David Eisenhower was born in 1890 in a tiny house next to the railroad tracks in the small north Texas town of Denison. While still an infant, his father found work out of state and moved his wife, Dwight, and two older brothers to Abilene, Kansas. The Eisenhowers were devout Mennonites when he was born but later became members of the new group known as the Jehovah's Witnesses. As such, the Bible and the pacifist faith of the Mennonites formed staples of Eisenhower family existence, as did their later beliefs in Jehovah's Witness ideas and other typical Midwestern American values.

An excellent athlete and student, Eisenhower received a scholarship to the US Military Academy. Despite his mother's objections due to the family's Mennonite faith, Eisenhower entered West Point and began a career in the army. He graduated from West Point and married Mamie Doud. When World War I began, he served in a training command. Just before the army shipped him to Europe, the war came to an end. In between wars, he served in various capacities, most conspicuously as an assistant to the highly regarded Douglas MacArthur. During World War II, the two men came to serve as supreme Allied commanders in each of their respective theaters of operation.

When the war began, the army chief of staff George Marshall recognized Eisenhower's administrative and personal skills. As the United States and Great Britain began to organize an attack on Nazi Germany, Marshall recommended to President Roosevelt and Winston Churchill that they place Eisenhower in overall command of the Allied efforts to recapture North Africa, despite the fact that Eisenhower had never led a field command and had only led training commands and held staff positions. When North Africa fell under Allied control, Eisenhower then led the invasion of Sicily and Italy. After successful operations in southern Italy, the joint Allied command transferred Eisenhower to England to prepare for the invasion of Normandy. There, Eisenhower's tremendous administrative and political skills especially came into play. Eisenhower successfully navigated the difficult waters of joint command from not only US and British forces, but also from various other Allied forces in the West, including Canadian, Free French, Free Dutch, and other small commands. Furthermore, he struggled constantly to balance the demands of egotistical army, navy, and air force leaders and of powerful politicians like Franklin Roosevelt and Winston Churchill.

On 6 June 1944 Eisenhower launched the invasion of France with the greatest invasion armada in history since the Spanish Armada in 1588. In the months that followed, Allied forces in the West cooperated with Soviet forces in the East to liberate Nazi-occupied Europe. Despite setbacks, less than a year after the D-Day invasion, the Allies toppled Nazi Germany and the war in Europe came to an end. When the war ended, America recognized Eisenhower as one of its greatest heroes. He subsequently wrote and published *Crusade in Europe*, his memoirs of the war in Europe, and served as the army chief of staff.

In 1948 Eisenhower accepted the presidency of Columbia University. After two years, as the cold war heated up, President Truman selected Eisenhower to be the first commander of NATO (North Atlantic Treaty Organization). As the 1952 presidential election approached, however, Republicans drafted Eisenhower to serve as their presidential candidate. He won a smashing victory, ending twenty years of Democratic domination of the presidency. Americans reelected him by an overwhelming majority in 1956. Throughout the eight years of Eisenhower's presidency, the United States experienced unprecedented prosperity in domestic economics, and, as he had promised, he ended the Korean War, even though the peace was actually an armistice that has continued to the present day.

Despite these positive events, Eisenhower's eight years in office saw a continued rise in Cold War tensions, the failed Hungarian uprising against Soviet domination, the Suez crisis in the Middle East, the launch of *Sputnik*, the infamous U–2 incident, and the Communist takeover of Cuba. In domestic affairs, the Red Scare continued, the Civil Rights Movement began, and a recession hit in 1957. Eisenhower steered a middle course in economic policies, continuing many New Deal and Fair Deal programs, initiating the major interstate highway construction program while also insisting upon a balanced budget. He also suffered a heart attack that left Americans wondering if he could continue in office. Despite the difficulties he encountered, most Americans believed that their lives were more secure because they trusted Eisenhower.

When Eisenhower left the White House, he and Mamie moved to Gettysburg, Pennsylvania, where they had purchased a farm. He spent the remainder of his life as an elder statesman, honored by the country he had served. After continued health problems, his heart weakened and he died in 1969.

After attending West Point, Eisenhower never returned to his Mennonite or Jehovah's Witness upbringing. Eventually, he and his brothers all left the Jehovah's Witness faith. He frequently mentioned prayer in his public announcements during World War II. The phrase "under God" was added to the Pledge of Allegiance during his presidency. He also made a profession of faith in the Presbyterian Church and was baptized and confirmed only a short time after entering the White House, though some criticized this as a political ploy. Despite the criticism, Eisenhower remained active in the church until his death, becoming an active member at the Gettysburg Presbyterian Church after his retirement. He usually began his cabinet meetings with a silent prayer, giving cabinet members the choice of praying if they chose to do so. After coming to the White House, he also developed a close relationship with Baptist evangelist Billy Graham. After he left the presidency, he and Graham continued this friendship, and when Eisenhower lay dying, he asked Graham to come for a visit. The two friends talked of spiritual things. Only days later, as Eisenhower was in his last moments, he said, "I want to go: God take me." In many ways, the old warrior had ultimately become one of the nation's most religious presidents.[306]

Even though President Eisenhower had little musical background and preferred sentimental popular styles, he and Mamie filled the presidential mansion with a variety of musical entertainment. Eisenhower's taste in music was the exact opposite to his predecessor, but Truman and Eisenhower had one thing in common: "the latest innovative trends in American music at this time—bop, cool, jazz, and the new, explosive rock 'n roll—had no place in the White House."[307]

Under Eisenhower, activities in arts legislature were very significant as they began to thrive and even expand because of the patronage in both the public and private sectors. Mrs. Eisenhower was an excellent hostess, carefully planning the many White House social events. Music following state dinners reflected the first family's fondness of Broadway tunes and sentimental ballads. President Eisenhower truly loved hymns, especially those with strong, powerful, and realistic words. On some private occasions the Eisenhowers had "sing-along" sessions featuring old-time hymns and songs. Family and close friends gathered around the piano or Hammond organ as Mamie accompanied their singing; she played everything "by ear" since she didn't read music.

President Eisenhower could sing well, especially on songs he knew with ideals in which he believed. On 30 October 1952, a recording was made of his singing "God Bless America," an event conducted by Fred Waring. Eisenhower's voice was clear, true, and warm as he sang the Irving Berlin classic with the choir in front of throngs of people. He wrote a musical prayer for his 1953 inaugural address. The prayer was set to music by composer Richard Rogers and sung on 8 January 1957 by the all-black Howard University Choir.[308] Eisenhower especially enjoyed bass soloists. The best American basso, George London, sang selections from Mussorgsky's opera *Boris Godunov* on 21 October 1953, and reporters wrote that the president loved it.

The Eisenhowers also loved quartets, especially the Men of Song, the Revelers, and the Deep River Boys. In addition, they enjoyed choral groups, particularly Fred Waring's "Pennsylvanians" and the Mormon Tabernacle Choir. Other choral groups who sang at the White House were the Army Chorus, the Navy Sea Chanters, the Singing Sergeants, the Singing Idlers, the

Singing Strings, and the Singing Violins. The concept of strolling musicians in the White House originated with the Eisenhower administration.

Their most delightful musicale was on 18 May 1958 when a celebration of Broadway musicals was presented, featuring songs from *Pajama Game*, *West Side Story*, *The Music Man*, *New Girl in Town*, and *My Fair Lady*. President and Mrs. Eisenhower also invited noted pianists to play in the White House, including Artur Rubinstein, Leonard Bernstein, and Leon Fleisher. The president said, "The development of American music and the native development of any art is the development of a national treasure."[309] This concept linked Eisenhower with his successor, John F. Kennedy, and his wife.

The archivist of the Eisenhower Library noted that in April 1953, the president wrote a letter of appreciation to the minister of Reid Memorial Presbyterian Church in Augusta, Georgia, indicating his preference for the hymn "Lead, Kindly Light." In a pre-inaugural service on 20 January 1957, three of Eisenhower's most favored hymns were sung: "O God, Our Help in Ages Past," "A Mighty Fortress Is Our God," and "The Battle Hymn of the Republic." A Congregationalist minister, Frederick Fox, said that Eisenhower loved hymns based on the Psalms since their messages have been tested over the centuries. Fox listed the foregoing four hymns as well as seven others favored by Eisenhower: "Abide with Me," "God of Our Fathers," "My Country, 'Tis of Thee," "God Moves in a Mysterious Way," "America the Beautiful," "I Love to Tell the Story," and "God of Our Life." The president's favorite Christmas carols were "Silent Night," "Adeste Fidelis," and "The First Noel." These hymns are all singable, meaningful, strengthening, reverent, and hallowed by usage among devout people.[310] The hymns sung at the mourning of President Eisenhower's death included those already listed here, as well as "Faith of Our Fathers," "Onward Christian Soldiers," and "The Old Rugged Cross."

In February 1953 right after his election, Eisenhower asked for prayer support from Senator Frank Carlson and Billy Graham. The national leaders met with the new president to seek God's guidance in decisions about discerning right from wrong. One of his first acts was to begin opening cabinet meetings with prayer. Soon, he instituted the interdenominational Presidential Prayer Breakfast. George Beverly Shea, soloist for the Billy Graham team, was in attendance at the 1954 Prayer Breakfast. After the meal was served, he was asked to lead in singing "What a Friend We Have in Jesus," the president's favorite hymn. On the day following, *The Today Show* televised the singing of the hymn nationwide, showing the president singing along on the hymn, clearly indicating that he knew all of the lyrics and sang them with confidence. Thus, the nation learned about another favorite hymn that the president truly loved.[311]

Joseph Scriven was the author of the text for "What a Friend We Have in Jesus."[312] Born in 1820 in Dublin, Ireland, he graduated from Trinity College but became estranged from his family because he was spiritually influenced by the Plymouth Brethren. The tragic death of his fiancé by accidental drowning on the eve of their wedding day shattered his life. At the age of twenty-five he moved to Canada, where he lived a dedicated Christian life by ministering to others in great need. Initially, he lived with friends, serving as a private tutor and repairing homes of the needy. He would saw wood for those who could not afford to pay; often, he gave away his own clothes to those in dire need. He became known as the "good Samaritan" of Port Hope, Ontario.

It was not until a short time before his death that his friends knew of Scriven's poetic gift. A neighbor who was visiting Joseph during an illness noticed a handwritten copy of a poem in his room. Reading the poem with delight, the friend questioned Scriven and learned that it had been composed years earlier for his ill mother in Ireland. In 1857 he had sent the poem to his mother to comfort her and remind her of the never-failing friend—Jesus. Responding to the question as to how he had written it, Joseph stated, "The Lord and I did it together." For several years the lyrics were attributed to Scottish poet Horatio Bonar, who denied its authorship. The author was designated as "unknown" in a Richmond, Virginia, Sunday school song book in 1870.

Five years later, Ira Sankey was preparing the collection "Gospel Hymns No. 1" for the D. L. Moody campaign in England. Even though he had already chosen a hymn by Charles Converse, Sankey decided at the last minute to substitute Scriven's lyrics to Converse's music, listing the author as "unknown." He later explained: "Thus the last hymn that went into the book became the first in favor."[313] Combining six books of songs into one volume, "What a Friend We Have in Jesus" went around the world. When researchers discovered the 1869 small collection of poems by Scriven titled *Hymns and Other Verses*, they found the true authorship of the lyrics. But this was almost thirty years after it was written.

The hymn tune was composed by Charles C. Converse,[314] a well-educated lawyer and professional musician who had studied in Europe with Franz Liszt and Louis Spohr. Though he composed many works for orchestra and choirs during his day, he is best remembered for his simple music so well suited to Scriven's lyrics. Initially, the tune was called ERIE after the city where

What a Friend We Have in Jesus

Words: Joseph Scriven, 1857
Music: Charles C. Converse, 1875

8.7.8.7.D.
CONVERSE

1. What a friend we have in Je - sus, All our sins and griefs to bear!
2. Have we tri - als and temp-ta - tions? Is there trou-ble an - y - where?
3. Are we weak and heav-y lad - en, Cum-bered with a load of care?

What a priv-i-lege to car - ry Ev - 'ry-thing to God in prayer!
We should nev - er be dis-cour-aged, Take it to the Lord in prayer:
Pre - cious Sav-iour, still our ref - uge; Take it to the Lord in prayer:

Oh, what peace we of-ten for-feit, Oh, what need-less pain we bear,
Can we find a friend so faith-ful Who will all our sor-rows share?
Do thy friends de-spise, for-sake thee? Take it to the Lord in prayer;

All be-cause we do not car - ry Ev - 'ry-thing to God in prayer!
Je - sus knows our ev-'ry weak-ness, Take it to the Lord in prayer.
In His arms He'll take and shield thee; Thou wilt find a so-lace there.

Converse lived, but today it is known as CONVERSE and sometimes FRIENDSHIP because of the subject of the text.

This hymn is a good example of a biblically based poem, having many scripture references, including Proverbs 18:24, Psalm 55:22, 1 Peter 5:7, and Philippians 4:6–7. Since Eisenhower was raised in a strict religious home where Bible reading was a daily family activity, he was no doubt familiar with the scriptures. Additionally, he strongly believed in the power of prayer, having asserted in 1948 that he was an intensely religious man since "nobody goes through six years of war without faith."[315]

"What a Friend We Have in Jesus" extends the intimate characterization of Jesus to a friend who shares and bears one's sorrow, hears one's prayers, and carries them to God. The words emphasize different difficulties faced daily by Christians. It is easy to see why President Eisenhower chose this hymn, because in 1953 he was inaugurated with 2 Chronicles 7:14, which reads, "If my people, which are called by my name, shall humble themselves, and pray, and seek my face, and turn from their wicked ways; then will I hear from heaven, and will forgive their sin, and will heal their land." The essential message of this hymn is a call to prayer. This indicates his devotion to the act of prayer, setting an example and precedent for the country to follow thereafter. Most presidents have continued this tradition to the present day.

JOHN F. KENNEDY

1917–1963

Thirty-Fifth President (1961–1963)

Few American presidents have begun their presidencies with such great expectations as those that surrounded John F. Kennedy. Nor have many American presidents so energized the public with personal charisma and a spirit of optimism as he. At the same time, no American president has ever ended his time in office so tragically and with such unfulfilled promise as did Kennedy. One of the great unanswered questions of history for many Americans of the past forty years remains, "What if John Kennedy had not been assassinated?"

John Kennedy was born to Joseph and Rose Kennedy on 29 May 1917. He was their second born, following an older brother, Joseph, Jr., and preceding seven other children. His maternal grandfather, John F. Fitzgerald, also known as "Honey Fitz," was a prominent Boston politician, and his father, Joseph Sr., was a successful businessman and, later, US ambassador to Great Britain. In every way, young John was a privileged child and youth. Despite this privileged life, he struggled with illness that followed him from prep school to Harvard University, and indeed, for the rest of his life. Upon completion of his degree at Harvard, Kennedy published his first book, *Why England Slept.*

With war on the horizon for the United States, Kennedy volunteered to serve in the US Navy despite his health limitations. Seeing combat in the Pacific theater, he became a hero when a Japanese destroyer rammed his boat, *PT 109,* and temporarily marooned him and his crew. Even though the collision badly injured his already fragile back, Kennedy's efforts were instrumental in the rescue of the survivors. Ultimately, his injury led to his discharge from the navy.

After the war and severe illness from what was eventually diagnosed as Addison's disease, John Kennedy entered public service when Massachusetts's Eleventh Congressional District elected him to Congress after a vigorous campaign in 1946. After serving a rather undistinguished six years in the House of Representatives, Kennedy ran successfully for the US Senate in 1952. While serving in the Senate, Kennedy published his second book, *Profiles in Courage.* He also married the glamorous and well-placed Jacqueline Bouvier and became a father. All the while, he positioned himself for a run at the presidency.

His chance came in 1960. Though still considered an upstart by many leading politicians, Kennedy secured the Democratic nomination and defeated the incumbent Republican vice president, Richard Nixon, in a highly visible campaign famous for its televised debates. With his election, he became both the youngest man and the first Roman Catholic ever to hold the US presidency.

Almost immediately, a myriad of problems confronted Kennedy. He feared an economic recession, faced tense relations with Cuba over the Bay of Pigs invasion, struggled with problems relating to civil rights, debated the role of the United States in Southeast Asia, and dealt with the specter of nuclear warfare with the Soviet Union. At one crucial moment, US intelligence services located sites for missile bases in nearby Cuba. Intelligence experts informed Kennedy that the missiles there could not only reach the United States, but were capable of carrying nuclear warheads. Resisting the temptation to invade Cuba and risk war with the Soviet Union, but also feeling that he had to act, Kennedy opted to initiate a blockade of Cuba. With tensions at a peak, both Kennedy and the Soviet premier Nikita

Khrushchev finally reached an agreement for the removal of the missiles from Cuba. In many ways, it was Kennedy's finest hour.

As Kennedy faced these crises, his youthful vigor, his beautiful wife and children, and his dynamic and visionary speeches captured the imagination of the American public. While he made many mistakes early in his presidential administration, he also demonstrated a tremendous capacity to grow in the Oval Office. He launched a vigorous and inspiring campaign to expand American frontiers into outer space and to land the first man on the moon. He dealt fairly with issues between big business and labor. He gradually took a stronger, though somewhat unpopular, stand on civil rights. And in the crowning achievement of his presidency, he forced the Soviet Union to remove missiles with nuclear capabilities from Cuba without bringing on World War III. His attempts to make an even greater contribution to American history were cut short, however, when he was assassinated by Lee Harvey Oswald in November 1963 after less than three full years in office.

The depth of Kennedy's religious beliefs has been questioned. As a young man he visited Rome and, together with his family, attended the investiture of Pope Pius XII. Though reared a Roman Catholic, Kennedy's private faith was not generally visible to the public. This was in part due to the fact that he wanted to assure the public that his Catholicism would not dictate the way he governed or that he would not allow the Catholic papacy to meddle in US policy. His personal faith has also been questioned as his moral indiscretions have been made public. Nevertheless, he was proud of his achievement of becoming the first Roman Catholic president, marrying within the church, and receiving last rites at his death. Some biographers and admirers have also asserted that his faith contributed to his perseverance in the face of personal adversity, and it is unquestioned that Roman Catholicism was a significant part of his personal heritage.[316]

Even though Kennedy won the Pulitzer Prize for *Profiles in Courage,* which obviously dealt with words and images, music for the president was another matter. It has been noted that his musical tastes ranged from "middlebrow to non-committal." It is interesting that he studied piano as a child, but as one report indicated, "Anybody studying this boy's character when he was practicing scales would have said he'd never grow up to become President of the United States."[317]

When a question arose about Kennedy's favorite song, Jacqueline replied, "Greensleeves." This is an old English melody often put to the text "What Child Is This?" Another favorite was noted as "Silver Bells," one of the most recorded modern secular Christmas melodies. It has been noted that

Dave Powers, a special assistant to John Kennedy, recalls the president asking a strolling band at a White House staff party to play "Silver Bells."[318]

August Heckscher, cultural liaison for the Kennedy administration said, "It was not only that he didn't particularly enjoy [music] but I think it was really painful.... It hurt his ears. I really don't think he liked music at all except a few things he knew. Other forms of art, however, he felt differently about."[319] He liked poetry very much and in a practical way painting and ballet, perhaps mainly because his wife loved them so much. Heckscher states that the performing arts were Jacqueline Kennedy's forte. Not only did the First Lady write poems and stories, but she also drew her own illustrations. In addition, she took lessons in piano and ballet earlier in her life. Having studied in France during her junior year at Vassar, the French culture left its mark on her. She knew all the arts extremely well.

Mrs. Kennedy also had an astute advisor, press secretary in the Kennedy administration Pierre Salinger: "[He] had been a child prodigy on the violin.... His great musical knowledge was enormously helpful in suggesting artists [to appear in the White House]."[320] The president always had problems with classical music, even to the extent of applauding at inappropriate times. Therefore, the White House staff worked out a code system whereby the president would watch a certain door slightly ajar as the signal to applaud.

From Mrs. Kennedy, music critic Paul Hume of the *Washington Post* learned that both the president and Mrs. Kennedy enjoyed symphonic music with extra musical association, such as Debussy's "Prelude to the Afternoon of a Fawn." The Kennedys were eager to pay tribute to the nation's burgeoning talented youth. Their series called "Concerts for Young People by Young People" was very encouraging to many young musical artists. The Kennedys also expanded the traditions of the military musical groups, as can be noted in the following occasion.

In Washington, DC, in 1961 invited guests were transported down the Potomac River to Mount Vernon on boats with small orchestras playing music. This event was the first White House state dinner held away from the presidential mansion and was perhaps patterned after the regal festive barge concerts of King George I in 1717 on the Thames River in London. On that occasion the music of George Frederic Handel, composed especially for the event and now called the "Water Music," was first heard.[321]

According to Heckscher, toward the end of his life, President Kennedy "came to feel...that progress in the arts was intimately related to all that he wanted America to be." This is one reason that Kennedy supported the National Culture Center plans, which became the Kennedy Center for the

Performing Arts. In his administration the formation of the Federal Advisory Council on the Arts had a positive mission "to demonstrate that the White House itself could be an influence in encouraging public acceptance of the arts." The White House became a deliberate showcase for leading performing arts organizations. Mrs. Kennedy said her main concern was "to present the best in arts, not necessarily what was popular at the time."[322]

As to his use of hymns, a Kennedy Library spokesman stated that President Kennedy was a very private person concerning certain matters and that they did not know of a hymn that may have been his favorite. He simply assumed that "Eternal Father, Strong to Save" was loved by him since he served so nobly in the US Navy and this hymn had been adopted officially as "the Navy hymn."

However, in research on the music selected for his funeral by his family, there were other hymns performed in addition to "Eternal Father, Strong to Save." Among these are "O God of Loveliness" sung at the Capitol in Washington, DC, and "Pray for the Dead at Noon and Eve" as well as "Holy God, We Praise Thy Name," both sung at Washington, DC's, Saint Matthew's Cathedral as part of the funeral service. Other hymns heard during the ceremonies included "Ave Maria" and "Holy, Holy, Holy."

The music at Kennedy's funeral served to quell the nation's grief and eulogize John Kennedy in every venue and was very significant as millions shared the hymns dear to America's only Roman Catholic president. Music critic and historian Irving Lowens compiled a listing of the musical selections of the funeral of President Kennedy, which appeared in the *Washington Star* newspaper on 1 December 1963.

Probably these five hymns were known by President Kennedy; otherwise the family may not have chosen them. Obviously "Ave Maria" and "Pray for the Dead at Noon and Eve" are specifically sung for Catholic services. Reginald Heber's "Holy, Holy, Holy" was originally written for Anglican worship. The beautiful hymn "O God of Loveliness," while penned by Catholic bishop Alfonso de'Liquori, uses the music of a Silesian folksong sometimes referred to as CRUSADER'S HYMN. Most research and personal conclusions suggest that "Holy God, We Praise Thy Name" best represents John F. Kennedy as his favorite hymn choice. This strong Catholic hymn has also been widely accepted, with slight adaptations, by many Protestant denominations.

"Holy God, We Praise Thy Name" is a paraphrase of portions of the ancient "Te Deum," a fourth-century extra-biblical hymn that clearly states Catholic doctrine. Hymnologist Carlton Young said that "the earliest extant version of 'Te Deum' is contained in the late seventh-century antiphonary of the Celtic church monastery at Bennchar (Bangor) Ireland."[323] Since the

Holy God, We Praise Thy Name

Words: Ignaz Franz, 1744
Music: Anonymous, 1794

7.8.7.8.7.7.
GROSSER GOTT

1. Ho - ly God, we praise thy name; Lord of all, we bow be - fore thee; All on earth thy scep - ter claim; All in heaven a - bove a - dore thee. In - fi - nite thy vast do - main; Ev - er - last - ing is thy reign.

2. Hark, the glad ce - les - tial hymn An - gel choirs a - bove are rais - ing; Cher - u - bim and ser - a - phim, In un - ceas - ing cho - rus prais - ing, Fill the heavens with sweet ac - cord: Ho - ly, ho - ly, ho - ly Lord.

3. Lo! the ap - os - tol - ic train Joins thy sa - cred name to hal - low; Proph - ets swell the glad re - frain, And the white - robed mar - tyrs fol - low. And from morn to set of sun, Through the church the song goes on.

4. Ho - ly Fa - ther, Ho - ly Son, Ho - ly Spir - it: three we name thee, Though in es - sence on - ly one; Un - di - vid - ed God we claim thee, And a - dor - ing bend the knee While we own the mys - ter - y.

Kennedy heritage is Irish, this may have had a special significance for President Kennedy. The English text of this noteworthy hymn was prepared by Thomas Cranmer for the 1549 Anglican *Book of Common Prayer*.

However, in 1744 the Latin text was translated and metricized into German by Ignaz Franz. This version was consequently published in *Katholische Gesangbuch*, a hymnal requested by Maria Theresa of the Austrian Hapsburg Empire. "Holy God, We Praise Thy Name" is a versified form of the first section of "Te Deum," which in its entirety is too long for congregational song. Clarence Walworth's English translation and paraphrase in current use in England and America first appeared in England in 1853 in a "Redemptorist" mission hymnal.

The tune commonly titled GROSSER GOTT has been sung to the Franz text since 1744. The hymn quickly became a favorite congregational hymn in both German and French Catholic hymnals. According to hymnologist Carlton R. Young, the tune's first appearance in the United States was in Philip Rohr's *Favorite Catholic Melodies* of 1854.[324] Since that time it has been used in hymnals of various denominations under names such as FARMINGHAM, HALLE, TE DEUM, and HURSLEY.

GROSSER GOTT is an anonymous tune according to most scholars. Hymnologist Paul Westermeyer says that the German metrical setting of "Holy God, We Praise Thy Name" was wedded to a melody that possibly originated as a French folksong. However, it is eminently a congregation tune that, to this day, has received wide circulation in both Catholic and Protestant hymnals.[325] Another name for this tune, HURSLEY, comes from the fact that the Reverend John Keble, author of the hymn "Sun of My Soul, Thou Savior Dear," was vicar at the Hursley parish in England for thirty years. His text has also been universally sung to GROSSER GOTT.

The English text of "Holy God, We Praise Thy Name" reflects praise to God the Father. Stanza one emphasizes all creation bowing before holy God. This basic Christian doctrine is common in all denominations, being an ecumenical concept. The second stanza clearly points out that even heavenly creatures praise God in a climaxing chorus, closing with the Trinitarian phrase, "Holy, holy, holy Lord." The third stanza carries the idea of the Trinity, further addressing the "Holy Father, Holy Son, Holy Spirit" but noting that in essence they are only one. Closing with the mystery of this concept, this hymn contains one of the most important of all Christian doctrines—the Trinity.

Perhaps President Kennedy either sang or heard this hymn only in Latin since Vatican Council II convened from 1962–1965. The major results of this convocation in Catholic worship were the move from the liturgy in Latin to the vernacular and the strong emphasis on active participation in worship, including congregational singing. It is uncertain whether either of these edicts was in place in any Catholic service by November 1963, the month of Kennedy's assassination.

Kennedy was a believer in Roman Catholicism, and he participated in its church services. Therefore, the hymn "Holy God, We Praise Thy Name" could have influenced and reinforced his belief in God and the church's Trinitarian doctrine. It certainly is a strong hymn of praise to almighty God.

LYNDON B. JOHNSON

1908–1973

Thirty-Sixth President (1963–1969)

Like an earlier president named Johnson, Lyndon Baines Johnson assumed the presidency in the wake of a president's tragic assassination. Like this predecessor from a century before, he also served in one of the most tumultuous decades in American history. He sought to stamp his impression on the nation after winning a term in his own right by one of the greatest landslides in American history, but by the end of his presidency he had become instead a tragic figure, literally almost besieged in the White House and disappointed by his own unpopularity. After leaving the job that he had sought for so long, he died within a few years at a still relatively young age.

Lyndon Johnson was born in central Texas in the years prior to World War I. Both sides of his family at one time had been fairly prosperous, but by Johnson's childhood had fallen on hard times.

His father did serve for a time in the Texas state legislature, and through his father's experiences Johnson got his first taste of politics. Because of his family's financial difficulties, Johnson worked his way through the Southwest Texas State Teachers College in San Marcos. He also demonstrated some measure of adeptness in campus politics there. After graduation he went to work as a teacher in south Texas, teaching mainly disadvantaged and impoverished students of Mexican descent. He often referred to this brief experience as significant in forming his opinions about poverty.

In the 1930s, Johnson began to capitalize on his political ambitions, moving to Washington, DC, to become a congressional aide for Texas congressman Dick Kleberg. He then served as the Texas state director of the National Youth Administration, a New Deal program. Highly successful as an aide, Johnson revolutionized the work of congressional aides and convinced himself that he would make a great congressman. In 1934 he married the daughter of a wealthy Texan. The gracious and genteel Claudia Taylor, better known as "Lady Bird," became a chief asset for Johnson in his political ambitions. In 1937 voters in his home district elected Johnson to the US House of Representatives. Pledged to the New Deal programs of President Franklin Roosevelt, Johnson worked diligently to promote rural electricity, especially in Texas. After losing a tightly contested race for the US Senate, Johnson volunteered for the US Navy and served for a time in the Pacific theater of operations, mainly in legal and administrative capacities, during World War II. After his service, he returned to the House of Representatives. In a highly controversial and contested election in 1948, Texas voters elected Johnson to the US Senate by a supposed eighty-seven votes. Within a few years he became the Senate minority leader, and when Democrats gained control of the Senate, he became the Senate majority leader. Highly effective in this position, Johnson quickly became one of the nation's foremost politicians. In 1960 after he lost the Democratic Party's nomination for the presidency, he accepted the party's position as vice president on John Kennedy's ticket. When Kennedy was elected, Johnson became vice president. As vice president his main responsibility was to oversee the nation's space program. When Lee Harvey Oswald assassinated Kennedy in November 1963, Johnson became the nation's thirty-seventh president.

In 1964 Johnson, now typically called "LBJ," diligently pushed through a new civil rights bill that had been stalemated in Congress. In 1964 he also won reelection in a landslide over Republican Barry Goldwater. Perceiving this election as a mandate, Johnson initiated an agenda he dubbed "The Great Society" program. Included in these initiatives were attempts to eliminate poverty in the United States, significant national aid to education, and continued promotion of civil rights, especially voting rights for African Americans. He promoted medical attention for low-income families through Medicaid and for the elderly through addition of Medicare to the nation's Social Security program. LBJ also continued a highly successful exploration of outer space through the *Mercury, Gemini,* and *Apollo* programs.

Despite Johnson's efforts to eliminate poverty and support civil rights, civil unrest continued. He continued and expanded US involvement in Southeast Asia. Johnson had supported President Kennedy's decision to send supplies and advisors to the corrupt but anti-Communist South Vietnamese government in their attempts to resist North Vietnam's attempts to unify the divided country under Communist rule. By 1965 American involvement had grown to more than 100,000 combat troops and included US Air Force and Navy bombardments of supply routes from North Vietnam to South Vietnam. Eventually, these aerial attacks targeted routes along the Ho Chi Minh Trail in neutral Laos and Cambodia.

Military buildup in relationship to the Cold War continued as well. By 1968, American combat troops numbered more than half a million. As American participation increased and casualty rates grew, internal opposition to the war expanded. Increasingly, inflation dogged the US economy, despite substantial growth, as LBJ continued to support the expensive war effort, the innovative space program, widespread social reform and high technology, and Cold War-related military programs. Due to the growing stress and his widespread unpopularity, Johnson chose not to run for reelection in 1968. He died only four years after leaving the White House.

Johnson maintained a persona that was larger than life. He did worship publicly but was generally regarded as rather "rough" in his language and lifestyle and regularly demonstrated an "earthy" sense of humor. He was affiliated with the Disciples of Christ but made little comment on his personal faith, although like many US presidents after Eisenhower, he frequently spoke with Billy Graham and considered him an advisor. He did strongly support the American concept of separation of church and state and promote equality in American life consistent with progressive religious ideals. In his social concerns he demonstrated compassion for the downtrodden and underprivileged, and he agonized over the loss of life incurred in Vietnam.[326]

Evidently Lyndon Johnson had limited musical talent. He studied violin for several months as a boy and took a few dancing lessons. Early in life his mother insisted that he practice elocution, and he grew up with a sort of grassroots expression in the arts. Because of the tremendous emphasis placed on the arts by the Kennedys, the role that President Johnson played in developing the arts has often been overlooked. He felt that the arts belonged to the whole country and should come from small towns rather than just large cities. Abe Fortas, a Johnson advisor who had a love for music, said that the president had an extraordinary aesthetic sensibility, an untrained sense of art and music, but a natural appreciation of the arts.[327] The president certainly enjoyed western music, such as "Don't Fence Me In," "Wagon Wheels," songs from the musical *Oklahoma*, and "The Yellow Rose of Texas." But he also enjoyed some "highbrow" music, such as Strauss's "Blue Danube." Lady Bird Johnson came to appreciate ballet very much while in the White House. The Johnson daughters enjoyed the social dances held in the mansion, especially the variety of rock-inspired gyrations of the early 1960s. The president preferred dancing to "Alexander's Ragtime Band." On the word of some advisors, including Robert Kennedy, Johnson did not invite popular singer Frank Sinatra to the White House because of the reputation of certain friends of the crooner.

The Johnsons strove for high-quality talent, superb productions, and fresh ways to honor the arts. They had great pleasure in promoting the arts, choosing representatives of current musical trends very carefully. For the first time, jazz occupied a prime place in mansion musicales. Dave Brubeck, Charlie Byrd, and the North Texas State University Lab Jazz Band performed, but the appearance of Duke Ellington in 1965 was a highpoint of the Johnson years. There was an emphasis on children and youth music during this era. Eric Leinsdorf, conductor of the Boston Symphony stated, "I think the President was keenly aware of the enormous importance which music played in the creation of a better life for people."[328]

The result of President Johnson's action on the arts was the establishment of the National Council on the Arts in 1964, followed by the National Foundation for the Arts and Humanities in 1965 and the National Museum Act of 1966. The sheer magnitude and scope of these developments were impressive. President Johnson often spoke of the arts in American life. At the White House Festival of the Arts in 1965 he said, "Art flourishes most abundantly when it is free—when the artist can speak as he wishes and describe the world as he sees it…. [Artists] help dissolve the barriers of hatred and ignorance which are the source of much pain and danger. In this way [they] work toward peace…which liberates man to reach the finest fulfillment of his spirit."[329]

While protest singers, led by Bob Dylan, did not appear at the White House like the Hutchinsons of the 1840s, the vocal protestors did proclaim their message in song during the 1960s. Johnson attempted to correct racial, intellectual, and human injustice with his efforts to establish a "Great Society." The Johnsons were creative in programming "twin-bills" for state dinners at the White House. The mixing of folk, pop-folk, Baroque-pop, and nightclub styles with classical performers like pianist Van Cliburn was typical. For their final musicale in 1968 they invited opera star Robert Merrill to appear with the New Christy Minstrels.

Two hymns were noted by the Lyndon Baines Johnson Library as favorites of the president. The first, "Onward Christian Soldiers," was written by Englishman Sabine Baring-Gould in 1864. After first appearing in America in 1873, it became very popular. In 1910 it was sung at the World's Sunday School Convention held in Washington, DC. On 22 May of that year, the hymn was sung simultaneously in more than 100 nations world-wide, in as many languages, being translated and performed to show solidarity of the Christian church.[330] The hymn was the battle song for Theodore Roosevelt's campaign of 1912 and became a favorite song during World War I. President Woodrow Wilson liked the hymn very much, and it was selected to be broadcast nationwide on 6 June 1944 (D day), after a prayer voiced by President Franklin Roosevelt. The second hymn noted was "The Battle Hymn of the Republic," a moving hymn that has been favored by many presidents from Abraham Lincoln to the present. President Johnson especially liked singer Anita Bryant's rendition of this patriotic hymn. President and Mrs. Johnson claimed "Silent Night" as their favorite Christmas hymn.

The author of "Onward Christian Soldiers," Sabine Baring-Gould, was born in Exeter, England, in 1834 and graduated from Cambridge University in 1856. Being a man of unusual versatility, he spent much time in France and Germany as a youth. He wrote extensively on various subjects, including two volumes of hymns. Even though he has more book titles in the catalogue of the British Museum than any other writer of his time, he is best remembered as the poet of this simple but powerful hymn. The benediction hymn "Now the Day Is Over" also came from his pen.

The occasion for writing "Onward Christian Soldiers" was on Whitmonday of 1864 when Baring-Gould was curate at Horbury. During the Victorian era, this special day initiated several festival days for the Church of England. Customarily, Sunday school children marched to nearby villages, singing hymns as they processed. Feeling that he needed a march, the thirty-year-old minister stayed up late searching for the right hymn. Having the melody of the slow movement of Haydn's *Symphony in D* in mind, he wasn't satisfied with any text. Thus, he wrote his own, completing the lyrics in less than fifteen minutes. He later stated, "It was written in great haste, and I am afraid that some of the rhymes are faulty." Titling the poem "Hymn for Procession with Cross and Banners," because the children were to march

Onward Christian Soldiers

Words: Sabine Baring-Gould, 1865
Music: Arthur S. Sullivan, 1871

6.5.6.5.D. with refrain
ST. GERTRUDE

1. On - ward Chris-tian sol-diers, march-ing as to war, With the cross of
2. Like a might-y ar - my moves the Church of God: Broth-ers, we are
3. Crowns and thrones may per - ish, king-doms rise and wane, But the Church of
4. On - ward, then, ye peo - ple, join our hap-py throng, Blend with ours your

Je - sus go - ing on be - fore! Christ the roy - al Mas - ter,
tread - ing where the Saints have trod: We are not di - vid - ed,
Je - sus con - stant will re - main; Gates of hell can ne - ver
voic - es in the tri - umph song; Glo - ry, laud, and hon - or

leads a - gainst the foe: For-ward in - to bat - tle see his ban-ners go.
all one bod - y we, One in hope, in doc-trine, one in char - i - ty.
'gainst that Church pre-vail; We have Christ's own pro-mise, and that can-not fail.
un - to Christ the King; This thro' count-less a - ges men and an-gels sing.

On-ward Chris-tian sol - diers march-ing as to war,

With the cross of Je - sus go - ing on be - fore! A - men.

behind an elevated cross followed by various Christian banners, he never expected it to be published. The children were delighted to know that they were the inspiration for the new hymn and heartily sang the hymn in procession from Horbury Bridge to nearby towns.[331] After the text was printed in *The Church Times* on 15 October 1864, it became extremely popular, much to the author's surprise.

Much of this notoriety can be attributed to the tune composed for the text when Sir Arthur Sullivan was inspired by the lyrics in 1871. Having become famous for his composing, Sullivan was the musical part of the "Gilbert and Sullivan" team, but also was an organist. While visiting the home of Mrs. Gertrude Clay-Ker-Seymer, at Hanford, Doretshire, he composed this tune. The lady of the house said that they went into her private chapel and sang the new tune with Sir Arthur accompanying on the harmonium. Charged with the spirit of hope and triumph, the music was stirring and majestic. Sullivan named the tune ST. GERTRUDE in honor of his hostess. The tune has a meter of "6.5.6.5 doubled with refrain" and is ideally associated with this text. The new tune with the text was first published in the *Musical Times* in 1871, followed by the *Church Hymnary* in 1872. The complete hymn was first published in America in 1873 in John Sweney's *Gems of Praise* in Philadelphia. Charles Robinson commented, "This hymn meets an American ideal…in that it is simple, rhythmic, lyric, and has a refrain at the end of each stanza." It rates high among hymns in both England and the United States.

The main misconception of the hymn is that it concerns war. While it employs imagery of marching, the metaphors deal with life and the journey of faith, not war. Originally intended for use in the custom of banner bearing, it does contain the biblical expression of the church militant. The words call for engagement with the world rather than withdrawal from it. The hymn proclaims the unity of Christianity rather than any differences. Being firmly Christological in focus, it places the cross at the center of Christian living. The language is not so directly militaristic as it is carefully allegorical and metaphorical—*like* a mighty army and marching *as* to war. It also speaks to those who contend with evil forces in a fractured and broken society.[332]

The conflict that President Johnson inherited may have been one good reason for his selection of this hymn. Stanzas two and four contain words that are actually a celebration of Christ's victory over death and hell. The need for Christian unity is evident in stanza three, while stanzas one and five are rallying cries to unite under one banner of Christ. As with most presidents, President Johnson was always conscious of a praying nation: "No man could live in this house where I live and work at the desk where I work without needing and seeking the support of earnest and frequent prayer. Prayer has helped me to bear the burdens of the first office, which are too great to be borne by anyone alone."[333] Undoubtedly, President Johnson had many struggles in the office he inherited. He, along with other leaders, used great and relevant hymns to bolster his courage during difficult times.

RICHARD M. NIXON

1913–1994

Thirty-Seventh President (1969–1974)

Early in his career, Richard Nixon made a name for himself by his controversial attacks on Communist sympathizers and alleged Communists in American government and business. Throughout his meteoric rise to the vice-presidency and to the Republican nomination for the presidency in 1960, his name became synonymous with controversy. After two notable failures, Nixon staged a political comeback that astonished most political commentators. After a few years in the White House, he resigned in the greatest scandal ever to touch the US presidency. Before his death, however, he staged another comeback and, despite the lingering controversy associated with him, became recognized as an elder statesman.

Richard Milhous Nixon was born in California in 1913. Raised in the lower middle class, his family struggled with the onset of the

Great Depression. An outstanding student, when disappointed by failure to receive a scholarship to Harvard University, Nixon distinguished himself at tiny Whittier College, a small Quaker school in his hometown. He then matriculated at Duke University Law School, where he achieved an outstanding record. After graduation he became the first Duke Law graduate to pass the California bar exam. During his four years in a Whittier law firm, he married Patricia Ryan, by whom he had two daughters. Like Lyndon Johnson, he enlisted in the US Navy with the onset of World War II, serving as a legal officer from 1942 until 1945, with most of his experience coming in administrative posts.

Nixon's naval experience convinced him that he had a future in politics. In 1946 he ran for the congressional seat in his home district, campaigning on a conservative anti-Communist, anti-New Deal platform. Elected, he went on to become a leading anti-Communist, serving on the controversial House Committee on Un-American Activities (HUAC), which sought to expose Communists and Communist sympathizers in government, in business, and in Hollywood. Nixon served as the chief congressional examiner of State Department official Alger Hiss. His work on HUAC catapulted him to national prominence while still a freshman congressman. He parlayed this notoriety into election as US senator from California in 1950, recognized as a prominent "cold warrior." Even though he was only thirty-nine, the Republican Party chose Nixon to be Dwight Eisenhower's running mate in 1952, continuing his rapid rise in US politics. When charged during the campaign with accepting gifts, favors, and having a secret campaign fund financed by conservative California millionaires, Nixon utilized a new medium, television, in a famous nationwide speech, known as the "Checkers speech" after the dog his daughters had been given. This savvy political move saved Nixon's place on the ticket. Eisenhower and Nixon were elected in 1952 and reelected in 1956.

Throughout Eisenhower's presidency, Nixon assumed major roles despite the fact that Eisenhower didn't always approve of him. Nixon and the aging leader never became close friends, but the two did become close associates, and Eisenhower sought to keep Nixon fully informed on government issues. Eventually, Eisenhower and Nixon became related by marriage when Nixon's daughter Julie married Eisenhower's grandson David. Among the duties assumed by Nixon during those eight years was a prominent role in foreign affairs. Historian Stephen Ambrose states that Nixon knew more foreign leaders than any other US vice president. When Eisenhower suffered a heart attack in 1955 and a stroke in 1957, Nixon calmly and capably handled his responsibilities. In 1960 Republicans overwhelmingly nominated Nixon as their presidential candidate. However, John Kennedy defeated Nixon in one of the closest presidential elections in American history. In 1962 he suffered a narrow defeat in the California gubernatorial contest. Many people thought his political career was over.

In 1967 and 1968, however, Nixon staged a remarkable comeback. With the nation wracked by civil unrest and uncertainty over the Vietnam War, Nixon received the Republican presidential nomination and then defeated Vice President Hubert Humphrey and third-party candidate George Wallace. After stepping up the bombing of North Vietnam and US support of South Vietnam, including increased aerial bombing of Communist bases in Cambodia, Nixon ended the draft, started a program called "Vietnamization," an attempt to turn the war effort over to the South Vietnamese, and began withdrawing US ground troops. Despite his strident anti-Communism, he also opened negotiations with Communist China (The People's Republic of China), flying to China to meet Communist leaders Chou En Lai and Mao Tse Tung. He worked with Soviet leader Leonid Brezhnev to develop the landmark Strategic Arms Limitation Treaty (SALT), beginning a period known as détente. After an overwhelming reelection victory over Democratic candidate George McGovern in 1972, Nixon and his national security advisor Henry Kissinger agreed to a settlement with North Vietnam to end US involvement in Vietnam.

Unfortunately for Nixon, within a short period of time, allegations of corruption and a cover-up began to assail Nixon's administration. As the media and Congress became involved, Nixon insisted that he had not known about the infamous Watergate break-in during the presidential campaign and also maintained that he had not tried to prevent investigation by the Justice Department. Throughout summer 1973 and following, increasing revelations demonstrated that Nixon actually had tried to prevent the investigation. At the same time, other unrelated allegations emerged that led to the resignation of Vice President Spiro Agnew and the nomination and approval of Gerald Ford as vice president. As Congress continued to collect evidence and as Nixon faced impeachment, he resigned in August 1974. He is the only president in US history ever to do so.

After his resignation, Nixon retired from the public scene but gradually became a prolific author. Over the years prior to his death, he was gradually re-embraced by the Republican Party as a senior statesman. He died in April 1994.

Nixon was reared a Quaker by his devout mother, and until his days in college, he adhered to strict Quaker teachings. When he married Pat, she converted to the Quaker faith to please Nixon's mother. However, after his college days he generally was considered a nominal Quaker, and Stephen Ambrose notes that he had serious doubts about many Quaker doctrines. In the White House, like Eisenhower before him, he became quite close to Baptist evangelist Billy Graham, and Graham continually lent his moral support to Nixon in the climactic days of the Watergate scandal and impending impeachment proceedings.[334]

Richard Nixon became a fine performer after studying piano and violin as a boy. Growing up, he spent considerable time at the East Whittier Friends Meeting House in Southern California. Not only did he play the piano for various weekly church services, but he also taught Sunday school and sang in the choir. Playing hymns and popular songs was enjoyable for him: "Playing the piano is a way of expressing oneself that is perhaps even more fulfilling than writing or speaking. In fact, I have always had two great—and unfulfilled—ambitions: to direct a symphony orchestra and to play an organ in a cathedral. I think to create music is one of the highest aspirations man can set for himself."[335] He was the first president since Truman to play the piano for White House guests. Sometimes on trips he had a piano moved into his suite at hotels, and during Watergate he played late at night in the mansion's family quarters.

President Nixon often spoke of his mother's faith. She was a godly woman who reared her children to fear the Lord and to honor his word. Once in his political life she said, "Richard, don't you give up. Don't let anybody tell you you are through." Her favorite hymn was the Quaker tune "Simple Gifts," which also was one of Richard's most loved songs. In 1926 Nixon's father took his three sons to a Paul Rader evangelistic crusade in Los Angeles, where each of the boys committed his life to Christ.[336]

President Nixon brought a reserved way of life to the White House, preferring formal attire, traditional art, and conservative music. The president and First Lady favored foxtrots and waltzes for social dancing. Some of the media criticized the president's artistic tastes as deplorable. However, between 1969 and 1974 there was a variety of styles represented in the musicales: twenty-four popular performers, nineteen classical artists, six jazz programs, three country music acts, three dance recitals, and one musical theater performance.[337] Included in these events were Elvis Presley, Johnny Cash, Sammy Davis, Jr., Beverly Sills, Richard Tucker, Nicol Williamson, and the complete Broadway musical *1776*. The president felt that music should reflect not only the gamut of American tastes, but also his own eclectic preferences. For this reason he personally made all decisions as to who would be invited. Hardly a national holiday, family birthday, or even a White House church service passed without some musical event. President Nixon was the first to acknowledge significant world events with commemorative musical tributes. These included the achievements of the *Apollo 11* astronauts, the United Nations' twenty-fifth anniversary, and the returning Vietnam prisoners of war. Performers reflected American musical styles, some of which made intense social statements; being difficult to control, they were sometimes embarrassing to the administration.

Instead of attending Friends Meetings in Washington, President Nixon planned a series of twenty-six non-denominational Sunday worship services in the White House. This ecumenical effort had an order of service patterned after Protestant worship. Regardless of the belief of the participants, "The Doxology" was required to be intoned. Then, an appropriate hymn was sung, a twelve-minute sermon without notes was presented, another hymn was sung, followed by a benediction. In addition, a musical rendition by a soloist or choir was used. Typically choirs like the Vienna Choir Boys, the Danish Boys Choir, and several Jewish choruses sang. It is unclear who selected the hymns for these services. It is possible that the president himself chose them because he was a deeply religious, although private, man. Dr. Billy Graham, a confidant of the Nixons for two decades, said of Nixon, "He doesn't wear his religion on his sleeve."[338]

At the first Sunday service, Billy Graham was the speaker, and gospel soloist George Beverly Shea sang "How Great Thou Art." Afterward, President Nixon sat down at a piano upstairs and began accompanying himself as he sang, "He will hold me fast, for my Savior loves me so, He will hold me fast." When asked about where he learned that old gospel song, the president related that when he was thirteen or fourteen, his father took him to Paul Rader meetings in Los Angeles; that was the signature song the choir sang every night,[339] and it made a deep impression on him.

The Nixon Presidential Library found no information about Nixon's favorite hymn. He evidently loved "The Doxology," the most sung hymn of Christendom. Other sources indicate that he enjoyed a Christmas song based on a medieval legend called "Little Drummer Boy." He appreciated the navy hymn "Eternal Father, Strong to Save," as did other presidents who served in the navy. Several other hymns heard at his funeral were "The Battle Hymn of the Republic," "Amazing Grace," "The Old Rugged Cross," "Nearer, My God, to Thee," "America the Beautiful," and "He Will Hold Me Fast." Since at this service Dr. Graham referred to the story of the president's connection with "He Will Hold Me Fast" and the influence it may have had on his conversion and life, it seems to have been a most cherished hymn.

The lyrics to "He Will Hold Me Fast" were written by Ada Habershon, an English woman born in 1861. Having been raised in a Christian home by believing and praying parents, Ada devoted her entire life to God's service. When she met Dwight Moody and Ira Sankey during their 1884 crusade in London, she became interested in their ministry. At their invitation and because of her knowledge, she went to America and delivered Old Testament lectures, which were later published. After becoming ill in 1901, she began writing sacred poetry. She penned "He Will Hold Me Fast" at the request of Charles M. Alexander, the music leader for evangelist Ruben A. Torrey. Alexander asked her to write some gospel song texts in 1905; by 1906 she had written 200 hymns.

Robert Harkness composed the music for "He Will Hold Me Fast."[340] He was the son of the mayor of Bendigo, a town in Victoria, Australia, where an evangelistic crusade was being planned in 1903. Since the local committee was to provide lay help for the campaign, including the accompanists, Robert's dad insisted that he audition for pianist. Reluctantly, Robert auditioned for the Torrey-Alexander team. He purposely played a non-traditional improvisation to "O That Will Be Glory." Memorizing the hymn quickly, he tried different improvisations of the chorus to try to displease Alexander. But instead, Charles said, "Keep it up. That is what we want." To further confuse the director, he played the chorus, doubling the melody at the octave, which greatly pleased Alexander. Dr. Torrey asked Robert if he was a Christian, to which Harkness replied, "No, I am here to play the piano." After the Bendigo meetings, Alexander talked with Harkness about spiritual matters, suggesting that he ought to accept Jesus Christ and become an out-and-out Christian. Riding his bicycle on his way home, he did just that, beginning a relationship with the team that lasted twelve years. He helped develop a new paradigm for revival music, lasting to the present day, while writing over 2,000 songs as well.

"He Will Hold Me Fast" was copyrighted by Tabernacle Publishing Company in 1906. It is incredible that President Nixon was able to play and sing this hymn forty-three years after he first heard it, and while hearing it, he was perhaps affected in such a way that he became a Christian. This is why it was a favorite.

Stanza one states that Christ will protect a believer from fear and temptation. The following stanza is a confession that this can't be done alone. Stanza three speaks of Christ's delight in saving a person, and the last stanza assures that because of the price Christ paid, sinners can be forever saved. The refrain is significant as it points out the reason for holding the lost sinner in his hand—"He loves me so." In his life, President Nixon had determination to the very end, as his mother had advised him; he never wavered in his belief in his position, taking the unprecedented step of resignation. This hymn

He Will Hold Me Fast

Words: Ada Ruth Habershon, 1905
Music: Robert Harkness, 1906

7.5.7.5.5.5.7.5.

1. When I fear my faith will fail, Christ will hold me fast;
2. I could nev-er keep my hold, He will hold me fast;
3. I am pre-cious in His sight, He will hold me fast;
4. He'll not let my soul be lost, Christ will hold me fast;

rall.

When the tempt-er would pre-vail, He can hold me fast.
For my love is oft-en cold, He must hold me fast.
Those He saves are His de-light, He will hold me fast.
Bought by Him at such a cost, He will hold me fast.

a tempo

He will hold me fast, He will hold me fast;
hold me fast, hold me fast;

For my Sav-ior loves me so, He will hold me fast.

summarizes Christ holding the Christian fast (strong). This is strengthened by the verbs near the end of each stanza: "he can," "he must," "he will." This is also echoed in Ephesians 6:10: "Be strong in the Lord."

GERALD R. FORD

1913–2006

Thirty-Eighth President (1974–1977)

Individuals who have assumed office in the middle of a presidential term face innumerable odds. While in all but one case these vice presidents have been elected as part of the presidential ticket, they may have to lead a cabinet they did not select or promote programs and ideas they do not support. Frequently, vice presidents have been chosen "to balance the ticket" either geographically or politically. Of course, most vice presidents who have assumed the president's office have done so upon the unexpected death or assassination of their predecessors. Only in the case of Gerald Ford has a vice president not been elected to his office, and, in that same case, he had to assume office in an event other than death. Gerald Ford was the first and only person to assume office upon the resignation of a president.

Gerald Ford was born in Nebraska in 1913 but grew up in Michigan. He attended the University of Michigan, where he was a star center and linebacker on the football team. He studied law at Yale University and then served in the US Navy during World War II. After the war, he married Elizabeth "Betty" Bloomer, with whom he had four children, began his law practice in Michigan, and became involved in Republican politics. In 1949 voters in his home district elected Ford to the House of Representatives. He achieved a reputation of great integrity, and voters reelected him to twenty-four years of service in Congress. In 1963 President Johnson appointed Ford as one of the members of the Warren Commission to investigate the assassination of President Kennedy. Subsequently, Ford served as the House of Representatives minority leader from 1965–1973.

In the early 1970s the country continued to be torn by dissension from the Vietnam War, and the economy began to experience a major economic recession. Worst of all, charges of corruption and deceit riddled the Nixon administration. In 1973, Nixon appointed Ford as vice president to succeed Spiro Agnew, who had resigned due to charges of tax evasion. In the months that followed, the Watergate scandal erupted and Nixon was forced to resign. Ford faced nearly insurmountable problems in the weeks and months that followed. He moved quickly to address the demoralization that the nation felt. He nominated former New York governor Nelson Rockefeller of the famed Rockefeller family and formed a cabinet. Seeking to calm the tumult that was ripping the country apart, he pardoned Nixon rather than see the former president placed on trial to the international shame of the country. This controversial decision cost Ford some respect from Americans wanting to see Nixon punished.

In his limited time in office, Ford dealt with major problems of inflation and a stagnated economy, the collapse of pro-American governments in Southeast Asia, and continued tension with the Soviet Union. He sought to stop inflationary pressures but also sought to stimulate the stagnated economy. Facing a Democratic Congress with a heavy majority, Ford utilized the presidential veto thirty-nine times, attempting to limit the growth of the federal bureaucracy and especially federal regulatory agencies. He brokered a temporary truce between Israel and Egypt while offering financial and military aid to both nations. He continued to promote détente with the Soviets, agreeing to the SALT II agreements limiting nuclear weapons. He refused to intervene when South Vietnam and Cambodia fell under resurgent Communist attacks, avoiding a new insertion of US forces in Southeast Asia. However, when Cambodian Communists captured an American merchant ship, the *Mayaguez*, Ford sent marines to free the crew and ship. President Ford survived two assassination attempts while president.

Despite strong opposition from Ronald Reagan, Ford secured the Republican nomination for president but lost the election to Jimmy Carter. Carter recognized Ford's contributions to healing the nation in his presidential inauguration. Ford devoted the remainder of his life to corporate and charitable causes while serving as a senior statesman, working on his presidential library and his autobiography. He died in 2006.

Ford was an Episcopalian and regularly attended St. John's Episcopal Church while he was president. He mentioned God and God's help upon occasion during his presidency and, upon addressing the Southern Baptist Convention in 1976, discussed at length the importance of religious liberty as well as the significance of churches, religion, and the Bible to the nation's health. He also stressed the role of Christianity in the development of culture at an address at Hope College. He remained active in the Episcopal Church until his health declined.[341]

Since Gerald Ford was not particularly fond of serious music, presentations of music at the White House during his administration were very relaxed, spontaneous, and entertaining, with styles leaning more toward the popular than they had been under Nixon. Ford's longtime press secretary commented, "As long as I've known him, he's never been interested in painting or sculpture or anything of that kind. He doesn't understand classical music. It just doesn't mean anything to him."[342] However, the future president had been a member of his high school glee club and was often moved to tears by listening to some emotionally moving songs, even hymns.

With First Lady Betty Ford, the arts were quite a different matter. Serving as White House hostess for her husband's administration, Mrs. Ford took charge of all the programming of musical events. Mrs. Ford had been a professional dancer with famed choreographer Martha Graham, so dancing was often the focal point. Even though the First Lady danced in Carnegie Hall in Graham's 1938 "American Document" program, the president himself didn't possess much dancing talent. President Ford insisted that the band play music to which he could dance, usually jazz and swing. Some members of the press wrote that he did the same two-step no matter what the meter of the music was.

Society writers often commented on the entertainment of the Ford years. They said that White House tastes were either "dismal," "establishment," or just plain "low brow." The choice in music was more indicative of Americans' musical tastes in the late 1970s: "Less innovative than inventive, less radical than romantic. It was a period for reworking, reconsidering, and the drive to protect society's ills unabashedly in song was less urgent."[343] However, the Fords were very successful in matching musical programs to the liking of state visitors. In 1975 there were fourteen state dinners representing thirteen different nations. The Captain and Tennille's big hit "Love Will Keep Us Together" was quite appropriate when Queen Elizabeth and Prince Philip of England visited America on 7 July 1976. Pearl Bailey, the outgoing blues singer, invited an embarrassed Egyptian leader, Anwar Sadat, to dance with her on stage at one event. Interestingly, the warm informality of this experience aided in bringing the two nations together. In 1974, one of the numbers at the dinner for King Hussein of Jordan was "You've Got to Be a Football Hero," obviously in honor of President Ford, but it was very entertaining as well.

The most important musical event was the 20 July 1976 White House gala, the celebration of America's bicentennial. Sponsored by Broadcast Music Incorporated, it included a wide range of conservative, mainstream, popular performers, such as Roger Miller, Ella Fitzgerald, Tammy Wynette, and "The Jordanaires." During Ford's term, there were many notable people from the arts who received the Medal of Freedom, America's highest civilian honor. Among these were Artur Rubinstein, Martha Graham, Irving Berlin, and Arthur Fielder.

The Gerald R. Ford Presidential Library states that the navy hymn "Eternal Father, Strong to Save" was President Ford's favorite hymn, due to his World War II naval service. Being a choice of five other presidents because of their naval service, the hymn story is covered under President George H. W. Bush's chapter. Hymns heard at President Ford's funeral included "Holy Ghost, with Light Divine," "My Country, 'Tis of Thee," "America the Beautiful," and "God Bless America." At the National Cathedral on 2 January 2007 "Holy, Holy, Holy," "The King of Love My Shepherd Is," and "For All the Saints" were sung. But the most significant hymn for President Ford was performed at St. Margaret's Episcopal Church in Palm Desert, California, to begin the six days of mourning his death. This Isaac Watts hymn, "O God, Our Help in Ages Past," was certainly familiar to the president since he regularly attended Episcopal churches and the hymn is included in *The Hymnal of the Protestant Episcopal Church 1940* and its replacement, *The Hymnal 1982*. (The life of Watts is included in President Zachary Taylor's chapter.)

Noted hymnologist John Julian wrote that "O God, Our Help in Ages Past" was undoubtedly one of Watts's finest compositions and his best psalm paraphrase. Its use is now universal, although only six of the original nine stanzas appear in most hymnals. The omitted stanzas are not equal to the

O God, Our Help in Ages Past

Words: Isaac Watts, 1719
Music: William Croft, 1708

C.M.
ST. ANNE

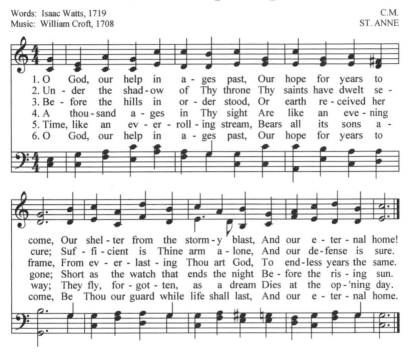

1. O God, our help in a - ges past, Our hope for years to
2. Un - der the shad - ow of Thy throne Thy saints have dwelt se -
3. Be - fore the hills in or - der stood, Or earth re - ceived her
4. A thou - sand a - ges in Thy sight Are like an eve - ning
5. Time, like an ev - er - roll - ing stream, Bears all its sons a -
6. O God, our help in a - ges past, Our hope for years to

come, Our shel - ter from the storm - y blast, And our e - ter - nal home!
cure; Suf - fi - cient is Thine arm a - lone, And our de - fense is sure.
frame, From ev - er - last - ing Thou art God, To end - less years the same.
gone; Short as the watch that ends the night Be - fore the ris - ing sun.
way; They fly, for - got - ten, as a dream Dies at the op - 'ning day.
come, Be Thou our guard while life shall last, And our e - ter - nal home.

others and actually impede the flow of thought.[344] Based on Psalm 90, this hymn is the second of five paraphrases of verses from this chapter set by Watts. Traditionally, the psalm has been ascribed to Moses; Watts's version does speak with a certain authority. But other scholars believe that Psalm 90 was written because of a Jewish national calamity. After young King Josiah wiped out idolatrous religions, the nation of Israel should have received the blessing of God. However, when Josiah was killed in battle while still a youth, the psalmist reminds the people that tragedies often occur but "after the nation has atoned for its sins, God the changeless and eternal will still be man's refuge and strength."[345] Subtitled in the original "Man Frail and God Eternal," Watts presents man's universal condition in contrast to God's reliability and stability.

Watts wrote this paraphrase shortly before the death of England's Queen Anne in 1714. At this time the country was in a state of anxiety about her successor, primarily because the Schism Act had been passed recently by Parliament. Not only did it forbid independents from operating schools, but it also implied greater levels of persecution for dissenting religious groups. Since Queen Anne died on the very day this act was to be enforced, many independents regarded her death as the "Protestant Passover."[346] With this hymn, Watts sought to calm the fears of his countrymen by encouraging them that the same God who had been their help in the past was their hope for the future.

Even though the hymn was not published until 1719 when it appeared in Watts's *The Psalms of David Imitated*, during five years it had been "lined out" in congregations throughout England. Ironically, in 1719, George I, who had replaced Queen Anne as monarch, repealed the Schism Act, thus justifying the faith expressed by the hymn. Originally titled "Our God, Our Help in Ages Past," this hymn became a bugle call to "stay the course, not only in worshiper's personal faith, but also in their relationship to the state and its laws."[347] In 1737 John Wesley changed the opening words to "O God," which turned the hymn to a broader community rather than just to the Calvinistic "gathered church" of the elect.[348] This guaranteed a more universal prayer rather than one to a limited sectarian deity.

The text of "O God, Our Help in Ages Past" is one of the grandest in all of hymnody. Being biblically based, it covers the entire scope of history, the mystery of time, faith in God, and the solidarity of a nation in times of crises when hope is placed in the eternal. Stanza one portrays the human perception of God as a force in the past and future, followed by stanza two, which ensures stability with the words "sure" and "secure." This long-term stability of God is celebrated in stanza three, after which man's concept of time is contrasted with God's time in stanza four. This thought continues to be reinforced in stanza five in graphic terms. Finally, Watts returns to the "eternal home."

The sturdy ST. ANNE tune by William Croft was first matched with Watts's text by the editors of *Hymns Ancient and Modern* in 1861. The setting ensured the enduring value of the hymn, especially as a national hymn in England. It is so well written that both George Handel and J. S. Bach often borrowed it. (The tune's history is covered in the chapter on President John Adams.) "O God, Our Help in Ages Past" has become an adopted hymnic expression for many Americans who see the United States as God's country just as eighteenth-century England was believed to be God's chosen nation. Carrying the torch of a blessed people, Christians have become the "chosen people." Thus, in America, the hymn perfectly fits in many national events such as presidential funerals as well as times of stress, which proves the universal appeal of this paraphrase of Psalm 90.

President Ford felt that the country needed healing and assurance when he made his final decision concerning Richard Nixon. Gathering up strength, on 18 September 1974, he offered a full pardon, stating, "I do believe, with all my heart and mind and spirit, that I, not as President but as a humble servant of God, will receive justice without mercy if I fail to show mercy."[349] Ford's action in this precedent-setting event is not only reflected in this hymn, but it is also consistent with the biblical passage President Ford chose when he took the presidential oath on 9 August 1974. Not only did he open the Bible to the following scripture for that ceremony, but he repeated these words as a prayer every night during his presidency. Proverbs 3:5–6 reads, "Trust in the Lord with all thine heart; and lean not unto thine own understanding. In all thy ways acknowledge Him, and he shall direct thy paths."

Known as an openly friendly, honest, and considerate person, President Gerald Ford made remarkably few enemies in his thirty years of public service. He often prayed for guidance in making particularly difficult decisions, which is consistent both with his choice of scripture as well as his choice of a favorite hymn.

JAMES E. (JIMMY) CARTER

1924–

Thirty-Ninth President (1977–1981)

Americans have sometimes known their presidents by physical characteristics. Americans recognized Abraham Lincoln, for example, by his gangly height, while they remembered William Howard Taft for his girth and John F. Kennedy for his handsome face. In the 1970s a political underdog rose to the nation's highest office and was often recognized for his toothy and famous smile. At the time, his southern friendliness seemed to reassure Americans in the wake of one of the nation's worst scandals.

James Carter, or Jimmy, was born in Plains, Georgia, in 1924. He was the first American president to be born in a hospital, unlike his predecessors, who were all born in homes. He was reared in a farm family with traditional rural family values, including a deep devotion to Christianity as expressed in his Baptist church. He excelled as a student and was appointed to the US Naval Academy during World War II, graduating as a submarine officer in 1946 and serving in the navy's experimental program to develop nuclear submarines. After seven years of service, he returned to Plains, where he became a successful peanut farmer. During the years of the civil rights movement, Georgians identified Carter as a progressive on racial issues. He ran successfully for the state senate and served for eight years. Not only did Georgians recognize Carter for his anti-segregationist viewpoints, but he became known for his efforts to improve government efficiency. Mainly because of his strong views on racial equality, Carter was defeated in his first bid for the governorship by segregationist governor Lester Maddox in 1966. In 1970, however, Carter was elected as Georgia's governor.

Four years later following the Watergate scandal, Jimmy Carter announced his presidential candidacy despite the fact that he was relatively unknown. He cast himself as a "new" Democrat, different from the liberal George McGovern whom Richard Nixon had defeated in 1972. He ran as the ultimate underdog and upset the political establishment with his candid campaigning and winsome smile. Winning the Democratic nomination, he narrowly defeated the more experienced Gerald Ford in the presidential election of 1976.

Unfortunately for Carter, the public's confidence in the national government was at low ebb due to the Vietnam War and Watergate. He advocated government efficiency and honesty, but high inflation and economic stagnation plagued his administration. Further hampering his efforts were the country's growing reliance on foreign oil and the creation and advancing strength of the Organization of Petroleum Exporting Countries (OPEC). Despite President Carter's efforts to urge the nation to reduce oil consumption and develop alternate sources of energy, spiraling inflation and interest rates increased the nation's economic woes. Despite some substantial achievements in deregulation and civil service reform, the American electorate grew impatient with Carter's administration. An uncooperative Congress also blocked his efforts to protect consumers, often viewing Carter as an outsider. Despite these difficulties, President Carter made significant strides in protecting the environment and in including women and minorities in significant government positions.

Congress, and especially resurgent conservative Republicans, criticized President Carter's foreign policies, oftentimes unfairly, including the agreement to turn over the Panama Canal to the nation of Panama. Conservatives opposed his recognition of Communist China, which continued Nixon's policy to include that nation in the broader international community. They also criticized Carter's responses to the Soviet Union's invasion of Afghanistan. An outspoken proponent of human rights, he found that international leaders usually rejected his pleas for improvement in this area. His greatest problem in foreign affairs came with Iranian militants' capture of the US embassy in Tehran and the subsequent hostage crisis. Carter's inability to secure the release of these hostages, despite diligent efforts and a failed rescue attempt, along with extensive television coverage and Iranian propaganda, ultimately led to his defeat in his reelection bid in 1980, despite the fact that he did negotiate the release of the hostages shortly before he left office.

President Carter's greatest achievement, however, came in the arena of international affairs. His groundbreaking efforts led to the agreement by Egypt and Israel to the Camp David Accords in 1978. His historic mediation between Egyptian President Anwar Sadat and Israeli leader Menachem Begin achieved peace between nations that had been at war for thirty years, and the agreement between the two has lasted until the present time.

In 1980, Carter's reelection bid fell victim to the Iran hostage crisis, a stagnant and inflationary economy, and a conservative resurgence led by Republican Ronald Reagan. In the years that followed, however, Carter set a new standard for the achievements of former presidents. He became an unofficial world emissary for peace and human rights. Through the work of his Carter Center, based in Atlanta, he has led international work to eradicate disease and has sought peaceful resolutions to conflict in locations like Haiti and North Korea. He receive the Nobel Peace Prize in 2002. He also became widely recognized for his work with Habitat for Humanity. He and his vivacious wife, Rosalynn, whom he married in 1946, humbly labored on countless Habitat projects. Their involvement and promotion dramatically increased the exposure of the organization's work and contributed significantly to its success.

Jimmy Carter is generally recognized to be the first American president to be openly evangelical and "born again." For many years he has been a deacon and Sunday school teacher in his local Baptist church, and he regularly attended the First Baptist Church of Washington, DC, throughout his presidency. Many of his human rights initiatives, beliefs about racial equality, and efforts for international peace may be directly traced to his deep Christian faith. He maintained a strong emphasis upon religious liberty and separation of church and state. He has also written several inspirational Christian books since his retirement. Originally Southern Baptist, Carter now identifies himself as simply "a Baptist," rejecting the more fundamentalist and conservative direction taken by the Southern Baptist Convention in the past two decades. Recently, he has sought to establish closer connections between all Baptist groups in the United States and to break down racial and ethnic barriers between the groups.[350]

The choice of President Carter's inauguration scripture gives an indication of his approach to his presidential leadership style. Initially he considered 2 Chronicles 7:14, but because of possible misunderstanding of the words "wicked" and "sin," he chose Micah 6:8: "He hath showed thee, o man, what is good; and what doth the Lord require of thee, but to do justly, and to love mercy, and to walk humbly with thy God."[351] This choice is also reflected in his most favored hymns.

President Carter's love of music is credited to a schoolteacher, Julia Coleman, who exposed him as a lad to classical music, art, and literature. Even though Jimmy was baptized at age eleven, according to his own admission, he did not become a devoted Christian until much later in life. Following his gubernatorial defeat in 1966, he came to a close relationship with God with the counsel of his younger sister, Ruth. This experience encouraged him to live a dedicated life of service to the church, community, state, and nation.

Having obtained an appreciation of great music, Carter spent most of his extra money as a midshipman at Annapolis on classical records.[352] Since he sang the moving navy hymn "Eternal Father, Strong to Save" along with classmates each Sunday morning at chapel, he developed a love for good hymns. He listed this outstanding Trinitarian hymn as one of his favorites. It was a selection of five other presidents and is covered elsewhere in this book. President Carter has requested that it be sung by the Navy Glee Club at his funeral. The Carter family has a hymn heritage common among Baptists, which includes singing "Blest Be the Tie That Binds," by John Fawcett, following the Lord's Supper, usually while holding hands as an expression of fellowship. This is also a favorite hymn.

Few presidential families have enjoyed classical music as much as the Carters. Former Marine Band director John Bourgeois said that of all the chief executives, President Carter had the most extensive knowledge of classical music. Occasionally the president would be brought to tears listening to a string quartet. The Carters invited some of the finest classical musical artists to perform at the White House. More significantly, they shared these events by having five one-hour programs televised nationwide on the Public Broadcasting Company. Initiated in 1978, these concerts included Vladimir Horowitz, Leontyne Price, Mikhail Baryshnikov with Patricia McBride, Mstislav Rostopovich, and Andrea Segovia. Following his desire to make it the people's White House, these events originated in the East Room. Like the president, Mrs. Carter also enjoyed listening to rehearsals for concerts at the mansion. This practice helped to relieve tension for the evening performance. When pianist Rudolph Serkin played at President Carter's first state dinner for Mexico's president Lopez Portillo in 1974, Mrs. Portillo, a former concert pianist, also played two Chopin selections. This was "an impromptu delight that melded elegance and informality in the typical Carter style."[353]

President Carter also recognized ethnic traditions by featuring folk musicians, including Bob Dylan, the Allman Brothers, and Paul Simon. In addition, the president said that jazz was the truly American indigenous music because of its "individuality and free expression of the inner spirit." When Dizzy Gillespie performed, Carter requested him to play "Salt Peanuts," and the president joined in with the bop artist, shouting the phrase "salt peanuts" on cue in the musical breaks. A comment was made that it was the "first presidential hot chorus in history." At a musicale honoring the Black Music Association in 1979, Chuck Berry, Patti LaBelle, Andrea Crouch, and Billy Eckstine were among those to perform. At the "Old Fashioned Gospel Singing" musicale, the president made some significant remarks, saying that "most of the gospel programs the Carters knew are '24-hour sings.' We had to shorten the White House event to three hours," drawing laughter from the crowd. Continuing, he stated, "Gospel music is really rural music. It has both black and white derivations; it's not a racial kind of music.... It's a music of pain, a music of longing and a music of faith."[354]

This is precisely a description of the favorite hymn of President Carter as he wrote, "Having been written by a former slave runner, 'Amazing Grace,' a universal favorite, had special meaning for Christians in the Deep South during the long struggle for civil rights. A close analysis of the lyrics is still inspirational, and the melody is simple and beautiful. I have sung the last verse several times on the stage with Willie Nelson, with him carefully holding the microphone nearer to his own mouth than mine."[355]

The author of "Amazing Grace," John Newton, was born in 1725, the son of an English sea captain. As a child, he had only two years of formal schooling, but his mother found great joy in teaching John scripture passages and hymns. She prayed that he might one day become a minister. Unfortunately, she died when he was only seven years of age; thus, he had to make his own way without her guidance. John's father made him go to sea at age eleven. Through the influence of evil companions, he lived a godless life. Being pressed into naval service, he soon deserted and, when captured, was flogged and degraded. Eventually, John fell into the hands of an unscrupulous African slave trader, who reduced him to the abject condition of a slave.

Amazing Grace

Words: John Newton, 1779
Music: Anonymous, 1831

C.M.
NEW BRITAIN

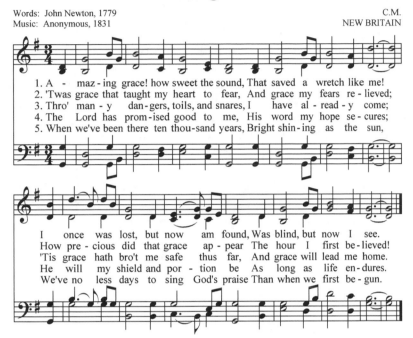

1. A - maz-ing grace! how sweet the sound, That saved a wretch like me!
2. 'Twas grace that taught my heart to fear, And grace my fears re-lieved;
3. Thro' man - y dan-gers, toils, and snares, I have al-read-y come;
4. The Lord has prom-ised good to me, His word my hope se-cures;
5. When we've been there ten thou-sand years, Bright shin-ing as the sun,

I once was lost, but now am found, Was blind, but now I see.
How pre - cious did that grace ap - pear The hour I first be-lieved!
'Tis grace hath bro't me safe thus far, And grace will lead me home.
He will my shield and por - tion be As long as life en-dures.
We've no less days to sing God's praise Than when we first be-gun.

It seemed that the memory of his mother and the religious teaching were lost on the teenaged boy.

Since at that time slave dealing was considered an honorable and lucrative profession, Newton eventually became the captain of a slave ship. However, he could not find peace with God. But with his deliverance from a debilitating fever and the reading of Thomas à Kempis's *The Imitation of Christ*, plus going through a terrifying storm at sea, he was brought as a penitent sinner to the throne of grace on 21 March 1748. After his marriage to his childhood sweetheart in 1750, he was appointed tide surveyor in Liverpool. During this time, Newton was closely acquainted with evangelical preacher George Whitefield, who greatly influenced him. After studying Greek and Hebrew as well as theological books, he accepted the pastorate of the Olney parish, ministering there for sixteen years. At Newton's invitation, poet William Cowper settled in Olney, and they became firm friends. Because of felt needs, Newton began having midweek night meetings. Cowper aided Newton in the ministry, and together they produced a book of Christian hymns for use in the Tuesday services. When *Olney Hymns* was published in 1779, 268 were by Newton and 68 were penned by Cowper. In this collection "Amazing Grace" first appeared, along with other notable hymns.

John Newton eventually had a strong influence on the abolition of slavery in England. Having many conversations with his friend William Wilberforce, the leader of the movement, Newton aided greatly in the success of the abolishment of English slave trading. "Amazing Grace" was written for a sermon Newton preached on 1 January 1773. Based on 1 Chronicles 17:16–17, the hymn was titled "Faith's Review and Expectation." Even though it is autobiographical, the hymn underscores the points of Newton's sermon. Author Steve Turner wrote:

> Phrases in the notes appear to have been paraphrased: "Blinded by the god of this world" became "was blind but now I see." "Millions of unseen dangers" became "through many dangers, toils and snares"; "the never to be forgotten hour" became "the hour I first believed" and "yet a little while and we shall be home" became "grace will lead me home."… Like the sermon, "Amazing Grace" outlined the Christian pilgrimage from conviction of sin ("taught my heart to fear"), repentance ("a wretch like me"), and faith ("the hour I first believed"), through the earthly journey ("brought me safe thus far") and on to life eternal ("a life of joy and peace"), with the focus remaining on the activity of "grace."[356]

No one knows which tune was first sung to the words of Newton; any number were possible because of its meter. Countess Huntingdon (a strong Christian and relative of George Washington) was the first to include the words in a hymn collection other than *Olney Hymns*. For some reason, the hymn never became popular in England. The tune sung today to "Amazing Grace" is called NEW BRITAIN. It first appeared in the shape note tune book *Columbia Harmony* in 1829, published in Cincinnati but with another text and with the tune name of GALLAHER. Some scholars believe NEW BRITAIN was a Scottish tune because of its use of a pentatonic scale in a specifically "Scottish way." Others think it was a slave melody, while some say it is a folk tune from the Shenandoah Valley. In 1831 the tune book *Virginia Harmony* included the tune HARMONY GROVE, which is almost identical to NEW BRITAIN. But William Walker is credited with first printing NEW BRITAIN and matching it to Newton's text in his 1835 tune book *Southern Harmony*. It may be that the printer in New Haven suggested the name because the only New Britain in America is a parish outside of Hartford, Connecticut.

The marriage of NEW BRITAIN to "Amazing Grace" proved to be a tremendous success since *Southern Harmony* sold an estimated 600,000 copies in America, which had a population of only twenty-three million in 1850.[357] The hymn was further spread by such evangelical movements as Dwight L. Moody and Ira Sankey campaigns in the late 1800s. Another reason for its success could be that "the words corresponded to the American experience in a unique way, not only by delineating the archetypal evangelical conversion but by articulating the groans of a people who frequently had to struggle with poverty, sickness, and the elements to survive."[358] Having learned the hymn from their owners, the black slaves of America also related well to this hymn; their heritage of slavery was inherent in the hymn's origination. These same types of situations may have affected the Carter family since President Carter wrote, "It is accurate to say that all three of these hymns have been favorites of several generations of my family."

President Carter would agree with John Newton when he wrote, "The views I have received of the doctrines of faith are essential to my peace. I could not live comfortably for a day, for an hour, without them."[359] The president was quoted by a *Washington Post* reporter in 1967 as stating, "I formed a very close, intimate personal relationship with God, through Christ, that has given me a great deal of peace."[360] His strong stand on desegregation and his work toward world peace and human rights seem to meld with the essence of the lyrics of "Amazing Grace." This hymn has become a worldwide phenomenon as is evidenced by the Library of Congress devoting an entire website to "Amazing Grace." Through the donation of an audio collection and the development of a database, this hymn has gained the distinction of being one of the best-known and most frequently recorded musical works in the world.

RONALD W. REAGAN

1911–2004

Fortieth President (1981–1989)

Some states in the Union bring to mind certain images or stereotypes. One such state is California. Some perceptions of California are right on the mark. The state is most often identified as Hollywood's home. Most people would readily admit that Hollywood and California create legends larger than life. Reflecting America's fascination with entertainment, the American president dubbed "the Great Communicator" got his start in the entertainment business in Hollywood and went on to use his considerable media skills to become the nation's fortieth president and bring about a period of change sometimes called "the Reagan Revolution."

Ronald Reagan was born in Illinois in 1911. From the time he was in high school, he demonstrated personal charisma, good looks, and athleticism. While attending Eureka College, a small institution affiliated with the Disciples of Christ Church, he played football but also began to study acting and to participate in school plays. After graduation, "Dutch," as he was known, became a radio sports broadcaster. Given a screen test because of his good looks, in 1937 he began a career in Hollywood that lasted for more than two decades. At one point, Warner Brothers, his studio, reported that only Errol Flynn received more fan mail than Reagan. His first marriage to actress Jane Wyman failed, but he fathered two children with her. In 1952 he married another actress, Nancy Davis, with whom he also had two children. Nancy would become a great asset and a significant influence in his political career. His acting colleagues elected Reagan as the president of the powerful Screen Actors Guild. He also spent time as a television host and became a leading spokesman for conservative politics in the late 1950s and early 1960s. He utilized this springboard to become heavily involved in California politics.

In 1966 Reagan won a narrow victory as Republican governor of California. Espousing conservative values during a time of civil unrest during the Vietnam War, he became the darling for conservatives around the country and began to be mentioned as a potential presidential candidate. He won reelection in 1970 and in 1976 unsuccessfully challenged the incumbent president, Gerald Ford, who narrowly defeated him for the Republican Party nomination. However, his speech before the convention clearly marked him as the frontrunner for 1980. After Carter's administration struggled with inflation and the demoralizing Iran hostage crisis, Reagan swept to the Republican nomination and then soundly defeated Carter in 1980 by more than a 400-vote margin in the Electoral College. Four years later, he won an even more impressive victory when American voters chose him over Carter's former vice president, Walter Mondale.

Reagan's first term began with difficulties. The nation dropped into an economic recession his first year in office, and less than three months after his inauguration an attempted assassination critically wounded him. Even as he faced surgery, his trademark sense of humor rallied the country behind him and strengthened his popularity. In the following years Reagan aggressively sought to remake the federal government by what he called "the Reagan Revolution," emphasizing stimulus for economic growth, efforts to limit inflation, to lower unemployment, and to both reduce taxes and government expenditures except in the area of national defense.

Even when huge deficits loomed and critics alleged that he was contributing to growing tensions with the Soviet Union, however, Reagan's popularity appeared to grow. Reagan's greatest contribution appears to have been his tremendous confidence in the American way of life and his superior communication skills that transferred that confidence to the public. He also stood strong against Communism, especially in Central America. His advocacy of a strong national defense led to tremendous popularity with veterans' groups, and his aggressive, though expensive, military programs have sometimes been regarded as a major reason for the collapse of Soviet Communism. He dealt aggressively with terrorism, even though American peacekeeping forces suffered terrible casualties in a terrorist bombing in Lebanon. Other antiterrorist activities included Reagan's hostile isolation of terrorist sponsor Libyan dictator Moammar Khadafi, whom Reagan regarded as one of the chief sponsors of international terrorism. Ultimately, Reagan ordered a US bombing strike in retaliation for Khadafi's activities.

Reagan's greatest accomplishment in foreign affairs was his series of negotiations with Soviet leader Mikhail Gorbachev that reduced nuclear weaponry and assisted Gorbachev as the Soviet Union instituted *glasnost* and *perestroika*. While the Berlin wall remained intact during his presidency, it may have first begun to crumble during Reagan's administration. Unfortunately, however, the notorious Iran-Contra scandal that involved the trading of weapons for hostage releases and subsequent illegal funneling of financial support for anti-Communist fighters in Nicaragua marred Reagan's second-term foreign policies. On the other hand, with an overhaul of the nation's income-tax system and continued emphasis on budget cuts in domestic programs in his second term, the nation's stock market soared and economic prosperity became widespread despite a growing gap between rich and poor. Perhaps his greatest overall achievement was the restoration of public morale in the aftermath of Vietnam, Watergate, and the Iran Hostage Crisis.

Reagan retired in 1989 at the age of seventy-eight, the oldest president in American history. After traveling, speaking, and enjoying retirement for a time, he was diagnosed with Alzheimer's disease. This public announcement did much to further public awareness of the disease. After a long illness, he died in 2004 and was mourned in a highly publicized series of funeral services.

Reagan's mother was a devoted member of the Disciples of Christ, and he spent most of his early life as a member of that denomination. As an adult, Reagan joined the Presbyterian Church and proclaimed that he was a born-again Christian. He openly professed his personal faith and frequently drew upon Christian values and terminology in his public addresses (for example, in his speeches and public prayers offered in the aftermath of the *Challenger* space shuttle disaster). At Reagan's funeral, his adopted son, Michael, spoke openly of his father's faith and its influence upon him.[361]

Although young Ronald was not a performing musician, he was the drum major for the YMCA Boys Band in Dixon, Illinois. He was selected for that particular honor because he could keep time marching and pumping the baton even though he could not play an instrument. His son Ron recalled his father singing to him as a child, but that was the extent of his dad's musical talent. At age fifteen, Ronald led in Dixon's Easter sunrise service when about forty worshipers from the Disciples of Christ Church sang the hymn "Arise and Shine" for the service near the railroad bridge. He also taught a young boys' Sunday school class and regularly attended worship services, where his favorite boyhood hymns were "Rock of Ages" and "The Old Rugged Cross."[362] In Reagan's high school yearbook, the caption under his picture read, "Life is one grand, sweet song, so start the music." Throughout his life he was always moved by patriotic music. Songs that reached people with the spirit of America were always inspiring and meaningful to the future president.

As a former actor and actress, Ronald and Nancy Reagan knew the entertainment business well. As First Lady, Nancy brought an image of class, good taste, and elegance to the White House, while the president added his charm. Since she gave the final approval to all performers at the mansion, the quality of music was guaranteed. While preserving White House traditions was important to the Reagans, they added their own unique touch. Ultimately, the delight in the programs was in the music itself and in its various genres; there was much variety during the Reagan era. They believed what Isaac Stern once said: "The world weeps, cries, loves and laughs better through music than in any other way."[363]

Soon after taking up residence in the White House, the Reagans began to plan a series of televised concerts, mainly from the East Room, titled "In Performance at the White House." The unique format of these programs was that the invited musical artist would bring a young budding performer who would also be showcased, often performing a duet with the older musician. The programs were very well received with such participants as Rudolf Serkin, Itzhak Perlman, Beverly Sills, Gene Kelly, and Leontyne Price, as well as the Julliard String Quartet and four generations of jazz artists. Merle Haggard brought a young fiddler for his appearance at the California White House. One program featured talented gospel and spiritual singers at the Washington historic Shiloh Baptist Church. This event was reminiscent of the Fisk Jubilee Singers who had sung for President Chester Arthur 100 years earlier. In addition, the Reagans hosted ten state dinners each year. On 26 March 1984, President Reagan presented Ernie Ford with the Presidential Medal of Freedom for his distinct service. Hymns played a valid role in this honor since in 1956 Ford's first album, titled simply *Hymns*, consisted entirely of favorite hymns. Incredibly, the album was at the top of the charts for 277 consecutive weeks, indicating the nation's love of hymns.

During his presidency, Ronald Reagan made mention of many favorite hymns, including "How Great Thou Art," "He Leadeth Me," "Jerusalem," "Amazing Grace," "Near to the Heart of God," "America the Beautiful," and "Lord, Make Me an Instrument of Thy Peace." His most loved Christmas song was "Silent Night," one of the carols sung around the piano in the grand foyer at the Reagans' first White House Christmas party.

But according to the Ronald Reagan Library, the president's favorite hymn was "The Battle Hymn of the Republic." This choice may be related to the following vignette, which Reagan told about his good friend Jeanette McDonald. Early in World War II, Reagan was stationed in San Francisco. Since there was no USO at the time, he was asked to contact someone to sing the national anthem for "I Am an American Day." When he called Jeanette, she said yes without hesitation. At the event she ended up singing a concert for the entertainment-hungry soldiers; she sang her entire repertoire. Because they wanted to hear even more, she finally sang a great favorite of hers, "The Battle Hymn of the Republic." Reagan said, "I will never forget her, nor forget how she sang; these 20,000 boys came to their feet and finished singing the hymn with her."[364]

"The Battle Hymn of the Republic" was written following a review of the troops near Fairfax, Virginia, on 20 November 1861. Present were President Abraham Lincoln, General George McClellan, cabinet members, Massachusetts governor John Andrew, Reverend James Clarke, Dr. Samuel G. Howe, and his wife, Julia Ward Howe. Following the ceremony, as they traveled by carriage back to Washington, DC, they heard soldiers singing "John Brown's Body," a song named for a self-styled abolitionist who was hanged for his efforts to free the slaves. Her former pastor said to Mrs. Howe, "Why do you not write some good words to that stirring tune?" She answered that she would: "Late that night while lying in her room in the Willard Hotel in Washington, Julia received an inspiration. She jumped out of bed and scribbled on a piece of paper the words 'Mine eyes have seen the glory of the coming of the Lord.' Then she sat up the rest of the night, and by candlelight, completed her poem."[365] The words first appeared in the February 1862 edition of *The Atlantic Monthly*. The editor paid Mrs. Howe five dollars and, since it had no name, titled the poem "The Battle Hymn of the Republic." Soon the entire nation was singing her words.

Julia Ward Howe, born in New York City, was raised in an evangelical Episcopal church. Already disagreeing with strict Calvinistic doctrine, she

The Battle Hymn of the Republic

Words: Julia Ward Howe, 1861
Music: William Steffe, 1858

Irregular
BATTLE HYMN

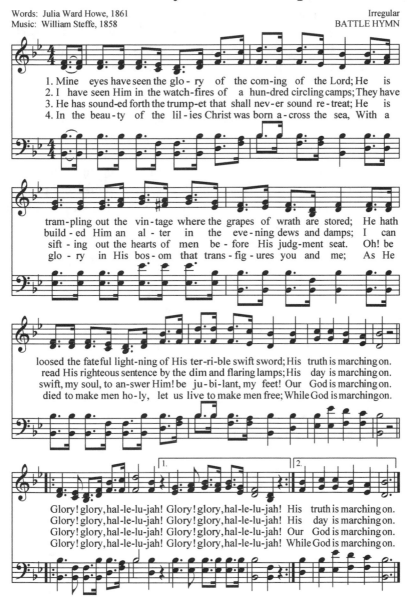

1. Mine eyes have seen the glo - ry of the com-ing of the Lord; He is
2. I have seen Him in the watch-fires of a hun-dred circling camps; They have
3. He has sound-ed forth the trump-et that shall nev-er sound re-treat; He is
4. In the beau-ty of the lil-ies Christ was born a-cross the sea, With a

tram-pling out the vin-tage where the grapes of wrath are stored; He hath
build-ed Him an al-ter in the eve-ning dews and damps; I can
sift-ing out the hearts of men be-fore His judg-ment seat. Oh! be
glo-ry in His bos-om that trans-fig-ures you and me; As He

loosed the fateful light-ning of His ter-ri-ble swift sword; His truth is marching on.
read His righteous sentence by the dim and flaring lamps; His day is marching on.
swift, my soul, to an-swer Him! be ju-bi-lant, my feet! Our God is marching on.
died to make men ho-ly, let us live to make men free; While God is marching on.

Glory! glory, hal-le-lu-jah! Glory! glory, hal-le-lu-jah! His truth is marching on.
Glory! glory, hal-le-lu-jah! Glory! glory, hal-le-lu-jah! His day is marching on.
Glory! glory, hal-le-lu-jah! Glory! glory, hal-le-lu-jah! Our God is marching on.
Glory! glory, hal-le-lu-jah! Glory! glory, hal-le-lu-jah! While God is marching on.

became more theologically liberal when she married and moved to Boston. But she insisted, "Nothing of what I heard or read has shaken my faith in the leadership of Christ in religion which makes each man the brother of all, and God the beneficent Father of each and all."[366] She always had a belief in a personal God and his overruling power. But because she believed that people can make a difference, she was active in various causes, including women's suffrage, world peace, and the abolition of slavery.

The tune universally sung to "The Battle Hymn of the Republic" is called BATTLE HYMN. Its history is difficult to trace, but it seems to have begun in the 1850s when a Charleston, South Carolina, fire company commissioned a composer to write a chanty for the words "Say, hummers will you meet us." Borrowing the catchy tune, the Methodists changed the words to "Say, brothers will you meet us...on Canaan's happy shore" and printed in *The Union Harp and Revival Chorister* in 1858.[367] In Charles Claghorn's study, South Carolina-born William Steffe, the organist and choirmaster of the Indian Fields Camp Meeting Fesitvals, wrote the music for "Say, brothers will you meet us." Others say the tune was a "work song" or a "plantation air" useful to pick cotton by; it may have originated with slaves. The tune BATTLE HYMN has true marks of southern folksongs. One scholar said the tune "is so simple and repetitive that it is hardly possible to speak of 'writing it'; rather it's a question of inventing it, spontaneously or otherwise, to go with the appropriate words and metric pattern. This particular pattern A-A-A-B was quite popular and simply 'in the air' in the 1840s and 1850s."[368]

At Fort Warren, Massachusetts, a quartet of sergeants regularly sang for various events. One evening they made up the words of "John Brown's Body" to the tune of "Say, brothers." After whistling the melody to band director Patrick Gilmore, he revamped and harmonized the tune. The band first played it at a flag-raising ceremony in May 1861. Although Gilmore wrote "When Johnny Comes Marching Home," he is best known for his band arrangement of what became BATTLE HYMN.

Charles C. McCabe, known as the Civil War "singing chaplain," did much to promote "The Battle Hymn of the Republic." While at a Christian commission meeting in February 1864, attended by President Lincoln, McCabe sang it, after which Lincoln requested a repeat performance. The hymn has been endeared by generations of Americans. Sung at numerous presidential funerals (including President Reagan's), it was even requested by British prime minister Winston Churchill to be sung at his funeral.

A study of the hymn reveals it is much more than just a song written during a national crisis. There were fine grape vineyards near Manassas where a major battle would occur. The pulsating rhythm of the tune illustrates the "trampling" of the stored grapes, matching it with the "marching" metaphor. There are unmistakable references to lightning-quick vengeance through swift retribution concerning John Brown in stanza one. Stanza two contains a clear picture of the "watch fires" that circled the city of Washington, DC, during this early period of the war when the Union feared that the Confederates would overtake the city and government. The "evening dews and damps" refer to the humid July weather in Virginia, while the "dim and flaring lamps" reflect the troop's camp conditions.

The allusion of the coming of the kingdom with its trumpet call in stanza three is not only biblical but also was prompted by the troop review. The judgment day as outlined in these phrases is a reminder to answer God's call for quick justice. While there are warnings, the emphasis on freedom is in stanza four, beginning with "Christ was born across the sea," a stanza that two other presidents wanted to eliminate or revise because it was too "Christian." The culture of freedom and morality inherent in the American psyche, especially during this civil crisis, is climaxed by the reminder that God's truth continues to "march." The last phrase's biblical image, "As He died to make men holy, let us live to make men free," was very appropriate at this time in American history.[369] It is very significant that this hymn was sung at the closing of the 6 June 1944 broadcast of D-Day. Following President Franklin D. Roosevelt's moving prayer, two hymns were heard: "Onward Christian Soldiers" and "The Battle Hymn of the Republic."

It is not surprising that President Reagan loved this hymn so much. It capsulizes his entire approach to liberating those oppressed behind the iron curtain. His accomplishments in world affairs are reflected in meeting the challenges presented in these lyrics. The positive tone of the text, which leads to victory over evil, is evident and consistent with Reagan's belief in God's divine plan. However, he also strongly believed in man's free will, which can determine his own destiny. Mankind has the guidelines to live by in the Bible; it's up to each person to decide whether he will follow those God-given instructions. What a powerful hymn chosen by a president who was able to carry out so much of the message of the poem.

GEORGE H. W. BUSH

1924–

Forty-First President (1989–1993)

Newsman and writer Tom Brokaw identifies the young men and women reared in the Great Depression and who served in World War II as "the Greatest Generation." Brokaw argues that this era produced a generation shaped by the hardships of the Depression who then saved the world from fascism and militarism with their selfless sacrifices. One such young man served as a naval aviator in the war and then went on to a career in public service that ultimately led him to the highest office in the land. Like John Adams, one of the founding fathers, this president, George H. W. Bush, also holds the distinction of fathering an American president as well.

George H. W. Bush was born in Massachusetts in 1924. Both his parents were interested in international affairs, and his father, Prescott, was a successful businessman who went on to become a US senator from Connecticut after George was an adult. Prescott saw that his son received a superb education, sending him to the prestigious Phillips Academy in Andover, where the younger Bush excelled as a student leader. When World War II erupted, George Bush volunteered for the US Navy, where he became the youngest pilot in the navy to receive his wings. He flew fifty-eight combat missions in the Pacific and was shot down near the Chichi Jima, part of the same island group that includes Iwo Jima. Fortunately, a nearby US submarine rescued Bush and saved him from nearly certain death. He received the Distinguished Flying Cross, the navy's highest honor.

After the war, Bush attended Yale University and married Barbara Pierce. He excelled in baseball and was Phi Beta Kappa, one of Yale's highest academic honors. He moved to Texas, where he and Barbara raised their family. Jeb eventually served two terms as governor of Florida, and their eldest, George W., eventually became two-term governor of Texas and the nation's forty-third president. George H. W. Bush became successful in the oil business and, like his father, became involved in politics.

From 1967–1971 Bush served his Texas home district as a member of the US House of Representatives. However, he also lost his bid for the US Senate. President Nixon appointed him as the US ambassador to the United Nations, continuing his interest in foreign policy. Afterward, he served as the chairman of the Republican National Committee as that party struggled with Watergate. Due to his foreign policy experience, he was selected to serve as head of the liaison service being conducted with the People's Republic of China. In 1976, President Ford tapped him as the director of the Central Intelligence Agency.

After Jimmy Carter's election in 1976, Bush returned home to Texas and prepared to run for the presidency in 1980. After a vigorous campaign, Ronald Reagan defeated him for the nomination but chose Bush to be his running mate. After Reagan's election, Bush served as vice president for the full eight years of Reagan's presidency, becoming a key advisor in the area of foreign affairs and representing the United States on many foreign trips, utilizing his considerable diplomatic skills. He quickly became the frontrunner for the Republican nomination in 1988 and won a victory over the Democratic nominee, Michael Dukakis, largely through a strong posture on defense and international relations, promises for "a kinder, gentler nation," and with the words, "Read my lips. No new taxes."

Bush rode the crest of prosperity for the first two years of his administration and benefited from the collapse of Soviet Communism in Eastern Europe. He celebrated the fall of the Berlin wall, but the celebration was short-lived. He sent troops into Panama to topple Panamanian dictator

Manuel Noriega, who had been indicted in the United States on drug charges. In summer 1990, Iraqi dictator Saddam Hussein invaded Kuwait and threatened US ally Saudi Arabia. Bush responded vigorously. He initiated "Operation Desert Shield," positioning hundreds of thousands of US military personnel, and assembled an international coalition, including many Arab nations, to oppose Saddam Hussein's aggression. When negotiations failed, the US-led coalition invaded southern Iraq, thrashed Saddam's huge army, and liberated Kuwait. Due to international pressure and other political and diplomatic considerations, however, coalition forces stopped short of ousting Saddam from power.

With the end of the war in 1991, Bush looked unbeatable in his reelection campaign for the following year. Unfortunately for him, the American economy entered a recession in the months that followed. Forced to raise taxes, his failed campaign promise hovered over his head, and Democrats reminded the voters of it frequently. The youthful Bill Clinton seemed an antithesis to Bush and his conservative approach to the economy. Third-party candidate Ross Perot also harmed Bush's chances, and Clinton defeated him in 1992.

Bush retired to Houston, Texas, but has remained active and visible. He supported sons George W. and Jeb in their political campaigns and went skydiving, much to the entertainment of the masses. He also performed critical roles in fundraising and administrative organization for disaster relief for tsunami victims in Asia and hurricane victims on the US Gulf Coast. He and Barbara have become beloved figures in US life.

The Bushes have been active members of the Episcopal Church in both Houston and in Kennebunkport, Maine. He has served as a vestryman for years in both churches on occasion. They both are active in many charity organizations and have shared public comments about their personal faith. While not as outspoken as his son, Bush frequently stated the importance of his personal faith during his war years and as president. On one occasion he shared that he believed that no one could be president without a belief in God. While some of his comments seem to have blurred the lines of church-state separation, he maintains that he upholds religious liberty. Either way, it is obvious that personal faith has been important to Bush.[370]

George Bush grew up in a family that possessed some musical talent. His father was a leader in the Yale Glee Club while in college and sang in the Silver Dollar Quartet, as well as being a lifetime member of the famed choral group the Whippenpoofs. Although his dad could not read music, he had a true bass voice and loved Fred Waring's chorus, the Pennsylvanians. Each one of George's three brothers and his sister had fine voices as well as an ear for music. But by his own admission, George never could carry a tune, even though he thoroughly enjoyed music, especially if it had rich harmony. As a teenager, he memorized the navy hymn "Eternal Father, Strong to Save," which may be partially responsible for his choice of military service. This hymn has beautiful harmony, enhanced by an exceptional melody.

In his adult life, George's musical tastes ranged from country and western music to Broadway tunes. His love for country music began in 1948 when he and Barbara moved to Odessa, Texas, to work in the oil business. On long trips to and from rigs, radio stations played only country music. Realizing that a good country song was like a Norman Rockwell painting, he said, "It captures the essence of the American spirit and portrays experiences that those who work hard and play by the rules can identify with. It is devoid of cynicism and can make you laugh or cry. To me, the same timeless qualities that make country music so appealing have also made our nation great."[371]

When George Bush decided to run for office, he thought that country music could be a natural match for politics. For his first campaign in 1964, he enlisted the help of a pure country group, the Black Mountain Boys. By 1977 George admitted that he really began to love country music. As vice president, beginning in 1981, he met some of the stars of country and western music. In his 1988 campaign for the presidency, Bush knew many performers who were willing to entertain at his political rallies. Among these were Crystal Gayle, Loretta Lynn, Roy Acuff, Moe Bandy, Bill Monroe, Vince Gill, Reba McIntyre, Ricky Skaggs, Barbara Mandrell, Randy Travis, Jimmy Dean, Naomi and Wynonna Judd, the Gatlin Brothers, and the Oak Ridge Boys.

Upon becoming president, George and Barbara recognized music as a vital gesture of American life. Music underscored every important national event in their White House. Continuing the concerts "In Performance at the White House" and having the Marine Band play 150 times a year meant there was much variety in musical events during the Bush era. They invited the American Ballet Theater, the Bolshoi Ballet, and the Houston Ballet to perform. In addition to country music stars, operatic singers included Roberta Peters, Fredica Von Stade, and Jessye Norman. Popular entertainers Pete Fountain, Harry Connick, Jr., Johnny Mathis, Gloria Estefan, and Joel Grey appeared, as well as some of the cast of *The Phantom of the Opera*. Classical instrumentalists were Yitzhak Perlman, Isaac Stern, Yo Yo Ma, Van Cliburn, and the National Symphonic Orchestra, among others. Christian musicians also sang, including Amy Grant, Michael W. Smith, Sandi Patti, and Lee Greenwood. In 1995 the president participated in the Twenty-Fifth

Annual Dove Awards by giving a taped greeting in which he stated, "Gospel music has meant a great deal to me. It touches the soul and our hearts, brings out the best in people. I salute you all."[372] During the Bush years, the first family hosted twenty-seven state dinners and at least twenty other special White House events, all of which involved musical performances.

President Bush sometimes referred to hymns in his speeches. In 1991 he spoke at the Australian World Congress Center in Melbourne, saying, "We hope this center will cause future generations to say of America and Australia, in the words of the great hymn, 'Blest be the ties that bind.'" In November 1992, George W. Bush coped with his father's failed reelection bid in consolation as he, his father, and campaign manager Mary Matalin cried on Air Force One when they listened to the Oak Ridge Boys sing "Amazing Grace." President Bush referred to William Cowper's hymn with these words: "You ever heard the expression 'The Lord works in mysterious ways?'... We had that in our family at the time, even with some bad things.... And if I had won that election in 1992, my eldest son would not be president.... So, what more can a dad ask? I think the Lord works in mysterious ways."[373] The office of President Bush clearly states that of all the hymns he loved, "Eternal Father, Strong to Save" was his most favored "because it expresses our dependence on God for peace and strength." This choice is consistent with his statement in 1989 at Phillips Academy in Andover, Massachusetts: "Without God's help we can do nothing. With God's help there is nothing we cannot do."[374]

In response to an ad in 1858 in the newspaper *The Guardian,* in which the English High Church invited submissions for a new hymnal, William Whiting, choirmaster at Winchester College, sent the poem "Eternal Father, Strong to Save." It was included in the 1861 collection titled *Hymns Ancient and Modern* because it also had translations of early Greek and Latin hymns. The hymn was written especially for one of Whiting's students who was planning to sail to America in 1860. Even though Whiting grew up on the coast of England and knew of the power of the ocean, it was not until age thirty-five that he experienced the fury of a storm at sea. Similar to John Newton's story when he came to God during a raging storm, Whiting prayed for God's help in keeping the boat afloat. Although he was assured of his salvation, the event prepared Whiting to write a powerful prayer hymn of encouragement for his student.[375] Interestingly, Whiting did not ask for any royalties for the poem; had he required them, he would have profited greatly because of its use even until today. It has been published in numerous hymnals and used regularly for worship services, solemn public gatherings, and state occasions since its publication in 1861. Hymnologist John Julian wrote, "The lack of

Eternal Father, Strong to Save

Words: William Whiting, 1860

Music: John B. Dykes, 1861

8.8.8.8.8.8.

MELITA

hymns for those at sea, together with its merits as a hymn, rendered it exceedingly popular from its first publication and its use has become most extensive in English speaking countries."[376]

The music for "Eternal Father, Strong to Save" was written by English clergyman and composer John Bacchus Dykes, who also wrote the music for Reginald Heber's "Holy, Holy, Holy." After receiving the poem and hearing of Whiting's sea experience, Dykes found a melody that fit the words perfectly. He called the tune MELITA, the ancient name for the Mediterranean island Malta, where the Apostle Paul was shipwrecked (Acts 28:13). Dykes's original harmonization of the melody is a sophisticated one, characteristic of the Romantic period of music. In a span of only twelve measures, he created a distinctive chordal motion that swells like the ocean it depicts. The MELITA tune is an example of musical originality in a conservative Victorian idiom, which demonstrates Dykes's musical skills as a gifted text painter.

The hymn was soon adopted by the English Navy, which spread it around the world. When in 1879 the choral director of the US Naval Academy heard the moving prayer for sailors, he started using it as the final hymn for every Sunday's service in the chapel at Annapolis. Becoming well loved by all midshipmen, the hymn soon became the official US Navy hymn. In 1995 "Eternal Father, Strong to Save" was one of four hymns sung at the fiftieth anniversary of the end of World War II. Since 1960 the words have been adapted for various branches of the military. Besides George H. W. Bush, five other presidents have listed it as a favorite hymn.

The Bible tells us much about the sea. Isaiah 51:15 reads, "God who stirs up the seas so that its waves roar." The writer of the Psalms describes those who go "down to the sea in ships [who] saw the deeds of the Lord" (Psalm 107:23–27). Paul experienced danger at sea: "No small tempest raged, all hope of our being saved was at last abandoned" (Acts 27:14–20). Both Paul and the sailors in the Psalms were saved, but their savior was the Lord (Psalm 107:28–29). Jesus also had some watery experiences. He walked on the water (Matthew 14:22–33) and encountered the storm at sea (Matthew 8:24). But "even the waves and sea obeyed Him" (Matthew 8:27).

"Eternal Father, Strong to Save" is not only the perfect navy hymn; it is also one of the greatest Trinitarian hymns ever written. While it addresses several biblical sea stories, it also outlines the work of the Trinity. Stanza one tells of the Father Creator, who appoints the limits of the sea and land. Stanza two speaks of Jesus, the performer of the two nautical miracles. Stanza three discusses the Spirit, who moved over the waters at creation. Stanza four addresses all three persons of the Godhead serving as the powerful protector to keep all sailors safe at sea—if not physically, at least spiritually.[377] MELITA is itself a "stormy" tune, which alone is a reminder of "those in peril on the sea."

This hymn has special significance for President George H. W. Bush because of the traumatic experience of having to parachute from his plane into treacherous ocean waters when shot down in the South Pacific. Fortunately, he was rescued by a US submarine, but it is certain that his memory of the hymn helped carry him through this experience. "Eternal Father, Strong to Save" is a powerful and meaningful prayer hymn, not only for those at sea, but also for Christians as they face the storms of life.

WILLIAM J. (BILL) CLINTON

1946–

Forty-Second President (1993–2001)

American presidents Woodrow Wilson, Franklin Roosevelt, and Grover Cleveland held the nation's highest office during times of war or economic depression. Calvin Coolidge and Dwight Eisenhower were blessed to serve during times of great prosperity and peace. The same is true of Bill Clinton, who presided over one of the lengthiest times of both peace and prosperity in US history. Perhaps because of this, he succeeded where no Democratic president had succeeded since Franklin Roosevelt, that is, in winning a second full term of his own. Unfortunately for Clinton, his second term was marred by a scandal involving his personal life.

Bill Clinton was actually born William Jefferson Blythe III in Arkansas in 1946. An automobile accident killed his natural father three months before Clinton was born. When his mother remarried a few years later, she changed young Bill's family name. Despite a difficult childhood, Clinton shone as a student and demonstrated exceptional talent as a saxophone player. He enjoyed music so much and exhibited such skill that he considered becoming a professional musician. However, a life-changing encounter with President John Kennedy while Clinton served as a delegate to Boys Nation redirected Clinton toward a life in politics. He attended and graduated from Georgetown University and received a prestigious Rhodes Scholarship to attend Oxford University. He completed a law degree at Yale University and returned to Arkansas.

His first foray in politics, a 1974 campaign for the US House of Representatives, ended in defeat. In 1975 he married fellow Yale Law School graduate Hillary Rodham. She proved to be a vigorous campaigner and advocate for him. His next campaign ended more successfully when Arkansas voters elected him state attorney general at the age of thirty. Two years later they elected him governor. Defeated in his reelection bid in 1980, he styled himself the "Comeback Kid" and ran again successfully in 1982. Arkansas subsequently reelected him in 1984 and for four-year terms in 1986 and 1990. Casting himself as a centrist, his main efforts included education reform and hiring of minorities in key positions in state government. Democrats began to recognize him as a potential presidential candidate and chose him to deliver a keynote address at the 1988 Democratic National Convention. Despite a lackluster performance he grew in popularity after he admitted his poor performance and poked fun at himself. In 1991 while many leading Democrats eschewed running against the incumbent president George Bush at the height of his popularity following the Persian Gulf War, Clinton declared his candidacy. He quickly became the frontrunner, and when Bush's popularity plummeted and Ross Perot formed a viable third-party candidacy, Clinton capitalized and won the election despite receiving a minority of the popular votes.

Clinton promised to be a "new Democrat" but was hurt by a failed attempt to bring about healthcare reform led by his wife Hillary and by his position regarding gay soldiers in the military. His first term, however, was largely successful despite the fact that Republicans won control of Congress for the first time in almost forty years. He concentrated his efforts on welfare reform, education reform, and anticrime legislation. In foreign affairs, he ordered US troops into Somalia as peacekeepers under United Nations' auspices and ordered air attacks on Serbian troops in Bosnia, which eventually forced Serbia to agree to an uneasy peace. Likewise, he also used air strikes against Iraq because of Saddam Hussein's violation of treaty agreements. As he had in Arkansas, he promoted minorities and women to key positions in the government. Like Ronald Reagan, Clinton was an effective communicator. His rapport with younger Americans was especially effective in helping him win reelection in 1996 as he soundly defeated the Republican nominee, Bob Dole.

Unfortunately for Clinton, he encountered severe problems in his second term. Earlier questions pertaining to the so-called "Whitewater scandal" in Arkansas ultimately uncovered charges of Clinton's alleged infidelity. Denying any such behavior, including testimony taken before individuals investigating the Whitewater scandal, Clinton ultimately confessed that he had engaged in inappropriate conduct with a female White House intern, Monica Lewinsky. His attempt to cover up ultimately led to his conviction in impeachment proceedings before the Republican-controlled House of Representatives. Found guilty on several counts, Clinton faced removal from office in trial before the Senate, but the Senate failed to convict.

Despite the Lewinsky affair and his ongoing battles with the Republican Congress, Clinton's popularity remained high, and he presided over the longest period of peace and prosperity in the nation's twentieth-century history. Due to a strong economy and budget cuts in several areas, toward the end of Clinton's tenure, long-running national budget deficits were eliminated. Unfortunately, partisan squabbling and increasing polarization in US politics marred this period and it remains to be seen how Clinton's presidency will be judged. Before they left the White House, New York voters elected Hillary as US senator. She was reelected in 2006 and has announced her candidacy to become the first female president of the United States. Bill Clinton supports her efforts. He has maintained a high profile in the Democratic Party and has worked with former president George H. W. Bush in tsunami and hurricane relief efforts.

Bill Clinton made a public profession of faith when he was a child. He frequently has mentioned his admiration for evangelist Billy Graham. Even though he experienced great difficulties growing up, he regarded himself a Southern Baptist and was a member of the Immanuel Baptist Church in Little Rock while governor, often singing in the choir and occasionally playing his saxophone. His positions on abortion and gay rights put him at odds with conservative members of the Southern Baptist Convention and even more moderate Baptists. He did profess to have renewed spiritual commitment during his White House years in the wake of the Lewinsky scandal and made a "pilgrimage" to the Holy Land that he called "life-changing." He also counted evangelical leaders such as Tony Campolo and his former pastor, Rex Horne, among his spiritual advisors.[378]

Bill Clinton was one of our most musical presidents, not only in appreciation but also in performance of music. Inspired by his experience of hearing live jazz played by Al Hirt in New Orleans, he played the tenor saxophone solo in the "Crescent City Suite" while in high school. His interest increased when he played a saxophone solo arrangement of Gershwin's "Rhapsody in Blue" at band camp in Fayetteville, where he earned first chair in his section, becoming one of the best saxophone players in Arkansas. He also played in a jazz trio at Hot Springs High School; wearing dark glasses, the group called themselves the "Three Blind Mice." Because of his hairstyle, he often performed impressions of Elvis Presley for his friends or at parties. From ninth grade on, his main subject was music, as he grew to love all styles—jazz, rock 'n roll, classical (especially Bach), and most certainly gospel.

However, after becoming an accomplished saxophonist, at age sixteen he decided to pursue public service as a vocation. He said, "I loved music...but I knew I would never be John Coltrane or Stan Getz"[379] (great saxophone players). Therefore, he pointed his life in another direction. Roger Clinton, his half-brother, said that religion and church were always important to his older brother. Bill was baptized at age nine and regularly attended Park Place Baptist Church in Hot Springs. Growing up, he loved singing hymns, especially gospel music.[380] As governor he joined state representative Ted Mullinex on stage singing gospel songs. At the governor's mansion, Clinton often sat on the piano bench, requesting that hymns be played. These sessions were accompanied by Carolyn Staley, the daughter of the pastor of Second Baptist Church in Hot Springs, who lived next door to the Clintons when he was growing up. On the day he formally announced his candidacy for president, a few friends and a handful of cousins lingered at the Clinton house around the piano singing the moving hymn "Amazing Grace." In 1993 President Clinton referred to hymn singing as having the ability to bring about political agreement by observing that "everyone was singing out of the same hymnal."[381]

While governor of Arkansas, he played an upbeat saxophone version of George Gershwin's "Summertime" on Johnny Carson's television show. After becoming president, Clinton continued to play his saxophone. At one inaugural ball, he played a saxophone duet of "Night Train" with Clarence Clemons. President Clinton took every opportunity to bring all styles of music to the White House. Included were Lou Reed, Yo Yo Ma, Placido Domingo, Jessye Norman, the group Earth, Wind and Fire, and many other musicians. From 1993 to 1998 nearly 100 musical events featuring a variety of guest artists appeared in the White House.[382]

During Bill Clinton's second term as president, he was invited to be a guest conductor of the Washington National Symphony playing at the Kennedy Center. He gladly accepted the invitation but asked to see the score of the number he was to conduct so he could be properly prepared. The director of the symphony, Leonard Slatkin, was very surprised at this request since he had not been informed that the president had won awards in college as student concert band conductor. Being somewhat nervous at the beginning, President Clinton did quite well on the symphonic arrangement of Sousa's "Stars and Stripes Forever," commenting that he hoped that Mr. Sousa would have been pleased.[383]

In regard to Clinton's favorite hymn, he loved to sing "Amazing Grace," but—according to the Clinton Presidential Library—he also enjoyed singing the contemporary song "In the Presence of Jehovah," written by Geron and Becky Davis. He appreciated the unique songs "Holy Ground" and "Mercy Saw Me," also by the Davises. Other favorite hymns of Bill Clinton are "Be Not Afraid" and "Goin' Up Yonder."

Geron Davis was born in 1960 into a pastor's home that was very musical. Davis related this story of the composition of "In the Presence of Jehovah."[384] Shortly after he married Becky, they moved from Irving, Texas, as ministers of music at Christ Temple to the Pentecostals of Alexandria Church in Louisiana. Traveling in the smallest U-Haul truck, because they had no furniture, Geron began to form the chorus of the song in his mind. On the next day after their arrival in Louisiana, he took a group of singers to a special event in New Orleans, teaching them the new chorus on the trip. Soon after their return, Becky wrote the first stanza of the song, followed by Geron penning the second stanza of "In the Presence of Jehovah." The choir at Alexandria was well trained by these two creative musicians, and grew steadily during their ministry there to 150 voices singing beautiful sacred music.

The Davises were often invited to direct the music at the annual summer camp meetings of Pentecostals in Redfield, Arkansas, thirty miles south of Little Rock. Dianne Evans, the daughter of Pentecostal ministers, worked in the office of the attorney general, Bill Clinton. She invited her boss to the camp, jokingly saying that her denomination had all their fun at church. Clinton went to the camp meeting, where about 3,000 worshipers were present. He said, "The service got going with music as powerful and rhythmic as anything I had heard in black churches. After a couple of hymns, a beautiful young woman…sat down at the organ, and began to sing a gospel song I had never heard before—'In the Presence of Jehovah.' It was breathtaking. Before I knew it, I was so moved I was crying."[385]

In the Presence of Jehovah

Words: Becky and Geron Davis, 1983

Music: Geron Davis, 1983

Irregular

1. In and out of sit-u-a-tions that "tug-a-war" at me; All day long I struggle for an-swers that I need. Then I come into His pres-ence, all my questions become clear; And for a sa-cred mo-ment, no doubt can in-ter-fere. In the pres-ence of Je-ho-vah, God Al-might-y, Prince of Peace. Trou-bles of the King.

2. Through His love the Lord pro-vid-ed a place for us to rest; A place to find the an-swers in hours of dis-tress. There is nev-er an-y rea-son to give up in de-spair; Just slip away and breathe His name, He will come and meet you there! In the van-ish, hearts are mend-ed in the pres-ence

Cue notes 2nd time

Harmony

The unforgettable night impressed him so much that he attended the meeting every summer but one between 1977 and 1992. After a few years, the Pentecostals discovered that Clinton sang in the Immanuel Baptist Church choir in Little Rock and invited him to sing with a quartet of balding ministers called the Bald Knobbers. The future president loved it and fit in quite well except for the hair issue. Clinton sang "In the Presence of Jehovah" at Lonoke, Arkansas, First Pentecostal Church as a duet with Danny Thomason, a fellow tenor from the choir at Immanuel Baptist Church.[386]

Eventually, when Governor Bill Clinton was elected president of the United States, he invited the choir from Alexandria to sing "In the Presence of Jehovah" and "Holy Ground" at the pre-inaugural service in Washington, DC, at the Metropolitan African Methodist Episcopal Church. On this trip, the choir also sang these songs in the Capitol rotunda with its excellent acoustics. Sometimes President Clinton would invite Pastors Anthony and Mickey Mangun of the Pentecostals of Alexandria to the White House, where invited guests would gather around the piano and sing gospel songs and hymns. The accompanist for these hymn-sings was Mickey, who had sung "In the Presence of Jehovah" when Clinton first heard the song.[387] So the Clintons joined the group of several presidents who had "hymn-sings" in the White House.

President Clinton's love of gospel songs probably influenced his mother's choice of music. Her funeral service featured the hymns she loved, including "Amazing Grace," "Precious Lord, Take My Hand," "Just a Closer Walk with Thee," and "His Eye Is on the Sparrow." In addition, "Holy Ground" was sung at the funeral; it so inspired Barbra Streisand, who was present at the service, that she made her own recording of hymns and inspirational songs, including one written in memory of President Clinton's mother called "Leading with Your Heart."[388]

Geron Davis offered these insights into why presidents loved hymns so much. He stated that hymns provide an oasis of rest, giving help in the middle of anxiety of tough decisions. Since hymns often present the principles of God set to music, it serves as communication with the Father in order to "recharge one's spiritual batteries." These thoughts illustrate well the premise of this book.[389]

In application of "In the Presence of Jehovah" to the presidency of Bill Clinton, one can see the comfort the text brings to believers who come into God's presence. There is no doubt that these words lingered in President Clinton's mind as he made tough decisions on the war in Serbia and other critical situations. The first stanza clearly calls for answers that are needed concerning the daily struggles faced by the commander in chief. Followed by the encouragement of the chorus as it promises "troubles vanish, hearts are mended," it must have been comforting to the president. In stanza two the same thoughts prevail as it speaks of a place of rest, away from distress. The last phrase urges those who struggle not to despair, which is reflective of the scripture stated in President Clinton's inaugural speech. From Galatians 6:9 he quoted these words: "And let us not be weary in well-doing; for in due season we shall reap, if we faint not." Since the essence of the entire song is the entering into God's presence, the challenge of this song is an experience for which all Christians should strive.

GEORGE W. BUSH

1946–

Forty-Third President (2001–2009)

In a controversial presidential election in 1824 that ended up being decided by the House of Representatives, Americans chose John Quincy Adams as the nation's sixth president. Not only did the House's decision make the election unique, but also the election was notable for the fact that Adams's father, John Adams, had also served as US president. Until the beginning of the twenty-first century this never happened again. Ironically, the second time a president's son was elected president, it came in an equally controversial election that ultimately was decided not by the US Congress but by the US Supreme Court.

George Walker Bush was born in Connecticut in 1946 but spent his childhood and adolescence in Texas. As noted in an earlier chapter, his father, George H. W. Bush, was a successful businessman and heavily involved in Republican Party politics. The younger George earned his bachelor's degree from Yale University like his father and then served for a time as a fighter pilot in the Texas Air National Guard during the Vietnam War era, though not seeing combat in the war. He then attended Harvard, where he earned a master of business administration and moved back to Texas, where he became involved in the oil and energy business. He married Laura Welch and failed in his first attempt to win public office, being defeated for a congressional seat in 1978. After nearly ten years in private business, Bush served as his father's campaign manager in the elder Bush's successful run for the presidency in 1988. An avid baseball fan, like his father, he organized a partnership that purchased the Texas Rangers major league baseball team. He became the team's managing partner and for almost five years was the face of the franchise.

In 1994 Texas Republicans drafted Bush to run against popular Democratic governor Ann Richards. Selling his part in the Texas Rangers, Bush capitalized on political networks he had built managing his father's presidential run and in the Texas oil business. He defeated Richards. Four years later, Texas voters overwhelmingly reelected him for a second four-year term, the first time in the state's history that had occurred. In his time as governor, Bush was known for bipartisan collaboration with Texas Democrats on issues such as welfare, education, tort, and medical care reform. He also presented himself as a "compassionate conservative," and Republicans nationwide recognized him as a potential presidential candidate.

In 2000 Bush received the Republican nomination over veteran politicians like Senator John McCain of Arizona. In one of the most controversial presidential elections in US history, Bush won a victory over Democratic vice president Al Gore with a narrow victory in the Electoral College, despite losing the popular vote. The outcome of the decisive electoral votes from Florida, where Bush's brother was governor, was finally accepted in a court decision that ultimately reached the Supreme Court. In the months that followed, Bush faced significant Democratic opposition in Congress and among Democrats in the public who regarded his victory illegitimate. He was also forced to deal with a recession. With the help of the Republican-controlled Congress, he pushed through tax-relief legislation and extensive educational reforms called "No Child Left Behind." The focus of his administration dramatically shifted on 11 September 2001. On that day terrorists struck US soil in spectacular fashion by crashing airline jets into both towers of the World Trade Center and the Pentagon. In the aftermath, Bush's approval ratings soared because of his response to the terrorism.

In the months that followed, Bush aggressively pursued antiterrorist legislation and the creation of the Homeland Security Agency and better coordination between different government departments and agencies. He utilized US and NATO forces to end the Taliban's control of Afghanistan and use of that nation as a militant Islamic terrorist training ground. In 2002, the Bush administration also began to try to solidify the United Nations' support against Saddam Hussein with charges that Iraq was violating peace agreements and was assembling weapons of mass destruction. Despite lack of substantial evidence to that fact, in March 2003 the United States and a few allies launched an invasion of Iraq designed to topple Saddam Hussein and establish a democratic Iraq. Less than two months later and with minimal casualties, Bush declared that "major combat operations" had ended. This success, along with the leadership exhibited by Bush in the aftermath of 9/11, played a significant role in Bush's reelection over John Kerry in fall 2004.

Unfortunately, the attempt to establish a democratic Iraq has proved more illusive. Despite the capture, imprisonment, and ultimate execution of Saddam Hussein and many of the former leaders of Iraq for crimes against humanity since 2003, there has been a rising tide of sectarian strife, and both former supporters of Saddam and militant Muslim terrorists who moved into the country have engaged in intensive terrorist activities. As this book is going to press, the end of US involvement in Iraq is not in sight, thousands of American soldiers and marines have been killed or wounded, and a completely stable government has not been established.

Bush's approval ratings have plummeted with the ongoing conflict in Iraq; unfortunately, his domestic agenda also has been sidetracked. The US economy rebounded after a recession that worsened after 9/11 and the US stock market continues to soar as this book goes to press. However, worsening budget deficits, created in part by the continued war in Iraq and the war on terror, have led to criticism of Bush's administration. These deficits, as well as concerns about Iraq, caused the Republicans to lose control of Congress in midterm elections in 2006. At this time it remains to be seen what President Bush's lasting legacy will be.

President Bush has been one of the nation's most outspoken presidents regarding the important role of his personal faith. He openly testifies about the spiritual change that led to the end of his alcohol abuse, and he frequently invokes personal references to his Christianity. He regards a conversation with evangelist Billy Graham in 1985 as the turning point in his spiritual pilgrimage. In fact, he has been so outspoken about his faith that some have questioned his commitment to separation of church and state. He and Laura are active members of the United Methodist Church although he and that denomination do not always see eye to eye on particular issues. In many ways he more closely affiliates with more conservative and evangelical forms of Christianity. Regardless, Bush indicates that his faith is an important part of his life.[390]

George W. Bush learned many lessons from his father, including always doing the right thing, striving for excellence, giving something back to his country, not shrinking from his responsibility, and being religiously faithful.[391] President George H. W. Bush invited Christian musical artist Michael W. Smith to play a concert for a White House Christmas program in 1989. During that visit, George W. played tennis with Smith, developing a close friendship; he appeared at the White House numerous times. At the fifty-first Annual Prayer Breakfast, the president said: "I want to welcome Michael W. Smith and his wife here.... They've been great friends of Laura and me and my family. It is a treat to have him here, to lend his God-given talents to this important breakfast."[392] Shortly after 9/11, Michael Smith was asked by President Bush to write a song about the attacks. In response, Smith wrote "There She Stands" and performed it at the 2004 Republican National Convention. The song celebrates the American flag and America's ability to rise from the ashes and remain strong even after such horrific events.[393]

Both Bush presidents enjoy country music. In addition, President George W. Bush is a fan of the southern rock band ZZ Top and other classic rock groups. He enjoys feel-good music, with his iPod playlist containing music that helps him get over the next hill while jogging or on his mountain bike. However, at some White House events, music of Vivaldi has been heard played by a string quartet. Music at the White House during his term has been quite varied. One of the first special events involving hymns was on 14 September 2001 at the service for the National Day of Prayer and Remembrance. The hymns chosen were "God of Our Fathers," "Amazing Grace," "God Bless America," "Father, in Thy Gracious Keeping," "O God, Our Help in Ages Past," "America the Beautiful," "A Mighty Fortress Is Our God," and "The Battle Hymn of the Republic." This service honoring the 9/11 victims, held in the Washington National Cathedral, proved to be timely and reassuring to America; the hymns were wisely selected and effectively presented.

Having begun the discipline of daily devotions before he reached the presidency, President Bush was spiritually prepared for this tragic situation. He found the book of Psalms especially helpful, particularly Psalms 27 and 91, which resonate with themes of moral steadfastness in the face of conflict. He regularly read from Oswald Chamber's classic *My Utmost for His Highest*, a devotional book written for soldiers with illustrations drawn from sports and nature, the language the president speaks.[394]

In the 2002 televised program "The White House Salute to Gospel Music," President Bush said, "Millions of Americans have turned their faith into song through gospel music. From its roots in rural churches to its popularity on radio, this music has lifted our hearts and lightened our burdens for generations. The Psalms tell us to make a joyful noise to the Lord. Tonight's performers will share some of the gospels' most joyful sounds. The sounds provide us comfort and hope when we need them most. They open up our hearts to a deeper faith and they bring us closer to God." The hymns sung included "The Doxology," "When We All Get Together," "Oh, the Blood of Jesus," "Soon and Very Soon," "Above All," "I Surrender All," "God Bless the USA," and "Let Freedom Ring." Joining co-hosts Michael W. Smith and CeCe Winans were several gospel groups including The Martins and The Gaither Vocal Band and soloists Steven Curtis Chapman, Twila Paris, and Jaci Velaquez. First Lady Laura commented, "Music has a way of seeing us through every chapter of our life. In song we find deep spiritual fulfillment. Gospel music, while uniquely American, is the reflection of what it means to be human, to feel pain and loss, healing and joy. Songs of praise can be the most powerful praise of all."

On 22 June 2004 President Bush proclaimed Black Music Month as he had done in 2001. He encouraged all Americans to celebrate the remarkable role of African American composers in their contribution to the nation's heritage. Honored at this event were Lionel Hampton, Shirley Caesar, Bobby Jones, James Brown, and others. In December 2005 First Lady Laura Bush announced the holiday theme at the White House was "All Things Bright and Beautiful," a hymn written by Cecil F. Alexander in 1848.

As his father did, President Bush referred to some hymns in his speeches. He spoke of the "wonder working power" in the faith and values of the American people, a phrase that comes directly from the hymn "Power in the Blood." In a 2001 press release he made reference to the third stanza of the Christmas hymn "O Holy Night" by stating, "Truly He taught us to love one another, His law is love and His gospel is peace, Chains shall He break for the slave is our brother, And in His name all oppression shall cease." This is a powerful and justifiable reference to America's role in the Iraq conflict.

One of George W. Bush's most cherished hymns is "Amazing Grace." After he became a committed Christian, there are many instances where this hymn became extremely meaningful to him. On Palm Sunday 2002, the president, who hates to miss church, was aloft aboard Air Force One, so he decided to have a worship service on the plane. Secretary of State

Condoleezza Rice led the group in hymns after which speechwriter Karen Hughes gave a short sermon. They concluded by singing "Amazing Grace." President Bush commented, "There were a lot of religious people on the plane. It was a packed house...and to be able to worship with people with whom you work in a unique spot is a special moment. I did feel the presence of God amongst my friends on Air Force One."[395] While serving as governor, he, along with a group of fifty-five prisoners—including a convicted murderer—sang "Amazing Grace" in Huntsville, Texas. The future president said, "Standing up there, singing that song, reminded me that all of us need to think about our hearts, our lives. We're all human. We all make mistakes."[396]

Perhaps the most influential hymn for President George W. Bush, the one that became the theme of his life, is Charles Wesley's "A Charge to Keep I Have." Alive with a sense of duty and a powerful call to destiny fulfilled, this hymn has been the president's inspiration during his life as a public servant. The hymn's first phrase became the title for his autobiography. This Wesleyan hymn written in 1762 was inspired by the words of *Matthew Henry's Commentary on the Bible,* a Christian classic. Henry wrote his reflections on Leviticus 8:35, which instructs the temple priesthood to "keep the charge of the Lord" with these words: "We have everyone of us a charge to keep, an eternal God to glorify, an immortal soul to provide for, needful duty to be done, our generation to serve, and it must be our daily care to keep the charge, for it is the charge of the Lord our Master, who will shortly call us to an account about it, and it is at our utmost peril if we neglect it. Keep it that you die not; it is death, eternal death, to betray the trust we are charged with; by the consideration of this we must be kept in awe."[397] Wesley formed Henry's words into the well-loved Methodist hymn often sung at the close of conferences as "a charge to keep" in order to change the world.

Charles Wesley, along with his brother John, not only founded the Methodist denomination, but also wrote or translated many hymns. Charles wrote over 6,500 hymns in his lifetime. After being ordained as Anglican ministers, they traveled to Georgia in 1735 to serve as missionaries. When John published the first American hymnal, *The Charles-Town Collection* in 1737, none of Charles's hymns were included since he had not yet become a Christian and begun writing hymns. They were both converted in 1738 in London under the influence of Moravians. Because of their beliefs, the brothers and their followers met vicious opposition and persecution. The established church accused them of blasphemy and urged people to run them out of town. The strong faith of these believers is revealed in "A Charge to Keep I Have." Hymnologist William Reynolds said, "Trials and tribulation

A Charge to Keep I Have

Words: Charles Wesley, 1762
Music: Lowell Mason, 1832

S.M.
BOYLSTON

1. A charge to keep I have, A God to glo - ri - fy, A nev-er-dy - ing soul to save, And fit it for the sky.
2. To serve the pres - ent age, My call-ing to ful - fill; O may it all my powers en-gage To do my Mas - ter's will!
3. Arm me with jeal - ous care, As in thy sight to live, And oh, thy se - vant, Lord, pre-pare A strict ac-count to give!
4. Help me to watch and pray, And on thy-self re - ly, as - sured, If I my trust be-tray, I shall for - ev - er die.

faced them daily, yet they confronted life with assurance and confidence and faced the certainty of death with faith in the Lord."[398]

From the beginning Methodists perceived their charge to glorify God with a dual thrust stated in this hymn. With the Wesleys' strong Puritan background and their association with Moravian pietism, they felt that Christians must have a felt religious encounter, termed a "heart-warming experience," as a part of their personal faith. On the other hand, their movement must be understood in terms of their present age. With the changing values of the Industrial Revolution and conflict between predestination and deism, the movement identified with the dissenting sects of the middle class, according to theologian James Warren.[399] Both approaches had to be respected.

"A Charge to Keep I Have" first appeared in Charles Wesley's *Short Hymns on Select Passages of Holy Scriptures* under the title "Keep the Charge of the Lord, That Ye Die Not." Besides the Leviticus reference, other scriptures used are 2 Peter 1:10, Hosea 6:2, and Matthew 25:30 and 26:41. Many hymnals associate 1 Corinthians 4:2 with the text: "Now it is required that those who have been given a trust must prove faithful."

The tune sung to this hymn is the fourth of ten Charles Wesley hymns that Lowell Mason composed. (Mason's life is covered in the chapter on President McKinley.) Originally written for a text beginning "Our days are as grass," Mason named the tune BOYLSTON either after a Massachusetts town or a street in Boston. The tune first appeared in Mason's 1832 collection *The Choir or Union Collection of Church Music.* The melody reflects Mason's attention to psalm-tone chants since there is a similarity between this tune and HOBART, which was definitely arranged from an ancient chant in the 1849 tune edition of the *Methodist Hymnal.*[400]

A painting inspired by the hymn "A Charge to Keep I Have" was loaned to George W. Bush soon after he became governor by his longtime friends Joe and Jan O'Neil. The German immigrant artist W. H. D. Koerner depicts a western rider spurring his horse up a difficult hill. Governor Bush was so moved by the painting that he placed it directly opposite his desk in Austin; it now hangs in the White House Oval Office. After receiving the artwork, he sent a memo to his staff, which said in part, "I thought I would share with you a recent bit of Texas history which epitomizes our mission. When you come into my office please take a look at the beautiful painting of a horseman determinedly charging up what appears to be a steep and rough trail. What adds complete life to the painting for me is the message of Charles Wesley that we serve One greater than ourselves." The combination of the painting and the hymn is a graphic vision of President Bush's leadership style: "He has taken the words of a Puritan, passed them through the lyrics of a Methodist hymn writer, and wrapped them in Texas boot leather to send them charging over a rugged hill in search of destiny."[401]

Since George W. Bush is one of a small number of presidents who had a profound religious transformation as an adult, it is fitting that "Amazing Grace" became a most loved hymn. The stanzas certainly reflect President Bush's experience. Author Paul Kengor wrote, "In his life and presidency, Bush has endured many such toils and snares—from [the death of little sister] Robin and the bottle [alcohol] to Osama and Saddam. Some carried embarrassment, some bitter criticism; one simply brought pain. George W. Bush is certain that he has overcome the adversities with God's help. He is confident that God's grace will continue to carry him—eventually all the way home."[402]

The hymn "A Charge to Keep I Have" is a motto that speaks of determination and direction, calling the country to a higher purpose. Stanza one centers on praise to God for the opportunity to tell others of God's provision of salvation. Stanza two underscores a Christian's privilege to serve God in his present age, yielding to the calling given to him, possessing the power to do the Master's will. The hymn calls for each one to obtain his highest and best. The third stanza reminds us that God charts the course and his people should accept God's will as they advance. The fourth stanza cautions Christians to stay humble as they follow the guidance provided by God in the charge to obey on the spiritual journey.

What an appropriate hymn, full of relevant thoughts about this country's reaction to the current world situation. In proposing a worldview to resolve the many crises faced by the nation, all should acknowledge that God's view is the primary consideration.

~

PRESIDENTAL PRAISE

~

Bibliographical Note

There have been many sources contacted during the writing of *Presidential Praise: Our Presidents and Their Hymns.* Dr. Michael Williams, in discussing the administration of each president, including their political journey and their faith, utilized several websites as well as many books. These are in the Notes at the end of the text. However, the two books consistently consulted were *Prayers of Our Presidents* by Jerry MacGregor and Marie Prys (Grand Rapids MI: Baker Books, 2004) and *God and the Oval Office: The Religious Faith of Our 43 Presidents* by John McCollister (Nashville: W. Publishing Group, 2005). Most of the other sources deal with a specific president and are documented.

Dr. Edward Spann, in writing about the music and hymns of the presidents, used as his primary resource *Our Presidents and Their Hymns* by John Benjamin Merrill (Los Angeles: The Wellmer Company, 1933) and *Music at the White House: A History of the American Spirit* by Elise K. Kirk (Urbana: University of Illinois Press, 1986). These two books were vital to the research, but Dr. Spann utilized more than 100 other resources in his research, most notably *A Dictionary of Hymnology* by John Julian (New York: Dover Publications Inc., 1892, Rev. 1907). Complete documentation is included in the Notes section following the text. Citation is made of any book, journal, website, personal correspondence, telephone interviews, etc., throughout the book.

Notes

[1] Mark A. Noll, *A History of Christianity in the United States and Canada* (Grand Rapids MI: Wm. B. Eerdmans Publishing Co., 1992) 134. Joseph Ellis, *His Excellency: George Washington* (New York: Alfred A. Knopf, 2004) 269.

[2] Joseph Ellis, *His Excellency: George Washington* (New York: Alfred A. Knopf, 2004); Richard Brookhiser, *Founding Father: Rediscovering George Washington* (New York: Free Press Paperbacks, 1996); James Thomas Flexner, *Washington: The Indispensable Man* (Boston: Little, Brown and Company, 1974); Bruce Chadwick, *George Washington's War* (Naperville IL: Sourcebooks, Inc., 2005); Henry Wiencek, *An Imperfect God: George Washington, His Slave, and the Creation of America* (New York: Farrar, Straus and Giroux, 2003); Mark A. Noll, *A History of Christianity in the United States and Canada* (Grand Rapids MI: William B. Eerdmans Publishing Co., 1992); Mark A. Noll, *America's God: From Jonathan Edwards to Abraham Lincoln* (New York: Oxford University Press, 2002); and Jon Meacham, *American Gospel: God, the Founding Fathers, and the Making of a Nation* (New York: Random House, 2006).

[3] Elise K. Kirk, *Music at the White House: A History of the American Spirit* (Urbana: University of Illinois Press, 1986) 7.

[4] John Tasker Howard, *Our American Music: A Comprehensive History from 1620 to the Present* (New York: Thomas Y. Crowell Company, 1965) 42.

[5] John Tasker Howard and George Kent Bellows, *A Short History of Music in America* (New York: Thomas Y. Crowell Company, 1957) 35.

[6] Irving Lowens, *Music and Musicians in Early America* (New York: W. W. Norton and Company, Inc., 1964) 111.

[7] Jane Hampton Cook, *The Faith of America's First Ladies* (Chattanooga TN: Living Ink Books, 2005) 179.

[8] S. E. Boyd Smith, "The Effective Countess: Lady Huntingdon and the 1780 edition of 'A Select Collection of Hymns,'" *The Hymn: A Journal of Congregational Song* 44/3 (July 1993): 26–32.

[9] John Julian, *A Dictionary of Hymnology* (New York: Dover Publications, Inc., 1892, rev. 1907) 926.

[10] Robert McCutchan, *Hymn Tune Names: Their Sources and Significance* (Nashville: Abingdon Press, 1957) 159–60.

[11] David McCullough, *John Adams* (New York: Simon & Schuster, 2001); "John Adams," http://www.ipl.org/div/potus/; "John Adams," http://www.whitehouse.gov/ history/presidents; and "The Religious Affiliation of US President John Adams," http://www.adherents.com/.

[12] Elise K. Kirk, *Music at the White House: A History of the American Spirit* (Urbana: University of Illinois Press, 1986) 21.

[13] Ibid., 23.

[14] Ibid., 370n9.

[15] James I. Warren, *O for a Thousand Tongues: The History, Nature, and Influence of Music in the Methodist Tradition* (Grand Rapids MI: Francis Asbury Press, 1988) 74.

[16] Lester J. Coppon, ed., *The Adams-Jefferson Letters*, vol. 2 (Chapel Hill: University of North Carolina Press, 1959) 394. Jefferson's letter is found in his chapter in this book.

[17] John Julian, *A Dictionary of Hymnology* (New York: Dover Publications, Inc., 1892, rev. 1907) 737.

[18] J. R. Watson, *The English Hymn* (New York: Oxford University Press, 1999) 107.

[19] Quoted from Erik Routley, *The Music of Christian Hymnody* (London: Independent Press Limited, 1957) by Paul Westermeyer, *Let the People Sing: Hymn Tunes in Perspective* (Chicago: GIA Publications, Inc., 2005) 172.

[20] Edwin S. Gaustad, *Sworn on the Altar of God: A Religious Biography of Thomas Jefferson* (Grand Rapids MI: William B. Eerdmans Publishing Co., 1996); Joseph J. Ellis, *American Sphinx: The Character of Thomas Jefferson* (New York: Alfred A. Knopf, 1997); Jon Meacham, *American Gospel: God, the Founding Fathers, and the Making of a Nation* (New York: Random House, 2006); and "Thomas Jefferson," http://www.whitehouse.gov/history/presidents.

[21] John Tasker Howard, *Our American Music: A Comprehensive History from 1620 to the Present* (New York: Thomas Y. Crowell Company, 1965) 42.

[22] Julius Portney, *The Philosopher and Music: A Historical Outline* (New York: The Humanities Press, 1954) 208.

[23] Elise K. Kirk, *Music at the White House: A History of the American Spirit* (Urbana: University of Illinois Press, 1986) 29.

[24] Ibid., 35.

[25] Douglas Alvin Snow, *Revive Us Again: Chronological Anthology of American Gospel Hymnody* (Benton AR: Blessed Hope Publications, 2004) xiv-xv.

[26] Rochelle A. Stackhouse, "Changing the Language of the Church's Song Circa 1785," *The Hymn: A Journal of Congregational Song* 45/3 (July 1994): 16–18.

[27] Lester J. Coppon, ed., *The Adams-Jefferson Letters*, vol. 2 (Chapel Hill: University of North Carolina Press, 1959) 386.

[28] Adams's response is found in this book in the John Adams chapter.

[29] John Julian, *A Dictionary of Hymnology* (New York: Dover Publications, Inc., 1892, rev. 1907) 305.

[30] Frank Colquhoun, *Hymns That Live: Their Meaning and Message* (Downers Grove IL: InterVarsity Press, 1980) 32.

[31] Julian, *Dictionary of Hymnology*, 489.

[32] Robert Allen Rutland, *James Madison: The Founding Father* (Columbia: University of Missouri Press, 1987); Richard Labunski, *James Madison and the Struggle for the Bill of Rights* (Oxford: Oxford University Press, 2006); Jon Meacham, *American Gospel: God, the Founding Fathers, and the Making of a Nation* (New York: Random House, 2006); "James Madison," http://www.ipl.org/div/potus/; "James Madison," http://www.whitehouse.gov/history/presidents; and "The Religious Affiliation of US President James Madison," http://www.adherents.com/ people/.

[33] Elise K. Kirk, *Music at the White House: A History of the American Spirit* (Urbana: University of Illinois Press, 1986) 35.

[34] Ibid., 36.

[35] John Julian, *A Dictionary of Hymnology* (New York: Dover Publications, Inc., 1892, rev. 1907) 865.

[36] Albert Edward Bailey, *The Gospel in Hymns: Backgrounds and Interpretations* (New York: Charles Scribner's Sons, 1950) 9.

[37] Paul Westermeyer, *Let the People Sing: Hymn Tunes in Perspective* (Chicago: GIA Publications, Inc., 2005) 169.

[38] Harry Ammon, *James Monroe: The Quest for National Identity* (Charlottesville: University of Virginia Press, 1990); "James Monroe," http://www.whitehouse.gov/history/presidents; "The Religious Affiliation of US President James Monroe," http://www.adherents.com; "James Monroe," http://www.ipl.org/div/potus; Jerry MacGregor and Marie Prys, *Prayers of Our Presidents* (Grand Rapids MI: Baker Books, 2004); and John McCollister, *God and the Oval Office: The Religious Faith of Our 43 Presidents* (Nashville: W. Publishing Group, 2005).

[39] Elise K. Kirk, *Music at the White House: A History of the American Spirit* (Urbana: University of Illinois Press, 1986) 41.

[40] Ibid., 39. Quoted in Harry Ammon, *James Monroe: The Quest for National Identity* (New York: McGraw-Hill, 1971) 400.

[41] Robert P. Watson, ed., *American First Ladies*, 2d ed. (Pasadena CA: Salem Press, Inc., 2006) 46.

[42] Elsie Houghton, *Classic Christian Hymn-Writers* (Fort Washington PA: Christian Literature Crusade, 1992) 203.

[43] Ibid., 205.

[44] John C. McCollister, *God and the Oval Office* (Nashville: W. Publishing Group, 2005) 29.

[45] John Julian, *A Dictionary of Hymnology* (New York: Dover Publications, Inc., 1892, rev. 1907) 498.

[46] Robert McCutchan, *Hymn Tune Names: Their Sources and Significance* (Nashville: Abingdon Press, 1957) 54.

[47] Paul C. Nagel, *John Quincy Adams: A Public Life, A Private Life* (Cambridge MA: Harvard University Press, 1997); Robert V. Remini, *John Quincy Adams* (New York: Times Books, 2002); "John Quincy Adams," http://www.ipl.org/div/potus; "John Quincy Adams," http://www.whitehouse.gov/history/presidents/; and "The Religious Affiliation of US President John Quincy Adams," http://www.adherents.com/people/; Jerry MacGregor and Marie Prys, *Prayers of Our Presidents* (Grand Rapids MI: Baker Books, 2004); and John McCollister, *God and the Oval Office: The Religious Faith of Our 43 Presidents* (Nashville: W. Publishing Group, 2005).

[48] Elise K. Kirk, *Music at the White House: A History of the American Spirit* (Urbana: University of Illinois Press, 1986) 42.

[49] Ibid., 47.

[50] David W. Music, "John Quincy Adams: A Hymn Writing President," *The Hymn: A Journal of Congregational Song* 53/3 (July 2002): 30.

[51] Ibid., 31.

[52] W. Thomas Marrocco and Harold Gleason, *Music in America: An Anthology from the Landing of the Pilgrims to the Close of the Civil War, 1620–1865* (New York: W. W. Norton and Co., Inc., 1964) 98.

[53] Albert Christ-Janer, Charles W. Hughes, and Carleton Sprague Smith, *American Hymns Old and New: A Historical Singing Book* (New York: Oxford University Press, 1980) 600.

[54] Charles W. Hughes, *American Hymns Old and New: Notes on the Hymns and Biographies of the Authors and Composers* (New York: Oxford University Press, 1980) 594.

[55] Ibid., 292.

[56] Edith L. Blumhofer, *Her Heart Can See: The Life and Hymns of Fanny J. Crosby* (Grand Rapids MI: William B. Eerdmans Publishing Company, 2005) 63.

[57] Louis F. Benson, *The English Hymn: Its Development and Use in Worship* (Richmond VA: John Knox Press, 1962) 462n52.

[58] H. W. Brands, *Andrew Jackson: His Life and Times* (New York: Doubleday, 2005); "Andrew Jackson," http://www.ipl.org/div/potus; "Andrew Jackson," http://www.whitehouse.gov/history/presidents/; "The Religious Affiliation of US President Andrew Jackson," http://www.adherents.com/people; Jon Meacham, *American Gospel: God, the Founding Fathers, and the Making of a Nation* (New York: Random House, 2006); Jerry MacGregor and Marie Prys, *Prayers of Our Presidents* (Grand Rapids MI: Baker Books, 2004); and John McCollister, *God and the Oval Office: The Religious Faith of Our 43 Presidents* (Nashville: W. Publishing Group, 2005).

[59] Elise K. Kirk, *Music at the White House: A History of the American Spirit* (Urbana: University of Illinois Press, 1986) 50.

[60] Ibid., 51.

[61] J. Joyce Cusmano, writer of album cover notes for "Christmas at the White House: The Favorite Carols and Hymns of America's Presidents," sung by Burl Ives (New York: Caedmon Records, Inc., 1972).

[62] Clint Bonner, *A Hymn Is Born* (Nashville: Broadman Press, 1959) 45.

[63] McCollister, *God and the Oval Office*, 39.

[64] H. Augustine Smith, *Lyric Religion: The Romance of Immortal Hymns* (New York: Fleming H. Revell Company, 1931) 69.

[65] Ibid., 70.

[66] As cited in Joel H. Sibley, *Martin Van Buren and the Emergence of American Popular Politics* (Lanham MD: Rowman & Littlefield, 2002) 117.

[67] Sibley, *Martin Van Buren;* "Martin Van Buren," http://www.ipl.org/div/potus; "Martin Van Buren," http://www.whitehouse.gov/history/presidents/; "The Religious Affiliation of US President Martin Van Buren," http://www.adherents.com/people/pv/; Jerry MacGregor and Marie Prys, *Prayers of Our Presidents* (Grand Rapids MI: Baker Books, 2004); and John McCollister, *God and the Oval Office: The Religious Faith of Our 43 Presidents* (Nashville: W. Publishing Group, 2005).

[68] Elise K. Kirk, *Music at the White House: A History of the American Spirit* (Urbana: University of Illinois Press, 1986) 52.

[69] Ibid., 53.

[70] Ivor Forbes Guest, *Fanny Elssler* (London: Adam & Black, 1970) 136–38. Quoted in Kirk, *Music at the White House*, 51.

[71] McCollister, *God and the Oval Office*, 42.

[72] Whitsuntide (also called Pentecost) celebrates the coming of the Holy Spirit. Whitsuntide is the week after Whitsunday, which is always the seventh Sunday after Easter.

[73] Elsie Houghton, *Classic Christian Hymn-Writers* (Fort Washington PA: Christian Literature Crusade, 1992) 86.

[74] Robert McCutchan, *Hymn Tune Names: Their Sources and Significance* (Nashville: Abingdon Press, 1957) 105.

[75] "William Henry Harrison," http://www.whitehouse.gov/history/presidents; "William Henry Harrison," http://www.ipl.org/div/potus/; "The Religious Affiliation of US President William Henry Harrison," http://www.adherents.com/ people/; Jerry MacGregor and Marie Prys, *Prayers of Our Presidents* (Grand Rapids MI: Baker Books, 2004); and John McCollister, *God and the Oval Office: The Religious Faith of Our 43 Presidents* (Nashville: W. Publishing Group, 2005).

[76] Elise K. Kirk, *Music at the White House: A History of the American Spirit* (Urbana: University of Illinois Press, 1986) 53.

[77] Ibid.

[78] McCollister, *God and the Oval Office*, 47.

[79] Elsie Houghton, *Classic Christian Hymn-Writers* (Fort Washington PA: Christian Literature Crusade, 1992) 49.

[80] Ibid., 50.

[81] Albert Edward Bailey, *The Gospel in Hymns: Backgrounds and Interpretations* (New York: Charles Scribner's Sons, 1950) 34.

[82] John Julian, *A Dictionary of Hymnology* (New York: Dover Publications, Inc., 1892, rev. 1907) 783.

[83] Robert McCutchan, *Hymn Tune Names: Their Sources and Significance* (Nashville: Abingdon Press, 1957) 140.

[84] Ibid., 25.

[85] Edith L. Blumhofer, *Her Heart Can See: The Life and Hymns of Fanny J. Crosby* (Grand Rapids MI: William B. Eerdmans Publishing Company, 2005) 55.

[86] J. R. Watson, *The English Hymn: A Critical and Historical Study* (New York: Oxford University Press, 1997) 118.

[87] Edward P. Crapol, *John Tyler: The Accidental President* (Chapel Hill: University of North Carolina Press, 2006); "John Tyler," http://www.whitehouse.gov/history/presidents; "John Tyler," http://www.ipl.org/div/potus; "The Religious Affiliation of US President John Tyler," http://www.adherents.com/people/; Jon Meacham, *American Gospel: God, the Founding Fathers, and the Making of a Nation* (New York: Random House, 2006); Jerry MacGregor and Marie Prys, *Prayers of Our Presidents* (Grand Rapids MI: Baker Books, 2004); and John McCollister, *God and the Oval Office: The Religious Faith of Our 43 Presidents* (Nashville: W. Publishing Group, 2005).

[88] Elise K. Kirk, *Music at the White House: A History of the American Spirit* (Urbana: University of Illinois Press, 1986) 55.

[89] MacGregor and Prys, *Prayers of Our Presidents,* 54.

[90] Kirk, *Music at the White House,* 59.

[91] Ibid., 61.

[92] Letitia Tyler Semple, "When Tyler Ruled: Recollections of White House Life in the Forties—Told by His Daughter," *Washington Evening Star,* 10 June 1893, quoted by Kirk in *Music at the White House,* 55.

[93] Robert Seager II, *And Tyler Too* (New York: McGraw-Hill, 1963) 350–51. Quoted in Kirk, *Music at the White House,* 56.

[94] Edith L. Blumhofer, *Her Heart Can See: The Life and Hymns of Fanny J. Crosby* (Grand Rapids MI: William B. Eerdmans Publishing Company, 2005) 56.

[95] Kenneth W. Osbeck, *101 More Hymn Stories* (Grand Rapids MI: Kregel Publications, 1985) 213.

[96] Paul Westermeyer, *Let the People Sing: Hymn Tunes in Perspective* (Chicago: GIA Publications, Inc., 2005) 200.

[97] CNN.com, "Th Presidential Prize: 'Splendid Misery,'" November 21, 2000 at http://archives.cnn.com/2000/ALLPOLITICS/stories/11/21/recount.theprize.ap/index.html

[98] This slogan referred to the extreme northern boundary of the Oregon Country.

[99] "James K. Polk: Biography," James K. Polk Ancestral Home, http://www.jameskpolk.com/new/biography.asp; "James K. Polk," http://www.whitehouse.gov/history/presidents/; "The Religious Affiliation of US President James K. Polk," http://www.adherents.com/people/pv/; Jerry MacGregor and Marie Prys, *Prayers of Our Presidents* (Grand Rapids MI: Baker Books, 2004); John McCollister, *God and the Oval Office: The Religious Faith of Our 43 Presidents* (Nashville: W. Publishing Group, 2005); and Joel H. Sibley, *Martin Van Buren and the Emergence of American Popular Politics* (Lanham MD: Rowman & Littlefield, 2002).

[100] MacGregor and Prys, *Prayers of Our Presidents,* 58.

[101] Elise K. Kirk, *Music at the White House: A History of the American Spirit* (Urbana: University of Illinois Press, 1986) 64.

[102] Milo Milton Quaife, ed., *The Diary of James K. Polk during His Presidency, 1845 to 1849* (Chicago: McClurg, 1910) 366–67. Quoted in Kirk, *Music at the White House,* 64.

[103] Kirk, *Music at the White House,* 62.

[104] Edith L. Blumhofer, *Her Heart Can See: The Life and Hymns of Fanny J. Crosby* (Grand Rapids MI: William B. Eerdmans Publishing Company, 2005) 66.

[105] Bernard Ruffin, *Fanny Crosby* (Cleveland OH: United Church Press, 1976) 58.

106 Frank Colquhoun, *Hymns That Live: Their Meaning and Message* (Downers Grove IL: InterVarsity Press, 1980) 124–25.

107 Albert Edward Bailey, *The Gospel in Hymns: Backgrounds and Interpretations* (New York: Charles Scribner's Sons, 1950) 122.

108 Paul Westermeyer, *Let the People Sing: Hymn Tunes in Perspective* (Chicago: GIA Publications, Inc., 2005) 296.

109 K. Jack Bauer, *Zachary Taylor: Soldier, Planter, Statesman of the Old Southwest* (Baton Rouge: Louisiana State University Press, 1985); "Zachary Taylor," http://www.ipl.org/div/potus/; "Zachary Taylor," http://www.whitehouse.gov/history/presidents/; "The Religious Affiliation of US President Zachary Taylor," http://www.adherents.com/people/; Jerry MacGregor and Marie Prys, *Prayers of Our Presidents* (Grand Rapids MI: Baker Books, 2004); and John McCollister, *God and the Oval Office: The Religious Faith of Our 43 Presidents* (Nashville: W. Publishing Group, 2005).

110 Elise K. Kirk, *Music at the White House: A History of the American Spirit* (Urbana: University of Illinois Press, 1986) 64.

111 Quoted by Samuel Eliot Morison, *The Oxford History of the American People* (New York: Oxford University Press, 1965) 516.

112 Ernest K. Emurian, *Stories of Christmas Carols* (Grand Rapids MI: Baker Books, 1958) 65.

113 William J. Reynolds, *Christ and the Carols* (Nashville: Broadman Press, 1967) 93.

114 Edith L. Blumhofer, *Her Heart Can See: The Life and Hymns of Fanny J. Crosby* (Grand Rapids MI: William B. Eerdmans Publishing Company, 2005) 79.

115 William J. Reynolds, Milburn Price, and David Music, *A Survey of Christian Hymnody* (Carol Stream IL: Hope Publishing Company, 1999) 56–57.

116 J. R. Watson, *The English Hymn: A Critical and Historical Study* (New York: Oxford University Press, 1997) 144.

117 Waldo S. Pratt, *The Significance of the Old French Psalter*, The Papers of the Hymn Society IV (New York: The Hymn Society, 1933) 12–18.

118 John Julian, *A Dictionary of Hymnology* (New York: Dover Publications, Inc., 1892, rev. 1907) 934.

119 Frederich Blume, *Protestant Church Music: A History* (New York: Norton, 1974) 530.

120 "Millard Fillmore," http://www.ipl.org/div/potus/mfillmore.html; "Millard Fillmore," http://www.whitehouse.gov/history/presidents/; "The Religious Affiliation of US President Millard Fillmore," http://www.adherents.com/people/; Jerry MacGregor and Marie Prys, *Prayers of Our Presidents* (Grand Rapids MI: Baker Books, 2004); and John McCollister, *God and the Oval Office: The Religious Faith of Our 43 Presidents* (Nashville: W. Publishing Group, 2005).

121 Robert McCutchan, *Hymn Tune Names: Their Sources and Significance* (Nashville: Abingdon Press, 1957) 104.

122 Elise K. Kirk, *Music at the White House: A History of the American Spirit* (Urbana: University of Illinois Press, 1986) 69.

123 Ibid., 69.

124 Samuel J. Rogal, "Helen Maria Williams and Her Contributions to Congregational Song," *The Hymn: A Journal of Congregational Song* 35/1 (January 1984): 11–15.

125 Ibid., 13.

126 McCutchan, *Hymn Tune Names*, 117.

127 Henry Wilder Foote, *Three Centuries of American Hymnody* (Harvard College MA: Archon Books, 1968) 185.

128 Rogal, "Helen Maria Williams," 12.

129 "Franklin Pierce," Grolier Multimedia Encyclopedia, http://ap.grolier.com/article; "Franklin Pierce," http://www.whitehouse.gov/history /presidents; "Franklin Pierce," http://www.ipl.org/div/potus/; "The Religious Affiliation of US President Franklin Pierce," http://www.adherents.com/people/ presidents; Jerry MacGregor and Marie Prys, *Prayers of Our Presidents* (Grand Rapids MI: Baker Books, 2004); and John McCollister, *God and the Oval Office: The Religious Faith of Our 43 Presidents* (Nashville: W. Publishing Group, 2005).

130 Elise K. Kirk, *Music at the White House: A History of the American Spirit* (Urbana: University of Illinois Press, 1986) 72.

131 Ibid., 72.

132 Edith L. Blumhofer, *Her Heart Can See: The Life and Hymns of Fanny J. Crosby* (Grand Rapids MI: William B. Eerdmans Publishing Company, 2005) 86.

133 Albert Edward Bailey, *The Gospel in Hymns: Backgrounds and Interpretations* (New York: Charles Scribner's Sons, 1950) 65.

134 Amos R. Wells, *A Treasury of Hymn Stories* (Grand Rapids MI: Baker Books, 1945) 348.

135 Stanley Sadie, ed., *The New Grove Dictionary of Music and Musicians*, vol. 7 (London: MacMillan Publishers Limited, 1980) 164.

136 J. R. Watson, *The English Hymn: A Critical and Historical Study* (New York: Oxford University Press, 1997) 175.

137 Bailey, *The Gospel in Hymns*, 64.

138 William A. DeGregorio, *The Complete Book of the U.S. Presidents* (Fort Lee NJ: Barricade Books, 2001) 199.

139 "James Buchanan," http://www.ipl.org.div/potus/; "James Buchanan," http://www.white-house.gov/history/presidents/; "The Religious Affiliation of US President James Buchanan," http://www.adherents.com/people/; Jerry MacGregor and Marie Prys, *Prayers of Our Presidents* (Grand Rapids MI: Baker Books, 2004); and John McCollister, *God and the Oval Office: The Religious Faith of Our 43 Presidents* (Nashville: W. Publishing Group, 2005).

140 Elise K. Kirk, *Music at the White House: A History of the American Spirit* (Urbana: University of Illinois Press, 1986) 76.

141 Ibid., 77.

142 Elsie Houghton, *Classic Christian Hymn-Writers* (Fort Washington PA: Christian Literature Crusade, 1992) 183.

143 Albert Edward Bailey, *The Gospel in Hymns: Backgrounds and Interpretations* (New York: Charles Scribner's Sons, 1950) 131.

144 Noel Davidson, *How Sweet the Sound: The Absorbing Story of John Newton and William Cowper* (Greenville SC: Emerald House, 1997) 157.

145 David W. Music, "The Tune MANOAH: Rossini in the Hymnal?" *The Hymn: A Journal of Congregational Song* 31/2 (April 1980): 105.

[146] Susan Wise Bauer, "Stories and Syllogisms: Protestant Hymns, Narrative Theology, and Heresy," *Wonderful Words of Life: Hymns in American Protestant History and Theology*, ed. Richard J. Mouw and Mark A. Noll (Grand Rapids MI: William B. Eerdmans Publishing Co., 2004) 220–21.

[147] Madeleine Forell Marshall, *Common Hymn Sense* (Chicago: GIA Publications, Inc., 1995) 93–97.

[148] Ann Richmond Sewell, *The Sounds of Joy* (Searcy AR: Hymnspirations, 1990) 130.

[149] William A. DeGregorio, *The Complete Book of the U.S. Presidents* (Fort Lee NJ: Barricade Books, 2001) 213.

[150] Mark A. Noll, *A History of Christianity in the United States and Canada* (Grand Rapids MI: William B. Eerdmans, 1992) 322; Allen C. Guelzo, *Abraham Lincoln: Redeemer President* (Grand Rapids MI: William B. Eerdmans, 1999); David Herbert Donald, *Lincoln* (New York: Touchstone, 1995); *Lincoln: A Life of Purpose and Power* (New York: Alfred A Knopf, 2003, 2006); Garry Wills, *Lincoln at Gettysburg: The Words That Remade America* (New York: Touchstone, 1992); Mark E. Neely, Jr., *The Last Best Hope of Earth: Abraham Lincoln and the Promise of America* (Cambridge MA: Harvard University Press, 1993); Stephen B. Oates, *With Malice toward None: A Life of Abraham Lincoln* (New York: HarperPerennial, 1977, 1994); and Joshua Wolf Shenk, *Lincoln's Melancholy: How Depression Challenged a President and Fueled His Greatness* (Boston: Houghton Mifflin Company, 2005).

[151] Douglas L. Wilson and Rodney O. Davis, *Herndon's Informants: Letters, Interviews, and Statements about Abraham Lincoln* (Urbana: University of Illinois Press, 1998) 107.

[152] Carl Sandburg, *The American Songbag* (New York: Harcourt Brace and Company, 1927) 152.

[153] Elise K. Kirk, *Music at the White House: A History of the American Spirit* (Urbana: University of Illinois Press, 1986) 78.

[154] Kenneth A. Bernard, *Lincoln and the Music of the Civil War* (Caldwell ID: Caxton Printers, 1966) 312.

[155] Edith L. Blumhofer, *Her Heart Can See: The Life and Hymns of Fanny J. Crosby* (Grand Rapids MI: William B. Eerdmans Publishing Company, 2005) 201.

[156] Bernard, *Lincoln and the Music of the Civil War*, 298.

[157] John Julian, *A Dictionary of Hymnology* (New York: Dover Publications, Inc., 1892, rev. 1907) 804.

[158] Irving Lowens, *Music and Musicians in Early America* (New York: W. W. Norton and Company, Inc., 1964) 184.

[159] Donald P. Hustad, "Favorite Hymns of Famous People," *The Hymn: A Journal of Congregational Song* 6/3 (July 1955): 101.

[160] Charles W. Hughes, *American Hymns Old and New: Notes on the Hymns and Biographies of the Authors and Composers* (New York: Oxford University Press, 1980) 476.

[161] "Andrew Johnson," http://www.whitehouse.gov/history/presidents; "Andrew Johnson," http://www.ipl.org/div/potus/; "The Religious Affiliation of US President Andrew Johnson," http://www.adherents.com/people/adh_presidents; "List of US Presidential Religious Affiliations," http://www.en.wikipedia.org/wiki/List_of_United_States_Presidential_religious_affiliations; Jerry MacGregor and Marie Prys, *Prayers of Our Presidents* (Grand Rapids MI: Baker Books, 2004); and John McCollister, *God and the Oval Office: The Religious Faith of Our 43 Presidents* (Nashville: W. Publishing Group, 2005).

[162] Alistaire Cooke, quoted in Elise K. Kirk, *Music at the White House: A History of the American Spirit* (Urbana: University of Illinois Press, 1986) 94.

[163] Charles Hamm, *Yesterdays: Popular Song in America* (W. W. Norton & Co., 1979) 254.

[164] Nancy Poore Tufts, *The Art of Handbell Ringing* (Nashville: Abingdon Press, 1961) 14.

[165] Albert Edward Bailey, *The Gospel in Hymns: Backgrounds and Interpretations* (New York: Charles Scribner's Sons, 1950) 135.

[166] Susan Wise Bauer, "Stories and Syllogisms: Protestant Hymns, Narrative Theology, and Heresy," *Wonderful Words of Life: Hymns in American Protestant History and Theology*, ed. Richard J. Mouw and Mark A. Noll (Grand Rapids MI: William B. Eerdmans Publishing Co., 2004) 212–13.

[167] Paul Westermeyer, *Let the People Sing: Hymn Tunes in Perspective* (Chicago: GIA Publications, Inc., 2005) 201.

[168] Robert McCutchan, *Hymn Tune Names: Their Sources and Significance* (Nashville: Abingdon Press, 1957) 99.

[169] Ron DiCianni, *The Faith of the Presidents: Our National Leaders at Prayer* (Lake Mary FL: Charisma House, 2004) 83.

[170] "Ulysses S. Grant," http://www.whitehouse.gov/history/presidents; "Ulysses S. Grant," http://www.ipl.org/div/potus/; "The Religious Affiliation of US President Ulysses S. Grant," http://www.adherents.com/people/adh_presidents; Steven Ambrose, *To America: Personal Reflections of an Historian* (New York: Simon & Shuster, 2003); Jerry MacGregor and Marie Prys, *Prayers of Our Presidents* (Grand Rapids MI: Baker Books, 2004); and John McCollister, *God and the Oval Office: The Religious Faith of Our 43 Presidents* (Nashville: W. Publishing Group, 2005).

[171] Elise K. Kirk, *Music at the White House: A History of the American Spirit* (Urbana: University of Illinois Press, 1986) 107.

[172] Edith L. Blumhofer, *Her Heart Can See: The Life and Hymns of Fanny J. Crosby* (Grand Rapids MI: William B. Eerdmans Publishing Company, 2005) 165.

[173] Kirk, *Music at the White House*, 104.

[174] J. Joyce Cusmano, writer of album cover notes for "Christmas at the White House: The Favorite Carols and Hymns of America's Presidents," sung by Burl Ives (New York: Caedmon Records, Inc., 1972).

[175] J. B. T. Marsh, *The Story of the Jubilee Singers* (London: Hodder and Stroughton, nd) 35.

[176] David W. Stowe, *How Sweet the Sound: The Music and the Spiritual Lives of Americans* (Cambridge MA: Harvard University Press, 2004) 109.

[177] Albert Edward Bailey, *The Gospel in Hymns: Backgrounds and Interpretations* (New York: Charles Scribner's Sons, 1950) 157.

[178] Elsie Houghton, *Classic Christian Hymn-Writers* (Fort Washington PA: Christian Literature Crusade, 1992) 226.

[179] John Julian, *A Dictionary of Hymnology* (New York: Dover Publications, Inc., 1892, rev. 1907) 765.

[180] Robert McCutchan, *Hymn Tune Names: Their Sources and Significance* (Nashville: Abingdon Press, 1957) 44, 54, 167.

[181] Blumhofer, *Her Heart Can See*, 220.

[182] Ibid.

[183] Hans K, Trefousse, *Rutherford B. Hayes* (New York: Times Books, 2002); "Rutherford B. Hayes," http://www.whitehouse.gov/history/presidents; "Rutherford B. Hayes," http://www.ipl.org/div/potus/; "The Religious Affiliation of US President Rutherford B. Hayes," http://www.adherents.com/people/adh_presidents; Jerry MacGregor and Marie Prys, *Prayers of Our Presidents* (Grand Rapids MI: Baker Books, 2004); and John McCollister, *God and the Oval Office: The Religious Faith of Our 43 Presidents* (Nashville: W. Publishing Group, 2005).

[184] Elise K. Kirk, *Music at the White House: A History of the American Spirit* (Urbana: University of Illinois Press, 1986) 113.

[185] Ibid., 128.

[186] Charles Richard Williams, *Diary and Letters of Rutherford Birchard Hayes* (Boston: Houghton Mifflin, 1914) 2:311, quoted in Kirk, *Music at the White House*, 383n3.

[187] McCollister, *God and the Oval Office*, 100.

[188] S. E. Boyd Smith, "The Effective Countess: Lady Huntingdon and the 1780 edition of 'A Select Collection of Hymns,'" *The Hymn: A Journal of Congregational Song* 44/3 (July 1993): 26–32.

[189] Millard Patrick, *The Story of the Church's Song* (Richmond VA: John Knox Press, 1962) 137.

[190] Frank Colquhoun, *Hymns That Live: Their Meaning and Message* (Downers Grove IL: InterVarsity Press, 1980) 99.

[191] Douglas Alvin Snow, *Revive Us Again: Chronological Anthology of American Gospel Hymnody* (Benton AR: Blessed Hope Publications, 2004) 41.

[192] Ira Rutkow, *James A. Garfield* (New York: Henry Holt and Company, 2006); "James A. Garfield," http://www.whitehouse.gov/history/presidents; "James Abram Garfield," http://www.ipl.org/div/potus/;

"The Religious Affiliation of US President James A. Garfield," http://www.adherents.com/people/adh_presidents; Jerry MacGregor and Marie Prys, *Prayers of Our Presidents* (Grand Rapids MI: Baker Books, 2004); and John McCollister, *God and the Oval Office: The Religious Faith of Our 43 Presidents* (Nashville: W. Publishing Group, 2005).

[193] Elise K. Kirk, *Music at the White House: A History of the American Spirit* (Urbana: University of Illinois Press, 1986) 132.

[194] McCollister, *God and the Oval Office*, 104.

[195] Robert J. Morgan, *Then Sings My Soul: 150 of the World's Greatest Hymn Stories*, vol. 1 (Nashville: Thomas Nelson Publishers, 2003) 61.

[196] Edith L. Blumhofer, *Her Heart Can See: The Life and Hymns of Fanny J. Crosby* (Grand Rapids MI: William B. Eerdmans Publishing Company, 2005) 220.

[197] John Julian, *A Dictionary of Hymnology* (New York: Dover Publications, Inc., 1892, rev. 1907) 954.

[198] Gilbert Chase, *America's Music: From the Pilgrims to the Present* (New York: McGraw-Hill Book Company, 1955) 306.

[199] Terry Teachout, "Our Gottschalt," http://www.commentarymagazine.com/article_print.asp?aid=12202063_1, 4.

[200] Kenneth W. Osbeck, *101 More Hymn Stories* (Grand Rapids MI: Kregel Publications, 1985) 126.

[201] "Chester Arthur," http://www.millercenter.virginia.edu/index.php/Ampres/essays/Arthur/biography/1;

"Chester Arthur," http://www.ipl.org/div/potus/; "Chester Arthur," http://www.whitehouse.gov/history/presidents/; "The Religious Affiliation of US President Chester A. Arthur," http://www.adherents.com/people/; Jerry MacGregor and Marie Prys, *Prayers of Our Presidents* (Grand Rapids MI: Baker Books, 2004); and John McCollister, *God and the Oval Office: The Religious Faith of Our 43 Presidents* (Nashville: W. Publishing Group, 2005).

[202] Elise K. Kirk, *Music at the White House: A History of the American Spirit* (Urbana: University of Illinois Press, 1986) 133.

[203] Erik Routley, *Hymns and Human Life* (Grand Rapids MI: William B. Eerdmans Publishing Company, 1952) 225.

[204] Kirk, *Music at the White House*, 135.

[205] Elsie Houghton, *Classic Christian Hymn-Writers* (Fort Washington PA: Christian Literature Crusade, 1992) 260–62.

[206] J. R. Watson, *The English Hymn: A Critical and Historical Study* (New York: Oxford University Press, 1997) 478–79.

[207] Henry Graff, *Grover Cleveland* (New York: Times Books, 2002); "Grover Cleveland," http://www.whitehouse.gov/history/presidents; "The Religious Affiliation of US President Grover Cleveland," http://www.adherents.com/people; Jerry MacGregor and Marie Prys, *Prayers of Our Presidents* (Grand Rapids MI: Baker Books, 2004); and John McCollister, *God and the Oval Office: The Religious Faith of Our 43 Presidents* (Nashville: W. Publishing Group, 2005).

[208] Elise K. Kirk, *Music at the White House: A History of the American Spirit* (Urbana: University of Illinois Press, 1986) 139.

[209] *Washington Weekly Star*, 11 June 1886, quoted in Kirk, *Music at the White House*, 386n4.

[210] Edith L. Blumhofer, *Her Heart Can See: The Life and Hymns of Fanny J. Crosby* (Grand Rapids MI: William B. Eerdmans Publishing Company, 2005) 86.

[211] Douglas Alvin Snow, *Revive Us Again: Chronological Anthology of American Gospel Hymnody* (Benton AR: Blessed Hope Publications, 2004) 203.

[212] Bernard Ruffin, *Fanny Crosby* (Cleveland OH: United Church Press, 1976) 226.

[213] Elsie Houghton, *Classic Christian Hymn-Writers* (Fort Washington PA: Christian Literature Crusade, 1992) 139.

[214] Frank Colquhoun, *Hymns That Live: Their Meaning and Message* (Downers Grove IL: InterVarsity Press, 1980) 192.

[215] Paul Westermeyer, *Let the People Sing: Hymn Tunes in Perspective* (Chicago: GIA Publications, Inc., 2005) 243.

[216] Ibid., 219.

[217] "Benjamin Harrison," http://www.infidels.org/library/historical/franklin_ steiner/presidents.html#2.5; "Benjamin Harrison," http://www.nndb.com/people/ 583/000044451/; "Benjamin Harrison," http://www.millercenter.virginia.edu/ index.php/Ampres/essays/ bharrison/biography/1; "Benjamin Harrison," http://www.ipl.org/div/potus/; "Benjamin Harrison," http://www.whitehouse.gov/ history/presidents/; "The Religious Affiliation of US President Benjamin Harrison," http://www.adherents.com/people/; Jerry MacGregor and Marie Prys, *Prayers of Our Presidents* (Grand Rapids MI: Baker Books, 2004); and John McCollister, *God and the Oval Office: The Religious Faith of Our 43 Presidents* (Nashville: W. Publishing Group, 2005).

[218] Elise K. Kirk, *Music at the White House: A History of the American Spirit* (Urbana: University of Illinois Press, 1986) 146.

[219] Undated clipping from *The Inland*, Benjamin Harrison Home, quoted in Kirk, *Music at the White House*, 387n19.

[220] Kirk, *Music at the White House*, 151.

[221] John Sutherland Bonnell, *Presidential Profiles: Religion in the Life of American Presidents* (Philadelphia: Westminster Press, 1971) 155.

[222] H. Augustine Smith, *Lyric Religion: The Romance of Immortal Hymns* (New York: Fleming H. Revell Company, 1931) 157.

[223] William J. Hart, *Hymn Stories of the Twentieth Century* (Boston: W. A. Wilde Company, 1948) 68.

[224] Kevin Phillips, *William McKinley* (New York: Times Books, 2003); "William McKinley," http://www.whitehouse.gov/history/presidents; "William McKinley," http://www.ipl.org/div/potus/; "The Religious Affiliation of US President William McKinley," http://www.adherents.com/people/adh_presidents; Jerry MacGregor and Marie Prys, *Prayers of Our Presidents* (Grand Rapids MI: Baker Books, 2004); and John McCollister, *God and the Oval Office: The Religious Faith of Our 43 Presidents* (Nashville: W. Publishing Group, 2005).

[225] McCollister, *God and the Oval Office*, 122.

[226] Jane Hampton Cook, *The Faith of America's First Ladies* (Chattanooga TN: Living Ink Books, 2005) 180.

[227] Elise K. Kirk, *Music at the White House: A History of the American Spirit* (Urbana: University of Illinois Press, 1986) 158.

[228] Ernest Edwin Ryden, *The Story of Our Hymns* (Rock Island IL: Augustina Book Concern, 1930) 299.

[229] "Tell Mother I'll Be There!" http://www.1timothy4-13.com/files/chr_vik/art01.html.

[230] Julia Ann Flora, *Suffering and Song: Lives of Hymn Writers* (Lima OH: Fairway Press, 1995) 33.

[231] H. Augustine Smith, *Lyric Religion: The Romance of Immortal Hymns* (New York: Fleming H. Revell Company, 1931) 266.

[232] Robert McCutchan, *Hymn Tune Names: Their Sources and Significance* (Nashville: Abingdon Press, 1957) 48.

[233] Douglas Alvin Snow, *Revive Us Again: Chronological Anthology of American Gospel Hymnody* (Benton AR: Blessed Hope Publications, 2004) 87.

[234] Nathan Miller, *Theodore Roosevelt: A Life* (New York: William Morrow, 1992); Edmund Morris, *The Rise of Theodore Roosevelt* (New York: Random House, 1979, 2001); Edmund Morris, *Theodore Rex* (New York: Random House, 2001, 2002); "Theodore Roosevelt," http://www.whitehouse.gov/history/presidents; "The Religious Affiliation of US President Theodore Roosevelt," http://www.adherents.com/people; Jon Meacham, *American Gospel: God, the Founding Fathers, and the Making of a Nation* (New York: Random House, 2006); Jerry MacGregor and Marie Prys, *Prayers of Our Presidents* (Grand Rapids MI: Baker Books, 2004): and John McCollister, *God and the Oval Office: The Religious Faith of Our 43 Presidents* (Nashville: W. Publishing Group, 2005).

[235] Elise K. Kirk, *Music at the White House: A History of the American Spirit* (Urbana: University of Illinois Press, 1986) 170.

[236] Ibid., 171.

[237] William J. Hart, *Hymn Stories of the Twentieth Century* (Boston: W. A. Wilde Company, 1948) 36.

[238] Ibid., 63.

[239] William J. Reynolds, *Songs of Glory: Stories of 300 Great Hymns and Gospel Songs* (Grand Rapids MI: Zondervan Books, 1990) 44.

[240] H. Augustine Smith, *Lyric Religion: The Romance of Immortal Hymns* (New York: Fleming H. Revell Company, 1931) 150.

[241] Amos R. Wells, *A Treasury of Hymn Stories* (Grand Rapids MI: Baker Books, 1945) 39.

[242] Wilson T. Hogue, *Hymns That Are Immortal* (Chicago: S. K. J. Chesbro, 1906) 216.

[243] Paul Westermeyer, *Let the People Sing: Hymn Tunes in Perspective* (Chicago: GIA Publications, Inc., 2005) 274.

[244] Robert McCutchan, *Hymn Tune Names: Their Sources and Significance* (Nashville: Abingdon Press, 1957) 36.

[245] MacGregor and Prys, *Prayers of Our Presidents*, 108.

[246] "William Howard Taft," http://www.nndb.com/people/583/000044451/; "William Howard Taft," http://www.millercenter.virginia.edu/index.php/ Ampres/essays/taft/biography/1; "William Howard Taft," http://www.ipl.ogr/ div/potus/; "William Howard Taft," http://www.whitehouse.gov/history/presidents/; "The Religious Affiliation of US President William Howard Taft," http://www.adherents.com/people/; "William Howard Taft Quotes," http://thinkexist.com/quotes/william_howard_taft/; Jon Meacham, *American Gospel: God, the Founding Fathers, and the Making of a Nation* (New York: Random House, 2006); Jerry MacGregor and Marie Prys, *Prayers of Our Presidents* (Grand Rapids MI: Baker Books, 2004); and John McCollister, *God and the Oval Office: The Religious Faith of Our 43 Presidents* (Nashville: W. Publishing Group. 2005).

[247] Robert P. Watson, *American First Ladies* (Pasadena CA: Salem Press, Inc., 2006) 183.

[248] Elise K. Kirk, *Music at the White House: A History of the American Spirit* (Urbana: University of Illinois Press, 1986) 189.

[249] Ibid., 201.

[250] John Julian, *A Dictionary of Hymnology* (New York: Dover Publications, Inc., 1892, rev. 1907) 1634.

[251] Paul Westermeyer, *Let the People Sing: Hymn Tunes in Perspective* (Chicago: GIA Publications, Inc., 2005) 237.

²⁵² Robert McCutchan, *Hymn Tune Names: Their Sources and Significance* (Nashville: Abingdon Press, 1957) 146.

²⁵³ H. W. Brands, *Woodrow Wilson* (New York: Henry Holt and Company, 2003); James Chace, *1912: Wilson, Roosevelt, Taft, & Debs—The Election That Changed the Country* (New York: Simon & Schuster, 2004); Jon Meacham, *American Gospel: God, the Founding Fathers, and the Making of a Nation* (New York: Random House, 2006); "Woodrow Wilson," http://www.ipl.org/ div/potus/; "Woodrow Wilson," http://www.whitehouse.gov/history/presidents/; "The Religious Affiliation of US President Woodrow Wilson," http://www.adherents.com/people/; Jerry MacGregor and Marie Prys, *Prayers of Our Presidents* (Grand Rapids MI: Baker Books, 2004); and John McCollister, *God and the Oval Office: The Religious Faith of Our 43 Presidents* (Nashville: W. Publishing Group, 2005).

²⁵⁴ Elise K. Kirk, *Music at the White House: A History of the American Spirit* (Urbana: University of Illinois Press, 1986) 92.

²⁵⁵ Ibid., 197.

²⁵⁶ Paul Kengor, *God and George W. Bush* (New York: Harper Collins Publishers, 2004) 175.

²⁵⁷ J. W. Storer, *These Historic Scriptures* (Nashville: Broadman Press, 1952) 96.

²⁵⁸ Ace Collins, *Stories Behind the Hymns That Inspire America* (Grand Rapids MI: Zondervan, 2003) 105.

²⁵⁹ "Warren G. Harding," http://www.whitehouse.gov/history/presidents; "Warren G. Harding," http://www.ipl.org/div/potus/; "The Religious Affiliation of US President Warren G. Harding," http://www.adherents.com/people/ adh_presidents; James Chace, *1912: Wilson, Roosevelt, Taft, & Debs—The Election That Changed the Country* (New York: Simon & Schuster, 2004); Jerry MacGregor and Marie Prys, *Prayers of Our Presidents* (Grand Rapids MI: Baker Books, 2004); and John McCollister, *God and the Oval Office: The Religious Faith of Our 43 Presidents* (Nashville: W. Publishing Group, 2005).

²⁶⁰ Elise K. Kirk, *Music at the White House: A History of the American Spirit* (Urbana: University of Illinois Press, 1986) 205.

²⁶¹ Ibid., 205.

²⁶² Kenneth W. Osbeck, *Singing with Understanding* (Grand Rapids MI: Kregel Publications, 1979) 184.

²⁶³ Ian Bradley, *Abide with Me: The World of Victorian Hymns* (Chicago: GIA Publications Inc., 1997) 98.

²⁶⁴ H. Augustine Smith, *Lyric Religion: The Romance of Immortal Hymns* (New York: Fleming H. Revell Company, 1931) 220.

²⁶⁵ Paul Westermeyer, *Let the People Sing: Hymn Tunes in Perspective* (Chicago: GIA Publications, Inc., 2005) 253.

²⁶⁶ "Calvin Coolidge," http://www.whitehouse.gov/history/presidents; "Calvin Coolidge," http://www.ipl.org/div/potus/; "The Religious Affiliation of US President Calvin Coolidge," http://www.adherents.com/people/adh_presidents; Jerry MacGregor and Marie Prys, *Prayers of Our Presidents* (Grand Rapids MI: Baker Books, 2004); and John McCollister, *God and the Oval Office: The Religious Faith of Our 43 Presidents* (Nashville: W. Publishing Group, 2005).

²⁶⁷ Elise K. Kirk, *Music at the White House: A History of the American Spirit* (Urbana: University of Illinois Press, 1986) 206.

²⁶⁸ Jane Hampton Cook, *The Faith of America's First Ladies* (Chattanooga TN: Living Ink Books, 2005) 181.

[269] Robert P. Watson, *American First Ladies* (Pasadena CA: Salem Press, Inc., 2006) 214.

[270] Kirk, *Music at the White House,* 214.

[271] Julia Ann Flora, *Suffering and Song: Lives of Hymn Writers* (Lima OH: Fairway Press, 1995) 127.

[272] H. Augustine Smith, *Lyric Religion: The Romance of Immortal Hymns* (New York: Fleming H. Revell Company, 1931) 301.

[273] Albert Edward Bailey, *The Gospel in Hymns: Backgrounds and Interpretations* (New York: Charles Scribner's Sons, 1950) 459.

[274] Smith, *Lyric Religion,* 302.

[275] Robert McCutchan, *Hymn Tune Names: Their Sources and Significance* (Nashville: Abingdon Press, 1957) 143.

[276] "Herbert Hoover," http://www.ipl.org/potus/; "Herbert Hoover," http://www.whitehouse.gov/history/presidents/; "The Religious Affiliation of US President Herbert Hoover," http://www.adherents.com/people/; "Herbert Hoover," http://www.historycentral.com/bio/presidents/hoover.html; Jerry MacGregor and Marie Prys, *Prayers of Our Presidents* (Grand Rapids MI: Baker Books, 2004); and John McCollister, *God and the Oval Office: The Religious Faith of Our 43 Presidents* (Nashville: W. Publishing Group, 2005).

[277] Elise K. Kirk, *Music at the White House: A History of the American Spirit* (Urbana: University of Illinois Press, 1986) 209.

[278] Ibid., 208.

[279] Robert P. Watson, *American First Ladies* (Pasadena CA: Salem Press, Inc., 2006) 222.

[280] John Sutherland Bonnell, *Presidential Profiles: Religion in the Life of American Presidents* (Philadelphia: Westminster Press, 1971) 200.

[281] Ibid., 203.

[282] Samuel J. Rogal, "A Survey of Hymns in Funeral Services for American Dignitaries, 1921–1969," *The Hymn: A Journal of Congregational Song* 45/3 (July 1994): 12–15.

[283] Kenneth W. Osbeck, *Singing with Understanding* (Grand Rapids MI: Kregel Publications, 1979) 106.

[284] Paul Westermeyer, *Let the People Sing: Hymn Tunes in Perspective* (Chicago: GIA Publications, Inc., 2005) 258.

[285] Albert Edward Bailey, *The Gospel in Hymns: Backgrounds and Interpretations* (New York: Charles Scribner's Sons, 1950) 204.

[286] Kenneth S. Davis, *FDR: The Beckoning of Destiny, 1882–1928* (New York: Random House and The History Book Club, 1971, 2003 ed.) 83; Jon Meacham, *American Gospel: God, the Founding Fathers, and the Making of a Nation* (New York: Random House, 2006); "Franklin D. Roosevelt," http://www.whitehouse.gov/history/presidents; "Franklin D. Roosevelt," http://www.ipl.org/div/potus/; "The Religious Affiliation of US President Franklin D. Roosevelt," http://www.adherents.com/people/adh_presidents; Jerry MacGregor and Marie Prys, *Prayers of Our Presidents* (Grand Rapids MI: Baker Books, 2004); and John McCollister, *God and the Oval Office: The Religious Faith of Our 43 Presidents* (Nashville: W. Publishing Group, 2005).

[287] Elliott Roosevelt, ed., *FDR: His Personal Letters, Early Years* (New York: Duell, Sloan and Pearce, 1947) 347, quoted in Elise K. Kirk, *Music at the White House: A History of the American Spirit* (Urbana: University of Illinois Press, 1986) 223.

[288] James Roosevelt and Sidney Shalett, *Affectionately FDR* (New York: Harcourt Brace, 1959) 69, quoted in Kirk, *Music at the White House*, 225.

[289] FDR to Davenport, 4 May 1942, President's Personal Files [PPF] 100, FDR Papers. Quoted in Kirk, *Music at the White House*, 395n12.

[290] Kirk, *Music at the White House*, 251.

[291] Ibid., 240.

[292] Albert Edward Bailey, *The Gospel in Hymns: Backgrounds and Interpretations* (New York: Charles Scribner's Sons, 1950) 290.

[293] Robert McCutchan, *Hymn Tune Names: Their Sources and Significance* (Nashville: Abingdon Press, 1957) 157.

[294] Kirk, *Music at the White House*, 225.

[295] William J. Hart, *Hymn Stories of the Twentieth Century* (Boston: W. A. Wilde Company, 1948) 52.

[296] David McCullough, *Truman* (New York: Simon & Schuster, 1992); *Harry S. Truman* National Park Service, Harry S. Truman National Historic Site Brochure, Independence, Missouri; Jon Meacham, *American Gospel: God, the Founding Fathers, and the Making of a Nation* (New York: Random House, 2006); "Harry S. Truman," http://www.whitehouse.gov/history/presidents; "The Religious Affiliation of US President Harry Truman," http://www.adherents.com/people; Jerry MacGregor and Marie Prys, *Prayers of Our Presidents* (Grand Rapids MI: Baker Books, 2004); and John McCollister, *God and the Oval Office: The Religious Faith of Our 43 Presidents* (Nashville: W. Publishing Group, 2005).

[297] Jonathan Daniels, *The Man of Independence* (Philadelphia: J. B. Lippincott, 1950) 70.

[298] Elise K. Kirk, *Music at the White House: A History of the American Spirit* (Urbana: University of Illinois Press, 1986) 254.

[299] Ibid., 261.

[300] Memo from the files of the Truman Library, 21 December 1979. Based on a telephone conversation with Paul Hume, 2.

[301] Kirk, *Music at the White House*, 265.

[302] Fact sheet number 132 from the Truman Library, "Nixon Donates Piano to Truman Library," *Time* (28 March 1969) and *Newsweek* (31 March 1969). See note 296. McCullough wrote in his biography of Truman a different version of this event, pg. 985.

[303] Letter from Rose A. Conway, secretary to Mr. Truman, to Lt. Colonel H.B. Collier (30 September 1959), from the Truman Library.

[304] Douglas Alvin Snow, *Revive Us Again: Chronological Anthology of American Gospel Hymnody* (Benton AR: Blessed Hope Publications, 2004) 589.

[305] Ace Collins, *Stories Behind the Hymns That Inspire America* (Grand Rapids MI: Zondervan, 2003) 27.

[306] Stephen E. Ambrose, *Eisenhower: Soldier and President* (New York: Simon & Schuster, 1990); Jon Meacham, *American Gospel: God, the Founding Fathers, and the Making of a Nation* (New York: Random House, 2006); "Dwight D. Eisenhower," http://www.whitehouse.gov/history/presidents; "Dwight D. Eisenhower," http://www.ipl.org/div/potus/; "The Religious Affiliation of US President Dwight D. Eisenhower," http://www.adherents.com/people/adh_presidents; Jerry MacGregor and Marie Prys, *Prayers of Our Presidents* (Grand Rapids MI: Baker Books, 2004); and John McCollister, *God and the Oval Office: The Religious Faith of Our 43 Presidents* (Nashille: W. Publishing Group, 2005).

[307] Elise K. Kirk, *Music at the White House: A History of the American Spirit* (Urbana: University of Illinois Press, 1986) 267.

[308] Ibid., 267.

[309] Ibid., 277.

[310] E-mail from Herbert L. Pankratz, archivist at the Eisenhower Library, "Dwight Eisenhower's Favorite Hymn" (11 August 2005), herb.pankratz@nara.gov.

[311] George Beverly Shea, *How Sweet the Sound* (Wheaton IL: Tyndale House Publishers Inc., 2004) 75.

[312] Julia Ann Flora, *Suffering and Song: Lives of Hymn Writers* (Lima OH: Fairway Press, 1995) 70.

[313] Ira D. Sankey, *My Life and the Story of the Gospel Hymns* (Philadelphia: P. W. Zieglar Co., 1906) 335.

[314] H. Augustine Smith, *Lyric Religion: The Romance of Immortal Hymns* (New York: Fleming H. Revell Company, 1931) 447.

[315] William A. DeGregorio, *The Complete Book of the U.S. Presidents* (Fort Lee NJ: Barricade Books, 2001) 530.

[316] Robert Dallek, *An Unfinished Life: John F Kennedy, 1917–1963* (Boston: Little, Brown, & Co., 2003); Jon Meacham, *American Gospel: God, the Founding Fathers, and the Making of a Nation* (New York: Random House, 2006); "John F. Kennedy," http://www.whitehouse.gov/history/presidents; "The Religious Affiliation of US President John Kennedy," http://www.adherents.com/; and "John F. Kennedy," http://www.millercenter.virginia.edu/.

[317] *New York Times*, 10 August 1962, quoted in Elise K. Kirk, *Music at the White House: A History of the American Spirit* (Urbana: University of Illinois Press, 1986) 287n11.

[318] J. Joyce Cusmano, writer of album cover notes for "Christmas at the White House: The Favorite Carols and Hymns of America's Presidents," sung by Burl Ives (New York: Caedmon Records, Inc., 1972).

[319] Kirk, *Music at the White House*, 287.

[320] Ibid., 288.

[321] Ibid., 289.

[322] Jacqueline Kennedy Onassis to Elise Kirk (3 February 1984), quoted in Kirk, *Music at the White House*, 287n8.

[323] Carlton R. Young, *Companion to the United Methodist Hymnal* (Nashville: Abingdon Press, 1993) 266.

[324] Ibid., 400.

[325] Paul Westermeyer, *Let the People Sing: Hymn Tunes in Perspective* (Chicago: GIA Publications, Inc., 2005) 150.

[326] Robert A. Caro, *The Years of Lyndon Johnson: The Path to Power* (New York: Vintage Books Edition, 1983); Robert A. Caro, *The Years of Lyndon Johnson: Means of Ascent* (New York: Alfred A. Knopf, 1990); Robert A. Caro, *The Years of Lyndon Johnson: Master of the Senate* (New York: Alfred A. Knopf, 2002); "Lyndon Baines Johnson," at http://www.whitehouse.gov/history/presidents; "Lyndon Baines Johnson," http://www.ipl.org/div/potus/; "The Religious Affiliation of US President Lyndon Baines Johnson," http://www.adherents.com/people/adh_presidents; "Lyndon Baines Johnson," http://millercenter.virginia.edu/; Jerry MacGregor and Marie Prys, *Prayers of Our Presidents* (Grand Rapids MI: Baker Books, 2004); and John McCollister, *God and the Oval Office: The Religious Faith of Our 43 Presidents* (Nashville: W. Publishing Group, 2005).

[327] Elise K. Kirk, *Music at the White House: A History of the American Spirit* (Urbana: University of Illinois Press, 1986) 305.

[328] Ibid., 308.

[329] *New York Herald Tribune*, 15 June 1965, quoted in Kirk, *Music at the White House*, 316.

[330] William J. Hart, *Hymn Stories of the Twentieth Century* (Boston: W. A. Wilde Company, 1948) 19.

[331] Guye Johnson, *Treasury of Great Hymns and Their Stories* (Greenville SC: Bob Jones University Press, 1986) 269.

[332] Ian Bradley, *Abide with Me: The World of Victorian Hymns* (Chicago: GIA Publications Inc., 1997) 242.

[333] John Sutherland Bonnell, *Presidential Profiles: Religion in the Life of American Presidents* (Philadelphia: Westminster Press, 1971) 236.

[334] Stephen A. Ambrose, *Nixon: The Education of a Politician, 1913–1962* (New York: Simon & Schuster, 1987); Stephen A. Ambrose, *Nixon: The Triumph of a Politician, 1962–1972* (New York: Simon & Schuster, 1989); Stephen A. Ambrose, *Nixon: Ruin and Recovery, 1973–1990* (New York: Simon & Schuster, 1991); "Richard M. Nixon," http://www.whitehouse.gov/history/presidents; "Richard Milhous Nixon," http://www.ipl.org/div/potus/; Jerry MacGregor and Marie Prys, *Prayers of Our Presidents* (Grand Rapids MI: Baker Books, 2004); and John McCollister, *God and the Oval Office: The Religious Faith of Our 43 Presidents* (Nashville: W. Publishing Group, 2005).

[335] Richard M. Nixon, *The Memoirs of Richard Nixon* (New York: Grosset and Dunlap, 1978) 9.

[336] Billy Graham, *Just As I Am: The Autobiography of Billy Graham* (San Francisco: Harper Collins, 1997) 440.

[337] Elise K. Kirk, *Music at the White House: A History of the American Spirit* (Urbana: University of Illinois Press, 1986) 319.

[338] John Sutherland Bonnell, *Presidential Profiles: Religion in the Life of American Presidents* (Philadelphia: Westminster Press, 1971) 244.

[339] Dan Wooding, *Evangelical News*, "I'd Rather Have Jesus," 21 June 2006, http://www.evangelicalnews.org/indiv_pr.php?action=display&pr_id=6201.

[340] Mel R. Wilhot, "Alexander the Great: Or Just Plain Charlie," *The Hymn: A Journal of Congregational Song* 46/2 (April 1995): 23.

[341] "Remembering President Gerald R. Ford," http://www.hope.edu/pr/pressreleases/content/view/full/12597; "Gerald R. Ford: Remarks at the Southern Baptist Convention in 1976," http://www.ethicsdaily.com/article_detail.cfm?AID=8343; "Gerald R. Ford," http://www.whitehouse.gov/history/presidents; "Gerald R. Ford," http://www.ipl.org/div/potus/; "The Religious Affiliation of US President Gerald R. Ford," http://www.adherents.com/people/adh_presidents; Jerry MacGregor and Marie Prys, *Prayers of Our Presidents* (Grand Rapids, MI: Baker Books, 2004); and John McCollister, *God and the Oval Office: The Religious Faith of Our 43 Presidents* (Nashville: W. Publishing Group, 2005).

[342] Elise K. Kirk, *Music at the White House: A History of the American Spirit* (Urbana: University of Illinois Press, 1986) 329.

[343] Ibid., 335.

[344] John Julian, *A Dictionary of Hymnology* (New York: Dover Publications, Inc., 1892, rev. 1907) 875.

[345] Albert Edward Bailey, *The Gospel in Hymns: Backgrounds and Interpretations* (New York: Charles Scribner's Sons, 1950) 55.

[346] Rochelle A. Stackhouse, "Hymnody and Politics: Isaac Watts's 'Our God, Our Help in Ages Past' and Timothy Dwight's 'I Love Thy Kingdom, Lord,'" *Wonderful Words of Life: Hymns in American Protestant History and Theology*, ed. Richard J. Mouw and Mark A. Noll (Grand Rapids MI: William B. Eerdmans Publishing Co., 2004) 47.

[347] Ibid., 51.

[348] Lionel Adey, *Hymns and the Christian "Myth"* (Vancouver: University of British Columbia Press, 1986) 11.

[349] Ron DiCianni, *The Faith of the Presidents: Our National Leaders at Prayer* (Lake Mary FL: Charisma House, 2004) 164.

[350] "Jimmy Carter," http://www.whitehouse,gov/history/presidents; "The Religious Affiliation of US President Jimmy Carter," http://www.adherents.com/; "Jimmy Carter," http://www.millercenter.virginia.edu/; Jerry MacGregor and Marie Prys, *Prayers of Our Presidents* (Grand Rapids MI: Baker Books, 2004); and John McCollister, *God and the Oval Office: The Religious Faith of Our 43 Presidents* (Nashville: W. Publishing Group, 2005).

[351] Jimmy Carter, *Keeping Faith: Memoirs of a President* (New York: Bantam Books, 1982) 19.

[352] Elise K. Kirk, *Music at the White House: A History of the American Spirit* (Urbana: University of Illinois Press, 1986) 338.

[353] Ibid., 338.

[354] Ibid., 344.

[355] Jimmy Carter, personal e-mail to C. Edward Spann, 22 February 2007.

[356] Steve Turner, *Amazing Grace: The Story of America's Most Beloved Song* (New York: Harper Collins, 2002) 82.

[357] David W. Stowe, *How Sweet the Sound: The Music and the Spiritual Lives of Americans* (Cambridge MA: Harvard University Press, 2004) 256.

[358] Turner, *Amazing Grace*, 126.

[359] Elsie Houghton, *Classic Christian Hymn-Writers* (Fort Washington PA: Christian Literature Crusade, 1992) 188.

[360] David Kucharsky, *The Man from Plains: The Mind and Spirit of Jimmy Carter* (New York: Harper & Row Publishers, 1976) 46.

[361] "Ronald Reagan," http://www.whitehouse.gov/history/presidents; "The Religious Affiliation of US President Ronald Reagan," http://www.adherents.com/; "Ronald Reagan," http://www.millercenter.virginia.edu/; Jerry MacGregor and Marie Prys, *Prayers of Our Presidents* (Grand Rapids MI: Baker Books, 2004); and John McCollister, *God and the Oval Office: The Religious Faith of Our 43 Presidents* (Nashville: W. Publishing Group, 2005).

[362] Edmund Morris, *Dutch: A Memoir of Ronald Reagan* (New York: Random House, 1999) 53.

[363] Elise K. Kirk, *Music at the White House: A History of the American Spirit* (Urbana: University of Illinois Press, 1986) 359.

[364] Sharon Rich, *Jeanette McDonald: A Pictorial Treasury* (Los Angeles: Time Mirror Press, 1973) 211, quoted in Kirk, *Music at the White House*, 348n28.

[365] Charles Eugene Claghorn, *Battle Hymn: The Story Behind the Battle Hymn of the Republic*, The Papers of the Hymn Society XXIX (New York: The Hymn Society of America, 1974) 12.

[366] Harvey B. Marks, *The Rise and Growth of English Hymnody* (New York: Fleming H. Revell Company, 1938) 191.

[367] Claghorn, *Battle Hymn*, 6.

[368] Ibid., 7.

[369] J. R. Watson, *The English Hymn: A Critical and Historical Study* (New York: Oxford University Press, 1997) 476–77.

[370] "George H. W. Bush," http://www.whitehouse.gov/history/presidents; "The Religious Affiliation of US President George H. W. Bush," http://www.adherents. com/; "George H. W. Bush," http://www.millercenter.virginia.edu/; "George H. W. Bush," http://www.ipl.org/div/potus/; James Bradley, *Flyboys: A True Story of American Courage* (Boston: Little, Brown & Co., 2003); Jerry MacGregor and Marie Prys, *Prayers of Our Presidents* (Grand Rapids MI: Baker Books, 2004); and John McCollister, *God and the Oval Office: The Religious Faith of Our 43 Presidents* (Nashville: W. Publishing Group, 2005).

[371] George H. W. Bush, "My Country and Western 'Tis of Thee," *Forbes* 153 (9 May 1994): 82.

[372] Stephen A. Marini, *Sacred Song in America: Religion, Music, and Public Culture* (Urbana: University of Illinois Press, 2003) 299.

[373] Paul Kengor, *God and George W. Bush* (New York: Harper Collins Publishers, 2004) 85.

[374] George Bush, *Heartbeat: George Bush in His Own Words*, ed. Jim McGrath (New York: Scribner, 2001) 21.

[375] Ace Collins, *Stories Behind the Hymns That Inspire America* (Grand Rapids MI: Zondervan, 2003) 47.

[376] John Julian, *A Dictionary of Hymnology* (New York: Dover Publications, Inc., 1892, rev. 1907) 356.

[377] Gordon Giles, *The Music of Praise: Meditations on Great Hymns of the Church* (Peabody MA: Hendrickson Publishers, Inc., 2004) 237.

[378] "William J. Clinton," http://www.whitehouse.gov/history/presidents; "The Religious Affiliation of US President William Jefferson Clinton," http://www.adherents.com/; "Bill Clinton," http://www.millercenter.virginia.edu/; "William Jefferson Clinton," http://www.ipl.org/div/potus/; Jerry MacGregor and Marie Prys, *Prayers of Our Presidents* (Grand Rapids MI: Baker Books, 2004); and John McCollister, *God and the Oval Office: The Religious Faith of Our 43 Presidents* (Nashville: W. Publishing Group, 2005).

[379] Bill Clinton, *My Life* (New York: Alfred A.Knopf, 2004) 63.

[380] Jack Roberts, *Our 42nd President: Bill Clinton* (New York: Scholastic, Inc., 1993) 14.

[381] Philip V. Bohlman, Edith L. Blumhofer, and Maria M. Chow, *Music in the American Religious Experience* (New York: Oxford University Press, 2006) 182.

[382] Elise Kirk, *Musical Highlights from the White House* (Washington DC: The White House Historical Association, nd) 164–70.

[383] Clinton, *My Life*, 45.

[384] Geron Davis, telephone interview by C. Edward Spann, 4 April 2007.

[385] Clinton, *My Life*, 250.

[386] Danny Thomason, script of PBS Television *Frontline* 11 May 1996 interview, "Stories of Bill," 4, http://www.pbs.org/wgbh/pages/frontline/shows/choice/bill/thomason.html.

[387] Clinton, *My Life*, 252.

[388] Ibid., 569.

[389] Geron Davis, telephone interview with C. Edward Spann, 4 April 2007.

[390] "George W. Bush," http://www.whitehouse.gov/history/presidents; "The Religious Affiliation of US President George W. Bush," http://www.adherents.com/; "George W. Bush," http://www.miller-center.virginia.edu/; "George W. Bush," http://www.ipl.org/div/potus/; Stephen Mansfield, *The Faith of George W. Bush* (Lake Mary FL: Charisma House, 2003); Jerry MacGregor and Marie Prys, *Prayers of Our Presidents* (Grand Rapids MI: Baker Books, 2004); and John McCollister, *God* and *the Oval Office: The Religious Faith of Our 43 Presidents* (Nashville: W. Publishing Group, 2005).

[391] Mansfield, *The Faith of George W. Bush*, 11.

[392] The White House Office of the Press Secretary quoting George W. Bush, "President Bush Addresses the 51st Annual Prayer Breakfast," 6 February 2003, from "The Healing Process," published in *CR Mag 84*, Tuesday 15 March 2005.

[393] "Michael W. Smith," http://en.wikipedia.org/wiki/Michael_W_Smith.

[394] Mansfield, *The Faith of George W. Bush*, 120.

[395] Paul Kengor, *God and George W. Bush* (New York: Harper Collins Publishers, 2004) 169.

[396] George W. Bush, *A Charge to Keep: My Journey to the White House* (New York: Harper Collins Publishers, Inc., 2001) 215.

[397] Matthew Henry, *Matthew Henry's Commentary on the Whole Bible*, 6 vols. (Brattleboro: Fessenden and Company, 1835) 1:388.

[398] William J. Reynolds, *Songs of Glory: Stories of 300 Great Hymns and Gospel Songs* (Grand Rapids MI: Zondervan Books, 1990) 9.

[399] James I. Warren, *O for a Thousand Tongues: The History, Nature, and Influence of Music in the Methodist Tradition* (Grand Rapids MI: Francis Asbury Press, 1988) 28.

[400] William J. Reynolds, *Hymns of Our Faith: A Handbook for the Baptist Hymnal* (Nashville: Broadman Press, 1964) 1.

[401] Mansfield, *The Faith of George W. Bush*, 13.

[402] Kengor, *God and George W. Bush*, 326.

Index of Hymns, Songs, and Musical Compositions

Index of Hymn Tunes Names

Tunes printed in four part harmony.

**Hymns that have no verified tune names.*

General Index

Credits for Presidential Praise CD Recording

The enclosed compact disk is a recording of several stanzas of each of the favored hymns. This is included to give the reader an idea of how each hymn sounded for the presidents. The performers are the Dallas Baptist University Presidential Hymns Ensemble which recorded the CD at Adamsound Studio in Dallas, Texas on January 14-16, 2008. The ensemble was directed by Dr. Stephen Holcomb, Director of Choral Activities at DBU, assisted by Dr. Terry Fansler, Director of the Music Business Program at DBU. The recording engineer for the project was Randy Adams. Sara Marantz was the pianist for "He Will Hold Me Fast" and "In the Presence of Jehovah." Dr. Edward Spann, retired Dean of the College of Fine Arts at DBU, was producer of the project. Funding for the recording was provided by a grant from Dallas Baptist University.

Members of the ensemble included:

Taylor Allen	Meredith Morris*
Jesse Cannon	Daryl Nelson
Andrew Clardy*	Lori Perkins
Robin Frazell	Alex Perry
Melissa Graham	Nathan Rees
Kara Martinson	Kami Reynolds

Soloist

CD Track Numbers

1.	George Washington	"How Happy Is He Born and Taught" (Wooten)
2.	John Adams	"How Lovely Are Thy Dwellings Fair" (Milton)
3.	Thomas Jefferson	"Hark, the Glad Sound, the Saviour Comes" (Doddridge)
4.	James Madison	"O God, My Strength and Fortitude" (Sternhold)
5.	James Monroe	"O Lord, I Would Delight in Thee" (Ryland)
6.	John Quincy Adams	"Send Forth, O God, Thy Light and Truth" (Whittemore)
7.	Andrew Jackson	"Come, Thou Almighty King" (Anonymous)
8.	Martin Van Buren	"Come, Holy Spirit, Come" (Hart)
9.	William Henry Harrison	"Lord, It Belongs Not to My Care" (Baxter)
10.	John Tyler	"O Happy Day That Fixed My Choice" (Doddridge)
11.	James K. Polk	"All Hail the Power of Jesus' Name" (Perronet)
12.	Zachary Taylor	"Great God, How Infinite Art Thou" (Watts)
13.	Millard Fillmore	"While Thee I Seek, Protecting Power" (Williams)
14.	Franklin Pierce	"When All Thy Mercies, O My God" (Addison)
15.	James Buchanan	"God Moves in a Mysterious Way" (Cowper)
16.	Abraham Lincoln	"How Tedious and Tasteless the Hours" (Newton)
17.	Andrew Johnson	"O for a Closer Walk with God" (Cowper)
18.	Ulysses S. Grant	"God Is My Strong Salvation" (Montgomery)
19.	Rutherford B. Hayes	"Rock of Ages, Cleft for Me" (Toplady)
20.	James A. Garfield	"Holy Ghost, with Light Divine" (Reed)
21.	Chester A. Arthur	"Abide with Me" (Lyte)
22.	Grover Cleveland	"Guide Me, O Thou Great Jehovah" (Williams)
23.	Benjamin Harrison	"I Love Thy Kingdom, Lord" (Dwight)
24.	William McKinley	"Nearer, My God, to Thee" (Adams)
25.	Theodore Roosevelt	"How Firm a Foundation" ("K" in Rippon's)
26.	William Howard Taft	"Deal Gently with Us, Lord" (Everett)
27.	Woodrow Wilson	"It Is Well with My Soul" (Spafford)
28.	Warren G. Harding	"Lead, Kindly Light" (Newman)
29.	Calvin Coolidge	"O Love that Wilt Not Let Me Go" (Matheson)
30.	Herbert Hoover	"Faith of Our Fathers" (Faber)
31.	Franklin D. Roosevelt	"Art Thou Weary, Art Thou Languid" (Neale)
32.	Harry S. Truman	"America the Beautiful" (Bates)
33.	Dwight D. Eisenhower	"What a Friend We Have in Jesus" (Scriven)
34.	John F. Kennedy	"Holy God, We Praise Thy Name" (Franz)
35.	Lyndon B. Johnson	"Onward Christian Soldiers" (Baring-Gould)
36.	Richard M. Nixon	"He Will Hold Me Fast" (Habershon)
37.	Gerald R. Ford	"O God, Our Help in Ages Past" (Watts)
38.	James E. (Jimmy) Carter	"Amazing Grace" (Newton)
39.	Ronald W. Reagan	"The Battle Hymn of the Republic" (Howe)
40.	George H.W. Bush	"Eternal Father, Strong to Save" (Whiting)
41.	William J. (Bill) Clinton	"In the Presence of Jehovah" (Davis)
42.	George W. Bush	"A Charge to Keep I Have" (Wesley)

Note: There are only forty-two hymn tracks (rather than forty-three) because Grover Cleveland was both the 22nd and the 24th president.